2022

STRENGTH
of
CHARACTER

A MOTHER AND DAUGHTER'S JOURNEY AGAINST ADVERSITY

HEATHER ROBINSON & BARB JOHNSON

ILLUSTRATIONS BY MIKE STINE

For all those living among us who challenge our perspective and helps each one of us discover our strength of character.

ACKNOWLEDGMENTS

To Jeff and Katie, whom I owe my heartfelt gratitude for tolerating my need for isolation during the years Heather and I wrote our book. Their love and support helped make *Strength of Character* a reality.

To my parents, Albert and Karen Gigowski, for always being there in our time of need. I would not have had become the person I am, without their support and guidance.

A huge Thank You has to go out to those, whom volunteered to be ours readers during the process of writing this book. Their encouragement inspired us to continue writing. Their excitement, when each received a newly written chapter, gave Heather and I the impression, our book was meaningful and would have an impact on others.

For over eighteen years, I carried with me a tattered photo of Heather. Barry Katcher, of *Smile Dog Productions,* is responsible for restoring my precious photo,which in turn, became the cover picture for our book.

Heather and I both feel honored to have included Mikey's artwork in our book. His talent and dedication he puts forth in his work, speaks for itself. Amazing job, Mikey.

We would like to thank Richard Ashland, for writing the forward, along with supporting Heather and I. Our book would have not been complete without the presence of his words.

To our best friend, mentor and Aunt. Thank you Marge, for being Marge.

Finally, I would like to acknowledge Sam Knopf, my technical adviser. When in doubt regarding issues with my computer, word processor and software, I always relied on Sam's input, even though the technology I was using may have been older than him.

FOREWORD

When Heather Robinson and her mother, Barb Johnson, asked me to write the forward to their book, *Strength of Character*, I was not only honored, but humbled by the opportunity.

My passion for writing has led me to speak to middle school and high school students about the importance of having goals in life and how critical it is to set your sights on something your heart can be joyful for. When you get up in the morning, be excited about what is ahead of you. I found out that my passion was not only for writing but inspiring others to do the same. That's when I met a school teacher from Greenville, Michigan, by the name of Karen Paulsen. Mrs. Paulsen contacted me after her husband, Doug, had read some of my writing. She asked me if I would be willing to work with one of her students who was very interested in being a writer. I said yes, but didn't know when I would get around to it because of my rather erratic schedule.

A few months later while skimming through some of my notes I saw the name Heather written next to her Facebook connection and a reminder that Mrs. Paulsen had requested that I contact Heather.

Mrs. Paulsen never mentioned that Heather was in a wheelchair, or that she had a captivating smile and piercing blue eyes. That information I discovered on Facebook. Have you ever seen someone that you never met before, but felt you knew them already? I sent a note to Heather and mentioned that Mrs. Paulsen had contacted me and asked that I connect with her to see if I could be of any assistance in her writing.

Heather had just graduated from high school and was very interested in having some help. We exchanged e-mail addresses and Heather sent some of her writing material to me. Her interest in writing love stories was not in my genre, but certainly I knew some of the elements of putting together a novel and wanted to at least give her some encouragement to move ahead.

We exchanged phone numbers and that's when I heard her voice for the first time. I hadn't realized until then that it was an effort for Heather to speak, that her legs were not the only thing affected by whatever it was that put her in that wheelchair. Our next step was to meet face-to-face.

It was a warm, sunny day and Ricky, Heather's boyfriend (now her husband) answered the door when I arrived at thier apartment. I did not know at that time what a life changing experience this would be for me. I knew there was something very special about Heather by the way she lit up and gave me a beautiful smile. It was like we were old friends,but we'd just met. I remember the mixture of emotions that I felt at our first meeting.One thing I knew for certain, was that this was not going to be the last time I would see Heather, and I also knew that there was a much bigger reason for being there, than trying to help this young woman write a novel.

We'd talked about the stories Heather had begun to write. It was obvious that she loved to write about characters, emotions, things that people say to each other, and about life and death. But I didn't feel that writing novels was the direction we were supposed to be going in. I asked Heather why she wanted to be a writer. She said,"What else am I going to do, work at Burger King?" We both laughed at that answer and there was my introduction to her spunky nature and her love of laughter.

So I asked the question most people want to ask and probably don't: "Heather, before we go any further, would you mind telling me how you ended up in a wheelchair?"

I had no idea of how the answer to that question would impact my own life or how much strength I would see blossom from this frail young woman who could barely raise her arms. She began to tell the story of how the life of a perfectly healthy toddler was transformed into a painful and torturous existence. How one normal childhood event turned into a lifelong struggle to survive. I was mesmerized by her words and how at times Heather had to stop because talking can be exhausting for her. Then she mentioned Barb, her mother, and I began to see how warriors are born. *Strength of Character*, is not just a story of someone's misfortune in life, but an epic journey of mother and daughter struggling against ignorance and indifference.

"Heather," I said, "This is the story you must write. The world is waiting to hear your story and see how you have overcome and rejoice in knowing that character has more value than all the things we can own in this life." Little did I know that Barb had already started working on a few pages.

Mother and daughter accepted the challenge of putting together the events of the past few decades. It was like a marathon. Barb would write on her word processor and Heather would in turn type every word on her laptop. For someone with delicate fingers and fragile hands, that was a great accomplishment. Heather sent me e-mails with each additional chapter and I would read them and wonder how I would have handled her constant battles with pain and disappointment, or how Barb managed to hold it all together through a tunnel that seemed to have no light at the end.

On a few occasions, during the writing of *Strength of Character*, Heather and Ricky came to our home. My wife and I would read her pages aloud while sitting in front of a blazing fireplace. Sometimes, Heather would cry and we asked her what it was that brought the tears. She said it was the realization of how much pain her mother had endured to care for her and to bring her through it all. My lip quivered a bit too.

As I look back at this experience I'm not sure that I did anything to help Heather. Oh sure, I encouraged the writing of this true-life journey, but I am truly blessed by having Heather, her husband Ricky, and her mother, Barb as my close friends.

Don't just read this book, absorb its pages and let your heart be opened wide. Laugh and cry with these pages and just know you have experienced some great spirits.

Richard Ashland
Author

*W*HEN MY DAUGHTER, HEATHER, BROUGHT home an invitation to her Graduation ceremony, I remember feeling such a great sense of gratitude for being given the privilege of sharing this event with her. I also caught myself reflecting back on all of Heather's accomplishments she had achieved throughout the time she attended school, along with the challenges she had endured along the way. In all honesty, I knew graduation day would be an emotional one for Heather, as well as myself; even if this was a graduation from preschool. The day before Graduation, Heather brought home a letter informing me that she had been chosen to lead her class, total of six, onto the stage at the beginning of the ceremony. The excitement shined in Heather's eyes when I read the news and I couldn't help but share in her enthusiasm. How fitting. Over time, Heather had become somewhat of a mother hen over her classmates at Little People Land, so leading her classmates up to the stage was a perfect way to end her preschool experience.

That evening with a bit of coaxing, I convinced Heather that she should go to bed earlier than usual. Following a life threatening illness a few years prior, she still was very susceptible to high fevers and bodily weakness whenever she became overly fatigued. It was crucial that she had plenty of rest each night.

Following her bath, I allowed Heather to choose the dress she wanted to wear to Graduation. Allowing a five year old to pick out clothing to wear in public is risky. As parents, we know the child is not concerned with making a fashion statement. The choosing is mostly based on whatever catches the child's attention at the moment, or the child's favorite article of clothing, which is usually torn, faded, and stained. Heather went with the latter as her choice. A floral print summer dress trimmed with lace and ruffles.

The dress had been worn so often, it was difficult to determine what type of flowers were printed on the material. However, the green of the stems and leaves seemed to retain their original color throughout all the washes. In the distance, the dress appeared as being blotches of pastel colors with distinct patterns of the stems and leaves. Up close, a few droplets of chocolate milk stains on the lace collar were quite visible.

I was not surprised by her choice. I actually expected it and had no problem with her wearing that dress. I knew it was her favorite and felt she deserved to wear whatever she wanted. After picking her choice of dress, Heather then pointed to a bedtime story for me to read. Even before finishing the story, Heather had drifted off to sleep. I sat in the quietness of her room for a short time, all the while gazing at this child whom had been through so much, but yet remained so full of life. I then carefully tucked the blanket around Heather leaving her to her dreams; knowing I soon would be marking an end to another chapter in her life.

Morning of graduation was filled with mixed emotions for Heather. She was giddy one moment and teary-eyed the next. I knew she was not really prepared to say good-bye to the school she had attended for three years, nor the teacher she adored. A teacher whom had taken the time to personally inform us about such a school that was designed for children with special needs. The very teacher whom contacted the necessary persons to get Heather registered, in addition to, helping arrange transportation.

Without Miss Kathy's help, Heather may not have had attended any type of preschool and would have missed out on the developmental gains preschools offer, in preparing children for Kindergarten. Little People Land was truly a gift for Heather. Not only was Little People Land a place to socialize, but the school provided the special help and assistance Heather needed at that time.

During the first year Heather attended Little People Land, she became a candidate for an augmentative communication device which would make it easier for Heather to communicate with others. Up until then, Heather was often asked to repeat herself or point to what she wanted, due to a speech impediment. The device was the size of a small lap top computer and was easily transported back and forth to school. Everyday objects, activities, and emotions were represented by pictures attached to the key pad. When a specific picture was pressed, a recorded response relative to the picture was heard. The pictures and responses could be changed whenever needed.

Heather was able to grasp the concept of usage quickly and could now inform others of her basic needs, discomforts, along with an activity she wanted to do. This also was a great approach to increase Heather's vocabulary over time. In fact, by the time she graduated from preschool, she began to speak more fluently where the device was no longer needed.

Heather was also quick to pick up on the procedure in recording responses on the Digivox as well and shared this know how with her brother, Mikey, six years older. Together, the two of them created their own recorded responses for the pictures. Fun as it was for the both of them, Miss Kathy viewed it differently and advised me not to allow the recordings to continue. I must admit, I did find many of their recorded responses quite creative and humorous.

During the time Heather attended Little People Land, she loved riding the bus even though the ride to and from school was over an hour long. The ISD (Intermediate School District) bus Heather rode on, traveled long distances throughout our county picking up other children, whom also had special needs. By far, Heather enjoyed the bus ride home the most. She had every reason for doing so.

Riding the bus along with Heather, were a few high school students who attended class in the same building as the preschool. Those students had been placed in a special classroom setting that addressed issues of disruptive behavior. At the beginning of the school year when Heather arrived home, I would meet the bus in our driveway in order to bring Heather into the house. Everyday the students offered to help carry Heather's belongings and often her to the house. Toward the end of the school year, I allowed them to bring Heather and her belongings to our house on their own. After bringing Heather to me and giving her hugs, the students made their way back to the bus. I was very moved by their gesture and credited the bus driver for allowing them to exit the bus as they did.

Throughout the course of the school year, a few of those students would bring Heather gifts. Something new would show up in her book bag from time to time, given to her by someone on the bus. It was absolutely amazing the impact she had on those kids. She just seemed to bring out the best in them. One would not have guessed those students were troubled.

As time approached for the bus to arrive Graduation morning, Heather and I went outside to wait. We remained relatively silent that morning. We both seemed to be lost in our own thoughts. With the heat of the morning sun, combined with the humidity in the air, Heather and I both started to break out into a sweat. As I was about to move Heather into the shade, she pointed toward the road where the bus appeared over the hill by the neighbors home a short distance from ours.

A smile appeared on Heather's face as we watched the bus approach the end of our drive and backed in. When the wheelchair ramp was lowered on the bus, I wheeled Heather over to the bus for the last time. Before the driver wheeled Heather unto the ramp, I bent down and gentle kissed her cheek and told her I would see her at school. I watched as the ramp was raised and Heather being placed in position to secure her wheelchair before I walked back toward the house.

It seemed like yesterday when Heather began attending Little People Land. I still remember how tiny and vulnerable she appeared as she was being driven away on her first day. I met her at school on her first day and spent the day in the classroom, in order to make sure Heather would adjust to the new surroundings with ease. Not at all surprising, I was the one who needed to adjust to Heather going to school. Heather acted as though she had been going to Little People Land all along. She didn't need to adjust to anything. Now, three years later, I would once again meet Heather at school. On this day, the purpose was to watch her graduate.

Accompanying me to Heather's graduation was my mom. When we walked into the gymnasium at Heather's school, we both noticed the stage had been decorated with balloons and banners. Since there would be other preschool classes participating in the graduating ceremony, the gym was already quite crowded with parents.

Most of the chairs set up for the parents had been already taken when we arrived. There were only a few chairs unoccupied toward the back of the gym, so Mom and I had no other choice but to sit there. The location was near the entrance where Heather and her class would enter, so this ended up being a perfect place to sit after all.

It didn't take long to notice how many of the parents and siblings of the graduating students were growing impatient for the program to begin. Thankfully, in a matter of minutes after Mom and I sat down, the head administrator walked onto the stage. She welcomed all who showed, then without further delay she gave the signal for the first group of children to walk in; Heather's class was first.

Before the program was about to begin, Miss Kathy approached me and asked if I felt comfortable in allowing Heather to walk up to the stage. Attempting to walk the sixty feet to the stage with the aid of her walker made me nervous, but if Heather wanted to try I was not going to stop her. I smiled with a nod. Miss Kathy smiled in return, then went back to her class.

Heather began school essentially confined to a wheelchair. With the help of physical therapy she received at school and outpatient therapy at the nearby hospital, Heather slowly regained strength in her legs that allowed her to begin taking steps and eventually walking short distances with the aid of a walker. Within seconds after Miss Kathy went back to her class, Heather appeared in the doorway of the gym. The sight of her standing there is one I will never forget.

So confident she was, my little stem and leaf girl. Her hair losing its curl from the humidity and there was a hole in her new tights. Maybe in a way she was making a fashion statement; *Do not measure me by my appearance, I am so much more.*

As with all the other children waiting to enter the gym, Heather looked around to see if she could spot where her family members were sitting. She didn't have to look long to spot Mom and me. We were only a few feet away from the entrance.

As soon as Miss Kathy gave the go ahead, Heather focused on me as she began her journey to the stage. The sight of her walking overwhelmed me as it had every time I had seen her walk. When Heather reached the chair I was sitting in she stopped. I instantly leaned over and asked if she was all right and in need of her wheelchair. She just stood there smiling, shaking her head no. In that moment I took a picture. Not with a camera, but with my heart and it remains as vivid even now.

After being nudged by a classmate, followed by me giving her a reassuring nod, Heather continue on her way. Her focus from then on was solely directed to the stage. Without help or falling, Heather wearily struggled up the ramp onto the stage and went directly to her wheelchair. I had tears streaming down my face and it didn't matter if others saw. For I had just witnessed a monumental moment.

Once all the children were gathered on the stage, they sang a couple of songs then the certificates were handed out. After receiving the certificate, the children were allowed sit with their family, if their parent(s) had attended the program.

After receiving her certificate, Heather chose to walk to Mom and me, instead of being wheeled to us. Heather made it down the ramp and no farther. She began to cry and looked to me for help.

I rose from my chair and walked to her. I lifted her up in my arms and carried her back to my seat with her Graduation Certificate in hand. Another parent offered to carry her walker. Once I was seated with Heather, I held her so close to me while she continued to cry; knowing that she understood what the day signified. Her last day at Little People Land.

Part One

*"Life's challenges are not supposed to paralyze you,
they're supposed to help you discover who you are."*
Bernice Johnson Reagon

CHAPTER ONE

THE MORNING OF SEPTEMBER 21,1989, I woke up with an abundant amount of energy, something I was not accustomed to. Being nine months pregnant and enduring the hottest summer in years for Michigan, accounted for the lack of energy I had been feeling. On that particular morning, the drop in temperature and lack of humidity was a welcome relief from the record-breaking temperatures that had been occurring. I dressed, then awakened my six year old son, Mikey, out of a seemingly deep sleep for school. It took a few minutes for him to adjust to his well lit room before he clumsily crawled out of his bed. Mikey had a easy going temperament which made my task of waking him easy. Not all children are morning greeters like Mikey seemed to be. Some children tend to resist and fuss. A trait I believe follows into adulthood. I would discover this trait in Heather.

When Mikey was picked up for school, the house became mine. I went about doing housework and decided to get started on the laundry. By the time the first load was washed, the morning sun was shining bright and there was slight breeze, making it perfect for hanging the clothes out to dry. I have always loved the comforting scent of sheets line dried, so this was my intention that morning. Living in the country as we did, it was best to take note if the neighboring farmers were fertilizing their fields. If so, it was wise to use the dryer. After detecting no odor of liquid fertilizer or any other farm manure, I chose to dry the sheets outside.

My first contraction hit while hanging the first load of sheets. Excitement and anticipation filled me as I imagined that this might be the day our baby may be born. Throughout the afternoon, the contractions grew in intensity and more frequent. Around 6:00 that evening, I told my husband, Alex, it was time to go to the hospital.

Without any complications, Heather Anne Moore, was born at 8:11 pm.

Alex and I elected not to know the sex of our baby during pregnancy, so I was elated when the doctor announced "you have a daughter." Weighing in at seven pounds and fourteen ounces, Heather was perfect, as all babies are in the eyes of the parents. She was born with a full head of black hair, punk rockers would envy— a natural mo-hawk. While in the delivery room, the doctor held Heather while Alex nervously performed the cutting of the umbilical cord, all the while displaying an overwhelming expression of being in complete awe of Heather, his first born child.

After the nurse cleaned and clothed Heather, I was allowed to hold her for a brief period of time before she was taken to the nursery. Later, when I was settled into my hospital room, Heather and I were once again reunited. The first thing I did was survey her fingers and toes which were all intact and accounted for. It was not until we had been home a week that I notice that she had a set of webbed toes on each foot. I remember thinking "Wow, this is quite unique. Guess I didn't survey her body with a very keen eye in the hospital. Were there any other additional features I overlooked?" Other than the webbed toes, no other distinct features were found.

Family members anxiously awaited our arrival home from the hospital. Heather was the first grandchild born on her father's side of the family, which automatically granted her special privileges while growing up. Ever notice how Grandparents tend to become more lenient with grandchildren, and how the grand children don't hesitate to take advantage of this? Babies have this overwhelming ability to bring out the tenderness in those who appear strict and reserved. Heather had this instant effect on her Great Grandma White, a woman quite stubborn and disciplined. Together the two of them would form a close net bond that remained until Heather's Great Grandma's passing thirteen years later.

HEATHER'S WORDS

Great Grandma White was a stubborn lady and a hard head, but would do anything for anyone; especially me. I was her first Great grandchild, so I got spoiled. I remember when I did something wrong while my father was with me at her house, she would always say "Oh Alex, leave her be." One such incident I remember was when I spilled a glass of chocolate milk on her carpet in the living room. No grandchild (not even dad) was allowed to drink in the living room. Not only did she allow me, she wasn't upset over the spill. Even today, it's a family joke of how I was her favorite. When I was older, I would spend every other weekend with Great Grandma White.

There was one time when she told my dad she didn't want me to stay the weekend, but called shortly afterward to see when the next time I would come over again. When I was at her house, I helped her fix breakfast, lunch, and dinner for the two of us. Oh, I can't forget her daily pills she had to take each morning and evening. The pills were counted out and kept in her spare ash trays placed on the kitchen table. I just couldn't get over how many pills there were in each ash tray. Great Grandma White was a smoker and I told her one day that she should stop smoking because they would kill her. She would only look at me and repeat what she always said, "*I'm going to die anyway.*"

I was ten years old when I started hanging out with her. We played Yahtzee and Skip Bow up until the news came on, then all her attention was focused on the television. I also remember Grandma Sandy, my father's mother, picking me up every Thursday for a weekly visit with Great Grandma White. We brought along food from Burger King and Wendy's. It was routine for us to stay and watch Wheel of Fortune and Jeopardy before leaving. I also remember how she loved Tiger baseball. Great Grandma was never afraid to express her opinion on any subject. A trait I have acquired from her.

Great Grandma White's health began to deteriorate when I was thirteen. One day when I returned home from a sleep over at my friend's house,, I asked if we could go to the hospital to see her. She had been in the hospital for four days. I was reassured that we would go see her the up coming weekend. It was later that evening that we received the call with the news of her passing. Great Grandma White died on July 20, 2000. I couldn't stop crying when I saw her laying in the hospital bed, but remember how peaceful and happy she looked. When it was time for us to leave the hospital, I kissed her forehead as a farewell gesture; for that day I lost my best friend.

That night, I was awakened abruptly from my sleep. I felt as though someone had just sat on my bed. When I looked to see who it was I saw my Great Grandma White sitting there looking at me. I sat up and she reach out and held my hand. She appeared younger, but I recognized her. She told me that she loved me and wanted to say good-bye. She also wanted me to tell my dad to relax and not get worked up over little things. Also to tell him good-bye. I never did tell my dad about her visit that night.

I had concerns over how Mikey would adjust to Heather being part of our family, since he had been the only child. Mikey's father and I separated when Mikey was barely two and divorced shortly after. It had been the two of us until I met and married Alex, three years later. The adjustment of having another man in the house was trying at times, as it is for most children. I guess, because there is always hope within most children that his/her parents will someday reunite. Mikey was no exception. His acceptance of Alex did not happen over night, but eventually he did acknowledge Alex as being a part of our life.

Mikey happily accepted Heather and grew into the role of big brother with ease. However, because of the age difference between the two, interacting with Heather was not a priority for him. It wasn't until Heather began walking and talking did the two begin spending time playing and fighting. Heather of course, became Mikey's shadow whether he liked it or not, along with granting herself free access to all of his belongings.

Every milestone an infant progresses to, such as rolling over, crawling, learning to stand and taking steps, to feeding one self, and eventually talking, Heather reached at the normal age range. She was a happy and inquisitive child with a streak of stubbornness, passed down from Great Grandma White. Heather liked order and neatness right from the get go, except for one distinct kitchen drawer containing plastic lids. Without fail, her first morning mission was to empty the drawer of lids onto the floor, not to play with them. She would just empty the drawer and move on the the next morning routine, checking the canned food cupboard to rearranged the cans to her liking. However, if Heather spotted any debris on the floor that shouldn't be there according to her, such as a shred of paper, thread, or the dreaded cat food crumbs, she would draw attention to it until someone or herself picked it up.

Heather, as with most young children, became attached to one special object; a pillow. A small white pillow with a light blue backing and a lamb appliqued on the front. Would not matter to Heather if the pillow was completely spoiled and smelled something awful, she didn't want to part with it. On the days I washed her pillow, she attentively stood guard in front of the washer and dryer refusing to move until the pillow was given back to her. I ended up mending the seams on countless occasions, recovered the pillow twice, having to sew the lamb back on so she did not suspect I had done anything to her cherished pillow, before she grew out her attachment.

Quoting a familiar adage, "It seemed like a blink of the eye," since Heather had been born and brought home almost twenty- two months ago. She was growing so fast while constantly exploring and discovering the world around her. Playing in the sand box with Mikey was a favored activity between the two. Heather also loved the water and would spend hours in it if allowed. As a reference to her eating habits, Heather was given the nickname "Piggy." She loved to eat, that child of ours, and couldn't be unsupervised for one second at any of Mikey's T-ball games, for she would quietly sneak off scoping out whether or not the other spectators had any snacks unattended. Which she would readily help herself to. There was one incident where she wandered off only to return with a box of Cheez-It snack crackers in hand. God only knew to whom those crackers belonged to.

Heather's most noticeable physical trait were her eyes. The most angelic hazel blue eyes, so full of emotion, unlike I had ever seen in a child. There was also an unexplainable presence that seemed to surround Heather, as one could feel so much love radiate from her. Something truly special resonated within her total being.

Heather was the picture of perfect health outside the occasional cold, flu, or when she had to be exposed to the chicken pox twice, before she became immune to it. Her health was never an issue for us to be concerned about. Alex and I especially made a point of keeping her immunizations up to date. Without questions or concerns, we handed over Heather's well being to a complete stranger at the health clinic where she received her vaccines, believing we were protecting her from so many harmful diseases. We did glance through the pamphlets that provided information including the risk factors connected to each vaccine. The risk factors seemed so low that I never believed Heather would ever experience any adverse reaction. Within a few days of receiving her latest DPT (Diphtheria, Pertussis and Tetanus) vaccination at twenty-two months of age, I would realized how mistaken my belief was.

CHAPTER TWO

OTHER THAN THE CHIRPY BIRDS outside my window, I woke to a quite house on Sunday, July 14,1991. Alex and I stayed out late with friends the night before and sleeping in was the only agenda I had in mind for the morning. Mikey was spending the weekend with his dad and Heather spent the night at her Uncle Larry and Aunt Karmen's house, so the morning was ours to do as we pleased. Well, that was the plan anyway. As with all plans, there is always a chance of a glitch which ultimately alters any plan and mine was about to be altered in a fashion that I was not prepared for.

With the ringing of the phone echoing throughout the house, I quickly rose out of bed and went to answer it, hoping the ringing didn't disturb Alex's sleep.

"Hello," I said in a sleepily tone of voice.

"Barb, sorry if I woke you, but something is wrong with Heather," Karmen announced in a distraught manner.

"Why, what's wrong? Has her cold worsened, or she running a fever?"

"No," Karmen replied. "It's something else. She seems to be feeling okay, but I noticed her dragging her left foot as she is walking. Her head is tilted downward to her left side and her fingers are rolled up into a fist. Grandma White is here and is quite worried. She thinks Alex and you should take Heather to the emergency room and have a doctor check her out. Grandma said, if she didn't know better, she would swear that Heather had a stoke."

A hundred questions and thoughts were popping into my mind all at once, making it difficult to grasp what Karmen had just said. The only systems Heather had been showing during the past week or so was those of a common cold.

"*WHAT*? Did you say stroke? Wait, did you say it look like Heather had a stroke?"

"That is the way Grandma White is describing Heather. Heather isn't fussing or seems to be in any pain," Karmen said. "I don't know what could have happened to her. She was fine last night. This just appeared this morning."

"Alex and I will be there shortly," I said. We said our good-byes to each other and I went to wake Alex, whom was already awake and dressing.

"Who was you talking to on the phone and who had a stroke?" He asked.

"It was Karmen. She said something is going on with Heather and they are worried. Grandma White said it looked as if Heather had a stroke because of the way she is acting."

"Acting? How is she acting?" He asked in a serious tone.

"According to Karmen, Heather is dragging her left foot when she walks, her head is tilted downward and her hand is rolled into a fist."

"Are they bringing Heather home?"

"I told Karmen we would go there and pick her up. She said Grandma White thought we should take Heather to the emergency room. It sounds serious, Alex."

"Maybe she fell and hurt herself without them seeing. Better get dressed so we can drive over there. It is probably not as bad as it sounds."

On our way to Larry and Karmen's house, Alex and I discussed possible causes for Heather's condition. We were speculating on so many possibilities. Maybe this happened, maybe that happened. So many maybe's without no real explanation for Heather's condition. The forty minute drive seemed like hours. It was as if time had slowed to a crawl. Alex and I became profoundly quiet as we neared the house. I guess we became lost in our own thoughts. I know I did. It just didn't make any sense. How could something like this happen? Were there signs I didn't pick up on? All she had was a cold. What did I miss? All those thoughts were playing themselves out over and over until we pulled into the drive and walked up to the door where Larry was waiting for us.

Heather was sitting on Grandma White's lap at the dining room table when Alex and I walked in. She immediately wanted down when she seen the two of us and started walking toward us. It was obvious she was indeed dragging her left foot. Her head was tilted just as Karmen had described and her left hand look like she had some type of paralysis. I felt like I was frozen in place and could not move. I just stood there bewildered. Alex, on the other hand, bent down to greet Heather and picked her up. She held out her arms for me to take her. Maybe she was just seeking out the comfort of Mom. I took her in my arms and held her as she laid her head on my shoulder while I stroked her hair.

We were all baffled by the condition Heather was in and decided right then we had better take her to the hospital. We assured Karmen and Grandma White, we would call them the instant we were home with any news we had. Alex and I left the house and drove directly to the emergency room at Kelsey Memorial Hospital back in Lakeview. On the way to the hospital, I kept watch over Heather wondering what was happening to her, fearful of what the doctor may say and saddened by the vacant stare of her eyes. This would mark the first time I felt completely helpless as a parent.

To our relief, there was no one in the waiting room when we entered. Before we even finished the paperwork handed to us by the receptionist, Heather's name was called and we were escorted to the room where we waited for the attending physician. While waiting, a nurse came into the room and took Heather's temperature, which registered one hundred and one degrees and recorded her weight at being twenty four pounds. She asked the reason for us being there and we described the symptoms Heather was experiencing. As the nurse was writing down the information we had given her, the attending physician on duty came into the room. My first impression of him was that he looked far to young to be experienced enough to diagnosis Heather. I began to think that Alex and I should have taken Heather to a different hospital.

CHAPTER THREE

"Hello, I'm Markus Greenwood the attending physician today." He announced while offering a cordial handshake to Alex and me. "What bring you folks in today?"

"Something is going on with our daughter, Heather," I announced. "She was fine yesterday, but this morning she is dragging her left foot when she walks, her head tilts downward toward her left side, and her hand looks as if she has some type of paralysis. Whatever it is, it seems to have only affected her left side," I said.

"Had she accidentally swallowed any poison you may not be aware of?"

"Not that I am aware of. She had spent the night with her Aunt and Uncle. There was no mention of Heather getting into anything like that."

"Has Heather been sick lately?"

"She started coming down with a cold over a week ago. Upper chest congestion along with a runny nose. She also seemed to be getting intermittent fevers."

He looked at Heather's medical chart and noticed that her temperature was one hundred and one degrees.

"Any coughing with the other symptoms?" Doctor Greenwood asked.

"There is some coughing, but not continuous."

"Any sign of ear aches that may be bothering her?"

"Not that I'm aware of. She hasn't been rubbing her ears to indicate that they are bothering her."

At that point of our visit, he began to check out Heather's ears and throat.

"There does appear to be some redness in both ears which may imply that a slight ear infection is present. Has her appetite changed any? There is some redness in her throat as well and her glands seems to be a bit swollen, but nothing serious."

"Yes, Heather hasn't been eating like she normally does. I just thought she had not been eating much due to her not feeling well." I said.

"Heather is how old?"

"Twenty two months old."

"Is her immunizations up to date?"

"Yes."

"What, if any medication is Heather on?"

"I have been giving her Tylenol for her fevers and Dimeatapp for the congestion and runny nose."

"Is she on any prescription medication?"

"No."

"Any unusual markings on her such as insect bites or bumps you may have noticed?"

"No, she did receive her DPT vaccine over a week ago. There was swelling on her leg where they poked her with the needle, which seemed to last a couple of days."

"The redness and swelling is quite normal after any vaccine, nothing to be concerned about."

As if those were not enough questions, we was then hit with a barrage of questions, most of which were already answered in the paper work we were asked to fill out. By this time, Heather was becoming fussy, Alex impatient and I tired of answering questions.

"Full term pregnancy?"

"Yes."

"Any complications during childbirth?"

"No."

"Any other siblings in the home?"

"Yes, Mikey, six years older than Heather."

"Is he in good health?"

"Yes."

"Any pets in the home?"

"Yes, we have a house cat and a dog."

"Notice any flea or tick bites on Heather?"

"No, I have not noticed any bites on her," I said, wondering where he was going with this.

"You said she didn't have any sign of insect bites, correct?"

"Not any that had caught my attention. Why do you ask about insect bites?" I questioned.

"Insects are known carries of infections disease. There may be a possibility that Heather was infected by an insect bite that you were not aware of. I would like to watch Heather walk now, so I can get a better idea of what you mean by her dragging her foot along."

I stood up with Heather in my arms and walked outside the room into the hallway. The doctor followed, while Alex stood in the doorway of the room. I walked down the hallway until the doctor told me to stop. I gave Heather a gentle hug and kissed the top of her head before standing her on the carpeted hallway floor. The doctor then called out to Heather in an effort to get her to walk toward him. When she didn't respond, he asked me to join him and call Heather over to the both of us. I called out to Heather, but she just stood there looking so tried and withdrawn. I called out again, this time more firmly while holding my arms out to her. Only then did she begin to slowly walk down the hall.

The receptionist and the nurses on duty all watched as Heather was making her way closer to myself and the doctor. I remember being bothered by this. It seemed like Heather had become a source of entertainment for them. I know the stares was out of curiosity, but it still bothered me. Here I was, watching my daughter struggling to walk down that hall looking so innocent and weak. The expression in her eyes in that moment was breaking my heart. It was as if she was pleading with me through her eyes." Please help me, hold me, I'm tried and want to go home." The closer she walked to me the more she had to struggle and soon began to softly whimper; to the point where the doctor finally said, " I've seen enough."

I went to pick up Heather and looked in the direction of the office area where the receptionist and nurses quickly turned away and resumed whatever they were doing beforehand. The four of us went back into the room where the doctor confessed to us that he has never seen such symptoms in a child so young.

"If she were elderly, I would say that she had a stroke."

"Does she need to be admitted for tests or observation?" I asked.

"Other then the fever, she does not appear to be in any immediate distress. I will have the nurse give her something for the fever and do advise you and your husband to contact your family physician for a complete examination."

"What do you think could have caused this to happen to Heather?

"Without further testing it is impossible to know. It does appear to be some type of neurological issue. She may have been fighting some type of infection for a while now which may be the cause of her intermittent fevers. Again, without further testing it is impossible to diagnosis Heather just by this examination."

"So we just take her home and pray she doesn't get any worse?" I asked.

"If her condition begins to deteriorate or shows any signs of convulsions, bring her in immediately."

"But, she is here now. Why not admit her now? What happens if she convulses while Alex and I are asleep? Are you willing to chance that?"

"Make the appointment with your family doctor. Keep a close watch over Heather and make sure she is getting plenty of fluids."

This was his response, followed by "It is possible that whatever has caused this to happen, most likely has run its course and no further developments will occur."

At that moment I thought to myself, "Right, give her Tylenol and fluids and all is well." The doctor rose and exited the room. Shortly afterward, a nurse came into the room to administer the Tylenol before we were told it was okay to go.

Walking to our car, I looked at Alex just shaking my head. I was dumbfounded by the lack of concern and angry at myself for coaxing Heather to walk when she was obviously so weak. When we arrived home, I called Karmen and Grandma White, offering no explanation for Heather's condition. I then called my mom to inform her, when it suddenly dawned on me, *No matter one's age, one still has the tendency to seek the comfort of mom. Just as Heather was seeking comfort from me earlier, I was seeking the same from my mom in that moment.*

CHAPTER FOUR

*I*N MY OPINION, THE GREATEST furniture design has to be the rocking chair. Astonishing just how many childhood aliments, wounded pride, and sleepless nights, are soothed by rocking with the child. In a way, it's like recapturing that intimate bond that existed before the child began to become more independent and engaged in discovering life apart from mom.

Heather looked so exhausted when we arrived home after our emergency room visit. When I finished making phone calls, I carried Heather into her room with the intention of laying her down in bed, but caught sight of the rocking chair in the corner of her room. Instead of laying her down, I decided to rock with her. Before the two of us sat down, I changed her diaper and began putting her in pajamas. Her body still felt very warm as her fever had not yet subsided. Once her pajamas were on, I gently picked Heather up, while grabbing her lamb pillow and a blanket. Then the two of us settled into the rocking chair. This is where Heather and I would end up spending the night.

When Mikey came home from his visiting his dad, I explained the best I could just how sick Heather was. He stayed in the room with us until his bedtime and went off to bed. Alex would check on Heather and I periodically before he too went to bed. A short time after the house become quiet and dark, with the exception of the moonlight shining through Heather's bedroom window, I noticed the silhouette of Mikey peeking into the room.

"Mom," He whispered. "I can't sleep. Can I sleep in here tonight?"

"Go grab your blanket and pillow." I whispered back.

Mikey must have known what my response would be, for he already had his blanket and pillow hidden behind him. He quietly came in the room and laid on the floor close to the rocking chair.

When I thought Heather had finally drifted off to sleep, I rose from the chair to lay her down on her bed. As soon as she felt me putting her down, she started to whimper and grabbed unto my shirt in an attempt to remain held, so back to the rocking chair we went. I attempted to lay her down a few other times throughout the night, but whenever I did, Heather sensed it and would wake up.

Alex woke early the following morning to find Heather and I still in the chair, along with Mikey asleep on the floor. Before leaving for work, he gave Heather and I a gentle kiss. The company Alex worked for manufactured prison cell doors. Shortly after Heather's birth, he began to travel with the work crew installing those doors at different locations in Michigan. This meant he would leave home every Monday morning and not return back until Friday afternoon. By this time, the kids and I were growing accustomed to his absences, but as a result, Alex appeared to gradually become more of an visitor than a father and husband.

After Alex had left for work, I again tried to lay Heather down on her bed. My body was tried and stiff from sitting in the chair all night and I needed to stretch. This time, Heather was sound asleep and didn't move when I laid her down. I too wanted to lay down to sleep, but there were phone calls to make.

I knew the doctor's office wouldn't be open for another two hours, but maybe the receptionist came in early. That was my hope anyway. I started calling at seven. This may seem a bit irrational, but it made me feel like I was at least making an effort. Perhaps, my calling was a way of easing the feeling of being so helpless.

Heather woke up crying thirty minutes later. When I entered her room, Mikey was already helping Heather out of bed. I stood in the doorway and watched as he took hold of Heather under the arms and tried to pick her off the bed, only to trip backwards on his blanket and Heather falling on top of him, then rolling onto the floor. Needless to say, the fall didn't help Heather's demeanor one bit. Her crying only heightened as a result. I went over to pick her up while giving Mikey a hint of a smile. Trying not to over react to what had happened, for this would certainly have had made him feel even worse than he already did.

Heather continued to feel warm. Her fever did not break during the night. I carried Heather into the kitchen and gave her some

Tylenol. She drank a few sips of water, but refused to eat when I offered her some cereal. Apparently, all Heather wanted was to be held. All I wanted was for time to speed up and reach Dr. Cottle. As for Mikey, he just stood by watching Heather with a worried expression on his face.

Following numerous attempts of reaching a live human, instead of an answering machine at the doctor's office, Sharon, the receptionist, answered.

"Hello Sharon," I said in a rapid tone of voice. "This is Barb Moore. I need to see John as soon as possible."

"Barb Moore?" She questioned.

"Yes. I know it has been a long time since I, or anyone in my family as been to see John, but I need to bring my daughter, Heather, in for John to examine her."

"Has your daughter ever been seen by Dr. Cottle?" She asked.

"No, by the time I became pregnant with Heather, he had chosen to stop delivering babies and Heather has never been that sick to where she needed to see a doctor until now."

"Well, his schedule is full today Barb. Dr. Cottle could see you tomorrow around three. Will that work for you?"

"Sharon, my daughter is very sick. She was taken to the emergency room yesterday. I need to see John today."

"What seems to be so urgent?"

"We don't know what is happening to her. She is running a fever and unbelievable as this will sound, her condition resembles that of a stroke victim."

"She wasn't admitted into the hospital?" Sharon asked in a bewildered tone.

"We were told to take her home and call our family physician. There didn't seem to be a lot of concern over her condition."

"Well, let me see what I can do. Is she in any pain? Is that her crying in the background?"

"Yes, it is Heather. From the moment she awoke this morning, her crying has been non-stop. As I mentioned earlier, she has a fever and is refusing to eat."

"What is her temperature now? Have you taken it?"

"The thermometer read a hundred degrees, that was around an half hour ago," I said.

"Barb, give me a few minutes to see if I can contact Dr. Cottle. I will call you back when I find out what he wants to do."

"All right Sharon, I'll be waiting for your call."

After ending the call, I felt quite discouraged. Sharon didn't seem alarmed by what I had told her and I was afraid she may be thinking I was just over stating Heather's condition. That fear was soon put to rest when the phone rang and Sharon asking "How soon can you get here?"

In a manner of minutes, Heather, Mikey and I were out of the door and on our way to Dr. Cottle's office. The office was not yet officially open to patients when we arrived, so we knocked on the door until Sharon let us in.

"Hi Barb, Dr. Cottle hasn't arrived yet, but he is on his way. While waiting for him, I need you to fill out some paper work and also need a copy of your insurance card."

Filling out paperwork similar to what was filled out in the emergency room seemed so time consuming. If I had known how many times I would be filling out similar paperwork for every doctor and specialist we would be seeing in the future, I would have made several copies of the original paperwork I filled out in the emergency room. I could have then just handed each receptionist a copy. Not an easy task filling out paperwork with a crying child sitting on your lap.

After updating my personal information and filling out the questions regarding Heather's medical history, Sharon took the three of us to a examination room. She took Heather's temperature, recording it as being one hundred and two and her weight was marked at being twenty-three pounds.

When we heard the shutting of the door at the back entrance of the building, I knew Dr. Cottle had arrived. Dr. Cottle, had been my family doctor ever since he took over the practice when the previous physician had left. Being a small town doctor, it was customary to be on a first name basis. John was in his mid to late thirties, so relating to him was easy. On the account of there wasn't a large age gap between us. What I admired the most about John, his approach to his patients was personal, which made me feel completely comfortable in his presence.

"It has been a while since you've been in to see me," Dr. Cottle stated, as he walked into the room. "I wasn't sure who Sharon was talking about at first. Is this little Mikey?" He asked over the cries of Heather. Mikey was one of the first babies John had delivered after he started his practice in Edmore.

"Yes, this is Mikey. Can you believe he is eight years old now?" I said while trying to console Heather.

"Eight years old. Time sure does fly by fast, doesn't it?" John remarked, while looking down at Mikey. "Sharon mentioned your daughter was taken to the emergency room yesterday and the attending physician advised you to bring her in today, is that correct? Was she sick prior to yesterday?" John asked.

"Yes, I just figured Heather was coming down with a cold. She had a runny nose and some chest congestion, along with intermittent fevers." I then went into describing Heather's symptoms she experienced at Karman's, along with her continuous crying which began that morning along with Heather's lack of appetite.

"How many days were the cold symptoms and fevers present before yesterday?"

"Maybe a week or so," I said

"Any rash at any time?"

"No, but she did have a lump and redness where she was injected with her DPT vaccination that lasted a couple of days afterward."

"So, Her immunizations are up to date?"

"Yes."

"How long after her vaccination did she come down with cold symptoms?" John asked.

"Maybe four or five days after her vaccine. Do you think this may be some type of a reaction from the shot?"

"She was perfectly healthy before her vaccination?

"Yes, she was normal; walking, saying a few words and playing. Hardly ever sick," I answered.

"Her temperature is one hundred and two degrees? What are you giving her for the fevers?"

"Some Tylenol. I gave her some this morning, but it doesn't seem to be doing anything to relieve the fevers."

"You say it looks like stroke symptoms that Heather has?"

"It's the best way to describe her condition," I replied.

"I notice the clenching of her hand and the tilt of her head, but I will need Heather to stand and maybe take a few steps in order to get an idea of her gait. Do you think we can could get her to do that?"

"I don't know, John. We can try.

I tried to put Heather down, but she began clinging on to me with all her might crying harder; if that was at all possible.

"Don't force her, Barb. Obviously, she is too upset. Right now, I am at a lost here. I haven't seen symptoms such as these in a child this young. I am going send you over to the hospital, in order to draw some blood from Heather. I will also arrange a CT (Computed Tomography) scan for Heather. The CT scan may be able to detect any abnormalities in the brain. The blood taken from Heather will detect if any infection is occurring. To be honest, I don't know what we are dealing with, Barb. I will be in contact with you as soon the test results come back. To help ease your worry, I will put a rush order on them."

"Do you think she should be admitted into the hospital?" I asked.

"Let's see what the test results reveal. What we need to do is lower that fever of hers. I'll order a stronger medication to be given her at the hospital. A word of caution Barb, don"t be alarmed if Heather needs to be sedated for the CT scan. It can be a frightening experience for a young child. Better plan on being at the hospital for a while." John said before escorting us out into the lobby.

A while? We were at the hospital for hours. Whatever was given to Heather for her fever, relaxed her to the point where her crying had stopped. That in itself was a blessing. Mikey was such a trooper throughout the day. I felt bad that he had to endure the waiting with nothing much to keep him occupied. Once the CT was completed, Mikey and I was allowed in the room where Heather was waking up from the sedative.

The two of us sat beside her bedside up until we were told it was okay to take Heather home. Again, no mention of admitting Heather for further testing and no insisting upon doing so from me. I just wanted to go home. I was exhausted and feeling frustrated, from not being any closer to knowing what was happening to Heather.

CHAPTER FIVE

OTH MIKEY AND HEATHER WERE drifting in and out of sleep on our way back home from the hospital. While we were at the hospital, Dr. Cottle had faxed over a message saying he had called in a couple of prescriptions in for Heather at our local pharmacy in Lakeview. The pharmacy had already closed by the time we arrived back in Lakeview, so I would have to wait till the next day to fill them.

Heather was still a little groggy from the sedative when we returned home, but her fever was gone, at least for the time being. What surprised me the most, as soon as I put her down in the house, she went straight to the can food cupboard and took out a can of Spaghetti O's and held the can out to me. It was an encouraging sign to see that her appetite was back. Once I took the can of Spaghetti O's from Heather, her and Mikey headed toward his room. Odd that it was, Heather's condition seemed to improve in the time it took us to reach home. What a relief it was not having to continuously hold Heather, while trying to do other things.

When we sat down to eat, I noticed Heather was having difficulty swallowing her food. At times she would appear to gag and cough when she swallowed. I took her bowl of Spaghetti O's away from her and mashed the noddles before giving it back. With the noodles mashed, she ate with no further trouble. This would mark the beginning of pureeing her food.

There was another symptom that had presented itself while at the table. One I hadn't noticed earlier. She appeared to be drooling. Drool was dribbling out the corner of her mouth. I figured it was from the previous gagging, but when she finished eating and was away from the table, the drooling continued. Even with these new symptoms, Heather seemed to be feeling better than she had been since this all began. She had stopped crying and wasn't fussy. After dinner, Mikey and Heather went back into Mikey's bedroom. I watched Heather as she walked behind Mikey and noticed she wasn't only dragging her left foot, she was staggering and had stumbled a few times before reaching the room. I thought the staggering may be from the sedative still working out of her body, so I gave it little thought.

I went about clearing the dinner dishes from the table before running a bath for Heather. While in the tub, she was having difficulty keeping her balance while sitting. This too I thought was from the sedative and being tired out from the day's activity. I ended up holding on to her while I washed her. Once Heather was taken out of the tub, she was reluctant to stand on her own in order for me to dry her off, so I wrapped Heather with a towel and carried her into her room. Mikey tagged behind, not wanting to leave her side. When Heather was dried off, I went to retrieve her pajamas.

As soon as she saw me picking out her pajamas, she began to whimper. I wondered what could be so upsetting about getting ready for bed? Was she afraid of going to sleep? Once her pajamas were on, I tried laying her in bed, but she didn't want any part of it. Her whimpers instantly turned into a full fledged crying session. I then thought if I took her into my room and had the three of us laying in bed, that might settle her down enough for her to fall asleep. This idea failed as well and I feared another night sitting in the rocking chair was in store for us.

A short time later, while Mikey was taking his bath, I noticed that Heather felt warm again. I wasn't sure if it was another fever or just from her crying, generating the warmth. I gave her a small amount of Tylenol as a precaution. After Mikey was out of the tub and dressed in his pajamas, he again asked if he could sleep in Heather's room with us. I told he might as well since I know he would be making his way there later anyway.

That night, Mikey would sleep in Heather's bed while she and I resumed our position in the rocking chair as we had the night before, with Heather straddling my lap in a sitting position facing me, while laying her head on the lamb pillow that rested on my chest. Mikey went about the business of arranging some toys in bed that he had chosen to sleep with. Afterward, he began play acting in front of Heather in an attempt to make her laugh.

As we settled down for the night, my mind began racing with so many questions, as I tried to make sense of Heather's condition. What could have possibly happened in two days time to cause this to happen? If she is physically regressing in such a fast rate, like she appeared to be doing, what is going to happen if this continues? Why hasn't she been admitted into the hospital? How am I going to manage her care, feeling this exhausted already? Why isn't Alex here to help, so I didn't feel so alone?

Right then the phone rang and I asked Mikey to answer it for me. He came back into the room announcing that it was Alex wanting to talk with me. I carried Heather, whom was still whimpering, into the kitchen where our phone was and thought maybe the sound of Alex's voice would lift her spirits.

She wanted nothing to do with the phone and started to break out crying, while laying her head on my chest. I filled Alex in about our day and the new symptoms that showed up after eating. To my surprise, he said that he was coming home the next day. The job was finished and he wouldn't be going on the road anymore. He mentioned something about the company he worked for was closing. I was having a hard time hearing with Heather crying, so most of what he said I didn't hear. Even though our conversation was brief, I was feeling better just with knowing he was coming home.

After I hung the phone up, I decided to turn off the ringer before going back into Heather's room. I didn't want anymore calls interrupting my efforts of trying to put Heather to sleep. Plus, I didn't feel like talking to anyone else that night. By then I was so tired and frustrated. I just wanted sleep.

Once again we experienced another restless night. Heather's breathing sounded raspy from her congestion. The decongestant I was giving her didn't seem to be loosening the phlegm and I feared that she may be at risk for pneumonia sitting in. Then I began wondering since she was already having such a hard time with breathing, what would happen if pneumonia actually did set in? Afraid of what the next thought would bring forth, I forced myself to stop thinking along those lines.

Heather woke up bright eyed and seemingly fine the following morning. She was ready to get down from the chair and I was ready to put her down. My body was achy and stiff from sitting in that chair.

When I helped her down from the chair, I noticed her pillow was drenched with drool. Made no difference to Heather, she grabbed her pillow from my hands and headed toward the living room. I followed carrying some toys for her to occupy herself with, as I was hoping to get a shower in while she played. When I stepped out of the shower, I heard the sounds of cartoons coming from the television. A sign that Mikey was awake and out with Heather. I peeked out into the living room to find the two of them sitting side by side in front of the TV, with Mikey's arm wrapped around Heather. It was a tender moment between the two, signifying a truce from pestering one another was in effect for now.

After breakfast and getting around to leave for town, I phoned Dr. Cottle's office in order to inform John of Heather's new symptoms. Sharon stated that John was busy with patients, but she would pass on the message. Sharon said if I preferred, I could call back later and talk with John. Soon after my call, the three of us left the house to go into town for Heather's prescriptions. I was hoping the medication John had prescribed would offer Heather relief from her congestion. Perhaps, even cure the other symptoms, or at least stop any further developments in her condition. Hope was all I had to fall back on, but in a manner of days hope itself would begin to waiver.

CHAPTER SIX

*B*Y THE TIME WE ARRIVED home from town, Alex had returned home as well and was waiting for us. As the kids and I enter the house, Heather became excited to see her dad and began to wiggle her way out of my arms before I had a chance to put her down. She immediately rushed over to where Alex was standing, stumbling along the way.

"Her walking is getting worse," Alex announced, as be bent down to lift Heather. "Did you call Dr. Cottle about this?"

"I called this morning, but he was busy with patients. I was told to call back later." I said.

The reunion between Alex and Heather was short lived as Heather motioned that she wanted down in order to play with Mikey, who had disappeared into his room as soon as he saw Alex. The relationship between Alex and Mikey was becoming quite troubling. The two just seemed to clash more often, leaving me with the impression, that I was some what caught in the middle by standing up for Mikey. Not a favored position to be in. With Alex being away during the week, the atmosphere in the household was carefree. Mikey was free to be himself. As soon as Alex returned home, the atmosphere instantly transformed into tension.

When we were alone, Alex proceeded to tell me about the possible closing of the shop he was working at and how he may have a chance of getting hired at Steel Parts Automotive, a well established company in Greenville, Michigan. This was good news because it would mean better pay for him and he would be home every night. Steel Parts Automotive was located near the factory where I worked; Northland Corporation.

I started working at Northland one year prior to Heather's birth. The work was hard, but the pay was decent. Northland had a history of laying off their work crew often, which proved to work out perfect for me. However, the work schedule was unpredictable. I might work one week and be laid off for two weeks, or I might work one day only to be laid off for the rest of the week. It was like having a part time job which allowed me to be home often with the kids.

While Mikey and Heather were off playing in Mikey's room, Alex and I talked for a few more minutes, regarding his week away and my week without him. He then mentioned something about going out and mowing the lawn.

"Mow the grass? I was hoping to nap since you were here to keep an eye on Heather," I said.

"She's fine playing with Mike. I'll have him come out and get me if something happens," Alex responded.

"Do you think that's a good idea?"

"Relax, Mike will come out and get me," He said sternly.

"Well, tell Mikey he can wake me if he needs to," I replied back.

"Then what's the point of him coming outside to get me?"

"I guess there isn't any, I'm just so tired and not thinking clearly."

"You tell Mike to come and get me if you want. I'm going to mow the lawn." With that, he walked out of the door. I just shook my head. It was plain to see how Alex and my priorities were completely opposite. Mowing lawn would have the furthest thing from my mind if I had a sick child.

I went onto Mikey's room to tell him that I was going to lay down for a nap. If Heather started to fuss, I told Mikey he could wake me or go outside and get Alex. I thought about calling Dr. Cottle's office before laying down, but decided against it. I would call when I woke up.

It seemed as though I just had fallen asleep, when I felt the sensation of being nudged. When I opened my eyes, there stood Heather holding a can of Spaghetti O's. "No Spaghetti O's today," I said sleepily. She just handed me the can and continued standing there with a pitiful expression on her face, as she said "ease?" With that kind of approach, I threw back the blankets and gave in to her request. I then called Dr. Cottle's office and was put through to John. I told him about the drooling and her issues with swallowing along with her balance difficulties.

"How about the fevers? Is she still feverish?" he asked.

"The fevers come and go," I answered. " I gave her the first dose of medicine you prescribed a couple of hours ago."

"No word on the test results yet, Barb. Most likely, I won't receive them until tomorrow."

"Do you think she should be admitted in to the hospital?" I asked.

"Let's wait until the test results are in before I decide. After our visit, I began been reading my medical journals, regarding the symptoms related to Heathers condition. I also have been consulting with my colleagues about Heather. We believe it would be in Heather's best interest to be examined be a neurologist."

"Did any of the doctors you have been talking with have an idea as to what may have caused this?"

"This is only speculation, but what may be occurring is some kind of inflammation in the brain. The symptoms that Heather displays coincides with an inflammation of that sort," John replied.

"So we wait for the test results? What then? Is her condition going to get worse. How can we stop the inflammation?"

"Barb," John said calmly. " I can't answer those questions. This is new to me as well. I'll get back to you with the results and also will begin making arrangements for Heather to be seen by a neurologist."

"John, what do I do in the meantime?" I desperately asked.

"Keep doing what you are doing. If, and this is very important Barb. If, she starts to convulse or show any signs of seizing, bring her to the emergency room immediately."

"What would cause her to have a seizure?" I asked.

"If an infection is occurring in the brain, any abnormalities of her nervous system can trigger a seizure."

"Do you think that is the reason for her crying as much as she does?"

"Most likely it is. What makes this so difficult, she can't communicate to us what she is feeling except for the crying."

"I feel so helpless with this," I said with tears forming in my eyes.

"Hang in there Barb. We should know something tomorrow."

"Alright, I'll be waiting for your call. Oh John?"

"What?"

"Would you call to let me know if you didn't get the test results also. It would make me feel that we hadn't been forgotten."

"I'll make sure Sharon calls you either way."

Shortly after ending the call with John, Alex came into the house. I repeated to him what was told to me by John. Alex just sat in silence with nothing further to add. I also sat in my own silence. When Alex returned from where ever he went in his thoughts, he mentioned that he was going to fix himself something to eat. I automatically glanced up at the clock and noticed it was close to dinner time. Where did the day go? I guess I was so preoccupied with Heather, time just seemed non-existent. Along with the life I had known before the morning we received the call from Karmen.

CHAPTER SEVEN

I T WAS LOOKING LIKE ANOTHER night in the rocking chair for Heather and I. Three nights in a row sitting in that chair, made me question why I didn't buy a chair with thicker cushions for comfort. Other than knowing how my body would be feeling the morning, I didn't see any other alternative for Heather to at least get some type of sleep.

I wish that I could declare myself as being a super mom during these pre-sleep formalities, but my patience was definitely challenged, along with me questioning my ability to handle what was taking place. I remember thinking at some point, prenatal classes should include a survivor's guide to help cope with uncontrollable crying caused by unknown factors.

Heather slept better than the previous nights. The congestion in her lungs seemed to be breaking up. This caused her to cough, but not to the extreme where the coughing interfered with her sleep. In the morning, she was once again ready to get down and play with Mikey. As I was sitting in the rocking chair and looking out Heather's window, I suddenly became aware of how I hadn't been outdoors, expect for our trips to the doctor, hospital and into town. Explains why I was beginning to feel somewhat imprisoned in my own home. I thought maybe later, if the sun was warm and there wasn't much wind, I would take Heather out for a brief period of time.

I remained in the chair thinking about all the particulars concerning her condition which were known to us. Her ongoing bouts with fevers, left side paralysis which was compromising her balance, the crying spells along with excessive drooling, swallowing issues, the congestion and runny nose. All these symptoms and still waiting for a diagnosis. Heather tried easily, but napping and bedtime appeared to bring about the crying episodes lately. What could be triggering

Heather's crying in these particular moments? A question, I would put forth to John when he called with the test results.

The crying sessions resembled those of a child whom awaken from a bad dream and was afraid to go back to sleep. Her crying lasted anywhere from 1-2 hours in duration. It was out of sheer exhaustion did she fall asleep, only to awaken a short time later. Naps generally lasted about an hour and her sleep was sporadic during the night.

At times, Heather would appear to be feeling better, as she would resume activities as she had prior to her illness. Emptying the lid drawer and rearranging the can food cupboard. However, in a moment's notice, signs of regressing appeared out of nowhere. Her balance became unsteady, causing her to stumble often and lifting her head seemed difficult.

What astounded me the most was Heather's adjustment to the limited use of her left hand and her mobility. If her balance became to unsteady she would crawl. She would use the side of her left hand or her palm to grasp objects requiring two hands. It was early on that we knew her dominant hand would be her right hand, so she experienced no limitation in that aspect. Maybe, without the sense of self-pity, adjusting to her limitations just came naturally. I have noticed this trait among other young children who have endured or are enduring some type of impairment.

In the beginning, I was determined to not assume the role of becoming an overly protective parent. By doing so, in my point of view, would only hamper Heather's ability to problem solve on her own. I also knew that becoming over protective of Heather could easily turn into becoming controlling over her. However, no matter what my intentions may have been in the beginning, becoming over protective of Heather just seemed to naturally occur.

The instant I heard the ringing of the phone, my few minutes of alone time came to a halt. I flew out of the rocking chair and rushed into the kitchen to answer the phone, in hopes the caller was John with the test results.

"Hello?"

"Barb, this is John. I have the test results here and the blood work definitely indicates an infection. Her white blood cell count is extremely high. However, the CT scan came back normal."

"So, what does this mean? The infection is not affecting her brain, like it was suspected?"

"No, it just reveals there are no tumors or other abnormalities that can be detected from a CT scan," John replied. "In order to get a more in-depth evaluation, I have been in contact with a neurologist in Grand Rapids, Michigan. I faxed over an order, requesting a MRI (Magnetic Resonance Imagining) be performed on Heather. The MRI can detect abnormalities which can not be picked up on using a CT scan."

"You still believe the infection is located in Heather's brain?

"Yes, the paralysis is connected with some type of dysfunction in her nervous system."

"Do you have any idea of what caused an infection to attack the brain?" I asked.

"This is something the neurologist will be better equipped at explaining to you. Dr. Vesser, the pediatric neurologist, will be out of his office until Monday. His secretary assured me that she will be in contact with you later today to arrange a suitable time to come in. I faxed over the tests results and Heather's file already," John commented.

"John, I have a question. Heather seems to cry the most before naps and bedtime. Do you have an idea of why this happens?" I asked.

"I would just be guessing, Barb. I honestly do not know."

"Well, maybe the neurologist will know. Thanks John for all you are doing. I would be clueless in knowing what kind of help I should be seeking, if it weren't for your help."

"Let me know how things go with the neurologist. I will get a copy of her MRI results sent to me. Perhaps, we all will also have a better understanding of what is happening to Heather. Any questions or concerns you might have before Monday, do not hesitate to call. You have my home phone number right?"

"Yes, I do and thanks again."

"We will find the cause, Barb." John said reassuringly." It's just going to take a while longer. If you have no further questions, I have patients waiting."

"No, I can't think of anything else." I replied.

"Good luck with Dr. Vesser and I hope all goes well. I'll be talking to you soon."

"Good-bye John."

It wasn't long after talking to John that I received the call from

Dr. Vesser's secretary and scheduled an appointment for the following Monday at 1:00 pm. I was excited, but also scared about going. I called Mom immediately with the news and this time arranged care for Mikey, because I wasn't going to subject him to another long stay, if need be, at a doctor's office or hospital. After hanging up the phone, I went and found Heather, picked her up and announced to both her and Mikey, "*Help is on the way!*"

CHAPTER EIGHT

HE DAY WAS TURNING OUT grand. The call from John was somewhat encouraging and Heather was feeling good and full of energy. The medicine Heather was taking was doing its magic on the congestion along with her runny nose. I figured that one more day on the medication her congestion may be totally gone. After Heather woke from a short nap and eating a pureed lunch(chicken noodle soup without meat, seasoned with Prednisone and a Flintstones chewable vitamin), Heather, Mikey and I were out the door to spend some time outside.

The sandbox was the chosen destination for the kids. I sat on the back stairs to our home and soaked up some mid afternoon sun. My attention was soon drawn to the swamp connecting to our back yard, noticing how it was bursting with life. There were black birds and Robins, peppering the branches of the swamp willows outlining the water's edge. Our returning pair of Canadian geese were busily raising their goslings and a lone Blue Heron was bobbing for frogs, something I wasn't pleased to see. My sister, Shirley, and I went to great lengths in catching those bull frogs at another location in order to stock our swamp. I absolutely loved the sound of bull frogs croaking in the evening. It soothed my soul so to speak.

I then turned my attention to the sandbox and watched the kids at play. Mikey was constructing roads for his match box cars and trucks, while Heather was busily shoveling sand into her pail just to empty it and begin the process all over again. We were outside close to an hour before Heather crawled out of the sand box and over to the stairs where I was seated. She pointed to the door, indicating that she wanted to go back inside. I stepped down to retrieve her and brushed the sand off her clothing, hands and whatever I could from her hair before taking her inside to change her.

While changing her, it dawned on me that she had not had a bowel movement since she had been home from Karmen's. I called Grandma Sandy and asked her advice, since she once was a registered nurse. Grandma Sandy gave me a couple of suggestions that would initiate a bowel movement. This would mark the beginning of administering enemas to Heather, since her bowels appeared to have stopped moving on its own accord.

Heather seemed fine after changing her and was content playing with some toys, while occasionally glancing up at the television. With Heather preoccupied, I did some laundry and other household chores. When the clothes in the dryer were ready to come out, I gathered them in my arms and headed to the living room to fold them, only to notice Heather had fallen asleep on the floor. I was taken back by this because there was no crying prior. Maybe the Prednisone was relieving the discomfort Heather experienced beforehand, or maybe the fresh air relaxed her. Whatever it was, I was thankful. Heather slept a good two hours longer than normal.

Upon waking, she was burning up with a fever and had trouble keeping her balance to where standing was impossible. Heather also wasn't able to sit upright without falling over sideways. I took her temperature and the thermometer read 104 degrees. At that point, I went to start a cool bath for her, hoping to bring down her fever. Without the ability to sit without falling over, I steadied her while splashing water on her body. When the water felt cold to the touch, I took her out and dried her off. Again, I was surprised by the absence of any crying.

Throughout the time I was changing her into some light weight clothing, she didn't even whimper. Then I became aware of the haunting blank stare of her eyes. The same expression that was present, while driving to the emergency room that past Sunday.

Mikey came into the house shortly there after, took one look at Heather then faced me with a panic stricken expression. Most likely, imitating the exact look I must have had at that moment. I remember saying to him, "I need to call Dr. Cottle, stay with Heather."

"What's wrong with her?" Mikey whispered with his small voice.

"I don't know Mikey. I need to call John." I said trying to retain my composure.

I called the office and thankfully Sharon was still there, but John had left for the day. She said she would page him and to wait for his call. Waiting for the call was agonizing for me. Should I really wait for John's call or should I take Heather to the hospital? I couldn't think of what was the right thing to do. I couldn't think at all. Thoughts were rapidly firing in my mind and I couldn't grasp on one long enough to even make a decision.

When Alex came home after work and walked in to the house, he instantly knew something was wrong. "Are you okay? Has something happened to Heather?"

"So much has happened." I exclaimed. "She is not doing well. Her fever is over 100 degrees. She can't stand, walk, or even sit without falling over."

"Where is she?"

"In her room with Mikey."

"You just left her alone with Mike?" Alex said in a agitated tone.

"She is fine with him." I stated firmly.

"Why are you in the kitchen if she is doing as bad as you say?"

"Waiting to hear back from Dr. Cottle," I replied, wishing he would leave the room.

"I'll go and be with her then." He remarked, as he was making his way toward Heather's bedroom.

In a matter of seconds, I could hear Alex ordering Mikey out of Heather's room. I watched as Mikey reluctantly went into his bedroom closing the door behind him. My first instinct was to go and console Mikey, but I also didn't want to leave the kitchen. I remained sitting next to the phone praying it would ring. Feeling angry at Alex, sorry for Mikey along with guilt for not being with Heather. As if on cue, the phone rang breaking the thought pattern at that moment.

"Barb, this is Dr. Cottle. Sharon said it was urgent?" John questioned.

I brought him up to date on Heather's condition, then asked if we should bring her to the hospital to be admitted.

"The symptoms you're describing are most likely stemming from the infection, and indicates that it is attacking her nervous system. With this type of inflammation, it is impossible to know what other area will be affected," John stated. "You asked in you first visit with Heather, if I thought her condition could be a reaction from her vaccination remember?"

"Yes, but you didn't respond to that question. Do you think the shot caused this?"

"I've been researching material on the adverse effects of the DPT vaccine. Although Heather's first symptoms didn't appear until days later, close to a week or so, it's difficult to say with certainty the shot is responsible, but is quite possible. My personal opinion is that too many of Heather's symptoms closely relate to the reported adverse reactions experienced by other children after receiving a DPT vaccination to reject the possibility of a connection."

"So what do we do? Do we take her to the hospital?"

"The rate that the infection is attacking her nervous system, I don't have any idea of what can be done to slow the process."

"What do you mean?" I asked fearfully.

"It could be possible her body is beginning to shut down. Or, this latest development could be just a temporary set back."

"Are you suggesting that we still wait and see what the neurologist recommends?"

"Try to listen to what I'm about to say," John said, in a matter of fact tone of voice. "If for any reason you do decide to take Heather to the hospital and her health deteriorates to the point where she in unable to sustain life without intervention, the hospital is obligated to use any means to keep her alive. Even if this requires the use of a life support system. Do you understand what I am saying here?"

I couldn't speak. I sat there numb. The silence between John and I lingered, until I heard him asking if I was still there. "I hear what you are saying, but do you think she is going to die? Is this what you are telling me?"

"Heather's body is fighting as much as it can against this infection. As hard as it is to say, at some point, the body will eventually give up the fight." He said in a sad way. "Because Heather's condition come on sudden and not recorded as being a terminal disease by an physician prior to taking her in the hospital, a parent has no say one way or the other regarding life support," John replied, again in a matter of fact tone. "Unfortunately, if she was hooked up to a life support system, you as a parent, would have to go to court and fight for the right to remove the life sustaining system."

"This is so overwhelming for me John. I need to discuss this with Alex."

"I wish there was something I could do, other than giving you this type of news."

"Thanks for calling back and taking the time to talk John. It is comforting to know you are there for support."

"If you need me for anything Barb, call the hospital and they will page me if you can't reach me at home," John said before we said our good-byes.

My first thought after the phone call was, "What the Hell just took place?" Were we just discussing Heather dying? Could Heather really be dying? In all honesty, if I was aware of another child with symptoms as Heather's, I would most likely assumed death was inevitable. However, as a parent of the child, death was inconceivable. No, Heather wasn't going to die. Maybe John is right about this being a temporary set back. Isn't it interesting how quickly the mind holds onto a scrap of hope, as an attempt to avoid the actual severity of the circumstance at hand?

CHAPTER NINE

I HESITATED A WHILE BEFORE GETTING up from the kitchen chair after talking with John. I had no idea as to how I was going to approach Alex with what John and I discussed. I sat there rehearsing in my mind how I could approach Alex with at least some type of composure. Really, how does one go about breaking the news of how their daughter may be dying? When I finally made my way back to Heather's bedroom, I peeked inside and discovered Alex and Heather had fallen asleep together. The two of them looked so peaceful that I couldn't bring myself to wake Alex.

No matter the status of our family unit, one thing remained untouched and that was how much Alex adored Heather. I backed away from Heather's doorway and headed toward Mikey's room. I asked if he wanted to go for a walk, which he anxiously nodded "yes."

I had in mind walking across the field to my parents home and telling them about Heather, when it occurred to me this would be a perfect opportunity for Mikey and I to talk about Heather. It was quite obvious that Mikey was still upset over Alex yelling him. Instead of running ahead of me and investigating what may be lurking in the tall grass like he normally did, he slowly tagged along behind me

There is a small hill behind my parents farm, where Mikey and I had often gone, when it was only the two of us. We would often pack a picnic lunch and laze around in the grass. In a way, it had become our special place to spend time together, with plenty of open space for Mikey to burn off his energy. When we reached the top of the hill, I packed down an area of the towering grass before motioning him to sit.

"It's okay if you feel angry at Alex," I said, in an attempt to break the silence between the two of us. "He shouldn't have had spoken to you in that tone of voice."

"I wasn't doing anything wrong, Mom," Mikey voiced back in a wounded tone.

"I don't think Alex is aware of how his choice of words and actions upsets you."

"He is always mad at me," Mikey said.

"Yeah, it seems that he is. Alex doesn't get to see Heather as much as we do. Maybe, he wanted to spend some time alone with her."

As soon as I saw Mikey look away, I noticed how my words were not reaching him. We both knew Alex was becoming more intolerant with him and no amount of making up excuses for Alex could mask that truth.

"Mikey, Heather is sicker than what I thought," I said in a lowered tone of voice.

"I know. I heard you talking with the doctor on the phone. Is she going to the hospital?"

"I don't know Mikey. Alex and I have to talk it over."

"Is she going to die?" He then asked.

The question caught me off guard. Hearing those words from an eight year old child, seemed so shocking in that moment. I wanted to say no. I wanted to tell Mikey, that Heather would get better and be as she was before this all happened. However, in doing so, I would be not only lying to Mikey, I would me lying to myself. I simply stated, "I don't know."

I didn't want Heather's experience become a secretive affair between Alex and myself. Mikey was observant enough to notice the changes taking place with Heather's health to sense she was not getting better. Like it or not, it was my responsibility as a parent to assist Mikey through whatever may happen and what was happening. Here again, how does a parent approach such an issue in a way which is understandable to a child?

"Did you know, the body can't move without the brain telling it to do so," I said breaking the silence.

"No," He replied, while shooing away a pestering horsefly.

"It's true. You can't walk, run, or play. You can't even eat or go to the bathroom if the brain doesn't tell the body what to do."

"No way!," He exclaimed. "The brain doesn't talk."

"Not actually speaking out loud silly," I said, as I turned and faced him with a smile. "Know how you have a controller for your video games and your remote truck?"

"Yes," He replied, as he rolled onto his side to face me.

"The brain is kinda like that. It sends messages to body parts in order for the body to move."

"So my brain is a control pad?"

"Well, not like the control pad at home, but yeah, something on that order. You see, Heather's brain is having trouble sending messages to her body parts."

"Is that why she can't walk right and use her hand like before."

"Yep," I answered, leaving the door opened for Mikey to ask more questions.

"So, her brain is sick? Is that why we got her that medicine?"

"Yeah. One medicine is to help her breathe better and the other is to help Heather move around better. Make sense?"

"Kinda. Will the medicine help her brain get better?"

"It doesn't look like it Mikey. If Heather's brain keeps on getting sicker, her body will stop working altogether. She could even stop breathing." I said in a broken tone.

"So, she is going to die. We better take her to the hospital so the doctor can make her better, Mom."

"That is why I am taking Heather to a special doctor on Monday. He might be able to help her," I said, trying to sound reassuring.

The questioning and suggestions of what could be done for Heather continued, until Mikey and I both ran out of each. We then just focused on the clouds. Occasionally, pointing out recognizable shapes the clouds were forming. Before rising and walking back home, Mikey and I embraced one another. I'm not sure which one of us felt better afterward. Perhaps, we both felt comforted by being together on our hill.

Even before Mikey and I were half way across the lawn, we could hear Heather's cries bellowing through the open windows of our trailer. Mikey chose to stay outside to play in the sand box while I made my way in the house, to find Alex was at his wits end dealing with Heather.

"I can't get her to stop crying," Alex said, while handing Heather over to me. "I don't know how you deal with this everyday."

"It does become overwhelming at times," I remarked, while cradling Heather in my arms. "Alex, we need to discuss a few things about Heather."

"Why? Did you hear back from Dr. Cottle? What did he have to say," he asked in a worried tone of voice.

I thought I had better try to calm Heather's cries before going into the conversation I had with John. I picked up Heather's pillow off from the floor and asked Alex to join us in Heather's room. I sat down in the rocking and began to rock Heather. Her crying gradually quieted to the point where Alex and I could actually hear ourselves speak. I related to Alex what John had told me and waited for his response, but no response was made. He just walked out of the room, leaving me alone with Heather. I guessed he needed time to allow what I had said to sink in.

My heart went out to him. Although Alex and I never openly discussed how he was feeling during this period, I knew there must have been a sense of helplessness within him, just as much as I was feeling. What made matters worse for Alex, Heather only wanted me to hold her most days. The companionship of Mikey seemed to also comfort her. In that aspect, the detachment of the family became more ingrained, again placing Alex as the outsider.

CHAPTER TEN

*H*EATHER REMAINED IN A STATE of aloofness throughout the afternoon and into the evening hours. Not wanting to eat and drinking a little. Her body was limp like a newborn baby. Her eyes vacant of any emotional expression. Whenever her eyes closed, I found myself nudging her body until she once again opened them. In my state of mind at that moment, Heather closing her eyes met dying; not falling asleep.

Mikey was in the room along with Heather and I, playing quietly and saying little. At one point, he stood beside us in the rocking chair. He took hold of Heather's hand and held it. Then he placed his other arm around my neck, while resting his head on my shoulder. It is said that children have a sort of sixth sense about dying and death, perhaps Mikey, in that moment, was saying his good-bye to Heather.

Later, when Alex came back into the room, he walked over and gently brushed Heather's cheek. When he glanced at Mikey and me, I noticed a tear welling up in his eye. He sat on the edge of Heather's bed for a short time with his head lowered before leaving the three of us. Alex never muttered a word. Tears began to run down my cheeks. Mikey gave me a hint of a hug when he caught sight of the tears. The tears were not for Heather or myself and not even for Mikey. The tears were for Alex. I was in the company of my children, while Alex was enduring this experience practically alone.

When nightfall approached, Heather went into a deep sleep and no longer responded to any of my attempts at waking her. I questioned myself as to whether or not, lay her in bed and allow her to sleep. Afraid if I did so, she might die if I left. Racing thoughts once again filled my mind. Finding the words to express what I was actually feeling is difficult. Only parents whom has experienced a similar situation will agree with me when I say, "There are no words to validate what is being felt."

I decided to lay Heather down and allowed her to sleep. I told Mikey to bathe and get around for bed. As I passed Alex on my way to our bedroom, I told him that Heather was resting peacefully. While I was in our bedroom, I felt this sudden urge to go outside, so I grabbed a sweatshirt and went outside. I headed toward the swing set and sat in one of the swings.

When challenging experiences become overwhelming, one more often than not, attempts to bargain with God. Maybe, its the hope that Divine intervention will occur, or perhaps the feeling of some comfort will be felt. I found myself doing just that as I slowly rocked back and forth in the swing. Even though I had long since stopped going to church, the concept of a "All powerful, All loving God," remained a belief. So, there was still a connection of some sort to God, felt by me. Besides, Heather had been baptized a year earlier, that act alone should qualify her for some type of help from God. Looking back, that type of rationalizing seems a bit desperate. I was desperate! Heather's health was deteriorating before my eyes and the threat of death was real.

I sat there for the longest time wondering how to approach God. One can not bargain with God, I thought. I'll just ask for a favor. No, even that is quite ridiculous. A favor from God? So I begged instead. "Please allow Heather to recover. Allow her live. Allow her to walk. Take away her pain without taking her away from us." Those were the only words spoken to God. No praying or praise. I left it at that.

I continued sitting in the swing while breathing in the crisp evening air. I found myself being entertained by the croaking bull frogs and the singing of the crickets. I absolutely loved this time of night. Suddenly, I then felt a wave of raw emotion sweep through me, so intense that I began to weep. There was no stopping the tears. Perhaps, without other distractions, my mind had no way of avoiding emotions waiting to surface.

For the first time since this all began, I allowed myself to feel all the heartache, frustration and anger that I managed to bury. I guess my body and mind needed this purification in order to regain strength for whatever was coming next. I sat and cried until Mikey called out to me, informing me that Heather was awake and crying.

Before going back into her room, I had an idea that might help in getting Heather to eat more. I went into the kitchen and rummaged through the cupboards for an old bottle and nipple that I may not have thrown away. To my amazement, I found the two and proceed to make some instant oatmeal. Added some maple syrup, another Prednisone and milk to thin its texture. I cut the tip of the nipple to allow the oatmeal to flow easier. I thought this would be a great method of getting some nourishment into Heather, since she wasn't eating like she should have been. With bottle in hand, I made my way to her room. Soon as I entered the room I found Alex holding onto Heather. As he handed Heather over to me, he asked what the bottle was for. "She needs to eat more than what she has been. This the only way I can think of to feed her."

Alex stayed and watched as I settled myself in the chair with Heather. I then offered the bottle to her. Maybe it was her body's determination to survive because with very little resistance, she began sucking. Alex and I both breathed a sigh of relief as we watched her empty the contents of the bottle.

With a full tummy, I thought for sure Heather would drift back to sleep, but it was not to be. Once again the usual crying session began. Alex left the room, not before giving Heather and I a kiss. He stated that he was headed off to bed. It wasn't long after Alex left when Heather let out this high pitched scream, which sent shivers down my spine. It brought both Alex and Mikey into the room in a matter of seconds. We all just watched as Heather would stiffen her body and scream. The screaming lasted close to thirty minutes. When the screaming ended, Heather drifted off to sleep. Most likely out of exhaustion. I laid her in her bed and snuggled beside her. Mikey made his bed on the floor and Alex went back to our room. Two more episodes of screaming would occur during the night. Each followed by sleep.

Although tired, Heather seem to be more alert in the morning than the night before. Once again I used the bottle as a means to feed Heather. Her body remained limp as she ate. However, the vacant look in her eyes had disappeared and seemed to be replaced with the familiar glimmer of life. Her smile returned as well. In the most unlikely moments throughout this experience, Heather would often manage a uplifting smile. Those smiles of hers is what kept me going. Maybe, it was a way for her to let me know how much she loved me.

The weekend passed with the similar pattern of feeding from

a bottle, crying and screaming before naps and bedtime, with no improvement in her muscle tone. Monday couldn't come fast enough. So much of my hopes laid upon the Neurologist finding a cure for Heather.

CHAPTER ELEVEN

*W*HAT I HAVE FOUND COMMON among medical physicians, no matter what status each is categorized, there are physicians whom personalize their patients, while others tend to view the patient as only a case file. Heather and I were about to meet a physician whom would view her not as a child, but by her illness itself. Highly respected and considered brilliant by his colleagues, Dr. Vesser displayed a sense of smugness that I found very offensive. In a short period of time, one could tell his passion was medicine and not people. What I mean by this is, his demeanor toward me was, "I'm the specialist and you are just the parent," kind of attitude.

I was told by his secretary to arrive 30 to 45 minutes before our appointment in order to fill out paperwork. Yes, paperwork that appears to be unread by the physician before he/she enters the examination room. The majority of questions that are usually asked by a physician are already answered in the medical file the doctor is holding. The concept of filling out paperwork just to re-answer verbally is idiotic, in my opinion.

To help ease the burden of filling out paperwork, the physician should consider filling in the necessary questions he is seeking answers to, while he is asking the questions. Better yet, take the time to read through the medical file before meeting with the patient.

Once again, I was hit with a bombardment of questions. When the questioning was over, he wanted Heather to be admitted into Blodgett Memorial Center, the following day. His exact wording: "We will try and find the cause of why your daughter is acting so bitchy." The audacity of him to speak of Heather in way he had.

He went on to say that his secretary would make the necessary arrangements and call me at home later with the details. Finally!

The need to admit Heather into a hospital had arrived. If I wasn't so offended by his crude remark, I would have hugged Dr. Vesser right then and there. Wouldn't that have shocked the smug bastard.

I drove the fifty miles back to Lakeview with a smile never leaving my face. Except for the crude remark pertaining to Heather, I felt confident Dr. Vesser was going to provide a diagnosis and treatment that would bring Heather back to us as she was before. I told Mom about our visit, before taking Mikey back home and begun calling other family members and telling them the news.

I received the call from Dr. Vesser's secretary later in the evening, informing me to have Heather at Blodgett by 6:30 am. Dr. Vesser arranged several test to be done shortly after our arrival, so no food or drink was to be given to Heather after midnight. I was also told to plan on Heather staying in the hospital for three to five days. Since rooming with Heather was not permitted, if I planned on staying with Heather, I would have to sleep in the family waiting room. With this said, she bid me a good evening and hung up.

I had a history of not liking hospitals. Without even a valid reason for my dislike, hospitals caused me such anxiety whenever I entered one. For instance, when my mom had surgery on her back, I made it as far as the doorway of her room and could not fully enter the room. As far as my sister, Shirley, whom was injured in a car accident, I managed to enter the room only to stop at the end of the hospital bed. That was how anxious I became inside a hospital. With Heather being admitted and I planning on staying there, my hospital phobia was about to be faced head on once and for all.

Mikey, was going to stay with his Grandpa and Grandma Stine while Heather and I were at the hospital. With everything that was going on at home, along with appointment with the neurologist, I completely forgot to call work in order to inquire about having more time off. I was scheduled to return back to work the next day. I called the receptionist hoping the plant manager was in, so I could arrange for some more time off. Either that, or inquire about what other options I had in order to stay with Heather. I knew I had some vacation days left and was willing to use them if needed.

After several rings, the phone was answered by Craig, the plant manager himself. I told him the condition of Heather, along with the pending hospital stay. I asked what options were available in extending my time off from work. Craig informed me that work looked to be slowing down and suggested I take another two week lay off. By extending my lay off, I could continue collecting unemployment benefits. After the two weeks expired and if I needed more time off, I would have to either use vacation days or take an emergency leave of absence. Taking a leave of absence would exclude any pay during the period I would be absent from work. Craig assured me that we would work something out. He wished me the best of luck and me to keep him informed of Heather's status.

After talking with Craig, Mikey asked if Heather could go into his room with him and play. Without the ability to balance herself. I didn't see anyway to prop her up in a sitting position without the risk of her falling over. Then I thought maybe I could use her car seat as a means of sitting Heather upright securely. I went and retrieved the seat from the car and brought it into the house. The car seat proved to be exactly what was needed, giving Heather the support to sit without falling. Sitting in the car seat also me the freedom from holding on to her as often as I had been. Her stroller was also used by Mikey at times when he wanted to move Heather from his room to hers, or just to stroll her around the trailer which Heather loved doing. By this time, I was starting to adapt to Heather's limitations, using whatever means available.

With Heather sitting in the car seat and Mikey entertaining her, I started gathering the items needed for our stay at the hospital. I remained ecstatic throughout the evening, anticipating the outcome of Heather's hospital stay. In my mind, Heather was going to be cured and life would return as it was before she became inflicted with whatever caused her condition. At no time, did I even consider any chance of permanent damage being an end result. I keep thinking all that was needed for Heather to get well, was a diagnosis and the right medication. Unfortunately, I was about to be given a very disturbing prognosis. Not only shattering my vision of Heather returning back into a typical toddler, but a challenge that would definitely test our strength of character.

CHAPTER TWELVE

At 6:15 AM the following morning, Heather and I entered Blodgett Memorial Medical Center in Grand Rapids, Michigan. Once I located the nursing station on the pediatric ward, I introduced myself and Heather, before asking where we were to go next. The nurse on duty typed Heather's name into the computer, which immediately began printing out documents confirming Heather's scheduled admittance. After signing several forms and Heather receiving her inpatient wrist band, we were shown to Heather's room to settle in. I asked the nurse before she left Heather and I if she had any idea what tests were so important for us to be there so early.

"This is the normal time patients are told to be here for admittance. Gives them a chance to settle in. I'm not aware of what tests have been ordered for Heather without looking at her file," She said sleepily. "My shift is about to end. After the shift change, I'm sure one of the nurses on duty will be in to see you and little Heather."

"When does Dr. Vesser make his rounds?" I asked.

"Dr. Vesser?" questioned the nurse, while giving me an odd look. "Dr. Vesser is a pediatric neurologist not an attending physician. He basically orders the various tests to be done on the patient, assesses the tests then recommends the type of treatment. Were you not aware of this?"

"Not really," I replied, feeling a bit awkward. "Will there be any doctor checking up on Heather?"

"I'm not for certain if Heather will need to be seen any physician, if she is only scheduled for various tests," She answered back with a heavy sigh. "A nurse should be in shortly to answer any questions you might have. You will have to excuse me. My shift is about over and I need to make my rounds before leaving. Hold tight someone will be in shortly."

"WOW, she was a bit standoffish." I thought. Boy, did I have a lot to learn about the workings of a bigger hospital. I would soon learn how Heather was on the schedule of those working with her, not the other way around.

After waiting four hours since being admitted, with no sign of a nurse alerting us of any tests, Heather was beginning to fuss. I knew she had to be hungry from not eating since dinner the night before. I carried her out to the nurse's station and inquired about getting Heather something to eat, then asked when she was going in for tests. The only nurse at the desk couldn't give me an answer. She began looking up Heather's information on the computer, but didn't locate anything on Heather.

"It seems that we have lost Heather's information on the computer," She said cautiously."What was your daughter admitted for?"

How does one reply back to a statement as such? I was tired, also hungry, frustrated and in a hospital. None of which added any charisma to my personality.

"Heather was admitted by Dr. Vesser," I said in a strained tone of voice. "The nurse admitting Heather this morning found her information. How is it possible that it is now lost?"

"I'm sorry," She replied back, in a similar manner as I had her. "It happens from time to time. I'll make some calls and see what I can find out."

"While we are waiting, is it possible to get Heather something to eat? She hasn't eaten since last night's dinner. I was told not to give her any food or drink after midnight," I remarked sarcastically.

"Well, since I don't have any idea of what tests are scheduled. It's best to wait until I get the information."

An hour later a lab technician came into Heather's room and drew blood. That would be the extent of any hint of a test performed on Heather during our first day. It was close to noon when food finally arrived for Heather. Before I began feeding Heather, I propped her up in a sitting position on the hospital bed using all the pillows and blankets available. Feeding her was a slow process. Since Heather could no longer hold her head upright on her own, I held her head while feeding her a tiny amount of food with a spoon. I didn't think of packing her bottle, nor did I think to bring her sippy cup. Heather tried sucking on the straw in her drink, but ended up coughing and gagging. So I ended up using the spoon as a means of delivering the juice to her.

When Heather had her fill of food and drink, she began to become fussy, indicating nap time was near. Without a rocking chair, I wondered how I was going to manage getting Heather to fall asleep. Rocking Heather as she fell asleep always seemed to work best at relaxing her. I went to the nurse's station and asked if it was possible to get a rocker for her room. I was told that rocking chairs were only provided in the nursery and bringing one into Heather's room would not be possible.

At that point, Heather was beginning to whimper. I knew what was about to follow shortly, so I took her back into her room and held her close while rocking back and forth on the edge of her bed. After thirty minutes of crying, she fell asleep. I paged the nurse and asked for more pillows and blankets to position around Heather for added protection against falling off the bed. I then informed the nurse that I was going to the cafeteria to eat. What I really needed was a cigarette by that time.

On my way back to Heather's room after eating and finally having that smoke, I stopped by the play area on the pediatric ward. I picked out a few toys, books and couple of movies to entertain Heather and I while we waited for Alex to arrive.

It was such a good feeling to see familiar faces walking into Heather's room later that day. Not only did Alex show up, but Grandma Sandy as well. We talked about the day's events and hoped that the following day would bring about more involvement from the medical staff. Alex and Grandma Sandy stay for over an hour before leaving. Their visit seemed so short.

I didn't imagine there would be such a feeling of isolation while at the hospital, but there was. By night's end, I begun to wonder why it was even necessary to admit Heather. The blood work could have been done at Kelsey Hospital back in Lakeview. Looking back on the experience at Blodgett, every test could have been an outpatient procedure and thus eliminating the need for a hospital stay altogether. But, in the moment, I didn't question the reasoning for us being there. I just went along with whatever was decided by Dr. Vesser. Why would I question the specialist whom was going to find the cause and cure which would bring Heather back?

Shortly after Alex and Grandma Sandy had left, I bathed and changed Heather into her pajamas. Heather still remained in a state of aloofness. Physically, she didn't seem to be in any pain, except when it came time to sleep. It was her absence of emotion which alarmed me. She would occasionally smile, but outside of that I could sense the essence of life within her diminishing. Heather's enthusiastic approach to life was dwindling and there was absolutely nothing I could do, but witness the process.

In a strange way, the ease at which Heather seemed to accept her condition was both intriguing and baffling to me. There wasn't any signs of panic or fear in her eyes. Just complete acceptance of whatever was happening to her. I guess being as young as she was, the fight for survival wasn't intense as it is for older children and adults. Heather's seemingly lack of fear of what was happening to her, prompted me to look closely at my own fears regarding unexpected physical limitations and even death. This caused such a sense of uneasiness within me, that I stopped all thoughts of self exploration. In that moment anyway.

Heather was showing the usual signs of becoming tired as bedtime neared. I grew worried as to how I would manage her cries and screams under the watchful eyes of spectators. I knew a lot of attention would be drawn to our room as soon as the high pitched screaming began. The thought of this only added to my anxiety I was already experiencing, but on the other hand, we were in a hospital. Maybe Heather could be given a mild sedative to help relax her. With that thought, I paged the nurse.

"In a short period of time Heather will begin screaming," I said even before the nurse fully entered the room. "She usually does at night before going to sleep. Is there any way we could get something to relax her?"

The nurse not being completely aware of Heather's medical condition, displayed a look of questionable doubt.

"Does she take any medication at home to relax her?"

As naive as it may sound, I never inquired about any form of sedative to help Heather fall asleep while talking with Dr. Cottle and more surprising he didn't mention using any.

"No," I replied. "I usually rock her while trying to console her the best I can. Since a rocking chair can not be provided for Heather, it's going to be difficult to get her to relax."

"I'll go check her file to see if any type of sedative may have been ordered by her physician."

"There won't be any mention of giving Heather a sedative in her file," I quickly responded. "The subject was never brought up with Dr. Vesser or her family doctor. Couldn't a sedative be ordered?" I asked.

"I will have to contact Dr. Vesser for approval," the nurse said, in a bothered tone.

"Why can't the doctor on duty prescribe the sedative?"

"Heather is the patient of Dr. Vesser. He would have to approve any medicine being given to Heather."

"Oh, okay, I'm sure Dr. Vesser will prescribe something for Heather. He must have some idea of how draining it is for her during these screaming spells." I said in a matter of frank tone of voice.

"I will see what I can do," She replied back, as she turned to leave Heather's room.

The thought of Heather actually falling asleep without having to go through a screaming session was encouraging. Upon her return to Heather's room, the nurse informed me that a mild sedative had been ordered and would be up soon.

Heather had already begun crying intensely by the time the sedative arrived. Thank goodness it was in liquid form and she drank it down without resistance. Either the sedative was too mild or given too late for it to make any difference, because Heather's cries once again turned into screams. I closed the door to Heather's room in order to avoid the stares from passing nurses and others. As I was sitting on the edge of the bed rocking back and forth with Heather in my arms, I felt so alone, helpless, and just wanted to go home. Her screams and crying lasted close to an hour before Heather fell asleep. Once I felt confident that Heather would remain asleep, I again positioned pillows and blankets around her and went to have a cigarette.

Day two: A team of doctors came in and evaluated Heather's muscle tone and more blood was taken. A MRI was scheduled for later in the afternoon. Other than that, Heather and I passed the time by either walking the halls, stopping in the play area or just staying in her room. Again, bedtime was challenging. The sedative given to Heather that evening would also had no effect on her screaming or crying as well.

Day three: Brought about more withdrawing blood, along with a physical examination of her ears, eyes, and throat. Again her reflexes were evaluated, but no visit by Dr. Vesser. I really believed he would have at least stopped by to see Heather and I.

Day four: Heather and I were scheduled to see Dr. Vesser before Heather's discharge from the hospital. I called Alex and informed him. We were both very anxious to learn the findings on Heather. Since Alex wouldn't be able to make it to the hospital in time for the consultation with Dr. Vesser, I was left to learn about Heather's possible fate on my own. The good news was Heather and I were going home. What a wonderful feeling that gave me. I was tired from lack of rest, upset by the experience of the hospital stay and homesick. Sadly, meeting with Dr. Vesser would only heighten the multiple list of mental anguish I already was experiencing.

CHAPTER THIRTEEN

HE OFFICE IN WHICH DR. Vesser occupied while consulting patients in the hospital, was located on the main floor. Upon entering his office, he motioned for me to take a seat which I did as I held Heather close. His office was not very professional looking as I imagined it would be. Files cluttered his desk and shelves. A couple of framed degrees hung on the otherwise bare walls. I spotted a photo of Dr. Vesser standing beside a beautiful woman whom I assumed was his wife. No children were in the picture with the two. There were no photos of children anywhere. I wondered if he had any children, but didn't feel the need to ask. I then noticed some images from Heather's MRI hanging on a huge lighted screen, attached to the wall behind Dr. Vesser's desk.

"What we are about to discuss are these images of Heather's brain," Dr. Vesser stated in a professional manner, as he pointed to the lighted screen. "With these images, it is possible to pin point the exact location of the inflammation that is occurring."

I sat there staring at the images feeling a sense disbelief, that is was Heather's brain being discussed. My thought, as Dr. Vesser began hanging the remaining images was; how it was only a short time ago Heather was healthy and happy. Here I am today viewing images of her brain that was being invaded by infection. I just couldn't grasp the realness of it all.

"What caused this inflammation?" I questioned. "I really believe it was from her DPT vaccination. Could a reaction from the vaccine be responsible? Dr. Cottle seems to think there may be a connection."

"Highly unlikely," He firmly stated. "Her symptoms began long after the vaccination was given. Reactions normally occur within a forty-eight hour time frame after the injection. Very unlikely there is any connection between the two."

"What can explain her rapid deterioration then?"

"The inflammation that is occurring now is what is referred to as being a secondary infection caused by the primary illness, consistent with post-infectious Encephalomyelitis. Heather's blood work came back negative for Herpes simplex, Rubeola, Lyme and tick disease along with measles. These are known diseases which triggers post-infectious Encephalomyelitis. However, without a cerebral biopsy the cause may never be determined."

The information Dr. Vesser was throwing at me, at the rate he was, made it difficult to comprehend what was being said. All that medical terminology he was using was definitely out of my range of understanding. I remained convinced the DPT vaccination was the cause.

"Is there anything in the DPT vaccine capable of causing the post-infectious Encephal ... however you pronounced it?" I asked, bringing his attention back to the vaccine.

"Once again, Heather's symptoms didn't occur within the forty-eight hour period. Therefore, it is my opinion, the vaccination had no role in her condition."

"Could it be some type of delayed reaction from the shot?" I asked.

"Mrs. Moore, I'm not going to continue a conversation on a topic that is not relevant, in my opinion, to the matter at hand."

He turned toward the images and pointed out the area where the infection was occurring, deep within the white matter of the brain. White matter is the part of the brain that makes it possible for nerves to communicate. Printed in a report by US Davis School of Medicine, I ran across an analogy that depicts the function of both gray and white matter which creates a easier understanding of the importance of each.

"If the nervous system were a computer network, gray matter is the portion that contains nerve cells and capillaries (tiny blood vessels). This area would be the computer and the white matter the cables. Diseased white matter impairs the nervous system much like a broken, frayed or poorly operating cables impair a computer network."

"White matter is full of Myelin, a fatty insulation that speeds up nerve impulses," Dr. Vesser stated. "Put simply, once the infection penetrated the blood-brain barrier (a protective shield that fights against foreign substances entering the nervous system,) the insulation around the nerve cells began to dissolve; short circuiting nerve impulses. The cloudiness you see in the image is where the infection is occurring. The entire centrum semiovale, the area in which white matter is located, has been affected in both the left and right hemispheres of the brain. The paralysis and other weakened body functions are caused by this. If the infection continues and more Myelin is destroyed, her breathing and other body functions will be effected."

"What about antibiotics? Wouldn't that stop the infection?" I asked.

"Encephalomyelitis is triggered by a viral infection. Antibiotics will be ineffective as a means of treatment. Viral infections do not respond to antibiotics."

"Nothing can be done to stop the infection then?" I asked in a distress tone of voice.

"We will keep her on the Prednisone to lessen the chance of swelling, but other than that, no. Keep her comfortable, give her lots of fluids and plenty of rest."

"Isn't there other medications available to stop the deterioration?"

"The viral infection has to run its course. What can be treated are some of the symptoms caused by the infection, such as the inflammation in her joints, muscles and perhaps rehab to help restore strength in muscle control afterward. Basically, what you see is what you get."

To Dr. Vesser, it may have seemed appropriate to make a statement such as "What you see is what you get." However, as a parent, it was nothing more than a cold hearten remark. I was unable to even reply back, as I was taken back by his lack of empathy. I just sat there feeling so angry.

CHAPTER FOURTEEN

*A*FTER A LONG PAUSE OF silence, Dr. Vesser brought my attention back to the matter at hand. He asked if I had any questions. I was still absorbing the last comment he had made. How could I even begin to ask questions? If I did ask questions would he respond in the fashion he did previously, when I pressed him on the DPT vaccine? Needless to say, I felt intimidated by him.

"Mrs. Moore, are there any questions that you may have?"

"What exactly does post-infectious Encephalo ... however it is pronounced mean?" I asked with hesitation.

"Post-infectious Encephalomyelitis is inflammation of the brain and spinal cord."

"So, her brain and spinal cord is infected?"

"With the images we have, the area in which the inflammation is taking place seems deep within the white matter and in the spinal region," he said, while again pointing to the cloudy area on the image. "Since the inflammation seems to have settled primarily in the brain and has not invaded the spinal region, it could be safe to diagnosis your daughter's condition as being post-infectious Encephalitis. which means inflammation of the brain."

"What causes the inflammation to occur in the brain?" I questioned.

"The inflammation is an infection most likely a viral infection, since you had mentioned Heather was showing signs resembling a cold."

"A cold caused all this?"

"Not likely. The cold symptoms could have stemmed from the initial presence of a virus. The chest congestion and runny nose were most likely the symptoms of the primary illness."

"I don't understand what is meant by primary and secondary

illness. Are you stating that a virus settled in her lungs which triggered a cold, which in turn attacked her brain?"

"The respiratory system may have been the initial target of the virus. The virus then can get into the blood stream. Once in the blood stream, the virus travels to the brain. If the virus breaches the blood-brain barrier which it had, the virus slips inside the brain cells. With me so far? " He asked.

"Yes, I'm understanding what you are saying."

"Unlike bacteria cells, virus cells can't live without host cells. Once healthy cells are invaded by a virus, the virus replaces the cell's original DNA with the virus's own genetic code. This damages and ultimately ruptures the infected brain cells. When cell breaks, it sends copies of the original virus to other cells. Unless the immune system is able to destroy the virus, the virus will continue to kill off the healthy cells."

"So, the cloudy area in the image is the virus destroying the brain cells?"

"Yes," he replied. "The cells of the immune system rush to the brain and start attacking the virus. The swelling of the brain is caused by this. The Prednisone your daughter is taking should help control the swelling. The Encephalitis is caused by both the virus and the immune system attempting to fight off the infection."

"Is the damage to her brain permanent?"

"It's difficult to say. The brain has an amazing ability to re-route nerve impulses. Once the virus has run its course, physical therapy can help your daughter regain muscle control. To what extent is hard to tell, depending on how much of her central nervous system has been affected."

"Is there a good possibility she can die?" I finally asked.

"Depending on the strength of her immune system. It will be her immune system that fights off this virus. If her immune system is weak, then the probability of death is likely."

"So, Encephalitis is not an illness by itself. It is just a medical term for the infection in her brain?"

"Yes. Like I stated early on Mrs. Moore, Encephalitis is not a treatable illness. Antibiotics will not destroy a virus because the virus is not a living organism. The immune system is the only weapon against any virus at this time. No antiviral drug has been approved as of yet," Dr. Vesser advised me.

We both eventually reached the point where there was nothing else to say. I sat there squeezing Heather ever so gently while staring at the images. I couldn't even make eye contact with Dr. Vesser. As much as I wanted to get up and walk out of his office, I seemed to have been frozen to my chair. After moments of silence, Dr. Vesser asked if I had any more questions. If not, he had another consult scheduled. I shook my head no, rose slowly from my chair and exited the office; not even acknowledging him on my way out.

I don't remember Heather and I returning back to her room. It was as if I was on auto-pilot. Back in her room, I finished packing our belongings and waited for Heather to be officially discharged. During our wait, I sat with Heather all the while fighting back the tears. Once I signed the discharge papers, I carried Heather and our belongings out of Blodgett.

During the drive home, I replayed the consultation over and over in my mind. Heather was no closer to being healed than before. Well, we did learn where the inflammation was occurring. No treatment to cure the inflammation and no cause was determined. It was all speculation. I still firmly believe this was a direct cause from her vaccination, but without any confirmation by a doctor I had no way of actually proving it. Dr. Vesser may have had disagreed with me, but that did nothing to deter my suspicion. Furthermore, I wasn't about to accept the prognosis of one Dr. Vesser.

I grew angrier as I neared home. There had to be a doctor somewhere that could help us and not easily dismiss my conviction of a reaction to my vaccine theory. I don't know where or how I formed this notion, but I truly believed if Heather's condition was caused by a vaccine, then it was possible to cure her. There just had be some form of treatment available that could offset the side effects of any vaccine. If there wasn't any such treatment, why place any child at such a risk in the first place by mandating vaccinations? Needless to say, my entire way of thinking was about to undergo a rude awakening.

By the time I pulled into the driveway of our home, I already decided Heather was going to the Mayo Clinic. One of the most accredited hospitals in the country. Yes, I believed it was there a cure would be found. For the first time since Heather became ill, I felt in charge and not helpless. A surge of energy begun to replenish my broken spirit.

Alex and I talked for hours about the test results, Dr. Vesser and his prognosis. I told him that I was going to take Heather to the Mayo Clinic. I had to find a cure for her. I planned to call Dr. Cottle in the morning, and hoped he might be able to arrange it. Alex said it was a good idea, but he wouldn't be able to go along with Heather and I, if John was able to arrange an appointment. He was expecting a call from Steel Parts Automotive for an interview any day. He couldn't risk not being available.

Being so involved with Heather, I began to realize how out of touch I was with Alex. We spent less and less time together and I could feel the distance between us grow. My reaction to his statement about not going was one of disbelief. How could he not go? I didn't push the subject any further. Instead, I called my sister, Shirley, and asked her if she would consider riding along if Heather and I went. Shirley believed she might be able to arrange time off at the animal hospital, where she worked as a veterinarian assistant.

I waited out the weekend in anticipation. I felt confident John could make this happen for us. I was adamant about going for I still believed that if the cause was established, then a cure was within the realm of possibility. I refused to allow the statement Dr. Vesser voiced, "What you see is what you get" become my reality.

CHAPTER FIFTEEN

BEING BACK IN THE COMFORT of my home and not tucked away in a hospital room was wonderful. However, our homecoming lacked the sense of being complete until Mikey arrived home early the next morning. Heather grew so excited when she awoke to find Mikey back home. The two of them just seemed to pick up at where they left off playing before Heather and I went to Blodgett.

After my stay with Heather at Blodgett, I formed a new found love for my old lumpy mattress at home. One thing was for certain, I would never again, after having to sleep on the most uncomfortable sofa in the hospital, ever complain about how lumpy my mattress was or insist upon replacing it. Never.

The weekend brought about visits from family members seeking updates on Heather, along with wanting to spend time with her. Heather's health had all of us worried. When I mentioned my intentions of taking Heather to the Mayo Clinic, Grandma White offered to loan us money for the trip when a date was set. I wasn't the only person to suspect the DPT vaccination had caused Heather's condition, others in the family had as well. There just didn't seem to be any other reasonable explanation for the sudden deterioration in her health.

The prognosis of possible death left everyone in the family stunned. Even though no improvement in her condition was evident, not one of us was willing to accept our little Heather may be in fact dying. It is so true when one says "A child should bury their parents and not for parents to bury their child." I guess because deeply ingrained in the psychic of parents and elders, the possibility of a young child dying within the family just seems contrary to nature. This was definitely my strong held belief and the basis upon which I was determined to find a cure for Heather.

Heather's condition remained stable throughout the weekend. She spent most of her time sitting in her car seat with Mikey close to her side. On several occasions, Heather managed to smile at Mikey as he creatively preformed skits with his actions figures. Her smiles were usually accompanied with a brightness in her eyes, radiating so much love toward Mikey. The two of them were becoming even more inseparable.

The only improvement in Heather's condition during the weekend was her appetite. Most likely because she was back home in familiar surroundings. I continued bottle feeding her different flavors of instant oatmeal, combined with a nutritional supplement along with her Predisone.

The pace at which Heather had regressed since July14, was astounding. It was as if she basically regressed into infancy. She was no longer able to hold herself upright and was barely able to move her head from side to side. The ability to stand, walk, and even crawl was now lost. Her left hand still remained clenched into a fist like position. Even her right side was showing signs of weakness. Heather had lost the ability to grasp and hold onto objects as well. Her drooling was excessive, as though she were teething. There still was no sign of being able to have a bowel movement on her own.

By the time we came home from Blodgett, Heather no longer could speak. She went back to making noises, resembling those of an infant prior to speaking. It was her crying and screaming before naps and bedtime, that had me baffled the most. For the life of me, I could not imagine what could be triggering the episodes, precisely at those times.

Heather was at least beginning to sleep longer while napping and during the night. Our nights we spent in the rocking chair had become a thing of the past. However, after she had fallen asleep at night, I would remain laying beside her in her bed, listening to every breath she took until I grew too tired to stay awake. Leaving Heather, in order to sleep in my own bed was scary at first. I'm not sure why I even did, because I was up and out of bed several times during the night just to check on her. I was so frightened that she could die unexpectedly. I kept thinking, that if she had died and I wasn't there to prevent her death in some way, how was I ever going to forgive myself?

I called Dr. Cottle's office early Monday morning, hoping to reach him before his patients began to arrive. Sharon answered the phone and put me through to John right away. John and I discussed the hospital stay, along with the prognosis Dr. Vesser had given to us. Afterward, I inquired about some type of sedative to help Heather relax before naps and bedtime. I then asked his opinion on taking Heather to the Mayo Clinic.

John suggested trying a low dosage of Valium to help relax her body before naps and bedtime. He later called in a prescription at the local pharmacy for me to pick up. Heather's temperament before sleep had John as baffled as I was. As for taking Heather to Mayo, he believed it was worth pursuing. Without any reservation, Dr. Cottle said he would see what he could do to arrange an appointment with a pediatric neurologist at the Mayo Clinic.

He informed me that it may take a few days to make the necessary arrangements. Once an appointment date was scheduled, he would get back with me. In the meantime, John suggested that I start gathering copies of Heather's medical files, along with her MRI films from Blodgett. I was to also obtain a copy of Heather's file at Kelsey Memorial. John assured me Sharon would prepare a copy of all his notes and test results he had on Heather. With all this information in hand, the neurologist at Mayo would not have to approach Heather's condition blindly.

I decided to wait until I heard back from Dr. Cottle before contacting work. No since in trying to second guess when I would again be needing time off. I absolutely dreaded the thought of returning back to work and placing Heather's care in someone else's hands.

Since the beginning of Heather's ordeal, I hadn't been apart from her. Perhaps, this was what just I was actually dreading. In such a short period of time, my life basically revolved around Heather. With the amount of time I spent caring for Heather, along with trying to maintain some kind of normalcy within the family unit, there didn't seem to be any time left to simple focus on myself.

I often was told by others how important it was to take care of myself during this time, but I found it impossible to place my needs and wants over everything else that was happening. As a result, I ended up putting myself on hold for the time being. The consequences of putting oneself on hold, is that it becomes easy to lose a sense of self after a while.

I received a call from John the following Thursday. An appointment with the pediatric neurologist at the Mayo Clinic, was scheduled for mid August; three weeks away. This was the earliest Dr. Scott at the Mayo Clinic could see Heather. For a procrastinator, which I am, three weeks would give me plenty of time to gather all the medical files and x-rays. Thankfully, Heather's condition had appeared stable. She wasn't getting better, but wasn't showing any indications of regressing further.

Reluctantly, I returned back to work on my scheduled date. I felt really out of sorts being away from Heather. My mind was constantly full of worry over how Heather was doing at the sitters. I kept expecting to be paged to the office, where I would receive news of some type of an emergency involving Heather. Thankfully, no emergency happened while I was at work. After working one week, I decided to take a leave of absence until I returned home from the Mayo Clinic if all went well.

Two days before Heather's appointment with Dr. Scott, my sister and I decided to leave for Minnesota. We estimated the drive to Minnesota would take close to thirteen hours. I was so happy Shirley went along with Heather and I. Shirley was more than just my sister, she had become my trusted friend, whose shoulder I would cry on whenever life became too overwhelming for me.

We arrived in Rochester, Minnesota, early the next morning, after fifteen hours of driving. With arriving a day early, it was possible to find accommodations and get settled in. Located on the hospital premises, are housing units for rent to accommodate outpatients. The entire Mayo Clinic complex was so enormous and impressive. The largest hospital I had ever been in was Butterworth (Spectrum) in Grand Rapids. The Mayo Clinic, at that time, made Butterworth look tiny in comparison.

The cost to stay in a housing unit was very reasonable. Each unit included a kitchen, bath, small dining area, with a living room/bedroom combo, where two twin beds along with small matching dressers were set up.

Shortly after obtaining our unit, Shirley and I began unpacking. Heather was calmly sitting in her car seat watching. Within a moment's notice, Heather began to fuss a little. When I turned toward her, I watched as her body stiffened as if she were going to have a seizure. I rushed to her side and began to unbuckle her seat belt. Even before I finished unfastening the straps, her body went limp and she made this gasping sound as if to catch her breath.

I quickly picked her up out of the car seat and held her close to me. This marked the first time I actually acknowledged the real possibility of Heather dying and that scared the Hell out of me. There were two other similar incidences that occurred during our first day at Mayo. Each time her body stiffened then went limp. I panicked and held on to her until the episode was over. I honestly felt if Heather were to die, her death would take place while at the Mayo. You could just sense that death was near.

Not only did those episodes scare me, I also noticed that haunting blank stare had returned. There was no spark of life what-so-ever shinning through Heather's eyes. She seemed completely detached from life and me. Throughout our stay, Heather drifted back and forth, to a state of absolute detachment, then back to being alert and smiling.

Heather's appetite lessened as well during that week and she began sleeping more than usual. She still continued to cry excessively before naps and bedtime. The Valium never seemed to have any calming effect on her. I didn't want to risk any harm to Heather by raising the dosage, so I kept to the prescribed amount. What seemed strange, while at the Mayo Clinic, was the absence of her screaming. Heather's eerie screaming had seemed to stop just as sudden as the screaming had begun. I wasn't sure if I was relieved by this new development, or more frightened that the absence of screaming was a sure sign her body was indeed shutting down.

Heather appeared to be in good spirits on the morning of our initial visit with Dr. Scott, the pediatric neurologist. He came across as being a kind and compassionate middle aged man, who took an interest in his patients, unlike Dr. Vesser. He advised me that several tests and examinations were already scheduled for Heather. In fact, another MRI was scheduled right after our meeting.

Only having briefly read through Heather's medical files and glancing at her latest MRI, he was already giving me his own hypothesis on Heather's condition. He too quickly dismissed the idea of Heather's condition as being any type of reaction to the DPT vaccine, when I confronted him with my suspicion. In his opinion, Heather's condition was more consistent with some type of Leukodystrophy, rather than a post-viral infection. The tests Dr. Scott had ordered for Heather were more extensive than she had experienced at Blodgett. A lumber puncture (spinal tap) was scheduled for the next day. Blood work and physical examinations by other specialists were also on the agenda. Each day, there was some form of testing or examinations taking place.

Because our stay exceeded the time limit Shirley arranged to be off from work, she had to leave the day of our final consultation with Dr. Scott. Alex and Grandma Sandy planned to drive out to the Mayo and bring Heather and I back home. The two of them would arrive sometime during the following day, which was a Saturday.

Both Shirley and myself dreaded the thought of her going home. I knew leaving was going to be extremely difficult for her, but as convincingly as I could manage, I reassured her Heather and I would be fine. It was her that I was most concerned about. It was a long distance to be driving alone.

At the Mayo Clinic, when an appointment is scheduled the patient doesn't have to wait a long period of time before being seen by the doctor. How cool is that? I'm not kidding. The time you are told to be there, is the time you are walking in the office and the doctor is there waiting. Every appointment Heather had with Dr. Scott was always in the morning or early afternoon. However, the final consult was set for 4:00pm. This in itself seemed discouraging. Shirley and I both feared bad news was about to be given to us.

We strolled Heather over to the building where Dr. Scott's office was, for the final consultation. After checking in with the receptionist, I went and sat next to the large fish aquarium in the waiting area and held Heather in my lap. Together, we sat gazing at the fish swimming so carefree in the crystal clear water.

Again Shirley and I sensed something bad was going to be said, for we noticed that twenty minutes had passed without being called into Dr. Scott's office. By now I found it more difficult to calm my mind of thoughts. I began wondering if the trip to the Mayo Clinic was even necessary, but instantly deflected the thought by reminding myself where it was that we were.

This was the Mayo Clinic, something had to have been discovered with all the testing done on Heather. But, what if a similar diagnosis was reached; did I cause Heather to weaken further by bringing her such a long distance and having her subjected to so many tests which were so draining on her? I couldn't refute that thought and begun to feel overwhelmed by guilt and could not shake it off. To the point that I becoming nauseous from the tension building within.

It seems that when one begin to feel any sense of guilt, the guilt automatically multiplies million times over within seconds. To where breaking the sense of guilt is impossible, unless the mind is suddenly distracted. Well, that distraction came about when Heather's name was called out by the receptionist, telling us Dr. Scott was ready to see us.

Even before Shirley and I took our seat, I knew my fear of receiving bad news was going to happen just by the way Dr. Scott was focusing on Heather in such a solemn manner. The images of the MRI were hung and he immediately began the consultation by pointing to the area in which the inflammation was located, while telling us that the infection had indeed spread considerably since Heather's last MRI.

"The appear of the inflammation is consistent with either a post-viral Demyelinating process (as suspected by Dr. Vesser) or a Leukodystrophy."

"So the inflammation is spreading and not subsiding?" I stated discouragingly.

"Yes, at the rate it is destroying the white matter, I'm afraid Heather will not have long before her body completely shuts down. With her recent breathing symptoms, lack of appetite, the stiffening and twitching of her muscles, this is an indication that her body is in the process of shutting down already. I'm so terribly sorry," He softly spoke.

I froze. No thoughts. No emotions felt. Just compete numbness swept over me. Dr. Scott , bless his heart, allowed me the time, however long it took, for me to begin speaking without pressing me to do so. I admired him for that amount of compassion bestowed on me during those moments of silence.

Where exactly do our thoughts derive from? I was just told the worst news a parent can possibly receive and here I was about to ask what Leukodystrophy was and if it was curable. Maybe out of the refusal to accept Heather's blink outlook, I blinded the realism with yet another distraction. Perhaps what the new suspected disease gave me was a speak of hope that Heather's life could be saved, unrealistic as that was.

"What is Leukodystrophy? Is it curable?" I asked.

"Leukodystrophy is a rare disease that effects the cells of the brain, specifically the white matter. The most common symptoms is a gradual decline in the child's health who previously appeared healthy. Loss in balance and body tone, speech, ability to eat, vision and hearing," Dr. Scott replied.

"Those are the symptoms that Heather has experienced except for her vision and hearing," I said. "How does a child become effected with this disease and why isn't it detected at birth?"

"Most Leukodystrophies are inherited disorders. There are some that seem to arise spontaneously after head injuries or by other types of infections. Either way, the disease stems from a defective gene that controls the production of Myelin. Leukodystrophy, in many cases, is overlooked as being a suspected cause. Therefore, many other diseases are tested for before Leukodystrophy is even considered."

"How is it possible to diagnosis Leukodystrophy?"

"MRI images are used to detect the degenerative process. Lumber puncture is to collect spinal fluid surrounding the brain and spinal cord. The fluid can be tested for certain diseases and the diagnosis of several infections which helps excludes other diseases and that minimizes the chance of misdiagnosing a disease. Blood tests can help diagnose most forms of Leukodystrophy by looking for mutated genes and measuring any abnormal levels of chemicals in the blood which could be indictors of the disease."

"Was anything found in Heather's test results that support your theory of this being Leukodystrophy?" I asked.

"Not exclusively. I'm recommending a cerebral biopsy (brain biopsy) be performed for a more through examination of her brain cells. Although the procedure is rarely used, often as a last resort when other tests have failed to provide a diagnosis, such as in Heather's circumstance," Dr. Scott explained. "I'm not going to lie to you Mrs. Moore. Heather's condition is critical and what I am about to propose may seem callus, but Heather is in a position to provide valuable insight to the medical field of neurology if a brain biopsy was conducted while her brain cells are still living. It is my opinion that her chances of making the trip back home alive is very slim.

However, if you allow a cerebral biopsy be performed here, there is a possibility of her dying during the procedure as well."

"You are asking if I will allow Heather to undergo a procedure at the risk of her dying, for means of medical research?" I asked, in a baffle tone.

"I realize this all must sound harsh, but with the data we will be able to collect, a better understanding of Heather's disease could be obtained and possibly help others in return."

"NO!" I said bluntly. "If Heather is going to die, then she will at home with family present. Not surrounded by strangers on a surgical table while being probed in her brain. No. No biopsy."

"I understand your position and accept your decision, but we will not be able to reach a conclusive diagnosis without the biopsy," He replied.

I already knew the diagnosis and cause. If only someone would take my suspicion seriously and not dismiss it or view it as being ludicrous. Why the reaction I received every time I mentioned a reaction to her vaccination was met with such skepticism, I don't know. What seemed to be occurring, in my opinion, was the specialists were more focused on diseases that were recognized in their field of expertise and not on the hypothesis of a parent.

With the consultation ending on a discouraging note, me not learning much of anything except for a new possible cause, along with Dr. Scott not getting a brain biopsy, Shirley, Heather and I left the building. Back at our housing unit, Shirley gathered her belongings and headed for home, leaving Heather and I alone.

Actually, it seemed strangely fitting that Heather and I were alone. Unbeknownst to me at that time, I was about to discover what my role as mother included, to this beautiful child I called mine.

CHAPTER SIXTEEN

*W*HILE ALONE WITH HEATHER AFTER Shirley had left, I sensed the urgency to call Alex, but could not bring myself to dial our number. Calling meant validating Dr. Scott's prognosis and I was not ready to do so. Instead, I sat on the floor facing the stroller Heather was still sitting in.

Seeing Heather in the condition she was in broke my heart. She was looking so worn and lifeless, as her eyes remained vacant of all emotion. Even though we were facing one another, Heather's gaze seemed to be looking straight through me, as if I wasn't there.

When Heather's body suddenly stiffened, terror immediately swept through me. I watched as her muscles began twitching, similar to muscle spasms. The incident lasted for only a brief moment, before her body went limp. Next came the gasping to catch her breath. Heather had not experienced an episode like such, since the first day we arrived at the Mayo.

I immediately reached out and unfastened the straps that were holding her in the stroller. I then carefully lifted her limp body out of the stroller and cradled her in my arms. As the two of us remained sitting on the floor, I began rocking back and forth, while Heather rested in my arms with her head laying against my chest.

Fragments of memories began to surface as I was rocking Heather. Each memory marking a moment of sheer delight I had experienced with her. Her birth. The times she would crawl unto my back, with pillow in hand, in order to lay on me while I was laying on the floor. The mornings she would wake me too early for my liking, but too precious to become upset over. The baths we had taken together, with her playfully scooping up bubbles in her tiny hands, for us to blow the bubbles into the air.

Memories of her growing, discovering, and challenging my

authority as she was becoming independent. With every fragment of memory that had risen, I revisited each experience, while being able to recapture all those emotions I had felt at that time. I was so fortunate to have had the time to create such memories with Heather to fall back on.

I felt so blessed to have Heather as my daughter and began wondering if she knew that. Did she feel the love I carried within me toward her? Was it even possible for a child, as young as Heather, to comprehend the meaning of love? I'm not sure, but I did know Heather felt a great sense of security and comfort while being around me. Just by the way she smiled and clung to me. Perhaps, this was Heather's way of assuring me she felt loved.

I wondered if she thought I was a good mother. A mother, whom would do anything to keep her with us, or if she could sense how my heart was breaking at the very thought of losing her. Being faced with the possibility of Heather dying, I felt such a strong need to believe that I was a good mother and that Heather felt the same as well.

When my legs began to fall asleep from sitting on the floor, I stood up with Heather in my arms and began staring out the window. I didn't even hear the ringing of the phone, until Heather began moving about in my arms. When I answered the phone, Alex was on the other end asking why I hadn't call him earlier. All I could manage to say was "I'm sorry."

Right off, Alex asked about Heather and what Dr. Scott had to say. I filled him in on every detail I remembered. There were several times where long periods of silence passed during our conversation, before talking resumed. The tone of Alex's voice sounded as defeated as I was feeling. He then said that him and Grandma Sandy would be leaving that night and not the next day as planned. I felt somewhat relieved the two of them were going to arrive sooner than I had expected. Deep down, I needed Alex there then. I was feeling so alone and frightened at the same time.

After ending the call, I sat on the edge of the bed holding Heather. I began to slowly rock back and forth while holding her tightly against my chest and begun to weep. There was no stopping the tears at that point. I ached deep within my total being.

Soon after my crying started, Heather motioned that she wanted to lean back on my lap. I thought I may have been squeezing her too hard, while not noticing I was doing so. I loosened my grip on her, but she motioned again to lean back. I placed my hand behind her head and the other across her back, to steady her as she pushed herself backward until our eyes met. Very slowly with her right hand, she raised her hand high enough to brush away the falling tears running down my cheek. For a split second, I could see compassion illuminating in her eyes which overwhelmed me even more. Perhaps, it was her way of showing me that I need not cry for her. Maybe, she sensed what her fate was and in her own way, cuing me to acknowledge the possibility of her dying. For her, as well as myself. There was no acknowledging anything, as I felt my mind searching for a distraction, any distraction that would take me away from the present moment.

Right then, I stood up and carried Heather into the kitchen in one arm, while dragging the car seat behind us with the other. I place the seat on one of the dining room chairs, secured Heather into the car seat and went about fixing something for us to eat. That was my distraction. It was only a distraction; for I knew Heather would eat little and I not at all.

After our dinner was cooked, I went to the table and sat in front of Heather in order to feed her. As I was about to feed her a spoonful of Spaghetti'Os, the most amazing and yet terrifying incident took place. Heather slowly turned her head away from me and in the direction of the dining room wall which the table was set against. She then began to smile and her eyes filled with joy. The same joy she would display whenever a loved one entered our home or when opening gifts on Christmas morning. Her expression was so vibrant and caught me by surprise, for there was absolutely nothing on the wall. No decorations, no window, nothing but a painted surface. Calling out her name didn't disrupt her focus on the wall. This is when I really became frightened.

It is my belief, we each have guardians watching over us throughout our lifetime. Maybe they're angels, or relatives that have passed, but a presence can sometimes be felt when the mind quiets and one is at peace with the Universe. This is what I believe Heather was experiencing at that time. I also believed her fate was being decided as well. Maybe, a Divine presence was there to guide her to the afterlife.

When I wasn't able to distract Heather's attention away from that wall, I leaned over and snatched her out of the car seat as fast as I could. There was no way I was going to allow Heather to die. She couldn't. What would I do without my Heather? No! I had to stop her from looking toward the wall, because I truly felt like a presence was there to help guide her through the process of death. I wasn't about to let go. I held her so close and began crying and pleading to God, to allow Heather to live.

I sat with Heather for the longest time. Once I gained my composure, enough that my crying had stopped, it came to me. I wasn't crying for Heather. I was crying for myself. My loss. My own need to be with her. Heather had become such a source of joy in my life, I didn't want that joy to ever be taken away from me. Once I allowed myself to step aside from my own fear of losing Heather, an amazing sense of calmness swept over me. It was then I finally knew without a shadow of a doubt, what my role as her mother included, which no preparation is offered in any parenting manual.

I was present with every milestone Heather had reached. Coaxing her, encouraging her, comforting her. I was there when she first rolled over, when she first crawled. I was present when she took her first steps. I heard her first word and watched her run for the first time. I was there to kiss her first skinned knee and wiped away her tears afterward. I was there to guide her through moments of uncertainty as every child experiences. The fear of touching grass without shoes on, the fear of being abandoned at the sitter's house. The fear of dogs, along with the fear of darkness. I have always played an important role in her life and I finally realized that I would in her death; if death was to occur.

What the whole experience at the dining room table taught me was this, I had no say what-so-ever if she were to live or die. Her fate was never in my hands. However, what I could do, was be there guiding her and comforting her while marking the moment, if death did occur.

In the back of my mind, I knew I wouldn't really be guiding Heather, she would be guiding me as she had been all along. However it may appear, I didn't give up on the notion of finding a cure for her. What it meant was, if the moment approached, I would be beside her, telling her how much she is loved and lovingly telling her that it is okay to go.

Chapter Seventeen

REGARDLESS, OF HOW EXHAUSTED I was feeling, the morning was already starting off glorious. Heather survived the night. As much as I possibly could manage, I fought sleep during the night, in order to watch over Heather. I listened to each breath she had taken. Several times during the course of the night, her breathing became seemingly laborious, only to return back to a normal breathing rhythm.

Alex and Grandma Sandy arrived later that morning. After one extremely long and worrisome night, it was a marvelous feeling to hear the sound of knocking. Quietly, I climbed out of bed and let the two of them in.

Not wanting to disturb Heather's sleep, we briefly chatted in whispers, before the three of us went and laid down to sleep. Following such an exhausting drive for both Alex and Grandma Sandy, the two of them fell asleep as the old saying goes, *even before their heads hit the pillow.* As a result, our room went from complete quiet to the sound of heavy snoring in a matter of minutes.

I found this quite amusing. Here, the three of us were concerned about waking Heather with our voice, but hearing how loud the snoring was and Heather not affected by it, we didn't need to be concern after all. I was so relieved to be in the company of familiar faces. The fear and loneliness I had felt during the night simply vanished.

While laying next to Heather, I remember looking up toward the ceiling and smiling. I felt such a strong sense of gratitude. Along with gratitude, hope was beginning to rise within me as well. Perhaps, if Heather made it through the night, she may very well continue to live. People say not to pin all your hopes on one certain outcome, but hope is all I had at that point and pinning them on the possibility that Heather would live is what I secretly did.

Having only slept for a few hours, Alex was ready to make the journey home. I too was ready to return to the quiet setting of our home in the country. Even though we had been at the Mayo for only a week, being there created such a sensation of being boxed in. I guess because we had spent the majority of time in our room.

Grandma Sandy and Heather remained asleep while Alex and I packed mine and Heather's belongings. When Heather did wake up, she was full of smiles and appeared more energetic than she had been in all our time at the Mayo. I think Alex and Grandma Sandy was responsible for her livelihood that morning. With everything packed and taken to the car, we were ready to leave. The only concern we had was how well Heather would tolerate the ride home. I still feared her condition would worsen as Dr. Scott predicted. We all feared it, but I knew if Heather suddenly quit breathing or went into convulsions, Grandma Sandy would know what to do. Thankfully nothing out of the ordinary happened on our way home. Other than a few episodes of fussiness, Heather remained in good spirits during the trip.

Grandma Sandy suggested that we check into obtaining a heart monitor for Heather when we arrived home. With a heart monitor, I would not have to spend each night trying to stay awake while Heather slept. I thought the idea was worth checking into and would call John the following Monday to inquire how we could obtain one.

A more serious discussion between the three of us on our way home, was what we would do if Heather did stop breathing while at home. After Dr. Cottle had spoken to me of how Heather would likely be hooked up to life support, Alex and I both agreed on not taking her to the hospital. As I reflect back, I wonder if we would have changed our minds in the actual event of Heather struggling to survive.

I guess because there would always be that disturbing question just under the surface of our subconscious of, whether or not, we made the right choice by allowing her to die without seeking medical help. Even though everything we were told by the specialists pointed in the direction of Heather dying. If such a decision were to be made, I would hope Alex and I would choose to allow Heather to die at home and not out of panic take her to the hospital where I believed she would die emotionally as she was kept physically alive by a machine. I prayed such a decision would never have to be made by us.

Following that discussion, Alex suggested that we have a family portrait taken as soon as possible. What a wonderful idea. I totally agreed and was grateful he thought of it. I really do not believe the thought of getting a family portrait taken would have ever crossed my mind.

Thirteen hours after leaving Rochester, Minnesota, we pulled into the driveway of our home. My first thought when we reached home, was how Heather had proven Dr. Scott wrong by surviving the trip home. Maybe, Heather would prove his entire prognosis inaccurate.

First thing Monday morning I called John at his office. We discussed the trip to Mayo and Heather's grim prognosis. I brought him up to date on Heather's present condition and asked for his help in obtaining a heart monitor. Whoever John had contacted, a heart monitor was delivered to our home the very next day.

The gentleman who delivered the monitor set it up and demonstrated how to hook the wires up on Heather. A set of electrode wires extending out of the monitoring box, were to be attached to Heather's chest. The function of the wires was to signal back to the monitoring box, Heather's heart beat. An alarm was set to go off in the event of irregular heart beats, or if she stopped breathing.

What a pain the monitor turned out to be. The alarm kept going off repeatedly during course of the night, because either one or both of the wires, taped to Heather had fallen off. The monitor was causing more stress on both Heather and the rest of the family, than when I alone was monitoring her breathing. We kept the monitor less than one week before returning it.

A few days after discontinuing the use of the monitor, Heather shown absolutely no signs of breathing difficulties. No gasping motions what so ever. Her breathing returned back to normal. Not only did her breathing return back to normal, the seizure like twitching also vanished. Whatever the reason may have been for this miraculous development, a new sense of hope began to emerge within the family unit. However, we still carried the fear of her regressing again without warning.

We went ahead and arranged for a family portrait to be taken. The portrait turned out beautiful. Heather was having a good day when the photo shoot was done. She just shined in the photo. Her eyes were so full of life that day. It was a good day for all of us. Days like that one became our source of strength and we didn't dare take them for granted. For in a moment's notice, Heather would suddenly appear unresponsive and frail. Other than the improvements with Heather's breathing and muscle spasms, we saw little improvement in her overall condition.

Alex and I, well more so Alex, because he was the one whom was always organized and planned ahead, decided to meet with the funeral director at the funeral home in Lakeview. We went to discuss funeral arrangements and to pick out a casket, if Heather were to die, as predicted by Dr. Scott. Her birthday was just a couple of weeks away. We should have been shopping for a birthday gift, not a casket.

I sat and listened as Alex and the funeral director discussed the matter of purchasing a cemetery plot for Heather. Holding a memorial service for Heather was also being talked over, while Alex and I looked through the variety of funeral programs that were available. None of what was being discussed really hit home, until the funeral director escorted us to a room where several models of caskets were displayed. Amongst the arrangement of coffins, were two child size caskets that looked no bigger than a shoe box. All I could think of was, "Had we really reached the point of expecting Heather to die?" We must have had. Because we selected a casket in which Heather would be laid to rest, in the event of her death.

The more I thought about the possibility of Heather having type of Leukodystrophy, the more I felt the need to learn whatever I could on the disease. I wrote to the Leukodystrophy Foundation and asked for some literature to better help me understand what we may be dealing with. When the information packet arrived, I was shocked to find just how many different types of Leukodystrophy there were at that time. Close to fourteen types. In the present day, researchers have categorized thirty-four types of the disease.

I began to receive a bi-monthly magazine from the foundation, filled with personal stories written by parents of children whom were affected, as well as, new discoveries on this horrendous disease. On the panel of researchers there was a name, Dr. Hugo Moser, an University Professor of Neurology and Pediatrics at John Hopkins University in Baltimore, Maryland. I was aware of John Hopkins Medical Center being ranked number one in the country, so I assumed the University followed suit. What I didn't know at the time was just how prestigious Dr. Moser was regarded. He was known around the world for his research and findings on Leukodystrophy.

With nothing else to lose, I decided to write Dr. Moser, along with sending him every scrap of information I had on Heather; including a copy of her MRI, lad results and the prognosis from Dr. Vesser and Dr. Scott. I asked if he would looked over the files and perhaps offer an opinion of what he believed Heather's condition was. It was within two weeks after sending the package to Dr. Moser, that I received a letter in response to my inquiry.

Dr. Moser offered two possible explanations that seem most likely to him. He agreed with Dr. Scott's suspicion that Heather's condition may have stemmed from a form of Leukodystrophy. Another possibility was metabolic brain white matter disturbances, which had an up and down course. Leigh's encephalopathy, known to be associated with this, is where the individual recovers to some degree only to regress again. Dr. Moser went on to say that in his opinion, Dr. Scott was one of the best pediatric neurologists in the world and considered him as being a good friend. Dr. Moser suggested that we reconsider a brain biopsy for a precise diagnosis. He also written that he would be pleased to review any additional medical files and lab reports on Heather that I may have.

There, I had the opinion of the leading researcher on Leukodystrophy in the country. World for that matter. That alone was amazing to me. I could now say and accept as my truth, I had done everything, short of consenting to a biopsy, in finding a cure for Heather.

Two months had passed since returning home from the Mayo and receiving the letter from Dr. Moser. Heather still remained in an infantile state. I noticed that she appeared to be losing weight which had me worried. I set up an appointment with Dr. Cottle in order for him to examine her. Her weight on that visit was twenty pounds. Not extremely underweight, but enough to be concerned about. John recommended adding more nutrient supplements in her food and increasing her calories intake. If this approach didn't produce positive result, then a feeding tube will have to be seriously considered as a mean of feeding Heather.

Since I was back to bottle feeding her on a regular basis, I would add a can of Ensure with her oatmeal. Sometimes I would mix

Carnation Instant Breakfast, along with other nutritional drink mixes to her oatmeal. Slowly Heather begun to gain back some weight and was looking much healthier. Thank goodness instant oatmeal comes in several favors because that had become the main menu for Heather for quite sometime.

Over the course the next couple of months, changes in Heather's overall condition began to occur. Some were subtle while others were major developments, as far as I was concerned. The most welcomed change was the ease at which Heather fell asleep. There was no longer any crying before naps or at bedtimes and no hours of rocking her in the rocking chair, before laying her down in bed. She took longer naps and slept through the night without waking as she had before. Another sign of improvement was the day she had a bowel movement on her own without us initiating it. Her first independent bowel movement since late July, close to four months. I was on the phone calling relatives, sharing the news of her independent bowel movement that day.

Heather stopped drooling in early November. Again, like the screaming, the drooling stopped as sudden as it had started. By Christmas and into the New Year, Heather began to slightly lift her head for short periods of time. She also could turn her head side to side, but still took great effort on her part to do so. Following next was the vocal sounds she began to make as if she were trying to speak. Although Heather still experienced bodily weakness, she was making attempts at moving her legs while sitting, along with showing more movement in both her arms and hands.

Heather still continued to have intermittent fevers, but not on a regular basis. The most noticeable change was the spark of life shinning once again in her eyes. This is what gave me the impression that Heather was really on the road to recovery. I can not help but believe that the incident at Mayo, when Heather smiled at that bare wall, had a lot to do with her improving health. Perhaps, it was the Divine intervention I begged for on the evening I sat in the swing.

CHAPTER EIGHTEEN

ITH ALL THE PROGRESS HEATHER was making in her recovery, the tension that once filled the house was beginning to subside. Alex was hired in at Steel Parts Automotive in Greenville,working second shift. Mikey was happier and doing better in school, and I, well I was feeling a bit lost. My emotions would shift back and forth from contentment to feeling such anxiety and back to feeling content.

Watching my child grow into a happy and healthy toddler, then regress into infancy and experience being on the verge of death had such a tremendous impact on me. One noticeable change that was taking place in me during that time, was how I began to feel more self confident. No longer did I view myself as the timid individual that I had been at the onset of Heather's illness. I was becoming more outspoken and self reliant. Not only when dealing with hospital staff and doctors, but also with Alex.

Watching Heather regain more strength and movement was exciting. She once again was able to eat soft foods without being bottle fed. She no longer choked or gagged while being fed. I still had to spoon feed her, but I believed it would be only a matter of time before she would be able to feed herself again. We were actually witnessing the beginning of Heather relearning everything she had accomplished before becoming ill.

Alex and I began to seriously consider pursuing a brain biopsy to rule out the possibility of Heather having any type of Leukodystrophy. I wasn't really in agreement with Dr. Scott or Dr. Moser's diagnosis of Leukodystrophy, after Heather began to show signs of improvement. Heather's symptoms may have been similar, but the fact that she was getting better in itself was proof that Leukodystrophy couldn't be the cause. Leukodystrophy was classified as being a terminal disease without a cure. However, the other disease Dr. Moser mentioned, Leigh's Encephalopathy remained plausible. The thought of Heather regressing again terrified us. Would she be able to survive a relapse? Asking ourselves that question was in fact the deciding factor in consenting to the cerebral biopsy. We wanted/needed to know if Heather's condition was Leigh's Encephalopathy. If she was tested positive for Leigh's Encephalopathy, it would give us some type of fore warning. At best, we may discover if another disease was responsible for Heather's regression. The other being a reaction to her DPT vaccination, as I had repeatedly spoke of.

In order to even to seen by a neurosurgeon, we had to get a referral. This met going back to Dr. Vesser. As much as I disliked his demeanor, if getting a referral met being in his presence; so be it. I was ready to correct him if he chose to make another inappropriate comment about Heather. I was that confident in my ability not to allow him to recreate that feeling of intimidation that he had in the past. I was ready to do battle with Dr. Vesser even before stepping in his office. That was how much I despised his arrogance. Unfortunately, the overflow of my feelings toward Dr. Vesser trickled down to the receptionist when I called to set up an appointment.

"Hello, Dr. Vesser office," the woman announced in a mild manner.

"Hello, this is Barb Moore calling to set up an appointment for my daughter Heather Moore."

"Has Dr. Vesser seen Heather before?"

"Yes, in late July of last year."

"What is the purpose of seeing Dr. Vesser?"

"To get a referral to see a Neurosurgeon regarding a cerebral biopsy.:

"I see, there is an opening Monday, February 3rd at 3:15pm. Is this a good time for you."

"Yes, that will work out great."

"Come in a few minutes early, in case there is any new information that may need to be filled out."

"There is no change in the insurance coverage. Any other information on Heather should have already been sent to your office by either Dr. Scott at the Mayo Clinic or Dr. Cottle." I said in a harsh tone.

"Well, you do realize Dr. Vesser doesn't consider giving a referral without an examination in order to decide if it is in your daughter's best interest," She replied back in the same manner as I voiced previously.

"I really don't see any reason he wouldn't refer Heather. Dr. Vesser was the one who first mentioned a cerebral biopsy."

"I'll put her down for Monday," She said soberly.

"Okay, thank you."

"Good bye, Mrs. Moore."

As a precaution, Heather and I arrived at Dr. Vesser's office at 3:00pm. Just in case there was some new paperwork that needed to be filled out. I walked up to the receptionist and announced that Heather was there. She gave a quick glance at us and told us to take a seat. Someone would come get us when the doctor was ready. No mention of paperwork.

We didn't have to wait long before Heather's name was called out and we were taken to Dr. Vesser's office. As soon as Heather and I entered his office, he invited us to take a seat and proceeded to briefly examine Heather before he began speaking.

"So, I see you decided to take Heather to the Mayo Clinic. Looking for someone to confirm your suspicion of a reaction to the DPT vaccination?"

I could feel the defensiveness in me begin to stir. Nothing would have given me more pleasure than to verbally destroy this man's conceitedness.

"There was a part of me that had hope my suspicion would be taken seriously," I replied. "I also believed there would be more of a effort put into finding out what was happening to Heather rather than telling me, *"what you see is what you get."* God, that felt good throwing that in his face.

"I see," he said, while nodding his head. "Did you get the results you were looking for?"

"I'm sure you are aware of Dr. Scott's diagnosis and his thoughts on the matter," I said gazing coldly into his eyes.

"Yes, I did receive a detailed letter from Dr. Scott, including the results of all the tests that he had ordered on Heather. Leukodystrophy is a continuation of regressing. However, Heather has made some major improvements since the last time I had seen her. I would have to disagree with the diagnosis Dr. Scott had stated. I also read that he suggested a cerebral biopsy while you were there, but you objected against having it done. Is there a specific reason you elected not to pursue the biopsy at that time?"

"Heather was very weak when we were at the Mayo. Dr. Scott felt that Heather might not even survive the trip back to Michigan. How could I have given my consent to a procedure when there was a good possibility that she may even had died during the biopsy? The need to know what caused her condition, no longer seemed as important then. If she was going to die, I wanted her home in the company of family."

"You feel that Heather is up to the biopsy now? What is it that you are hoping to gain from the biopsy?" He asked.

"I contacted Dr. Hugo Moser, a neurologist, at John Hopkins University, after returning home from the Mayo. Hoping to get his professional opinion on Heather, I sent all the files I had on her, including the copy of her MRI. He wrote back and suggested that a type of Leukodystrophy may be one cause, but another possible cause might be Leigh's Encephalopathy. In his letter, Dr. Moser stated that with Leigh's Encephalopathy, Heather may experience some improvement then may regress again. I guess the biopsy is for our own peace of mind. To rule out Leukodystrophy and know for sure if what she has is Leigh's Encephalopathy or not." I replied.

"Yes, I have heard of Dr. Moser and I'm familiar with the research he has done with Leukodystrophy. I must say, I'm impressed by your persistence in finding the cause of Heather's condition. Leigh's Encephalopathy maybe a possibility. The onset of the disease is similar to what Heather experienced, but in my opinion; I still suspect her symptoms stem from a viral inflammation. I will contact Dr. Herz, whom I believe to be the best neurosurgeon in this area and arrange a consultation for Heather."

"In your opinion, do you believe Heather is strong enough to undergo this biopsy?" I asked. "Could we be risking her health in doing so?"

"To be honest Mrs. Moore, I didn't even expect Heather to improve as much as she has. I understand your concern for her health, but I also understand the anxiety you and your family must be feeling in not knowing what to expect later in the future. I do recommend going through with the biopsy. Dr. Herz will determine whether or not if the biopsy is beneficial to Heather. I have seen only a few cases where the child had improved as much as your daughter has. One child went on to completely recover without any signs of suffering a brain inflammation of any kind. The brain is an amazing mechanism in the human body. The full potential of the brain has yet to be discovered." He stated with enthusiasm.

"So, we will be contacted by Dr. Herz then?"

"Yes, his secretary will be calling to arrange an appointment. You do not need to worry. Heather will be in good hands with Dr. Herz. Like I stated earlier, he is the best neurosurgeon in the area. I believe we have covered everything we needed to today. Do you have any other concerns or questions?"

"I can't think of any."

"Mrs. Moore, Heather is a very lucky little girl to have such a persistent mom as you seem to be. Your strength and determination, as well as your love for Heather, may have played a large role in her still being alive and with us today. A child can sense when a parent has given up hope. I would like to see Heather again after the biopsy has been done, if you wouldn't mind."

"Of course. Thank you Dr. Vesser for the referral. I'm sure you will be contacted with the results," I said.

I really didn't know what to make of the change in Dr. Vesser's attitude during the visit. He was headed in the direction of becoming cynical at first, but then he unexpectedly became sociable. Perhaps, during this particular visit, he allowed himself to view Heather as a child and not just another mystery case to solve.

The following Monday, I received a call from the office of Dr. Herz. A date was set to meet with the neurosurgeon. Heather's appointment was scheduled in the morning, making it possible for Alex to accompany Heather and I. By then, I was getting quite used of going alone with Heather to doctor appointments. In a way, it seemed odd that Alex would be going along with Heather and I.

Our first meeting with Dr. Herz was very casual. Before our appointment with him, he had reviewed Heather's medical files, along with her MRI's and CT scans. Based on the information he received on Heather's, his opinion regarding Heather's condition was similar to Dr. Scott and Dr. Moser. A type of Leukodystrophy may be a likelihood. During our visit, Dr. Herz performed a general physical examination of Heather, as well as a neurological exam.

What impressed me the most with Dr. Herz, was his up front honesty. He stated that under no circumstances, would he even consider going through with the cerebral biopsy, if it were putting Heather's health at risk, or if he thought it would not benefit Heather and us, for that matter. He stated that his utmost concern was always toward the patient. Before leaving his office, Dr. Herz handed us some literature pertaining to the biopsy. He suggested we read the material before returning for the next scheduled visit, where he planned to go be into more detail about the procedure, risks, benefits, and along with postoperative care, if we chose to go through with the surgery.

One would have had to have a medical degree to fully understand the reading material Dr. Herz headed to us. To me, the procedure sounded extremely complicated and risky. The more I read through the pamphlet, the more I was beginning to seriously doubt going through with the biopsy. That was until we returned for our second visit with Dr. Herz. The way in which he explained the procedure, in terms which I could easily understand, I felt satisfied that Heather would be in good hands.

The various equipment to be used during Heather's biopsy was set out for Alex and I to view. Right from the start, Dr. Herz had encouraged us to ask any questions that we may have had and to voice any concerns as well. He was so thorough in explaining the procedure, there wasn't many questions to ask. After discussing the biopsy in its entirety, Alex and I decided to pursue the brain biopsy. A date for the biopsy was set for March 18th, 1992.

CHAPTER NINETEEN

THE MORNING OF HEATHER'S BRAIN biopsy, she was expected to be at the hospital by 6:30 am. Again, Heather was not to eat after midnight, prior to her surgery. Her surgery was going to take place at Blodgett Memorial. In the back of my mind, I wondered if Heather would perhaps come up missing in the computer system. Upon our arrival, we checked Heather in and her medical information was instantly found. A good indication the day was going to be promising.

We were then escorted to the prep-surgical room where Heather would be prepped for surgery. Dr. Herz briefly came into the room and again asked if we had any questions or concerns regarding the surgery, before taking Heather into the operating room. Alex and I had no questions, but we both were full of concerns. Here was our twenty-nine month old daughter, barely three feet in height and weighing only twenty-six pounds, about to undergo a brain biopsy. Looking into her trusting eyes was the last image I carried with me, as Alex and I left the room and headed to the family waiting room.

The procedure itself would take about one hour. A special apparatus was attached to Heather's skull using screws to hold her head in place. The needle by which samples of brain tissue was to be gathered, would be guided by computer-assisted imaging. In Heather's case, she was placed in the CT scan machine as a means to obtain the correct position. The targeted areas in her brain, to collect samples of brain tissue was at the gray-white matter junction and also deep within the white matter. Six specimens of tissue were obtained during the procedure. Heather tolerated the biopsy well without any complications.

I remember sitting in the waiting area and getting a glimpse of Heather being wheeled into the recovery room. It appeared as if they had shaven a quarter of her hair off on the right side of her head. The bandage covering the wound looked quite small though. She looked so tiny on that hospital bed when I saw her.

We wasn't allowed into the recovery room until Heather became conscious. Barely awake, Heather still made an effort to smile when she noticed Alex and I standing by her bedside. Once it was felt that Heather's condition was stable, she was taken into the Intensive Care Unit and remained there throughout the duration of her stay at Blodgett. I stayed as well, not wanting to leave her there alone. I would once again have to sleep in the family room, but mostly I would be sitting next to Heather's bed.

On the second day after the biopsy, an incident happened while the nurse was cleaning and changing the bandage on Heather's wound. That incident, instantly took me back in time and became a definite sign that Heather was truly on her way back to us, as she was before the illness.

When the nurse came into the Intensive Care Unit, I had Heather sitting upright with me steadying her. The nurse removed the old bandage and cleaned the area, before removing some fresh gauze from its wrapper. As soon as the fresh gauze was removed, Heather's attention was immediately drawn to the floor and she began to fuss a little. At that time, the nurse believed Heather was becoming upset with having her bandage changed. She began making attempts at consoling Heather. When the nurse looked toward my direction, she noticed me smiling. For I knew the reason behind Heather's fussiness.

I told the nurse that Heather noticed a piece of the wrapper had fallen on the floor and it was bothering her. As soon as the nurse picked up the fallen piece, Heather once again smiled. As insignificant as this might seem, it was major to me. It meant Heather continued to be the little girl we had known her to be all along. She just wasn't capable of revealing this during her illness. It also was a sign that the inflammation may have not effected her mentally, which I was afraid that it may have had.

Heather and I left Blodgett and returned home three days later. It was if Heather never underwent a major procedure such as a brain biopsy. The only reminder of the biopsy still present today, is the area in which a small portion of her scalp was removed. Where her hair never grew back. A great show and tell story for her to share with classmates, if and when she started school.

On April 17th Good Friday, we received a call from Dr. Herz himself. Telling us that the final report of Heather's biopsy was back. The final diagnosis was "Focal perivascular inflammation and degeneration of white matter and consistent with post-infectious Encephalomyelitis." The exact diagnosis Dr. Vesser had assumed it was all along. No sign of Leukodystrophy or Leigh's encephalopathy and no sign of any virus present, which meant Heather's immune system had fought back and won!

Heather continued to regain more strength and mobility during the next couple of months. Her head control was to the point where she was able to keep her head in an upright position even while laying on her stomach. However, sitting was still impossible without having pillows supporting her, so she wouldn't fall over. More movement in her arms and legs was now occurring. She was even making attempts at crawling. The most heart warming moment in Heather's progress was when she said, "ma ma" and "da da."

She no longer was content with spending more time than needed sitting in her car seat. She would try her hardest to slide herself out of the seat. The experience of watching her regaining mobility was inspiring. Dr. Vesser was correct in saying the brain had the ability to re-route nerve impulses. Heather was indeed showing signs of this taking place. The intermittent fevers still occurred. Later, it was suspected that the fevers were brought on by food particles going into her lungs, which would trigger the fevers, indicating a possible infection.

In early June that year, a visitor came to see Heather and I. It was Mikey's Aunt Kathy, a teacher at Little People Land. Miss Kathy would have such an impact of Heather's recovery. I'm not sure to what extent Heather would have developed academically and physically if it wasn't for the help we received from her.

I had no clue of the programs available for special needs children. No information was offered to us after being discharged from the hospital. The suggestion of any type of rehabilitation was never mentioned by anyone and I didn't even consider it. I was under the impression that Heather would recover on her own, relearning everything in the same process as she had in infancy without intervention. That was how uneducated and really unprepared we were with raising a special needs child.

Miss Kathy contacted the Montcalm Intermediate School District personnel and suggested that Heather be evaluated for admittance into the school program. The evaluation would lead to Heather getting her the help, that was ultimately responsible for the remarkable accomplishments, Heather would achieve during her recovery. At the time of Heather's evaluation, she was thirty three months old.

As a means of evaluating Heather's various levels of functional abilities, the Peabody Development Motor Scale (PDMS) was used. This is one of the most reliable testing instruments used to assess related areas of development that are achieved early in life. The PDMS is used by pediatricians, Therapists, and Special Education teachers to help screen for and identify developmental delay. It's also used to determine treatment goals.

The therapists, whom participated in Heather's evaluation, placed Heather's receptive language skills (understanding what is said or read,) at a 27-30 month level. Her language expressive skills (speaking and writing,) was marked at the 12-18 month level. Fine motor skills (actions using thumb and fingers to grasp objects or tongue and lips to taste foods,) were estimated at the 17 month. Gross motor skills (actions requiring the movement of larger muscles for the purpose of walking, jumping, and dressing,) was at the 4 month level of development.

After the evaluation, it was felt by the therapists that Heather could benefit from an intensive rehabilitation program at Mary Free Bed in Grand Rapids, Michigan. The school contacted Dr. Kuldanek, the pediatric physician at Mary Free Bed. Heather was seen by Dr. Kuldanek, along with a team of therapists in early July. They also agreed that she had significant potential for improvement and arrangements were made for Heather's admission. Dr. Kuldanek recommended that a 4 to 6 weeks inpatient stay be scheduled. On July 21, 1992, Heather was admitted to Mary Free Bed Rehabilitation Hospital.

Heather would be involved in daily sessions of Speech/Language Therapy. Assisting Heather in various ways to help her communicate verbally while also teaching her some sign language. Occupational Therapy, addressing fine motor activities such as self care tasks and manipulating smaller objects using finger and thumb interaction. Physical Therapy, working with Heather on strengthening her muscle tone, endurance, and mobility.

Heather was also evaluated by the hospital's psychologist as part of her rehabilitation program. She also attended individual cognitive remedial interventions 4-5 times per week. The goal of those interventions was to discover the most constructive way in which Heather could learn new things and the ability to plan; implement and sequence motor tasks. Such as connecting blocks, completing puzzles, and any activity that requires thought process.

The separation anxiety I experienced while Heather was in Mary Free Bed seemed to fully engulf me. Making it difficult to focus on anything besides wanting to have Heather back home. Mikey and I would travel down to see her as often as possible during the week. After I arrived home from work and Mikey from school, we would go and stay with Heather until she fell asleep. Some nights we wouldn't leave the hospital until after 10pm. Driving the hour back home and getting a few hours of sleep before having to get up for work, was exhausting. Occasionally, Alex would go see Heather earlier in the morning before he went to work. He was able to attend several of Heather's therapies and watch her in action, so to speak. I, on the other hand, had to wait till the weekend to attend Heather's therapies and to be brought up-to-date on her progress.

Heather's therapies kept her busy during the day. It was the evening hours where Heather didn't have a lot of interaction with others. There were a few college students who would come and visit the children in the pediatric ward on certain days during the week. Mikey and I would go see Heather on their off days, just so she wouldn't feel alone and forgotten.

Before Heather's discharge, she was approved for a couple of weekend passes; where we took her home on a Friday night and return her back on Sunday afternoon. Having her home even for the brief stay was wonderful. What began as a 4-6 weeks stay, extended to a little over two months before she would be officially discharged.

CHAPTER TWENTY

ECAUSE OF THE DEDICATION OF each therapist working with Heather, she made some remarkable gains during her stay at Mary Free Bed Rehabilitation Hospital. The ability to relate to younger children, on the child's level of understanding, along with a tremendous amount of patience each therapist had shown to Heather, in my opinion, made all the difference in her attitude toward therapy. It takes a great deal of creativity on the part of the therapist to present tasks that are interesting to any child. While at the same time targeting the specific area the therapist is attempting to strengthen.

On the day of Heather's discharge from Mary Free Bed, I attended each of her therapies. Each therapist had commented on how delightful it was working with Heather. She was one of those children who was eager to participate in therapy without a lot of reluctance. In truth, Heather's eagerness was a direct result of the approach each therapist had taken in connecting with her. Without their continuous encouragement and direction, Heather wouldn't have progressed as much as she had. The credit goes to the therapists along with my ever lasting admiration.

By attending Heather's last therapy sessions, each therapist demonstrated various activities that were used in Heather's therapy program, which I continued to do with her at home. Regrading Fine Motor Tasks and Oral Motor/Feeding, I was given instructions and suggestions on helping Heather become more involved with her dressing and hygiene tasks. Stretching exercises were demonstrated as well, for Heather's legs and ankles to help reduce the tightness of her lower extremities.

At the time of her discharge, her receptive language skills remained at the 27-30 month level. She was able to identify basic vocabulary in books and was able to identify toys without difficulty. Expressive language skills also remained the same. Although Heather was able to to make the K,G, and M sounds. While in rehab, She had spoken on occasion the words "ma ma," "da da," "Ikey" for Mikey, and "addie" for Laddie our dog. Her ability to speak was marked as being moderately to severely impaired due to speech Apraxia (incapacity to program the positioning of speech muscles) and general weakness of oral muscles. This weakness in her lips, tongue, jaw, and cheek muscles contributed to her chewing and swallowing difficulties as well.

As an alternate means to communicate, sign language was taught to Heather. It was felt that this approach to communicating with others would help reduce the frustration Heather experienced from her speech impairment. Simple words such as: eat, drink, Mom, Dad, more, in, out, up, down, mine, and baby, were taught to her. When Heather had to go to the bathroom, she was encouraged to point or tug on her wet diaper. Before her illness, we had been in the process of potty training her and was making good progress at that time. So, this was encouraging to hear that she would make such gestures.

As part of her therapy, Heather had to be taught how to chew and when it was safe to swallow. On one of our day passes with Heather, the four of us went out to eat at a local restaurant. Before Heather was allowed to swallow any food, she had to show us how well she had chewed the food by opening her month so we could see. If she chewed the food well we would then tell her to swallow.

Well, those who were sitting near our table in the restaurant, appeared to become somewhat offended by Heather proudly displaying her chewed food to us. They even seemed more appalled when Mikey made Heather laugh and the chewed food came flying out of her mouth. One could have only imagined the thoughts going through their minds at the sight of that.

Table manners didn't apply to Heather during this time. Even though Alex became a bit uptight with Mikey's little stunt, I, on the other hand, saw humor in it. Mikey was just being a typical sibling mocking his little sister. Until Heather learned to chew her food well enough so she didn't choke when swallowing, she would have to be supervised at all times while she ate. Not only at home, but at school during sneak time.

Occupational Therapy (fine motor skills) was very successful in advancing Heather's ability to execute tasks regrading hand and eye coordination and finger and thumb activities. She was able to draw vertical and horizontal lines, align two or more cubes to make train and build a eight cube tower. These completed tasks placed her in the 24-31 month level. A giant leap from the 17 month level she was marked at before admittance into rehab.

Heather was able to place her arms in her shirt and assist with pulling the shirt down. Her dressing skills were marked at a 16-19 month level. As for feeding skills, Heather began assisting with her eating by using a curved spoon. Which made it easier for her to bring food to her mouth without spilling all of it. She developed more control on bringing her sippy cup to her mouth as well, but did tend to still gulp instead of sipping the liquids.

Physical Therapy (gross motor skills,) was also an area in which Heather excelled in. Heather was able to tolerate sitting on a small bench with minimal assistance up to fifteen minutes. She was able to tolerate prone (lying down) on her elbows with a small wedge. She made attempts at reaching for objects while in this position, alternating hands. Heather was able to pull to stand at a small table from the stool she was sitting on. She would tired easily and could only repeat the pull to stand exercise about 5-7 repetitions.

Not only did she achieve pull to stand from stool to table, she went even further in her physical therapy. She was able to crawl, combat style close to 5-10 feet before becoming fatigued. With minimal assistance, Heather was walking short distances using a reverse rolling walker. She was able to propel her wheelchair up to 200 feet with minimal assistance for steering. A pair of AFO's (leg braces) were made specially designed for her as well and to help support her legs and ankles. These would also cut back on her wanting to lean forward on her toes while standing, thus allowing her to stand up straight.

Because of Heather's limited verbal and motor skills, her performance on cognitive testing fell significantly below average. It was determined that a lot of visual activities were to be used as a means of learning, instead of using verbal instructions. It was noted that Heather did tend to become easily frustrated when too many requests were placed on her. It was best to approach Heather with limited options and to inform her what exactly was expected of her with each task before she attempted the task.

Her current level of general psychometric intelligence (ability to process information to plan and implement tasks,) was in the bottom of the low-average range. It was felt that Heather did have the potential to engage in new learning, if the activities were repetitive and short in duration as her attention span was limited. As long as she wasn't bombarded with a lot of requests of "do this and do that," her frustration and Apraxia would not interfere with her ability to respond. The more educational experiences that could be offered in an indirect way, a game or in a laid back manner, the better.

Also attending the last day of Heather's therapies sessions was the school staff from Little People Land. This gave them the opportunity to evaluate Heather and also work with the therapists in deciding what therapies and learning activities would best benefit Heather while she attended school. It was recommended that Heather attend school at least three times a week, along with arranging outpatient therapies in all fields: Occupational, Physical, and Speech at the nearest facility. Preferably, a facility whose therapists were accustomed to working with younger children, such as Heather. Participation in a school setting was greatly stressed. This would benefit Heather's social skills and gradually help her adjust to her disabilities in a classroom setting.

Heather started school at Little People Land one week after her discharge, which gave her time to settle in at home. We installed railings along the hallway in our home, which made it possible for her to walk down the hall from her bedroom and into the living room. During the week when I worked, Alex was in charge of getting Heather ready for school and get her on the bus. Regarding therapy outside of school, Heather was taken to Greenville Memorial Hospital's rehabilitation facility. This arrangement worked out prefect since we both worked in Greenville. Alex would drop Heather off at rehab before going to work and I would pick her up after I was out of work.

The therapists at school and at Greenville instantly fell in love with Heather. It was obvious that Heather was emerging into a "social butterfly." She experienced no difficulty adjusting to school or rehab in Greenville. Like I stated earlier, people were automatically drawn to her, especially in the rehab facility. She was the youngest patient receiving therapy there. Upon seeing her, one would want to go and hug her. She was that adorable.

"Experience is not what happens to you, it is what you do with what happens to you."

Aldous Huxley

What was so frustrating throughout the course of Heather's illness was the realization that I had absolutely no control as to what happened or would happen to Heather, outside of seeking medical help and comforting her the best way I knew how. That feeling of being so powerless was incredibly defeating because I always imagined I would be able to protect my children from any harm. Every once of faith, inner strength and courage I had was tested. Trying to manage family, work and life in general became extremely overbearing. Thankfully, I had a lot of support from family, friends and especially Dr. Cottle, who had made himself available whenever I needed anything pertaining to Heather. Not once did he dissuade my attempts to find a cure for her. No matter how extreme they may have sounded or had been.

Sadly, Mikey experienced what a lot of children most likely go through when a sibling has special needs; the sense of somewhat being forgotten and less important. With my attention being so focused on Heather, it was extremely difficult to provide him with the attention he craved. Mikey never once complained or showed outward signs of resentment. He was always eager to be near Heather and I. Entertaining her whenever possible and consoling me, when I should have been consoling him. What saddened me the most with Mikey was the estranged relationship that was taking place between Alex and him. I guess in a way, I was also growing distant from Alex. Heather, on the other hand, was in the process of becoming *daddy's little girl.* When the need for Mom wasn't predominate any longer, Dad became the light in her eyes.

I could have easily went into the direction of self pity and anger in my approach to life, while dealing with Heather's ordeal, but instead I was inspired by Heather. As I stated earlier, Heather didn't exhibit any type of self pity. Whatever developed with her condition, she seemed to naturally adapt to. By not becoming completely self-absorbed in this experience with Heather, I was able to discover the opportunity to experience who and what I was. My strengths and weaknesses, my beliefs and insecurities were all challenged.

The most valuable lesson I learned from the experience, was

accepting the truth of how our children are gifts, not any type of possession. Children are not born for the purpose to mold and shape into what we, as parents, would like them to be. Each child is born with their own specialness. The only requirements of being a parent, in my opinion, is protecting, providing for, loving the child and helping the child develop that specialness. I also came to realize how my children made it possible for me to discover qualities about myself, unattainable by any other means. I could only hope that in the future, I would do the same for them.

I never did gave up the notion the DPT vaccine caused Heather's condition. Shortly after being discharged from Mary Free Bed, the public became more aware of several cases of severe reactions to the DPT vaccine, administered to children between 1991-1992, in the state of Michigan. A law firm in Warren Michigan, Dobreff & Dobreff, was offering their services to families whom suspected their child experienced such a reaction. Alex and I contacted their office and met with the lawyers. Because of no mention of a possible reaction to the DPT vaccination was ever recorded in Heather's medical files, they were apprehensive in filling a case for Heather. It wouldn't be until 2007, when I actually saw the following statement in Heather's medical history completed by a medical physician: "Post- infectious encephalitis, due to DPT vaccination in childhood."

ALEX'S WORDS

When Heather became ill, I didn't know why or what to expect. Did she get sick from a baby shot or was it that we would never know. I took her to get her last series of shots and always felt some guilt. I didn't know what to think after coming home from the Mayo Clinic. I thought that there was no way this was happening. Such a beautiful baby girl. Our lives had been changed forever from this illness. We moved forward with funeral plans and tried to understand what to expect for Heather's final days. The bedtime ritual to get Heather to sleep was almost unbearable. As she had to be rocked and held by her mother. Sometimes an hour or more she would cry. When Heather started to show signs of improvement, we saw hope for her to live longer; regain mental and physical capabilities. She continued to get better, began school and never looked back.

DPT Vaccine

Call it mother's intuition or whatever, but without any signs of a prior illness or other indications of any inherited disorders, the rate at which Heather's health deteriorated so rapidly had to have been connected to her last DPT vaccination. It is interesting to note, because none of her symptoms, except for the slight fever and swelling around the injection site occurred within 48 hours after her shot, the possibility of any connection was quickly dismissed. Where exactly did this seemingly non-negotiable cut off point of 48 hours originate?

From January of 1978 to December 1979, the FDA (U.S. Food and drugs Administration,) paid for and organized a study at UCLA called: *"Pertussis Vaccine Project: Rates, Nature and Etiology of Adverse Reactions Associated with DPT Vaccine."* The results of the study were published in November 1981. The unpublished "Final Report" was submitted to the FDA in March of 1980.

The study had discovered a higher number of adverse reactions to the DPT vaccine than earlier recorded in literature. The most noticeable finding in the preliminary report is the high recurrence of persistent crying, episodes of convulsions and collapse. The study also uncovered that systemic reactions in the central nervous systems were present in 50 percent of the vaccinations.

Because the nature of the study could be potentially damaging, the FDA placed an arbitrary time limit of forty-eight hours in which a reaction had to take place. Even though scientists and other medical researchers had in fact documented, serious reactions do occur after the cut off. The forty-eight hours cut off was a way to limit the statistical data and hide the degree of the problem from the American population. What is interesting, the majority of funding for the FDA came from the companies that the FDA was seeking to monitor and evaluate.

In 1979, the FDA funded another study at UCLA which was published in 1981. This time focusing on the DPT and DT vaccinations. After evaluation 16,000 DPT and DT vaccination cases, it was determined that the Pertussis (P) antigen in the DPT shot was responsible for causing reactions. So, the 48 hour cut off was created by the very agency that was designed to protect the people from harmful drugs, along with food contamination. Perhaps, this is why the cut off is honored by many physicians and government itself.

The first whooping cough vaccine was created in 1912 by two French bacteriologists. The Pertussis bacteria was grown in large pots and then the bacteria was killed with heat, preserved with Formaldehyde. This vaccine was created 98 years ago, is quite similar to the whole cell vaccine used throughout the world today. In the 1930's and early 1940's, the idea of combining the Pertussis vaccine with Diphtheria and Tetanus was considered. Combining multiple antigens would reduce the number of required injections. So, for the sake of simplifying the lives of parents, busy doctors and the children, the DPT vaccine was created.

No large clinical trials of any kind were ever done in the United States to measure the effectiveness and safety of the Pertussis vaccine. Many of the adverse reactions suffered by children whom were given the DPT, are very similar to what Heather had experienced. Pain, redness, soreness or swelling around the injection site. Close to 50% of children developed a fever greater then 100 degree after one or more doses. Cough, runny nose, and ear infections were also common and are resistant to antibiotics and other medicines.

Two of the most frequent and most overlooked reactions to the vaccine were the high-pitched screaming and persistent crying. The high-pitched screaming and persistent crying is considered to be due to irritation to the nervous system. Some children has had recurring symptoms of this for weeks and up to months after the injection.

Slight paralysis on one side of the body, as was apparent with Heather. Paralysis of lower body including legs or paralysis of all for limbs have been reported in the literature written by scientists; to be a side effect of the Pertussis vaccine. Severe to mild neurological damage was also linked to the DPT vaccine. In fact, Pertussis bacteria has been used in a variety of laboratory experiments to help provoke Encephalitis and Encephalopathy in Mice. I wondered why I didn't find this information in the pamphlet at the clinic where Heather received her vaccinations.

While gathering information, I ran across a disturbing news article written by *Fresno Bee, California's daily newspaper in 1984,* seven years before Heather's reaction. The article mentioned that Michigan had made too much DPT in its Lansing laboratory and wanted to sell it to other states. In order to do so, the FDA would have to do some testing on the vaccine before the vaccine would be approved. After such testing, the FDA denied approval and returned the vaccine, saying it was 300% too potent. However, Michigan State Health officials disagreed and decided to test the vaccine on children in Ingham County (Lansing). Health officials released 400,000 doses of the DPT vaccine for use throughout the state one month later.

It was reported by the *Detroit News*, three children were left with permanent brain damage, after receiving the vaccine. The parents of the children decided to file suit against the Michigan Department of Public Health. The State of Michigan, asked that the parent's suits be dismissed, protesting that the doctrine of sovereign immunity protects the state government from claims arising from services that only government can provide. After which, the Michigan Supreme Court decided that the parents of children injured or killed by vaccines produced by the state couldn't sue the state.

"Who can parents and vaccine injured adults hold accountable for injuries caused by vaccines? The system is designed that no one neither a person or entity, can be tagged with accountability. Not the vaccine manufacturer, not the doctor who recommended the vaccines, not the person who administered them. Not the members of the Advisory Committee of Immunization Practices who added the vaccine to the pediatric schedule. Not the members of the Institute of Medicine,who perpetrate the mantra "vaccines are safe and effective" and stonewall opportunities for change and improvement. No one is to blame, that is except the "defective child" who could not tolerate the immunological onslaught caused by the vaccine," stated by Sherri Tenpenny, DO. (One of the most outspoken physicians in the country on the hazards of vaccines and vaccination.)

After so much controversy over the side effects of the DPT vaccine, along with the fear arising among parents, the DPT vaccine was eventually eliminated in the United States. Replacing the DPT vaccine is DtaP. However, the whole cell DPT is still being administered to children in third world countries.

Part Two

"Anyone who has ever struggled
with poverty knows how extremely
expensive it is to be poor."
James A. Baldwin

CHAPTER TWENTY-ONE

"Mom, we lost them!" Mikey shouted. "What are we going to do?"

"Hello!" I stated back. "No need to shout, you're sitting right next to me."

"Sorry," he replied. "But we lost them, Mom. Do you know where to go?"

"Not exactly. This circular drive is crazy. On top of that, we are in the wrong lane. I have to move over to another other lane before I can even think about catching up with them."

"Just move over then."

"See how many cars are driving along side of us? I have to keep circling until there is an open spot for us to move over."

"We've been going around in circles for a long time already. Do you think they'll wait for us?"

"They're not going to leave us behind," I replied back. "Hey you kids, tell me when you see an open spot in traffic on your right, so I can move over."

It was late June of 1993 and we were on vacation. Each year, my mom, would drive to Pennsylvania to visit her relatives. The brave woman, that my mother is, invited five of the grandchildren along. My sister's two children, Randi age fourteen and Professor Gus age thirteen. My brother's oldest daughter Jaimee who was eleven and my two. Mikey, who was now ten, along with Heather, age four.

At first glance, one would never have believed that Heather went through an ordeal which she had. However, since Heather used her wheelchair as a means of getting around outside of our home, people did noticed she had some type of disability. Whenever we were out and about in public, we would encounter a lot of stares from onlookers. The stares directed at Heather, were noticeably out of pity. At times, it felt as though these people had never seen a child in a wheelchair before. Not only was Heather exposed to those types of stares from onlookers, there were others who were clearly uncomfortable with being in the presence of a handicapped child. I often wondered, what exactly made others seemingly uncomfortable around those in wheelchairs and others whom have some type of noticeable disability.

Children were the most curious around Heather. Often we would be asked by children as to why she was in a wheelchair. The parents would quickly apologize for their child's questioning, but I would assure the parents that it was alright. I would just explain to the children that Heather became sick when she was younger and now she had to use the wheelchair.

Heather was once again happy and seemingly healthy. She continued to tire easily, which brought on fevers from time to time, but otherwise, her health posed no real concern for us. Heather was regaining a lot of muscle tone since her discharge from Mary Free Bed. It was absolutely amazing watching her regain her independence.

I decided to go along with the gang to Pennsylvania this trip. Getting away from home and work was exactly what I felt was needed. The emotional ups and downs I had experienced with Heather's ordeal had really taken its toll on me, both emotionally and physically. With seven of us going to Pennsylvania, I thought it would be best if I drove our Caravan. There would be plenty of room for all of us, our baggage, and Heather's wheelchair. Without schedules to keep or concerns about traveling with Heather, we left for Pennsylvania.

The trip's itinerary included driving into Canada, staying the night at Niagara Falls, driving through New York and down into Pennsylvania. We left my house before the sun rose and arrived in Niagara Falls later that evening. Before leaving Canada, we took the boat tour that took us close to the Falls. Once in New York, we made a stop at the Gorge in Watkins Glen State Park; located in Western New York.

To make it to the top of the Gorge without driving, one has to walk up 1.5 miles of stone stairs and cross a few bridges. There are a variety of 19 waterfalls in the Gorge, ranging from 3-60 feet high making the stairway quite slippery in spots. I carried Heather as we made our way to the top. Once there, Mom and I decided to take the road back down. The two of us had our fill of stairs. The kids, whose energy never ran low, chose to take the stairs back down and met Mom and I at the bottom of the gorge.

From there we headed for Corning, New York to visit the Museum of Glass. Mom thought the kids would be interested in how Corning Ware was made along with watching the process of blowing glass into vases and different styles of glassware. What the kids were most interested in was getting out of there. With the ovens set at 2300 degrees, it was so extremely hot in the viewing room. It didn't matter if there was a shield of glass dividing the work area and viewing section; the heat from the ovens was still unbelievable hot.

We reached my Aunt Betty and Uncle Dude's home in York, Pennsylvania, near nightfall. No matter how tired the kids appeared to be, the first question asked by them after unloading the van was "Can we go swimming in the pool?" No one in our family back home had a pool, so this was quite the luxury for the kids. The pool ended up being the source of entertainment for the kids on the days we were not traveling.

Mother Seton Shrine was another destination of ours, which is located in Emmitsburg, Maryland. In the garden at Mother Seton Shrine, there is a pool where one can fill containers with Holy water to take home with them. This was one of the main reasons Mom wanted to go there. She wanted to bring home some water for Heather. There is a belief that Holy water can bring about unexplained miracles. Although there are no documented miracles, many people have reported having an increased sense of well being after drinking the water in faith. We filled a couple of gallons to take home for Heather to drink.

For the grand finale, the pinnacle above all our destinations, was the day we toured Washington, DC. It was decided that the kids and I would follow my cousin Penny in our van, as she led the way to the city. Mom, Aunt Betty and Penny's daughter, Tiffany, rode in the car with Penny. We visited the National Aquarium, Washington Monument, Lincoln Memorial, and was headed for Arlington Cemetery when we lost my cousin in the circular drive from Hell. I lost count of how many times we had to circle before being able to exit and continue on our way.

CHAPTER TWENTY-TWO

*H*OW DOES THAT OLD SAYING go? "One needs a vacation after a vacation in order to recuperate?" The whole idea behind going out to Pennsylvania was to recuperate, but I arrived back home feeling as exhausted as when I left. Something else was taking place when I arrived back home as well.

There was no denying that my marriage to Alex had been struggling for some time, but that was understandable with all that we had been through with Heather. During Heather's illness, the focus on our marriage was shifted to Heather. For me, there really wasn't a lot of available time for meeting the needs of everyone in our home. I guess, I took it for granted that Alex understood and accepted that my priorities had to be with Heather, along with Mikey.

I guess I should have never taken that assumption for granted, because in a matter of time, he began to show signs of discontentment. How incredibly unfair it seemed to expect one person to meet everyone's needs, when he/she can't even meet their own needs. That was the position I felt I was placed in, and honestly, I felt a bit resentful.

Alex and I was getting to the point where communication and tolerance toward one another was strained and all that was needed to be said was "*our relationship is over.*" However, like many couples, we didn't say those words until resentment and anger over rode any feelings of mutual respect. Six months after returning home from Pennsylvania, Alex moved out.

Heather didn't appear to experience any set backs when Alex moved out. At the time of our separation, she was still very young and accustomed to not spending a great deal with her dad. T As for Mikey, he was now free from Alex's overbearing presence. It wasn't as if Alex and Mikey never formed a likable bond, but Alex had a different take on how Mikey should be raised. This created the majority of conflicts between the two of them. In spite of everything I was feeling, there was a positive side to Alex leaving. No longer did I have to feel like the mediator between Alex and Mikey. A role which certainly led to numerous confrontations between Alex and myself.

It would only take a few months after Alex had left, to recognize the direction the kids and I were headed toward; poverty. My income was not going to sustain us. Working a second job was out of the equation. I didn't want my children growing up in a household with me away so often. Until our divorce, Alex agreed to pay the mortgage on the trailer, instead of going to court and paying child support. I was relieved to know that at least the kids and I had a place to live. However, even with the mortgage being taken care of, I was still falling behind on the other bills. This is when I applied for and received Supplemental Security Income (SSI) for Heather.

Anyone who has ever applied for SSI knows the amount of frustration involved. So much paperwork was required; providing medical records confirming Heather's disability, as well as my proof of income. Then there was the waiting in line to see a case worker, in a facility which was clearly under staffed. My wait ended up being over two hours before I even talked with a case worker.

Being that my work schedule was unpredictable from week to week, the amount of money we received monthly from SSI varied. Even with the extra income I still remained struggling to make ends meet. I didn't qualify for any other state help such as food stamps or heating credit. According to State Regulations, I made too much money to qualify. Too much money? My argument with that State Regulation, is the basis on which one qualifies. One's income is calculated by gross earnings and not take home pay. Why is this?

Alex moved ahead with filling for divorce and arranged a court date with the Friend of the Court concerning child support and visitation regarding Heather. There was never any disputes between Alex and I pertaining to visitation. Whenever Heather wanted to see her dad, I made sure he was aware of it and he would make every effort to see her.

HEATHER'S WORDS

At the age of five years old, I don't remember dad moving out or the divorce, but I do remember going to dads every other weekend. He was living in a apartment in Lakeview. Mom told me if I wanted to go see him anytime, I could. She wasn't going to stop me from being with him. While I was over at Dads, we played broad games and he taught me how to play Sonic the Hedgehog on the Sega. His friend Rex lived in the same building, so he would come over to hang out with us often.

Early spring of 1994, I was invited out by a fellow co-worker, Mike, which I eagerly accepted. Throughout the ordeal with Heather and the aftermath of Alex and I separating, Mike had always took the time to ask how I was. Over the years of working together, we had talked often and a mutual friendship had already developed as a result. Mike's character was completely opposite from Alex. His was more of a laid back approach to life and wasn't the least bit judgmental. Mike also was a single parent of three children, making it easier for him to relate to my situation on a personal level. After our first date, we began to go out more often which naturally evolved into a serious relationship.

Within a few months of seeing one another, there was talk between Mike and I of moving in together at some point in time. Discussing the possibility of moving in together turned into planning for the move when I found out I was pregnant a short time later. Instead of jumping right into moving in together, we decided that it would be best to wait until school let out for summer break the following year. I didn't want to up and move while the school year was still in session and have Mikey try to adjust to a new school. On top of that, Heather was finishing up her final year at Little People Land.

Mikey wasn't pleased when I told him the news of being pregnant. At age 11, he responded with "That is all we need is another mouth to feed." After Alex had left, Mikey became more of a father figure to Heather than playing the role of big brother. He also did what he could to help me through my own periods of depression and frustration. What saddened me the most was, as with many children who are growing up in a broken home, Mikey seemed to be growing up before really had a chance to experienced a childhood.

Heather on the other hand, was excited about the baby. She wanted a baby sister. Mike's children took the news quite well. The only person who seemed to have an issue with the news was Alex. His concern was how I would manage taking care of Heather with a baby on the way. A concern he had every right to voice. However, what followed afterward, completely left me dumb-founded; as it did everyone in my family.

I received a letter from the Friend of the Court informing me that Alex had petitioned the court to stop paying child support. Addition to that, he was asking that I repay back past support money I had received while I was receiving SSI payments. There was no mention of seeking custody of Heather or increasing visitation privileges. For whatever reason, Alex felt that he shouldn't be paying child support since I had another source of income. What was so disheartening about this was, he knew we needed the extra income to keep afloat financially.

Before the court date, I elected to stop SSI payments. The whole process of monthly calculating my income and waiting for payments was becoming more of a burden than anything else. Receiving child support was something I could rely on without the worry of being lowered from one month to another.

I sought out no legal representation on the day Alex and I went to court. Therefore, I sat in the front of the judge alone at my table. Alex, on the other hand, obtained the representation of one of the most recognized attorney in the county. After reviewing the petition and questioning both Alex and me, the judge announced his decision. His reaction to Alex's petition was quite harsh. He commented on Alex's lack of consideration for Heather's well being and stated that receiving SSI had no impact on paying child support. Alex's request was denied.

Before leaving the courtroom, Alex's attorney approached me and asked what all was needed for Alex to apply for SSI, since I no longer was receiving any payments. The nerve of him even inquiring offended me. I informed him that unless Alex had custody of Heather, he was unable to collect any benefits. Plus, his income exceeded the amount the state allowed one to earn while receiving payments.

I walked out of the court house knowing life was going to become even more challenging, but you know what? I didn't care right then. I had no clue as to how the kids and I were going to survive without the extra income, but when I focused on what we did have; a house to live in, food to eat and each other, I knew we were doing just fine.

Chapter Twenty-Three

A S FOR 1995, THE YEAR was filled with closing doors on much of the past, as doors were opening to what I had hoped would be a positive step forward in life. Major events were about to take place. The first being Heather's Graduation from Little People Land. It was more than a celebration completing preschool, it was a celebration of Heather persevering against unthinkable odds. Then, on May 24th, less than a week after Heather's graduation, I gave birth to Katherine Eulonda Johnson. Weighing in at 6lb, 8oz., Katie arrived into our life with one healthy set of lungs. An indication of we could expect throughout her childhood; easily frustrated with unpredictable outbursts.

Heather's Words

When Mom was pregnant, I hoped the baby would be a girl so we could play together. Mikey and I still had a great bond, but I wanted to play with my kitchen play set and Barbie Dolls instead of action figures. After Katie was born, I held on to her and asked Mom if she could put Katie into the child swing so I could push her. I knew the swing was automatic, but I still wanted to push her. I usually sat in the front of the swing while pushing her. Sometimes I stood in the back of the swing leaning against the wall for support. Mom told me not to push to high or hard, so I gently pushed her.

Over the next two months, I gradually packed our belongings for the move to Mike's, while Mike remodeled portions of his home before we moved in. It is so true how one never really knows how much stuff he/she has accumulated until one moves. I ran across items that I had long forgotten I had. I think sorting what I wanted to take and what I didn't need, took longer than the actual packing.

We moved in with Mike and his children, Matt, age 12, Cori, age 10 and Bryant, age 8, in late July. With the eight of us living in Mike's home, it did become quite hectic at times. Outside of a few confrontations between the children, we all seemed to adjust to one another rather quickly.

HEATHER'S WORDS

I remember moving in with Mike, Katie's dad. Here I am only six and have three dads in my life. My dad, Mikey's dad, which I called "Daddy Al" and now Katie's dad. The town of Sidney was small with a bar, party store, along with a bank and post office. Mike lived on a busy road where cars were passing by the house all the time. In the summer and into the fall, the sound of the loud motorcycles would awaken me when the riders would start them up after leaving the bar. Mike had a Great Dane named Bo. I never seen such a tall dog as Bo. He was so lovable.

Mike's house seemed so big compared to our trailer. His house was three stories high counting the basement. At our trailer, I only had to climb stairs whenever I went in or outside. At Mike's house, there were outside stairs, stairs that led to the bedrooms and the only bathroom, plus stairs that went down into the basement to the boys room.

I called Mike, Big Mike when we first moved in. Then after a while he was just Daddy Mike. I never asked my dad if this bother him and he never mentioned anything to me about it doing so. My dad began dating shortly after moving out of the trailer. Denise Cole, the woman Dad was dating, worked with him at Steel Parts Automotive. On one of my weekend I spent with him, he took me to meet Denise . He told me that the two of them were living together. Even though Mom and Daddy Mike were already living together. I remember being up set when Dad told me about him and Denise. I still wanted Mom and Dad to get back together again, but they never did. My weekends with Dad began on Saturday mornings, because he worked second shift. I would miss Mom while with Dad and vice versa when I was with Mom.

Katie, Cori and me shared a bedroom together. We slept on bunk beds. I always wanted to sleep on the top bunk when Cori was away at her mom's house. All three of Daddy Mike's kids stayed the week at their mom's when school began. I did however, get to be on the top bunk a couple of times. Daddy Mike would lift me up there because I couldn't climb the ladder. If I had to use the bathroom during the night, I would call out to Mom. She would come and get me down. After using the bathroom, she put me in with Katie once again on the bottom bunk. I felt like I was on the top of the world sleeping on the top bunk.

All of us , Daddy Mike, his kids, and us were getting along so good when we moved in. Well most of the time anyways. Bryant became easily annoyed at Katie when she threw her fits, which was often. Then there were a few fights between Mikey and Cori that I remember. Today Bryant and Katie are best friends.

With having only one bathroom in the house, Katie and I took our bath together after supper. That way, I knew we would have hot water. It was also a good idea to wash at night because it took me longer than others to get undressed and into the tub. Mom would always help me and Katie into the tub. Katie had to always be in the front of the tub by the faucets. She would throw her fit if she was placed behind me. But, then again Katie was at that stage where she had to have her way with everything. Look out if she didn't get her way. I could only con her into sitting in the back a few times.

Even playing with the doll house when she was a little older, Katie would only allow me to play with the baby and she would be the parents. I guess she liked to be in control. We played for hours with the doll house; me being the baby, while Katie taking control of how we play. One of the biggest challenges for me while at Daddy Mike's was climbing the stairs. Sometimes the other kids would help me up and down the stairs. Most of the times I crawled up and down by myself. It would take long time for me to do this when my legs grew tired. There were a few times where I would slip and tumble down but, didn't get hurt, just my pride. I would have to crawl like Katie did up and down the stairs. The basement stairs were quite steep and someone would have to go behind me as I made my way down. I spent a lot of time with Mikey downstairs during the summer while Katie napped.

Eventually, Katie began to walk and I couldn't figure out why I didn't walk like the rest of the family or anyone. Walking looked easy for Katie as I watched her. She could stand and didn't fall until after her fifth step. I, on the other hand, struggled to stand and fell after the third step. I still carry the memory of thinking; why on earth couldn't I walk? I looked like the rest of the people who walked. I had two legs and feet. Maybe, if I practiced enough, I will walk one day without my walker. Not until I was older did I understand the reason for not walking. It seemed unfair.

Time went by quickly after the move and before we knew it, the next school year was about to began. I attended an Individual Education Program (IEP) meeting with the teaching and therapy staff, whom would be involved with Heather during her kindergarten year. Heather was going to be attending school in Stanton Elementary School. The school had been recognized as being one of the leading schools in our county, for accommodating special needs children.

It was my intention to place Heather in a main stream classroom environment. I believed she had the capability to function at the level of other children attending kindergarten. With the exception of her physical and speech therapy and spending a hour or so in a resource room, Heather was allowed to attend a regular classroom setting. The children in her classroom accepted Heather without any reservations. Her teacher Mrs. Eggleston was so patient with Heather, as she needed extra time to complete tasks unlike the other students in the classroom. Mrs. Eggleston had a gift for teaching young children and is remembered as being one of those teachers whom had a positive impact on her students.

The resource room was used more as a means for Heather to rest if she grew tired throughout the day and where she would receive individual help if it appeared she was falling behind academically. The only area Heather struggled in was reading. Vocalizing words was difficult for her, but by the end of the school year, her ability to sound out words improved greatly.

However, speaking was still frustrating for Heather. She was asked to repeat herself often because she would speak in such in a soft voice. If she didn't take her time in pronouncing the words or spoke in a soft tone, it was very difficult to understand what she was saying. Overall, Heather continued to amaze us all with her progress. Not only in school, but also at home. More and more she was beginning to dress herself without a lot of assistance. Heather also began taking several steps without the use of the walker. As Mrs. Eggleston had commented before promoting Heather to first grade. "The sky is the limit for Heather."

HEATHER'S WORDS

When I began Kindergarten, I remember the bus picking me up at Grandma Johnson's house whenever Mom worked. Because Grandma was so busy during the day, Katie was taken to a baby sitter until she was older and able to walk. On the days when I didn't have school, Katie and I would help Grandma around the house and garden. Her garden was the biggest garden I had seen, maybe big isn't the word for it. Enormous fits the description better. She was a master gardener at that time. I remember many people stopping by the house to walk through the garden. There were so many different kinds of flowers, statues and branches in the garden. Grandma also was a 4H leader. She gave Katie and I a rabbit to take care of while we were there. In my life time so far, I have never seen an animal go to the bathroom as much as rabbits do. Katie and I also played with the kittens on the farm.

I made one friend in kindergarten, Elizabeth Ritter. Elizabeth and I spent a lot of time together, in school and outside of school. I would go over to her house or she would come to ours. We were inseparable.

April 12, 1996, Dad and Denise married. I wasn't there for the wedding. From then on, I called Denise "Momma Denise." Denise was easy to talk to, more so than my dad. She would stick up for me whenever dad was being to hard on me. I was so happy that she was in my life. I remember it was during this time when Mom and Daddy Mike began fighting with each other.

CHAPTER TWENTY-FOUR

*T*HERE COMES A TIME WHEN some children begin to discriminate against other children who appear different. I knew no matter how hard I worked at trying to install a feeling of being normal within Heather, the day would arrive when she experienced being ridiculed for being handicapped. That day and days following, began shortly after Heather started first grade.

The first time the ridiculing occurred, Heather came home from school crying. It took a while to calm her down in order for her to tell me what happened. Her teacher sent home a brief note explaining what happened, but I needed Heather to open up and tell me what was said and how she interrupted the incident. With Heather telling me in her own words, I could get an idea of how she was processing the ridiculing in her mind.

"They called me stupid, Mom," Heather whispered, as she struggled to speak.

"They said I was a retard in a wheelchair."

"Who said this to you? The kids in your class?"

"Some of them did. The teacher took them in the hall. I think she yelled at them."

"Good for her."

"Am I stupid? They make fun of me because I go to the other room."

"The resource room?"

"Yes. Why do I have to go there? Why do I have to be like this?" She asked, before lowing her head.

I then took her out of her chair and held her as she began to cry uncontrollable, until she became exhausted by the crying. There was so much I wanted to tell Heather as I was holding her, but I knew she wouldn't hear, none the less believe what I said in that moment. Her spirit was broken for the time being.

Up until then, Heather had never encountered any type of ridicule from anyone. My concern was how Heather was going to respond. I was so angry at those thoughtless kids and yet I too was hurting. Heather's hurt became my hurt. We were so attached during her illness, it was as if I could feel her pain at times. This bond between Heather and I remained intact, even as she recovered.

When her crying subsided, Heather fell asleep in my arms. As she slept, I revisited the experience of her illness in my mind, asking myself why? If everything in life happens for a reason, then what's the reasoning for Heather going through what she had only to be mocked by her peers? Hadn't she been through enough hardships? No answers came to me.

I could only hope Heather wouldn't fall victim by the cruel remarks of others, to which her self-esteem would plummet. All along, Heather was treated as if she were a normal child. She wasn't babied or pitied by me or anyone in the family. If she fell, the fall was made light of, after seeing she wasn't hurt. If she struggled at a task, we allowed her to work through it and discover her own way of managing. Heather wasn't discouraged by us in trying whatever she wanted, that wouldn't physically harm her. In essence, Heather was never made to feel incapable of achieving.

When Heather had awaken from her brief nap, she appeared withdrawn. The effort from others in the household to cheer her up were futile. She didn't want to eat and asked if she could just go to bed. I carried her upstairs and into the bathroom where I began to draw a bath for us. I thought bathing with her in a tub full of bubbles, might cheer her up and provide me the opportunity to discuss her feelings. Feelings which she may not know how to express, but I was there to help her. As Heather and I sank into a tub full of bubbles, I waited for her to speak. We sat there for quite some time before she finally spoke.

"Mom?"

"Yes."

"Do you think I am stupid?" She asked, while scooping up bubbles with her hands.

"I know you are not stupid. Do you think you're stupid?"

"I go to the other room, where kids need help. Doesn't that make me stupid?"

"Do you feel stupid because you go there?"

"I didn't, but I must be if I go to that room."

"Is it because of what those kids said to you?"

"They were mean to me. They made fun of me and I cried. Everyone saw. Maybe, I should stay in the other room."

"The resource room?" I asked.

"Yes, the kids in there don't make fun of me or call me names. I don't want to go back to Mrs. Hanna's class."

"Heather, you belong in Mrs. Hanna's classroom. You are just as capable of doing what the other kids are doing. The resource room is where you can rest. You go there because you get tired easily. Know what? There are always going to be kids who will say mean things to you. Always."

"Why?" Heather asked. "I didn't do anything to them."

Good question. What's my answer? I had no answer. Actually, the kids who mocked Heather should be the ones answering, with their parents present.

"I guess some kids don't care if they hurt your feelings. Being different from other kids doesn't mean that you should feel sad about it. Maybe those kids who made fun of you, are mad because you get to leave the classroom and they can't"

"Why can't they go to the other class?"

"Because you go to physical and speech therapy. You miss out on some work the others kids in Mrs. Hanna's class has already done. Resource room gives you the time to do the work, plus you get extra help if you need it. You are always tired after therapy, so we thought if you needed to also rest or maybe nap; you could do that also," I said, hoping Heather understood. "Mikey was in a resource room when he was having trouble doing his work."

"He was? Did kids make fun of him too?"

"Yes, but he didn't listen to them and that is what you have to do. Don't let those kids make you feel bad."

"I can try not to listen," Heather replied, sounding a bit uplifted. "But what if they keeping saying mean things?"

"Mrs. Hanna knows who said those things to you. She will be watching them. Plus, other teachers will be watching too."

"Do you think they will stop making fun of me?"

"Since Mrs. Hanna took them in the hall, those kids might be to scared to say anything to you because they know they will get in trouble."

"I'm hungry now. Can we eat when we get out of the tub?" Heather asked in her usual upbeat tone.

"Of course," I replied. "I think we have soaked long enough. Look at how wrinkled my hands are. What do your hands look like." I asked. "Yup, we definitely soaked long enough."

The following day and days, the ridiculing continued. If not by the same few who first mocked Heather, it was by others. Heather began to cry before getting on the school bus and would cry when she arrived home. Her attitude toward school was changing. She always loved going to school, but now she dreaded going. I went to the school and met with Mrs. Hanna, the principal and the resource teacher. Mrs. Hanna and the resource teacher each voiced their concern of how Heather was becoming withdrawn and how her classroom participation had stopped.

We discussed the possibility of placing Heather in the resource room full time. I hated this idea. She was doing fine in the regular classroom setting before the mocking begun. Placing Heather in the resource room full time seemed more as a means of protecting her from the cruel remarks made by others. I decided against the idea and Heather continued her regular school schedule. Perhaps, Heather should have gone to the resource room full time. It became obvious that Heather was disliking school more and more.

Heather then started talking about wanting to move in with her dad. Moving to her dad's meant going to a different school. Did she think a change of school would stop the mocking from others? Yes, but how do you tell a child, running away from something he/she doesn't like, doesn't mean that it won't happen again. In a child's mind it's possible. Each time she returned home from spending the weekend with her dad and Denise, she would repeat the request of moving in with him. As time passed, I was faced with some very challenging questions, which required me to take a real close look at what is was I believed to be most beneficial for Heather. No matter how much I wanted Heather to grow up with me, was it in her best interest to do so?

While I wrestled with those questions, I also was facing the decision to end the relationship with Mike. In the past year living with Mike, his drinking began to escalate along with staying out late with his friends. As a result, I ended up feeling as though I was only there to take care of everything on my own without any support from Mike. I wasn't happy and the effects from this was trickling down to everyone in the household. This is when I ask Mike to choose between the family or his habits. Deep down, I knew what choice Mike would make and it broke my heart.

Watching Heather become more unhappy with school and seeing how she seemed intent on moving in with Alex. I knew what I needed to do, but how? How could I let go of her without losing a part of me? I knew she would get the best of everything living with her dad and Denise. I also knew she would be well taken care of and loved by them. I knew all this, but yet; I couldn't seem to let go. I knew I would still be in her life, but in a completely different manner. I wouldn't be the one tucked her in every night and see her face each morning. There would be so much I would miss out on while she grew up. I hated being in that position having to decide and then following through with it.

The decision to let Heather live with her dad, was the most difficult decision I think I have ever had to make. The decision was a very personal one, but I lost count after a while, of how many times I was asked by others, how I could just give up Heather. It was as if I committed a crime of some sort. It seemed as if others could not comprehend what was the most important factor; Heather's well being.

The school Heather would be attending was Cedar Crest, in Greenville. When I went to met with her teacher, Mrs. Shaw, I liked her right off. I was impressed at how the school was in the process of preparing to accommodate Heather's special needs. Heather would be the first student attending whom was in a wheelchair. The school also arranged for Heather to continue receiving therapies and have an aid if needed. By the end of my visit, I knew Heather would be well taken care of.

Shortly after Heather moved in with Alex, I found a place to rent. Mikey, Katie and I moved out of Mike's house, and moved back to Lakeview, which meant I was even farther away from Heather. Alex had said that he wasn't going to file for child support because he knew how hard it would be for me to manage being on my own again. Him and Denise were making good money and he saw no need for me to pay anything. I was surprised and thankful for his consideration, but yet there was some doubt of his words. Doubt that would become reality at the most unexpected time. Life just didn't seem to be granting any relief from the challenges I was facing.

CHAPTER TWENTY-FIVE

HEATHER'S WORDS

*M*OVING TO DADS WAS A little hard for me, because I missed seeing the family; especially Mom. Dad and Momma Denise treated me good and I didn't go without anything. I was given pretty much everything I wanted. Dad bought me new clothes and there was so much food in their house. Something I wasn't used to while living with Mom. My room at Dads was perfect for me. I didn't have to share it with anyone. That seemed strange, since I had always had to share a bedroom.

I would spend a lot of time in my room coloring, drawing or reading. It was a place where I could do whatever I wanted without being disturbed. When Dad was home, the two of us would play board games. On the weekend, Dad and I would watch football or NASCAR together. I was ready to start school at Greenville and hoped the kids there would not make fun of me.

---

*"God places the heaviest burden on those
who can carry it's weight."*
Reggie White

I believe somewhere in the midst of burden placement, God must have had misjudged the strength of my shoulders. The place where Mikey, Katie and I called home, after moving out of Mike's house, was undoubtedly the most dismal structure I had ever occupied. In truth, the trailer should have been condemned years ago. But then again, if one's home represents the occupants perspective toward oneself, then I guess the trailer was where I fitted in best. For at that time, I felt as decrepit as that trailer looked. I was emotionally broken from being away from Heather and dealing with the break up with Mike.

I remember being told by a co-worker shortly after the move, to try and make the best of a bad situation. It could be a lot worse. How? How could my situation be worse off than at that present moment? I was living in a run down trailer, no money to speak of and rumor had it at work, the union was considering a strike against the company. A strike meant such a drop in income, but if one is in the union, one is expected to be loyal to the union. No matter the cost it may bring upon the worker.

I hadn't even regained any footing financially after the move, before I received a letter of the Friend of the Court, stating that Alex was seeking child support payments. This was, as the saying goes, "the straw that broke the camel's back." Once again, I appeared in front of the Friend of the Court judge, alone at my table. Alex sat next to his respected lawyer across from me. An amount was agreed upon between Alex and I before going to court. I assumed this was just a formality to have the child support documented and filed with the court.

When the judge asked if the amount listed on the petition was agreed upon by both parties, I readily said yes. Alex's lawyer on the other hand, said his client would like the court to figure the amount of support, Alex was eligible to receive based on my income. Oh, one could only imagine the thoughts going through my mind at that time. I was asked to hand over my wage statements to the judge. After which, the judge then asked if there was anything I wanted to say on my behalf, before he left the courtroom to calculate the amount allowed to Alex.

I commented on how my earnings were not consistent every week and that lay offs from work were frequent. Did he not read the court file in front of him containing the information from our last appearance in court? Apparently not. The judge assured me that what I had told him would be taken into consideration, then he left the room. The courtroom was dead silent while we waited for the judge to return. Keeping my composure while my financial ruin was being decided was unbelievably difficult, to say the least. I was no doubt stunned by Alex's request. From that moment on, his words would never hold any truth. Whatever was spoken by him from that day on, would be completely meaningless to me.

On that day, I witnessed how his need for money over rode any consequence it may cause others. When the judge returned, I was literally shaking in my seat and for good reason. Based on the wage statements I provided, not taking into account monthly bills, Alex was allowed to receive $125.00 weekly. Unbelievable. $500.00 or more each month, out of the $1,000.00 I was bringing home if I worked steady, which was rare.

The judge asked Alex if this was the amount he wanted set for support payments. Alex declined and requested that child support be in the amount agreed upon by the two of us. I was sitting there trying to grasp the reasoning behind Alex's request of having the court calculate child support in the first place. Was it for future reference, if he decided to change his mind? Did it matter? What mattered at that time, was me getting out of that courtroom before I lost it altogether.

Adjusting to the lower income was difficult, but somehow we managed. I remember picking up my paycheck while being laid off and crying so hard, after seeing that the amount of my work check was only $35.00, after child support was taken out. Knowing that I wouldn't be receiving any income for another two weeks, just added more stress. This is when we struggled the most.

I envied those who kept warm during the winter months. Since I was a renter and not the owner of the trailer, I had to pay in full for fuel before it was delivered. This meant running the furnace as little as possible. In a trailer with no insulation, this can't be done without freezing. Many mornings we woke up to the sight of frost reaching halfway up our inside walls. Icicles formed on the upper window frames as well, inside the trailer. On the frigid nights, Mikey, Katie and I (Heather also, when she was there,) would gather in the smallest bedroom with a small space heater as a means of staying warm.

I envied those who couldn't decide what to fix for dinner. I forgotten what it was like to have a choice. Many weeks we ate cereal for dinner, Ramen noddles and scrambled eggs. There were nights when popcorn was our only food choice. Mom and my sister Shirley would occasionally bring over food for us. Katie's dad would at times do the same.

I envied those who couldn't decide what to wear and those who spoke of shopping trips. Outside of school clothes, the kids and I wore hand-me-downs or whatever was affordable at Goodwill. I envied those who spoke of the restaurants they ate at. Only on rare occasions could we eat out. McDonald's was a luxury to us.

HEATHER'S WORDS

I looked forward to my weekends with Mom and couldn't wait to see Mikey and Katie. The trailer they lived in looked like someone had placed it on the land and didn't take care of it. It was old and nasty. The inside walls were thin and the carpet looked like it had been there for years, but it kept us dry when it rain. Unless, you walked near a certain wall in Katie's room. The rain leaked down the wall and soaked the carpet.

Mom would have more food in the house when I came over. Dad had said that I wouldn't be allowed over there if she didn't have food. He was tired of me coming home hungry. Sometimes, Mom couldn't afford extra food. I didn't mind because I was there spending time with them. Playing house with Katie and hanging out with Mikey.

There were times when I wondered why we ate so little at Moms, but at Dads we ate full meals. I also questioned why Mom had to live like she was, while Dad was living in a nicer home. At that time, I thought Dad should have helped Mom. No matter if he was mad at her because I thought he was. I didn't understand why Mom was paying Dad to take care of me when he and Momma Denise could do it by themselves. I thought Dad should of just told Mom "If you have extra money, ask Heather what she needs" and not go to court and take it from her. I had so many questions and thoughts that I kept to myself. Oh well, the past is done and over with. We can't go back and that a good thing because I wouldn't like to see my mom, Mikey and Katie live that way ever again.

It would be so cold in that trailer. I remember gathering in Katie's room with a heater to stay warm. I do remember growing icicles inside the trailer. I thought it was unique. If anyone mentioned to me how cold it was, I would say to them; "Yeah, I bet you don't have icicles growing in your house like Mom does." We still talk about that to this day. When I look back, I don't know how Mom did it with barely no money. But what she did have was a sense of humor that kept us laughing.

On the really hot nights, the trailer was unbearable to sleep in. Mom would tell us to grab our blankets and we would all sleep under the stars, if it didn't rain. Katie would keep us up by her constant jabbering all night, along with jumping on Mikey and me. She was very hyper. When Katie did finally fall to sleep, Mikey and I would then keep waking her up. Of course she would throw a fit.

There were times when Mom had extra money saved and with that money, the four of us would do something special. Mom called it making memories. This was so important to her and the beginning of making family memories that we still create today.

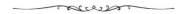

On my weekends with Heather, I would pick her up at either Great Grandma White's home or the sitters', after I got out of work on Fridays. Having the family united again was a joy beyond all joys. There was only one time when Heather said she didn't want to come home with me. I was heart broken and felt so afraid that I didn't matter as much to her anymore, when she had said that.

Because it is easy to jump to conclusions before thinking things through, I automatically assumed I was being replaced by Denise. I thought maybe Heather was ashamed of how we lived and didn't want to stay in such a place as that trailer. Leaving Grandma White's house without Heather that afternoon was devastating. I cried all the way home.

Twenty minutes or so later after I arrived home, a car pulled into the drive. It was Denise bringing Heather over. Denise described how Heather had burst into tears right after I left and wanted to come over. With eyes puffy from crying, I greeted Heather with the biggest hug of all time. So much of my identity as a mother rested on the reassurance from my children that I was someone they wanted to be around. Not because they had to be, but because they wanted to be. This was the reasoning behind my wanting to create family memories. I wanted each of them to have cherished memories from childhood as they grew up. Memories that included more than just being poor and the day to day struggles they experienced.

The kids and I would from time to time drive up near Baldwin, Michigan, and spend the weekend at my patent's cottage. The cottage was walking distance to Wolf Lake. The lake was quite clean and had a nice sandy shore line. The lake was where we spent a lot of time while up there. There where numerous trails to walk on, surrounding the cottage as well. Mikey would often carry Katie and I Heather, since many of the trails were too rough to push Heather's wheelchair on. Sometimes the four of us would make the five mile journey around the lake.

Going to John Ball Park Zoo in Grand Rapids was also a favorite of ours. The most memorable trip Mikey, Heather, and I had taken together was to Chicago. After receiving my vacation check from work, I purchased train tickets for the three of us. Katie was a bit too young and still unpredictable, temperament wise, to accompany us. The three of us boarded the Amtrak train in Grand Rapids, which made daily trips to Chicago. We were to spend the day in Chicago and arrive back in Grand Rapids later that night.

Heather, being the independent child that she was, decided to use the bathroom on the train without any assistance from me. It wasn't long after she had gone into the bathroom that I heard *Mom* being called out. When I checked on her, I noticed Heather had slipped downward and was stuck on the toilet seat. The train hit some rough patch on the track which threw Heather off balance while sitting on the toilet. She looked as if she was folded in half sitting on the seat. We laughed so hard while I lifted her off.

The three of us spent the day in in Chicago and luckily, was able to catch the train home later in the afternoon. Once in Chicago, we brought a watch at a dollar store. That way, we could keep track of the time and get to the train station before the train departed for home. All day we walked around the surrounding area. Shopping, marveling at the architectural designs of the buildings and visited the aquarium. When I noticed that the sun was beginning to descend behind the buildings, I asked Mikey the time, he announced it was noon. We never set the watch after we brought it. I asked a man on the street what time he had. According to his watch, we had twenty minutes to get to the train station and board our train. No way was it possible to reach the station in time by walking, so I hailed a taxi cab.

Back home in Lakeview, there are no taxi cabs. Our village is quite small in size. So, riding in one was exciting for us. What was amusing, when a cab driver did respond to my hysterical arm wailing, he hesitated before asking if we needed to use trunk of the cab. Here we are, loaded down with bags plus Heather's wheelchair. Of course we needed the use of the trunk. I was worried that maybe his trunk didn't open, which would have had explained his hesitation of asking. Now, that would be our luck. I guess he just didn't want to exit the cab to open it. Whatever the reason for his attitude, he did manage to get us to the station in time. Bless his heart.

The outings of ours is what created a sense of prosperity and not poverty. Yes, there were consequences that followed after spending more money then planned, but we always seemed to manage. The first thing we did when I received my tax return money, was go to the grocery store. Grab two shopping carts and fill each one with whatever we desired. We ate good for weeks after.

Any break from the day to day worries and stress of our living conditions, helped me maintain a sense of hope. How easy it would have become to just give up and become trapped in believing that life held no promise of hope. Discovering hope in the most inopportune times was what inspired me to trudge forward in my attempt to overcome the adversity we faced.

HEATHER'S WORDS

The trip to Chicago was amazing, besides getting stuck in the toilet on the train. Mom came in and rescued me. We both laughed when she lifted me off the seat and attempted to wipe off that blue liquid off my butt cheeks. Some children would be embarrassed if their parent was to come in the bathroom when they are in there. I, on the other hand, wasn't.

When we exited the train in Chicago, we couldn't believe how big Chicago was. I thought Grand Rapids, Michigan, was big, but its nothing like Chicago. Cars were honking their horns and there were tons of people walking on the sidewalks. My goal while in Chicago was to buy a pair of Nike shoes, but instead I gave my shoe money to a man who was sleeping in a box in a back alley. I don't know how we managed to get down that alley, but we did. Mom called it skid row. There were others along the alley who were also without homes. Mom said that many were winos, while others may be drug addicts.

At first, the three of just just smiled as we walked past the man I ended up giving some of my money to. After we passed him, I told Mom to turn back around. I really didn't need the money or shoes. When I handed him the money, he had a thankful smile on his face. So many other people walked past him without even bothering to say hello. I bet we made his day. Not only for the money, but noticing him. I kept a little of my money for shopping. Mikey, Mom, and I went into so many stores. Buying little, but looking at everything.

While we walked down this one sidewalk, there was a younger boy selling M&M's to help raise money for summer camp. Mom gave him a twenty and told him we didn't want the candy. Even being poor as we were, we always gave to others. Those people we saw on the street without a home, may have lost their job or just lost their way in life. Yes, the money I gave was most likely spend on wine or other substances, but it didn't matter to me.

Mom always told us kids that people, society has overlooked and those living on the streets give us the opportunity to see what kind of person we are. Was I, the kind of person that walks by another in need without offering help or a smile? Or am I the kind of person who notices and acknowledges them. I always take a second and smile or say hi. I give to those when I can. I know what it is like to be looked at differently and ignored by others. Maybe that is the connection Mom talked about when she used to say: "Everyone in life is connected by Life itself, but people tend to forget that."

CHAPTER TWENTY-SIX

THE SCHOOL STAFF AT CEDAR Crest, did an excellent job at accommodating Heather's needs. It become obvious right off that the move to her dad's, along with her placement in a new school environment was in fact, the right choice. Mrs. Shaw, Heather's first grade teacher was a blessing. Her approach to Heather, as well as her ability to install a sense of acceptance between the children in her classroom and Heather was phenomenal. The children from other classrooms at Cedar Crest would stare at Heather, whenever she was in the hallways, but never was she ridiculed the way she had been at Stanton Elementary.

Heather was assigned an aid as soon as she enrolled at Cedar Crest. Mrs. Marsh would assist Heather throughout the day at school. She helped Heather off the bus in the mornings, escorted Heather to her therapies and assisted her if she needed to use the bathroom. Then take Heather out to the bus after school was out. The two of them became good friends and shortly there after, became Heather's sitter after school while her dad and Denise worked.

It was during her elementary school year where Heather seemed to reach her peak at walking. She still fatigued quickly, but until she did her pace at walking was normally running speed. She would have to be reminded frequently by her aid or other school staff to slow it down. While in the hallways, Heather couldn't keep up with her classmates if she walked at a safe pace. Running was the only way she would not be left behind. Because of the classroom clutter and classmates, maneuvering her way around the classroom would at times become difficult. In the areas where using her walker was impossible, Heather would use the desks to support herself as she walked.

There was one incident where Heather took off running when she should have walked, in which she paid a hefty price for doing so.

The price, a trip to the ER, along with receiving five stitches in her chin. Heather was bound and determined to run through the parking lot of Lakeview High School in order to get inside before she missed her cousin Gus, along with Katie's brother, Matt, wrestling match. As soon as she was out of the car and had her walker situated, she took off without heeding my warning of how the pavement was slippery. Heather tripped and down she went cutting her chin wide open. Needless to say, we missed both matches. The fall didn't deter Heather in the slightest to slow down. She still chose to run whenever she had the chance.

In the third grade, instead of using the wheelchair lift on the school bus, Heather managed to climb the stairs into the bus. Then used her walker to get to her seat. The mobility Heather was gaining during her elementary years at Cedar Crest was impressive. She wanted so much to be like the other children and therefore, put all her effect in doing so.

Heather attended therapies just as she had in Stanton Elementary. In her physical therapy sessions during school, one of her goals was to sit without tipping while doing an activity for fifteen seconds. Fifteen seconds seems like such a brief period of time, but her upper body muscle tone was still incredibly weak. By the time she advanced into middle school, she was able to sit without support or tipping for five minutes. Balancing and stretching her lower extremities were done at each session. Transfers from floor to chair, wheelchair to a regular chair was worked on as well.

Due to the continuous discomfort of Heather's AFO's (leg brace), she wore them less and less. As a result, her medial arch in each foot collapsed. Because of the lack of support to her ankles and feet, her feet took on the appearance of being flat footed. She began to walk on the sides of her inside feet, causing the bone structure to become deformed. As painful as it looked, Heather complained of no pain. No matter the amount of persuasion we brought across to Heather, of how important it was to wear her AFO's; she resisted. Not only were the AFO's designed to support her ankles, they also helped reduce the spasticity in her legs.

Spasticity is a condition in which certain muscles are continuously contracted. The braces helped stretch Heather's Achilles tendon, thus preventing shrinkage or shortening. Which would have made it possible to walk heel to toe instead of just walking on the toes as Heather was after a period of time from not wearing her braces. Heather's spasticity was cause by her viral Encephalopathy. The virus had attacked the portion of the brain that controls voluntary movement of the muscles and tendons in her legs. The spasticity in Heather's legs were an ongoing concern since Heather objected to wearing her braces.

Another consequence of not wearing her braces and not receiving the proper amount of stretching was leg scissoring. Heather's left leg began to turn inward and cross over her right leg while she walked, tripping her up often. This development would result in spending more time in her wheelchair at school because she would fall more frequent than before.

It was suggested that since Heather's spasticity in her legs was becoming more tight, lengthening her tendons in each legs would relieve the tightness and increase her chances of walking without the restrictions she was experiencing. The downside of that suggestion was surgery and intensive physical therapy. Heather wasn't known for putting in a lot of effort when it came to stretching or exercising outside of school therapy. Without the initiative to commit to the amount of therapy required after surgery, Alex declined to have the procedure done. Instead Heather went into Mary Free Bed and received a series of Botox injections in each leg to help relax the spasticity. Heather received the injections only a couple of times, before refusing to endure the painful procedure.

HEATHER'S WORDS

Becky Knorel was my physical therapist at Cedar Crest. She would stretch my legs and had me do balancing exercises. Becky would put my AFO's on and we would go for a walk around the hallways in the school. The AFO's were uncomfortable to wear and gave me open sores. I can't even count the times Dad and I would go to Mary Free Bed to have them adjusted. I couldn't walk very good in them because they would rub against my ankles. I would have liked them if they didn't give me sores on my ankles. Dad would get mad at me because I didn't like to wear them. I did wish that he had to wear them and see how well he could handle the pain. I think he would not have lasted long. I also had night time AFO's. They didn't hurt as much, but annoyed me when I tried to sleep. The strips on the AFO's would get stuck on the other and I couldn't get them pulled apart. I couldn't wait till Dad came home from work when this happened because he would take them off. I did refuse to wear my AFO's. I told myself if I could walk and my feet didn't hurt why wear them.

Getting the Botox in my legs did help. Even though the shots last for only three-four months, Dad and I still went to Mary Free Bed to get them. Ten minutes before leaving the house, my dad would put some numbing cream on my legs that my doctor gave him. He then wrap my legs with plastic wrap so the cream wouldn't rub off. At the hospital, they had ten needles laid out and ready to be injected into my legs. Five shots went into each leg. It wasn't bad if the cream worked. I wished they had knock me out for the five minutes it took them to inject me, so I didn't have to feel the needle pinch.

Dad would become upset at me by my crying when I got the shots. I wished he had to get them. After we were in his truck going home, he asked me if it hurt that much. I would shake my head yes. I thought it was a waste of time and tears getting those shots. Eventually, I stopped getting them and yes, my legs became tight. But, I could walk with my walker, sit, lay, and more. To me, I think my doctor just wanted to see how the shots worked and how my legs would stretch better.

During Heather's years at Cedar Crest, her occupational therapist worked with Heather on cutting with scissors, ripping tape, dressing skills and stocking objects. Heather's penmanship wasn't really a concern, her writing skills was like that of her fellow classmates; messy, but still readable. To assist with fastening and unfastening her jeans, Heather was given a button hook to maneuver the button on her jeans. In time, she managed to learn how to make the hook work. Heather struggled the most with cutting, but would gradually learned the technique as she aged.

To watch the amount of effort it took her to perform simple tasks was perplexing to me. Even though I have watched her over the years as she struggled with simple tasks, I still found myself amazed at how much more effort it took her than I. I wanted so much to do the task for her when the task appeared to become a strain on her. And yes, there were many occasions where I did.

In speech therapy, the therapist concentrated on increasing the volume of Heather's voice. She spoke so softly at times which made understanding her difficult. Heather was also encouraged to talk about her disabilities in a positive manner and to start sticking up for herself. I thought this was a great approach in helping Heather resolve any hurt she may have carried with her from Stanton Elementary. The goal set for speaking louder was reached before she move on to the middle school. Because her word pronunciation is poor at times, she was and still is asked to repeat herself often.

Academically, Heather was an average to above average student at Cedar Crest. Her teachers would comment from time to time that Heather would become easily distracted from her class work, but she would always catch up on the work during her time spent in the resource room. Every teacher Heather had, believed that she had the ability to succeed in school and accomplish whatever she set her mind to. By the way Heather carried herself, one could tell that she also believed she was capable of achieving whatever she wanted to. Before we knew it, Heather was about be making the leap to middle school along with her fellow classmates.

Heather's Words

Pauline Garvin was my occupational therapist at Cedar Crest. She would stretch my arms. Afterward, I did hand exercises like cutting paper or picking up small objects. I was given a special fork and knife to help with eating. She showed me how to use them. Speech, PT and OT was once a week, but on different days. It was nice that the therapies wasn't all in one day. When I went to therapy, I would leave the classroom at the beginning or in the middle of class. I didn't like it because I missed some information given by the teacher.

The kids at school treated me well, but I still was stared at. Some of the kids would ask me why I had to use a walker. I would tell them I got sick as a baby. I didn't know what truly happened at that time, until I was older.

In second grade, my friend from Stanton Elementary; Elizabeth started school at Cedar Crest. Her family moved to Greenville and lived a couple of blocks away from the school. I was so happy to see her. We picked up where we left off from Stanton. I became a part of the family and like always, Elizabeth and I spend all the time together.

Before Elizabeth started school at Cedar Crest, my first friend was a boy named Troy. I thought he was really cute. Yes, I had a crush on him. We played board games and colored together. Then when we were in fifth grade, I asked him to be my boyfriend. He told me no because I was in a wheelchair. My heart felt like it was ripped out of my chest. I went home and called Mom to ask if she still had the video tape of me walking normal. I took the tape to school and the teacher let me play it. I wanted to show Troy that I wasn't born this way. When I look back on this, I laugh because why would anyone date at that age. I just wanted to hang out with him outside of school. Instead, we hung out during school throughout my elementary years.

My last year at Cedar Crest, I got my first power wheelchair. Becky and my dad thought it was a good idea because the middle school I would be going into was so much bigger than Cedar Crest. I thought the wheelchair was awesome. The only thing I had to do was move a level to make the chair go.

The person I was closest to at school was Mrs. Marsh. If I needed help or anything, she would be there for me. She became my babysitter outside of school. Her son Donald and I would hang out when I was at their house, playing games or watching movies. Mrs. Marsh and I would make pancakes, brownies or cupcakes. The kitchen would be a mess afterward, but she didn't mind. Just like Grandma Johnson, Mrs. Marsh had bunny rabbits. She let me pick one out and I picked a black and white one, named it spot. We lost touch after I began middle school. I did see her from time to time and we both would talk, to catch up on each other life.

Being the only child at Dad's and Momma Denise's, changed when my brother Kaleb was born in 1998. He was a cute little man. It wasn't long after he was born that we moved into a bigger house outside of Greenville. We all stayed at great Grandma White's house for a couple of weeks before we were able to move into the new home. I was happy because I didn't want to leave her side. I would sleep on the floor in her room at night. She had a steep driveway that was paved just off the highway. The bus would drop me off on the top of the drive. Instead of having to walk to the house, I would just sit on my walker and roll down the drive, since my walker had wheels on it. I wasn't scared about getting hurt or yelled at by anyone. No one dared to yell at me when Great Grandma White was near. I was her favorite.

Before Kaleb's birth, I was definitely a "daddy's little girl." I loved spending time with him and had to be constantly by his side. He taught me how to ride a bike. He tied my feet to the paddles so they wouldn't slip off and pushed me until I was able to steady the bike while paddling. He walked beside me as we went down the sidewalk and headed for Dairy Queen, which was a couple of blocks away. On our way back home, I would become tired and he have to push me back.

In our new home, I was allowed to pick the bedroom I wanted. I chose a bedroom that was downstairs. To get upstairs, I had to climb two set of stairs, since the house was three stories high. The downstairs had a living room, bathroom and another bedroom. I thought it was amazing that I had it all to myself. When dad came home from work, he would always come down to my room and check on me. On the weekends, I make him read my favorite bedtime stories; *"Just a Nap"* by Mercer Mayer and *"Tiger Bedtime"* by Stephanie Calmenson.

Before we moved to the new house, Grandma Cole's (Momma Denise's mom) cat had kittens. Dad let me pick one out to bring home. I chose a calico kitten and named her Sasha Kitty. When she was a couple of month older, she got out of the house without no one noticing. When I returned home from school, I called out for her, but she didn't come. Momma Denise and I looked everywhere. I started to cry and Momma Denise called Dad at work to ask if he saw Sasha before he went to work. Hearing how upset I was, he came home and help to look for her. Dad found Sasha hiding in some bushes in town, a few miles from where we lived. When he brought her back home, she had a broken jaw. No one could think of how she managed to get in town. Dad said he did see something skid on the road behind him near where Sasha was found, on his way to work. Sasha somehow jumped up under Dad's truck and rode under there before she fell off. Her jaw healed, but now she had a tooth that stuck out. Mikey always called her snaggle tooth from then on.

Holidays were special at Dad's house. Momma Denise would decorate the house for every occasion. Something we didn't do at Mom's. I was the one who hung the angel on our Christmas tree each year, until I got bigger and Kaleb did it. Dad would lift me up to hung it. Halloween was always fun at Dad's. Momma Denise, Dad, my Aunt Amy would take Kaleb and I, along with my cousin Tyler, who was Kaleb age, out Trick-or-Treating. Great Grandma White would give out the most candy. Living as close to the main highway, she didn't get a lot of visitors, so we scooped on the candy at her house.

In the summertime, I spent a lot of time at Grandma Cole's house, along with my cousin Morgan. Being so close to age, her and I hung out a lot. Grandpa and Grandma Cole had a swimming pool and Morgan and I would be in the pool for hours at a time. Didn't matter if it was cold outside or raining. I didn't learn how to swim so I had to wear Arm Band Swimmies. I hated them because my underarms would be raw from the bands rubbing against them. At least I could swim freely.

Morgan was such a tomboy. She wasn't afraid to get dirty or hurt. I watch as she climbed the trees at Grandma's and wished that I could do the same. One day while jumping on the trampoline, she manage to break her leg. Morgan had to use a wheelchair when Dad and Momma Denise took us to the fair. I thought was extraordinary because now I wasn't the only one in a wheelchair. People still stared at me because I show no signs of injury, unlike Morgan. On our camping trips with the family, Morgan and I had two play tents. The play tents didn't had a bottom to them. We would play in the tents and laughed. We were best friends and always up to something.

One day, Morgan went with Grandpa Cole and her dad to shoot their bow and arrow. After they were done, Morgan helped them pick up their arrows. She tripped and injured her eye. The end of one arrow with the feather part went into her tear duct. She is now blinded in her right eye.

CHAPTER TWENTY-SEVEN

Even though Mike and I had lived apart for three years, we continued to see one another as if we were a couple. There was a chemistry between us which didn't dissolve even through the most challenging times. I had always felt such an appreciation for knowing him and being included in his life. Within his eyes, the admiration he felt toward me shone as well. Several months after I had moved back to Lakeview, Mike came to me one morning while at work, smelling of alcohol and talking of suicidal thoughts. This is when I stepped in and arranged for his admittance into rehab.

He successfully completed his program and walked out of rehab with a fresh perspective on life, our future together and himself. He stayed with Mikey, Katie and I a few weeks at the trailer and began attending AA (Alcoholics Anonymous) meetings while I sat in the Al-Anon meetings.

After attending several AA meetings, Mike felt he needed to move back into his own home in Sidney. Not only to reconnect with his children, but also to begin living in his environment, where his temptation to drink and fall back into his old habits could be confronted. He felt confident that all would be fine. I felt leery of him actually being willing to say no to his friends when it came to partying.

Shortly after Mike returned home, the union of the company we worked for held a meeting to propose a strike. Votes were cast and the next thing I know, I was picketing against the company who had employed me for the past ten years. Personally, I didn't vote to strike. However, I did believe Northland Corporation owed it to their retired employees and those soon to retire the benefits promised by the company.

Some of the employees continued to work despite the hostility they encountered from the picketers. To show support to our cause, a few top union leaders came to our location and gave us the pep talk on how we were family and that our striking would create a change for the better. Better change for whom? Those men giving the pep talk wasn't living on $150.00 a week and receiving food from a food bank. They weren't out of a job and struggling to make ends meet like the majority of us carrying the picket signs.

I picketed and protested the company over a month before seeking other employment. It was impossible for me to provide for my family on the amount of money I received. Thankfully, my landlord allowed me to work off rent by mowing their lawn and doing other odd jobs, such as house cleaning. Eventually, I went to a temp service in order to seek work. Within a few days, I received a call from the agency and was informed about an opening for temporary help at Parker Hannifin, a local manufacturing plant in Lakeview. The only downside of accepting the job was having to work third shift. This meant Mikey and Katie would be alone during the night. Mikey was fifteen and capable of looking after Katie. We also had neighbors across the lawn and the landlords lived on the property as well. So if there was an emergency, the help was nearby.

Parker Hannifin had a reputation for being a respectable place to work. I was fortunate to start when I did, because the company was expanding their assemble department and word had it that some hiring was going to take place. I worked as a temp at Parker for four months before I was hired and still remain employed by the company today.

Life took off in a new direction from there. I slowly began to dig myself out of debt, Mike and I were heading in the direction of marriage and Heather was continuing to make incredible strides in her life. Everything in life was becoming positive.

After three years of living apart, Mike vowed that he was ready to commit to me and our family. In early June, of 2000, and in the presence of our children, Mike and I exchanged wedding vows. With Matt, Mike's son, and Heather, as being our chosen witnesses.

We were married in the surroundings of nature. When the flowers were in full bloom and baby birds were taking flight. Just as nature was in the process of renewing itself after enduring the hardship of the past winter. I believed the ceremony between Mike and I symbolized our own renewal as a couple, after enduring the hardships we experienced together over the past three years.

Katie and I once again moved into Mike's home in Sidney. Katie was now five years old. Mikey, at age seventeen, chose to move in with his dad and grandparents in order to finish out his senior year with his friends at Lakeview High School. Heather would be turning eleven that upcoming September and would be entering the middle school. The once crowded home of eight at Mike's, was down to three; Mike, Katie and myself. As for Mike's children, Matt had recently graduated from high school and was living with friends. Cori, whom was sixteen and Bryant now thirteen, stayed mostly with their mom.

Superstitions. It's fascinating what we, as individuals, choose to believe as being signs to upcoming disasters or direct causes of unwanted events that happen in our life. Very often it is said, "I should have had paid attention to the signs so this or that would not have happened." I'm not a very superstitious person, but I found it utterly amazing how the wedding ring, I personally designed, in a way, foretold the direction in which our marriage was headed even before I took notice. The ring was a sliver band with a diamond separating Mike's and my birth stones. "Two become one," was the meaning behind the setting.

Several months after the wedding, I noticed Mike's birth stone had fallen out of its setting on the ring. I thought this was interesting because Mike, at that time, began showing signs of growing restless and had begun to spend more and more time hanging out with his childhood friend.

I took the ring back to the jeweler and had the stone replaced. Six months or so after the birth stone was replaced, the diamond fell out without my knowing until the ring snagged my shirt. I didn't know where or when it fell out. At first, I was frantic in my search for the missing diamond, but soon my panic turned into anger at how cheaply the ring had to have been made. With an expensive ring as mine was, how could the stones be falling out of their settings?

About this time, Mike was beginning to drink more, staying out later than usual and then would fall into a depressive state for doing so. Our relationship was taking a turn for the worst. After giving up on finding the missing diamond, I found it! The diamond lay hidden in a crevice of the stairway, leading to our bedroom upstairs. Once again, I took the ring back to the jeweler. This time, the ring was entirely remade and was I informed that each stone had been securely set. None of the stones would fall out: *GUARANTEED*. Well, nothing in life is guaranteed. The day after confronting Mike, about him getting back into his old habits, his birth stone fell out of its setting. Coincidence? Not in my perspective. After three years of marriage, I ended our marriage and Katie and me moved out of the house.

To pin the failure of our marriage solely on Mike would be completely unfair. Right from the start, I had known there was that possibility of Mike returning back to his old habits. Instead of weighing the consequences, I followed my heart. I entered into a marriage, under the impression that somehow I could prevent Mike's relapse. In a way, by trying to prevent his relapse, I may have helped initiate it, by expecting him to be the type of man I believed he could be, instead of accepting him for who he really was and not go through with the wedding. This was a very hard lesson for me to learn, as it is for many others who find themselves in a similar relationship.

I found an apartment to rent back in Lakeview. Moving back to Lakeview meant seeing more of Mikey. He lived only a few blocks away from the apartment Katie and I moved into, so he was always popping in to visit. The apartment was nothing like that trailer we lived in before Mike and I were married. To us, the apartment was like living in luxury. There was such a positive energy filling the living space, unlike the dismal feeling experienced in that old trailer.

CHAPTER TWENTY-EIGHT

HEATHER'S WORDS

*W*HEN MOM TOLD ME THAT her and Katie were moving out of Daddy Mike's, I was very saddened. I knew I was always welcomed at his house and went several times with Katie when she visited him. Daddy Mike told me that if I ever needed anything to let him know. Whatever happened between him and Mom, it had no impact on how he felt about me. I was always going to be apart of his family and his life. After Mom moved out, Mikey and I would sometimes spend the weekend at Mike's, when Katie went there.

It seemed like old times with Daddy Mike. While playing games with all of us, he would be telling his famous non funny jokes, with him being the only one laughing. The house was always full of kids and Daddy Mike's friends. We would have bonfires and sit around the fire until late into the night. Usually on those weekends, Mikey would go get one of the neighbors; Trinity Evans. Trinity and Mikey became friends when Mom lived with Daddy Mike before they were married.

Mikey had been grounded for some reason and his punishment was to spend some time outside. He rarely went outside otherwise. While sitting on the front stairs, Trinity happened to walk by and stopped to talk to Mikey. From there, they became buddies and Trinity became an adopted brother of mine.

It was with Trinity's help that I learned how to use my crutches. It was Mom's idea to get the crutches and use them instead of my walker. The crutches were not the type for a broken leg that a doctor would give you. There were different. They were specially designed for children who had Cerebral Palsy, with metal arm bands and handles to grasp while walking. I didn't like them because I fell so often with them. Plus my upper arms would bruise from the metal bands pinching into my skin.

Trinity, Mikey, and Bryant worked with me as I learned to climb the front stairs of the house. Bryant said that the crutches were better than my walker because I would have more freedom do move around. Unlike with my walker, I couldn't stand back up as good as I did with my walker. I had to ask for help or else grab onto something to pull myself up. Using them in the winter was dangerous. I slipped on the ice and fell a lot, leaving me with wet pants. Not fun, but I used those crutches for several years to walk short distances. My legs would give out after a short time, when the scissoring of my legs was becoming more of a hindrance.

Daddy Mike would also bring his kids over to the trailer sometimes,on the weekends I spent with Mom. Together, we all played as if we had been living together all along. There was a big slide in the landlords yard and they allowed us kids to play on it whenever we wanted. Mikey helped me to the the top of the slide while Matty stayed at the bottom in order to catch me. I flew right off the end and hit my face on the ground, cutting my lip and inner mouth. I had to go to the emergency room because the cut looked so bad that Mom was afraid it was really serious. No stitches, but the cut inside my mouth was very deep. I remember being so mad at Matty that I didn't talk to him the rest of the day.

Matty, Cori and Bryant were so much fun to be around. I never considered them being step brothers or sister. Mom always said there was no such thing as *step*. They are family and that is how I believe it to be. The three of them included me in so many things and my disability was never an issue to them. I love them so much for that.

As for living with dad, the family and I settled into the new house that him and Momma Denise bought after Kaleb was born. After the boxes and furniture had been moved into the new house, I went down into my bedroom and unpacked my belongings. So many things I didn't want but kept them anyway; not even knowing why. Back then, the American Girl doll collection was very popular. I had one. Even had a wheelchair for her as well. Grandma Johnson made me tons of clothes for the doll and Aunt Loni made some pieces of furniture to go along with my doll. Katie soon bought her own American Girl doll and the two of us would play for hours with them. I laid out the furniture and doll accessories in one corner of my room. The other corner of my bedroom became home to all my stuffed animals.

Arranging my room was so time consuming. I had to try and work around my cat Sasha while putting things away. She found it quite satisfying laying in the middle of my room, in the path of everywhere I needed to go. I had a lot of clothes to put away and hang in my closet. When I opened my closet doors, I was shocked to see how much room there was. I didn't want that closet and felt ashamed for having one as big as it was. Mom and Katie were using totes for their clothes. If I could, I would have torn out the closet and brought it over to their apartment.

My day to day schedule while living at dads was pretty routine because it took me a long time to get ready for school. I would get out of bed at 5:00 A.M. The bus wold pick me up at 7:00 am and middle school started at 7:30. Getting up that early gave me plenty of time to get around, but made for a long day. By the end of the school week, I would become very tired. Having my own bathroom was great. While I was getting ready for school, Momma Denise would join me because she didn't want to wake up the kids if she used the upstairs bathroom. After getting dressed, I would grab my school bag and crawl up the flight of stairs; out of the door I would go. The door led into our garage where my power wheelchair was kept.

After school, I would park my wheelchair in the same place where plugging it in to the battery charger was easy to do. I would then walk, more like wall surf back into the house. Grab a snack from the kitchen and head to my room. Wall surfing was using whatever was along the wall to grab onto in order to steady my balance.

My power wheelchair would at times die on me in the middle of our driveway, because of the battery going dead. I hated it when my chair did this because I was the one pushing it to the garage. As small and weak as I was, I was amazed how I managed push the wheelchair up the driveway; including struggling up the hill that led to our garage. I didn't understand why the batteries died.

There were two batteries that powered my chair. I found out that later those batteries were memory batteries. Dad told me to make sure the batteries were running low before I recharged them. I followed his instructions, but it didn't matter. At some point, the batteries were charged sooner than needed. Which meant that the batteries only held a short amount of power before going dead. Needless to say, I ended getting new batteries, very expensive batteries. I then took notes and figured out the amount of days my wheelchair would last. It was close to every couple of days. After that, I never had a problem of my wheelchair losing power in the driveway again.

At the new house, Grandma Cole was the one who baby sat my brother Kaleb. He was a grandma's boy. Kaleb would stay over at Grandpa and Grandma Cole's home a lot. I enjoyed those nights because it gave Momma Denise a break and time to herself. I also liked it because the house was so peaceful and still. You could hear a pin drop. Kaleb was around four years old at that time and he was full of energy and quite loud. If Kaleb spent the night with Grandma Cole during the week, I would have the house to myself after school. I could do whatever I wanted to do without getting yelled at. I would go up stairs and turn on dad's stereo and listen to music while doing my chores. I only had two chores; empty the dishwasher and fill the empty water bottles.

The dishwasher wasn't too hard, but I had to be careful not to drop the glasses. Once in a while a cup would slip out of my hand or knock one off the counter to by accident. The water bottles were a pain in my butt because we had a water filter which made the water run so slow; I thought anyway. The days when I am home during the week, I would turn off the filter and fill the bottles with unfiltered tap water. This way, I could fill the bottles faster. To me, the water tasted the same. After my chores were done, I usually grabbed a tons of sneaks to hide in my room and once in a while I would grab a small piece of sandwich meat for Sasha Kitty. Dad would tell me to pick out couple of CD's in his magazine that he ordered from, that was my allowance for doing chores.

At this time, I was around eleven years old and didn't become tired as fast. Going up and down the stairs was easy. As I made my way to my room after chores and gathering snacks, I would drop everything and grab my night clothes and headed toward the bathroom. Get undressed and lower myself into the tub. I loved taking a bath early after school because I didn't have to worry about it later and I had the rest of the afternoon and night to do my homework or whatever. While taking my bath, I would leave the door open for Sasha could come in and lay on the rug next to the tub to watch me. When I was ready to get out, I sprinkled some water droplets on her so she would move. She didn't lay on the rug often, but when she did I took my time and stayed in the tub longer.

I did my homework on the floor in my bedroom because when I sat in the wooden chair at my desk, my left leg would fall asleep. I laid my school books and notebooks out on the floor and my backpack would be getting laid on by Sasha. She loved to lay on it or go inside it while I was doing homework. Sasha was my shadow. No matter where I went while downstairs, she was right beside me. Which was nice because I didn't feel alone. I talked to her about my day, even though she didn't understand and just laid there staring at me.

While on the floor in my room, I would grab my blanket and wrap it around me. No matter what season it was outside, downstairs would always be freezing. Cold enough to turn my toes purple and sometimes black. The circulation in my legs was poor. I wore two pair of socks and a pair of slippers. Sometimes I had to sit on the edge of the tub with my feet soaking in warm water to get the color back.

Later I would found out that I had Raynaud's disease. Raynaud's disease caused the blood vassals in my legs to narrow more than what they do in the average person when a person gets cold. No real particular cause for this disease. To me, it was another thing to add to my list of problems. So why did I pick a bedroom downstairs? To be away and be by myself. I loved to have time to myself because I could think or just get away from everyone.

On April 20, 2000, my baby sister, Madison, came into this beautiful world. When she began to eat solid foods, she would eat here and there so dad gave her the nickname "Nibbles." I never used her real name and don't today, I continue to call her Nibbles.

As with Kaleb, I had to get used to having a shadow again when Nibbles grew older. She wanted everything that was mine which caught her attention. If I was playing with a deck of cards, she wanted them. Not another deck, but the deck I had. It was funny when Nibbles began to get into Kaleb's thing. He would get so upset at her. He must have forgotten that he did the same thing with my things when he was Nibbles age. Nibbles became my shadow and I had to make sure everything had to be place high in my room or else it would fall prey to Nibbles.

One thing I hated about having a younger sibling was the stair gate. Dad and Momma Denise put a stair gate at the top of the stairway leading down to the basement. I couldn't unlock it when I went upstairs because I was crawling up the stairs and not walking. Which meant I couldn't stand up on the stairs, due to the fact that there wasn't a railing to hold onto. I didn't want to lose my balance and fall down the stairs, so I would have to call out and have someone open it for me.

Kaleb, had the nickname "Pee Body." Like so many other young kids, Kaleb used to pee the bed when he was younger. I got so used of calling him that. I still call him "Pee Body" today. I was happy when he began school. This meant he was staying home all the time instead of going to Grandma's. Grandma Cole was still coming to our house in order to take care of Nibbles, so it wasn't like he didn't see her.

On one weekend when I had a friend over, I thought it would be funny to scare Kaleb. Dad had a skull mask and I knew where it was at. I asked Kaleb if he wanted to play hide-in-seek. He wanted to play, he would had to count first and try to find my friend and I. I put the mask on and hide in our storage closet. When he opened the door, he let out the loudest scream and cried to Momma Denise. My friend and I laughed so hard. I got grounded on the spot and my friend had to go home, but it was so worth it.

I can't even count how many times I got grounded at Dads. To me, the grounding was for stupid reasons. I remember being grounded because of a school grade. I got a C- in one of my classes and in dad's way of thinking, a C- is a D. He told me that I couldn't have any friends over or use the phone. I couldn't even call Mom. I couldn't believe what I heard from Dad. Not allowed to call my own mother. He must have been insane that day. When I was alone in the house, I made sure to call Mom to let her know what was going on, if I was coming over or not on the coming up weekend. When Dad said I couldn't have friends over, I didn't mind it because I saw them at school. Also the only one who usually came over was Elizabeth. My other friends, who I hung out with at school didn't come over. There were a couple of times one or two did come over and stayed the night.

Dad brought home a Kitty Cat snowmobile one year for Kaleb

and I to ride on. The snowmobile was small and perfect for little kids. It had wheels and ski's so we could ride it all year round. Most weekends I would be riding it, with Kaleb in front of me as I drove him around the driveway. Kaleb loved it as I did. One day while riding it alone, I was making a turn and leaned in the wrong direction. I tipped over. My elbow was bleeding and I had tears streaming down my cheeks, but that didn't stop me from getting back on and riding it. We also had a Go-Cart, but I was too short drive it. Which sucked because I wanted to so bad.

Dad taught me how to play Cribbage. I was glad because it was a game that the two of us enjoyed. Dad slowly explained the rules and how to play as I listened to his instructions. The game was simple to learn, even Cole would join in. Only three players could play at one time. Three players was a little hard for me, but I went with the flow. When I returned home after staying with Mom, I would go upstairs to play Cribbage with Dad. If NASCAR or football was on, dad and I sat on the floor in front of the TV to play. Pee Body and Nibbles would watch sometimes. Nibbles would be on my side, while Kaleb was on Dad's.

A memory that I will never forget and most heartbreaking one growing up, is when the family and I went and stayed at a hotel for the weekend. It was just to get away and also a place where we could swim. I didn't want to go because I was on my menstruation cycle. I asked Dad if I could go to Moms that weekend, but he said it was his weekend with me and I was going to spend time with the family. Yeah, spending time by myself in the room while they were by the pool was more like it. They asked me if I wanted to go down by the pool and watch them swim, but I said I would stay in the room and watch some TV. When the family came back for lunch, I asked Momma Denise if I could try using a tampon because I really wanted to go swimming. I went into the bathroom and tried inserting the tampon. I couldn't get it to work and felt disappointed. I came out of the bathroom and told them I'd be seeing them when they came back after swimming.

For whatever reason, Dad chose that moment to make the comment that I wouldn't be able to have sex. All because I couldn't insert the tampon. I didn't understand how the topic came up. To me, Dad was being Dad. While the family was having fun back at the pool, I was crying while laying on the floor seeing how far I could spread my legs. I couldn't spread them far so I thought maybe Dad was right. I was fourteen at the time and was getting in to the dating age, I guess. But, sex never crossed my mind because I was going to wait for the right person.

I wanted to know the point behind Dad telling me that I wouldn't be able to have sex. Was he scared of getting myself hurt? Or was he just in his hurtful mood again. Maybe , I can't have sex because I'm disabled. I did/do sometimes think that he wished I was a normal child. I was normal to mom and in my own eyes, but I always felt he wanted me to be like the rest of the people who could walk. Maybe he couldn't accept that I would be capable of living on my own, get married and start a family. I did promise myself that I would show dad that I would be able to have sex.

I felt horrible when Dad told me this. Whenever Dad told me that I wouldn't be able to do something, I felt like a failure. A failure that wouldn't be able to do things in life. I also began wondering, "Would I ever get married and have a man who would love me the way I am? Would he accept me if I couldn't have sex?" To me, sex is a bonus in the relationship. I was filled with so many concerns and questions after dad's remark that day.

One of the greatest difficulties I experienced while growing up was walking without falling. I guess falling was my favorite thing to do because I did it a lot. Never knew when or where I would fall. I would be walking down the hallway in the house and *BAM*, my left leg or my hip would give out. Crawling up the stairs I would lose my balance and be at the bottom before I knew it. I guess I couldn't wait to get there. I always laughed when I fell down.

When I fell in front of Mom, she would laugh along with me. No matter where we were at, like on a sidewalk or at someone's home. We had a good outlook when I fell. Now with Dad, I had to be careful because he held a different outlook when I fell. Around the house wasn't so bad, but out in public is where he cared the most. I did fall once in front of people out in public. I got back up and just shook my head. In my mind I was thinking "Only me."

In the background I could hear Dad make an angry sound. When we were out of the restaurant, he said I embarrassed him. I knew he didn't mean it because I was at the age of knowing that he spoke before thinking. So I let him have his fit, but couldn't wait to get home. Surprisingly, with all the falling I did while growing up, I never had a broken bone.

Middle school was difficult at first because there were so many kids together in one building. In Greenville, there were four different elementary schools. Middle school was when all for elementary going into middle school were combined. I was being stared at by the upper class mates along with the newly combined students. Several of the students would ask me questions, which I didn't mind. As the kids grew close to me, I didn't have to worry about the stares anymore; I found my place in school.

In sixth grade, Becky my physical therapist came to me and ask if I would like to be a guess speaker on what it was like being in a wheelchair. I would be speaking in front of students without any disabilities. I said yes and was excited because it would be a good opportunity for kids to get the feeling of what I had to deal with everyday. Becky was going to bring in wheelchairs, button hooks, sock aid and more adaptive devices; most of which I used.

Each of these sessions would last an hour. It wasn't as if the kids had to use the wheelchairs the whole day. I thought it would be interesting if the kids used the wheelchairs all day and out in public. Take a group to Walmart or somewhere where there were a lot of people around. To see how those kids reacted to the stares and being talked about.

Being in a wheelchair wasn't so bad, but when you are having trouble opening a door; many people just stop and watch without offering help. There are some who have a kind heart and do help. I did get mad at those who didn't help when I was younger, but now I don't mind it. I would just like to know what was going through their minds when they witness a disabled person struggling to open a door. I told/tell myself often that those people was/is missing out on a great opportunity to help another soul. And when people stare at me, I just wave or say "hi" to them. Just to let them know I'm human and not an alien; unlike when I was younger when I felt like an alien because of all the stares.

The class work in middle school was easy. I just had a hard time reading and taking tests. I never liked to read out loud because I didn't know how to pronounce some words and I didn't want my classmates to think I was dumb. I knew I wasn't dumb because I was getting good grades. I just had some trouble remembering what was taught to me. I had to work extra hard in school. Plus I never asked anymore to help me at home.

Momma Denise was busy with the kids and I didn't want to bother her. Dad worked second shift and during the times he did help me, he would become irritated quickly. Every so often, when there was going to be a big math test I needed help studying for, I would call Matty to see if he would come by. Matty, I thought was an expert in math. He took his time and showed me easy ways to do some problems. Never did he lose his patience with me.

In eighth grade, I was getting high honors and honors for each marking period. School seemed to be getting easier and I was proud of myself. I couldn't believe how many A's I had on each of my progress report cards. It was during my eighth grade year I began to hangout with Antwone. We began to hangout together more than usual; not only in school, but also outside of school. His mom and him would take me to their church on Wednesday nights. I was very excited the first time Antwone asked me to go church because this would get me out of the house and plus give me a chance to know him a little more.

He had a girlfriend, but she never went with us to church. I wished I was his girlfriend, but being friends was just important to me. I don't know if his girlfriend had a problem with me going to church with Antwone, I never asked. The only person who had a little trouble with me hanging with Antwone was my dad. The reason being, Antwone was African American. Antwone's mom was white and his dad, which Antwone didn't like to talk about was African American. I didn't care what dad thought about Antwone. Color didn't then and still doesn't cross my mind; we are what we are.

One day while I was staying the weekend at Mom's, Antwone and his mom picked me up on a Saturday, to go to church. He reached over and held my hand. We talked about school and life in general. I was a little confused when he held my hand because he had a girlfriend. So why was he holding my hand now? I let that question slip out of my mind. What ever happens, is supposed to happen. This is the belief that mom had installed in me.

After church, we gave his Aunt a ride home. On the way, we stopped at a gas station where Antwone's mom asked if we wanted anything. Antwone and I both say Reese's peanut butter cups at the same time. We laughed at one another. While his mom and Aunt were in the store, Antwone leaned over and kissed me. My first kiss. It was wonderful. I felt like I was floating on a cloud and I had a big smile hidden within me. I have been waiting for this day to come. I wanted to stay in that place forever, but couldn't because his mom and Aunt came back to the car and handed us our Reese's.

In school, Antwone and I went back to our lives. Him being with his girlfriend and I hanging out with my friends. I always knew I was in his heart because of the way he looked at me. I had a hard time figuring out why he couldn't be with me, but later on I began to accept the fact that maybe he didn't know how he would feel if everyone knew we were dating. With my disabilities, would everyone pick on him or stare? To me, if he really did want to be with me, he wouldn't care what the world thinks. So much peer pressure to be a certain way, dress a certain way, and talk to only certain students; went on in school. Slowly Antwone and I drifted apart. We still talked in school and had our secret together. The night of the kiss was the last time I went with Antwone and his family to church.

Being a mother of a special needs child was never an issue for me whenever the kids and I went out in public. Each and every outing would have at least one memorable moment we all would laugh at. Several of the those outing are still being remembered to this day as being so funny. Heather is correct when she wrote that she never knew when falling down was going to take place. Our reaction to her falling was so casual. If she fell, we helped her up and be on our way as if nothing out of the norm had taken place. In fact, many of her falls and flying out of her wheelchair were caused by me. Whenever I was pushing her in her chair, chances were good that she would end up on the ground if she wasn't buckled in.

Katie, Heather and myself went to the art museum in Grand Rapids one Saturday afternoon. As we were heading back to the car, I became distracted by the looking at the architectural designs of the surrounding buildings, not even paying attention to the shape of the sidewalk; I was pushing Heather down. Naturally, it would be Heather's luck that I would hit the hole in the sidewalk that would send Heather flying out of the chair. The three of us just started laughing. Heather wasn't hurt, so there was no need to over react. The reaction of shock and disapproval came from the onlookers we had attracted. The look on their faces was one of disbelief at how Katie and I were standing there laughing at the young woman sprawled out on the sidewalk.

Another experience with Heather that made those around us uncomfortable, was when the kids and I ate at TGIF's. Heather needed to use the rest room and choose to go in the stall alone. I went into the stall next to her. Afterward, while washing my hands, I heard Heather calling out to me. When I asked her what was wrong, she replied that she was stuck between the toilet and stall wall. The only way to get to Heather was by crawling under the stall door, since she locked her door. Without giving it a second thought, I dropped to the floor and scooted under the door and saved her. The looks on the faces of the women in the bathroom when Heather and I exited the stall was priceless.

There are countless individuals who seemed to be content in watching Heather and I struggle with opening doors. The doors that open inward are the most difficult. I would have to hold the door open with one hand, then maneuver Heather in her chair with the other. Many times we would be stuck in the doorway with me trying to get us through the door without being helped by anyone. The most memorable and funny moment where we needed help, but no one helped was at a body building event. As I was placing Heather in her seat, Mikey forgot to hold the folding seat down. Heather slipped out of my grip and was practically sitting on the floor. There was very little room between the row and the chairs, so we were stuck. Here we were in the midst of body builders and not one offered any help. Everyone around us just watched as I struggled to place Heather in a chair.

Fortunately, there are others who are more than happy to lend a hand. Heather and I have encountered times, when individuals would call out and tell us to wait at a door, in order for them to open for us. I have told Heather over and over again she is blessing to everyone. In her presence, everyone is given the opportunity to discover what kind of person he/she really is.

CHAPTER TWENTY-NINE

THE APARTMENT IN LAKEVIEW KATIE and I moved into, was walking distance to school and less than one mile from where I worked. This location seemed like the perfect place to live. The village fire department along with the town police station was across the street. So, when my car caught on fire while being warmed up in the winter, the fire department didn't have to travel far to extinguish it. The other tenants living in the complex probably didn't know they could react as fast as they did when the fire broke out early in the morning. Each one had to rush out in the cold and move their cars out of the shared garage to avoid any damage to their cars. Before the fire was completely put out, my car had become valuable only to the scrap yard owners. Thanks goodness a co-worker also lived in the complex, so she gave me rides to and from work. In fact, she was the one who convinced the landlord that I would be a reliable renter which helped me get the apartment.

Once again, I became a single parent with no money in my savings and a lot of bills to pay. It was beginning to seem like I was destined to keep repeating starting over from scratch. There was definitely a pattern forming to my life which always circled back to struggling financially and included heartache. However, I never seemed to totally lose faith in the hope of finding a man with whom I would grow old with.

It was when I began to question whether or not I would meet such a man, I met Nathaniel. Funny how the law of attraction works and brings into one life's, a mate. Nathaniel and I worked in the same building for quite some time. I hadn't even noticed him until he came over to work on the side of the factory where I was working. When he walked into the break room during lunch, our eyes met and I instantly felt chemistry between us. It was the feeling that I knew him. So strong was this feeling, but the crazy thing way; I had never met him.

The most stand out feature that caught my attention were his eyes. Nathaniel's green eyes were so memorizing that I had a hard time keeping myself from staring at him all the while he was there. He was considered charming by all the women he worked along side of. Word had it that he was interested in me, but was to shy to ask me out on a date. Just as if it were high school, where friends instigated a date with someone you were interested in, this was the same technique used on Nathaniel. Eventually, he asked me out after a bit of persuasion from the women at work.

Spending time with Nathaniel just reinforced that sense of familiarity I felt when I first saw him. I couldn't shake the feeling that I knew him somehow. On our first date, we spent our time in nature. Talking for hours until the mosquitoes became too much of a nuisance. Nathaniel was a romantic at heart. More charming than what I was told he was, which made it difficult not to automatically drop my guard. Fearing that I may once again overlook signs of misleading attributes in his character, I fought against believing everything he was telling me. Impossible to do when one is swept off one's feet, so to speak. His charm and sincerity offset any doubt that may have risen. Even before he brought me back to the apartment, I knew the two of us was going to enter into a serious relationship and the thought overwhelmed me.

I received a card from Nathaniel a few days after our first date was taken by surprise at how expressive this man was with words. He thanked me for a wonderful day in such a poetic manner that I had to share his words with friends. Showing them that I found a true romantic. He had such a way with expressing emotions, for his words flowed with passion and I was consumed by each and every sentence.

I finally introduced him to Mikey, Heather and Katie. As skeptic as the kids were becoming by my choice of men, they seemed to like Nathaniel right off. At least the girls did. Mikey however, was a little apprehensive, but sociable toward him. Nathaniel and I spent most of our time together and began talking about the possibility of moving in together. This created some concern among the kids, but seeing how happy I've become since meeting Nathaniel they didn't completely reject the idea.

Heather began coming over to stay more often after we moved in the apartment. Alex was beginning to be more lenient with visitation, where before visitation was followed to the exact way the court had it written. As Heather was growing older, she wanted to be around us more. Right before the end of her eighth grade school year, I received a pamphlet from Mary Free Bed regarding a sport's camp for the disabled. I believed Heather would benefit greatly from the experience; so I called for more information.

The Jr Wheelchair Sport Camp lasted five days in August at Grand Valley State University. The camp was sponsored by Grand Rapids Sports Association, along with Mary Free Bed Rehabilitation Hospital. To qualify for the camp, the campers had to be physically disabled and require the use of a wheelchair to play sports. Sports like basketball, hockey, tennis, including softball and even riding specially designed bicycles were part of the program. Heather had never really played any of these sports. She would shoot baskets with her brother Kaleb at times, but not in a group setting. The day camp was free for those living close to GVSU who could be dropped off in the morning and picked up in the afternoon. The fee for overnight campers, living more than 45 miles from the campus was $150.00.

I spoke to Heather about the camp and she was willing to give it a try. I believe her decision to try had something to do with hearing that boys would be attending as well. Heather was at the boy crazy stage. She had only gone to one other summer camp; Wah Wah Tay See. But, that was a few years back along with her cousin Morgan. At the wheelchair camp, Heather would know no one, but that didn't concern me. Heather was a social butterfly who made friends with everyone.

HEATHER'S WORDS

I went to Wah Wah Tay See, with my cousin Morgan and another cousin. Our cousin didn't stay long because she became homesick. Morgan and I stayed for what seemed like forever. While there, we did a lot of activities. Morgan and my favorite activity was swimming, of course. We made friends with so many campers and I found out that one of the campers was going to be in middle with me. His name was Roger. He was a grade higher, but I didn't care. I was going to be new at the middle and now I knew someone already going there.

Roger and I began to hang out together while Morgan went off with her friends. He was out going and would make me laugh. I enjoyed being around him. He told me about his twin sister Nora and I couldn't wait to meet her when school started. Roger and I became boyfriend and girlfriend before school started. In school we held hands and nothing further. His sister Nora, was easy to get along with and I was glad. I wasn't long before I found out that Roger found another girlfriend. He didn't even tell me. I was mad for a while, but we still remained friends throughout middle school and high school. We lost touch after he graduated.

When Mom asked me if I wanted to go to a wheelchair camp, I said yes. This would give me the opportunity to be on my own for five days. I thought the sport would be easy to do, boy was I wrong. On the first day of camp, I was given a light weight wheelchair to use while I was there. My wheelchair was an older model and very heavy for me to push. As I looked around at the other campers, I couldn't believe how many were there in their wheelchairs. It wasn't the first time I had seen a person in a wheelchair, but it was the first time where I was surrounded by many younger kids in wheelchairs and how I wasn't the only one in a wheelchair in my surrounding; like I was at home in Greenville.

Some of the campers were paralyzed from the waist down. Some had no legs while there were others with only one leg. Either they were born with the defect or else was involved in an accident in some sort. I thought it was amazing that I wasn't getting stared at. There was no outsiders present that normally stared at those in wheelchairs. Everyone on campus was connected by their disability. We were family even before we had met one another.

Some of the campers went home in the afternoon, while others stayed on campus as I did. The dorm I stayed in was big. In the building, the boys roomed in the East wing and the girls had the West wing, but we all gathered in the lobby to chat or play games before we went to bed. The food was okay, but I was missing my parents cooking.

The first day of camp we were divided into groups. I believe the groups were organized by group A,B and C. I was in group B. I was the oldest in my group because it was my first time being there. Group A were my age and knew how to play the sports and group C was younger kids. I jumped in and tried to play. Floor Hockey was my worst nightmare because there were about ten players plus two goalies wheeling around on the floor. The Hockey sticks were too long and I would get my stuck in the wheels of the other players every time I played. I thought the Hockey sticks should have been shorter. I wished I was paralyzed while playing Basketball and Tag Football because we would collide into each other very hard.

Because I wasn't used to wheeling myself around in a wheelchair, since I mostly walked or else used my power wheelchair. I practiced wheeling the borrowed chair in the building where I was staying. I went up and down the hallway to get the hang of pushing. While I was practicing, I noticed a guy who was watching me at the end of the hallway. His name was Josh. He asked me what I was doing. I told him I didn't know how to turn that well. He then asked one of the counselors if we could go outside and was told it was alright to go. I felt like an idiot and didn't want to follow Josh. Outside, we talked about why I didn't know how to work a wheelchair. I then pop the question of why he was in one. The only thing I remember him telling me was that he was paralyzed.

We spent about an hour outside before I had the routine down. I was still slow, but was very proud of myself for learning. I thanked him and we both went back inside. That evening when everyone gathered for dinner, I sat with my room mate and noticed that Josh was staring at me from across the room. I just looked away and pretended that I was listening to the people around me. I think Josh wanted to get to know me better. After dinner I went to my room to get ready for bed. The bed was a little high for me to get into so I asked a counselor, who was standing in the hallway to help me up. She came into the room with a smile on her face and told me that Josh had told her that I was beautiful and he liked me. How could a person like someone by only spending an hour with them. That was what I was thinking after the counselor had told me. I guess my blue eyes caught his attention. Mom always told me that I captivated people with my eyes.

As the days went by, Josh and I became close. I met some of his friends and one of them became very protective over me, so I had myself a bodyguard. His friends would joke around with Josh. Like saying, "Are you going to hold her hand or what?" or "Get a room." From then on, after we finished our schedule for the day, the boys and I would play tag football. Josh was on my team. I should have stayed out of the game because it wasn't tag football we were playing. It was whoever had the ball attack them. I was getting hit and fell out of my wheelchair so many times. But, I was bound and determined to not let those boys get the best of me. I would get back into my chair and try my hardest to beat them. I cheat a little when I asked a counselor to push me around the floor since I was slow at pushing my chair.

My time at camp flew by and before I knew it, the last day arrived. Family and friends were invited to spend the day watching their child play sports. Mom was the only one who came from my family. I introduced Josh to her and she liked him. I also introduced her to many other friends I made; even my bodyguard. Before leaving for home, Josh and I exchanged phone phone and he gave me a kiss on the cheek. Josh lived in Eaton Rapids Michigan, near Lansing. Mom and I planned a trip to visit him, but before we got around to doing so; Josh invited me to a basketball game in Grand Rapids. Mom, Nathaniel, Katie and I went down to watch Josh and his team play. I called Matty and asked if he wanted to meet us there since he was staying in Grand Rapids. He said that it sounded like fun and would meet us.

I was amazed at the game. Yes, I played basketball at camp, but it was nothing like how these guys were going at it. Wheelchair basketball is one tough game. If anyone has never seen it played, then watch the movie; "Muderball." These players showed no mercy when playing. There was a lot of tripping over and slamming into each other. Mom just kept commenting on what a good thing it was that many of the players were paralyzed.

While waiting for Josh to arrive with his team, I noticed him walking into the gym with a girl. I thought it was his sister or a friend. At half time, I wheeled my old heavy chair over to where he was sitting and stayed there for a while. After Josh went back on the floor to play, the girl and I talked for quite some time and I asked her if she was his sister. She said no. Of course, I got cheated on again. Even though we lived far apart and having a relationship wasn't going to last, he at least could have said something before that day.

After the game I went up to Josh, shook his hand and told him good game and also have a good life. He knew that I found out about his girlfriend and his eyed told me he was disappointed with himself. Matty came up to me and gave me a hug and told me that he loved me, before leaving the gym. It was when we got into the car where I broke down and cried. Why couldn't Josh have told me that he didn't want to have a relationship with me, so I didn't have to find out the hard way? Once again my heart was ripped. Mom asked me if I still wanted to go to the mall and I said yes. I wasn't going to let a boy ruin our plans. So Mom, Nathaniel, Katie and I went to the mall and had a great time.

A few weeks after the sports camp, Nathaniel moved into the apartment with Katie and I. Since he had lived alone for quite some time, adjusting to his new surroundings took a bit of getting used to for him. He had already left Parker Hannifin before the move and was now employed at another factory. Nathaniel didn't work there long before he was hired in at yet another manufacturing company. Within a few months time, Nathaniel worked three different jobs before he landed a job working for an electrician, whom Parker Hannifin brought in from time to time, to do electrical and maintenance work. This meant Nathaniel was back working where I worked. This time not as a temporary worker, but as hired in help and making a lot more money as well.

Life for me took on an amazing turn that summer, with Nathaniel moving in. Shortly after he moved in, Heather stated that she wanted to come live with me. I was thrilled to say at least. The thought of having my family united was so emotionally uplifting. I had wished for Heather to want to come live with us for so many years, but never pressured her to do so. Her moving in with me would have to be of her accord. In truth, I couldn't believe she would choose living where we had so little; unlike where she had so much. However, getting Alex to allow Heather to move in without going to court worried me. Heather kept asking Alex to let her move. Her persistence paid off because before the next school year was about to begin, Heather moved in.

The apartment became cramped really quick with the four of us living there. It had two bedrooms which meant Katie and Heather had to share one. On the positive side, there was a bath and a half in the apartment. So we weren't having to wait on Heather when she was in the bathroom. Heather took forever in the bathroom.

It wasn't long after Heather moved in before Nathaniel and I discussed looking for a bigger place to live. I remember thinking how wonderful life had become at that time. I met a man who brought me so much happiness and having Heather back living with me, filled that void I had felt within for so many years after she went to live with Alex.

Heather and I went to register her for ninth grade at Lakeview High School. Everything was set for her to begin school. Katie and her would go to the elementary school first each morning, where Katie attended school. After seeing Katie off, Heather would then follow the paved walkway with her power wheelchair to the High School across the field. If rain was in the forecast, the Intermediate School District (ISD) bus would pick up Heather up at the apartment; leaving Katie to walk with her friends to school.

HEATHER'S WORDS

I decided to move in with Mom, Nathaniel, and Katie at the end of middle school, which meant saying goodbye to my friends at Greenville. This was a tough decision to move, but I didn't want to live with dad anymore. I was lonely and always by myself. Kaleb and Nibbles were a lot younger than I and they were busy playing together or else staying near Momma Denise. Dad still worked second shift so I saw little of him and Momma Denise was with the kids.

At Mom's apartment, Mikey came and went often. Katie was ten years old now so I would have someone close to my age to hang out with. Of course, Mom would be there after work where I would see her everyday instead of here and there as I did when I was living with Dad. Dad's reaction to my wanting to move was typical of him. He wasn't very happy at the thought of me moving in with mom. He said I wouldn't be taken care of there, because Mom didn't want me before. This why I was living with him. He went on to say that Mom would let me do anything I wanted and I probably would get pregnant. Dad also told me that I couldn't bring clothes that he and Momma Denise had bought for me. So I grabbed the clothes Mom had bought me, or anyone one her side of the family; it wasn't much. I didn't understand why I couldn't bring the rest of the clothes. They were just clothes and not that important to Dad, it wasn't like he was going to wear them. After I had been living with Mom for a while, Dad gave in and I had my whole closet of clothing at Mom's.

Katie always took some of my clothes and wore them without asking, which made me upset. There wasn't a lot of difference in our size. I was a bit taller than her, but other than that we could wear each others shirts. No if I wanted to wear one of her shirts, Katie would say "NO." I guess she was just being a little sister who thought; "What was hers, was hers and what was mine was hers as well."

Nathaniel was a very nice guy. I was happy that Mom had met someone. They looked so happy together. He would do anything for her if she asked. She never asked for much help because she was an independent woman. I could tell Nathaniel loved Mom so much because of the way he looked at her. The two of them were always laughing and cuddling.

In the Fall, I started my freshman year at Lakeview. I was surprised to see that two of my friends Sarah and Ethan were also going there. I guess they couldn't be away from me. Elizabeth and I still kept in touch. During the first couple of weeks at school, I ate lunch with my cousin Cristal. Afterward, I would hang out with Sarah. I didn't see Ethan until health class where we sat next to each other so we could talk.

After school, Katie and I hung out at the neighbor's house most of the time. There were two boys and two girls in that family. Two of them were my age and the other two were close to Katie's age. We always had a good time. It was all going great living with Mom. I felt like I had all the freedom in the world. I didn't have to worry about getting yelled at or having to be careful on what I did. It was nice, but I soon began to miss my friends and school at Greenville.

I told Mom that I wanted to go back to school in Greenville. That way I could still live with her and go to school in Greenville. Mom said this shouldn't be a problem. The ISD buses traveled all over transporting students to different schools. A bus must go to Greenville from Lakeview. After contacting the bus garage, mom found out that I couldn't be taken to Greenville on the ISD bus because I wasn't enrolled in a resource class. I had to be in special education in order to be transported. So, in order to go back to Greenville Schools, I had to move back in with Dad; which I ended up doing.

Chapter Thirty

$\mathscr{S}$TEPPING INTO THE APARTMENT AFTER work one afternoon, seeing Heather and Nathaniel sitting at the table in a deep conversation. I knew Heather had actually decided to move back to Greenville. She had been tossing the idea back and forth for over a couple of weeks, but not committing herself to a final decision. For the most part, her reluctance to move was her fear of hurting my feelings.

Once I saw Heather's expression when I walked into the apartment, I immediately felt that sense of loss I had felt when she first moved in with her dad. I did not want to lose her again, but I also did not want her to be in a situation where she wasn't happy. I assured Heather that everything would be alright and I wasn't angry. However, I would be angry if she decided to stay with me out of guilt. So, in a matter of hours, Heather's belongings were packed and she was going home with Alex.

After the last of Heather's belongings were loaded in Alex's vehicle, I turned away for I didn't want Heather to see the tears forming in my eyes. There was no comfort that would take away the sadness I was feeling that night. I felt bad for Nathaniel and Katie because I just withdrew into my own lonely world for the next few days. All their efforts to cheer me up were fruitless. Gradually, I began to interact with them and settled into what became an unbelievable happy period in my life.

Heather's Words

I felt bad leaving Mom to move back in with Dad because I didn't want to hurt her feelings or want her to think I didn't love her. I also felt bad about leaving Katie as we were just beginning to become close and I didn't want to lose that. Also leaving Mikey behind, my brother who helped take care of me when I was little. I know Mom was trying to hide her tears when Dad arrived to pick me up. I noticed the tears when I went to hug her goodbye after my things were pack into Dad's van. I tried to console Mom as I gave her a big hug and told her everything would be alright and that I would be over the following weekend. Mom always said to us kids "Do what makes you happy." I was doing half what I wanted and that was going back to school in Greenville. The other half of what I wanted was to stay with Mom and Katie.

When Dad and I arrived at his house, Sasha greeted me in my bedroom. I bent down and told her that I missed her too. Kaleb and Nibbles were happy that I was back as well. Even though I was away for a short time, the two of them seemed to have grown. Nibbles and I played together a lot more than before. Playing with play-doh was fun with Nibbles. She loved to make a mess with the stuff. She would have play-doh stuck underneath her socks or on her clothing. I had to watch her so she didn't get it on the living room carpet. Wouldn't Dad love that. NOT! He would have a cow if he saw play-doh stuck in the carpet.

Kaleb and I played video games. Basketball and NASCAR were the two we played the most of. I played football video game several times before I gave up playing with him. He was the biggest cheater. He had to be the one who always kicked the football at the start at the game. He would kick it in a way that he was able to catch it and score. So I gave up. Dad and Kaleb loved to play the war games together. If Dad was home, Kaleb and I didn't play the war games with each other. We knew that Dad would watch us and begin telling us how to play and what we were doing wrong. He couldn't just watch us play without interfering.

To me, I thought if we didn't die during play, we were doing awesome. Kaleb and I also shot baskets together. I would ride my power wheelchair down to our basketball hoop and stood using the chair to support me as I shot baskets. I threw the ball underhand instead of overhand. Under hand was the easiest for me and how I made the most baskets between Kaleb and I. We had a lot of fun shooting baskets together.

I didn't see much of Dad during the week, but he would come down into my bedroom sometimes after returning home from work to check on me. He just wanted to say "Hi" and see how I was doing. I really didn't like him waking me because I was never in the mood to talk. I don't like being woken up when I am sleeping. I tend to get a little crabby. I knew Dad liked having this time with me so I went with the flow. He didn't do it often, so I can't complain. On the Sunday nights after spending the weekend with Mom, I would routinely unpack my clothes down in my bedroom, then go up stairs to spend time with the family. Dad would either be watching football or NASCAR. I became a huge fan of those sports and basketball. Of course, dad and I would have to get in a game or two of Cribbage before bedtime.

On the weekends with Dad, there was always a big Sunday dinner where we all sat around the table and talked. At bedtime, Dad would come down and tuck me in. He told me that I was never to old to be tucked in by him. It was during this time when the two of us bonded the most. We would talk about old stories and especially Great Grandma White.

The story that remains a favorite today is when Dad and I went to see her. Dad went out to mow her lawn. While he was mowing, I took Great Grandma White's pills and cranberry juice to her in the living room. I then went back into the kitchen and made so chocolate milk for me to drink. My goal was to sit on her foot stool and talk to her, but that didn't happen. I slipped and spilled my chocolate milk all over her scanner she had, the wall, and on the carpet. She rushed up from her seat with a Kleenex tissues in hand to wipe up the chocolate milk. At that time, Great Grandma White had a bad foot so she was hopping on her good foot while trying to wipe off the scanner. I felt bad and started to cry.

When Dad came in after mowing the yard, she told him what I did. He started yelling at me which made me cry even harder. As always, Great Grandma White told him to stop yelling at me. It wasn't funny then, but now we laugh all the time when Dad or I bring it up; how Great Grandma White was hopping around on one foot trying to wipe up the chocolate milk.

My first day at Greenville High School was great. Dad and I went to get my class schedule at the counselor's office. There were four counselors and Mrs. Stafford was mine. She told me if I needed anything to let her know. I kept that in mind. We then went to the office where we met the vice principal, Mr Gates. I felt a very strong energy between us and couldn't wait to get to know him more throughout the year. Mr. Gates showed Dad and I around the school and where all my classes were. Greenville High School was a little bigger than Lakeview. I had six classes instead of four classes and a home room while at Lakeview. All my teachers were nice to me and offered to help me with anything I needed. I was given an extra set of text books to keep at home so I didn't have to take books back and forth to school. Also up and down the stairs to my bedroom.

I had two aids that helped me each day. One in the mornings and after school. They helped me get my folders and notebooks in/out of my bag. The female aid would help me when I needed to use the bathroom, but I often asked friends for their help. Otherwise, I was capable of taking care of myself during school hours. I rarely went to the bathroom during school. I have what is called a shy bladder. No matter how bad I had to go, it took forever to relax my body in order to go. On those days I couldn't go to the bathroom at school. I had better head for the bathroom as soon as I got home, most times I barely made it. I guess my bladder knows when I'm home or not. I still have trouble going in public and while visiting, but not as bad as it was in school.

I was allowed to leave class a few minutes early each say before lunch bell rang at school. I was glad because I could take my time and didn't get stuck in the crowd of students trying to get their lunches. In high school, some students left campus during lunch to eat. I never had the opportunity to do that.

Class work was easy, but like always I had trouble taking tests. If I wasn't a bad test taker I would have received higher grades. My grades wasn't that awful. I had mostly C's and couple of B's. Unlike I was getting in the eighth grade. It wasn't until the tenth grade when I was transferred to a resource room for English. All because of Julius Caesar, It wasn't totally his fault, my level of understanding literature and tenth grade English was below average. The English in the resource room was a little easier and I didn't have a lot of homework. There wasn't very many students in the class which I liked and Mrs. Bell take time to explain if I didn't understand something.

Back at Greenville school, Elizabeth and I once again picked up where we left off before I moved in with mom. She was part of a group who hung together at lunch and I joined in. We sat at the same table everyday. I didn't really like the idea of being in a clique, where you hang out with only certain people. I was more of a social butterfly as Mom always put it, wanting to talk to everyone. For the most part, I stayed around Elizabeth. Sarah and Ethan came back to Greenville as well. I laughed when I saw them. Like I stated earlier, they couldn't be away from me very long. I heard that Antwone moved away that year also, which made me sad because we had a very good friendship between us. I didn't even get to say goodbye.

Being in a new school and around new students, meant getting used of the stares from other and their talking about me. On top of that, I was a ninth grader. The upper class loved to look down at ninth graders. It wasn't as bad as I thought it would be, but there were a few students who were rude. I didn't understand why. Did they forget what it was like being a freshman? Or is it just an traditional role played out in high school, where the upper class picks on the ninth graders. God, I hope our class isn't like that when we get up there.

In the Common Hall, where the Senior and Juniors sit; there is a "G" for Greenville Yellow Jackets in the middle of the floor. If Freshman or Sophomores step on it, watch out. The upper class will become upset and begin yelling at those who dare to step on the "G." This guy asked me what I was doing running over the "G" with my wheelchair. I asked him what he meant. He told me that when Freshman or a Sophomore step or like you runs over it, it a show of disrespect to the school and the Yellow Jackets. I just stared at him like "How Stupid." I told him that I was sorry that I ran over his precious "G." I turned my chair around and ran over it again. No matter what, that symbol is going to get stepped on during the rushing of students going to their classes. It's in the middle of the hallway for God sake! I had a lot of respect for Greenville and their sports. The Yellow Jackets was our mascot.

As I was getting used to where everything was in school, I noticed a classroom where there were students who had different types of disabilities. The class I believe was separate from the school itself, but held in the high school. I think it was a class from the Intermediate school in Greenville. I thought it was unique that they had a class in public school. There was also one in the middle school where I used to hang out a lot at visiting. Since I was allowed to leave early for lunch, I began to walk with some of those students to the lunch room. Some of them sat with Elizabeth and I during lunch. I would see others when it was time to go home for they also rode the ISD buses. They truly looked up to me and I felt honored and somewhat protective over them.

On one occasion, two guys were talking very rude about the kids in the special education classroom. I felt I had to say something. I guess I was to become known as a "Bitch" by anyone who teased or mocked those students or me. I would stand up for those who couldn't do it for themselves.

I asked them what they were talking about. I knew what they were saying, but I wanted to hear it from them. They said that they wasn't talking to me. I replied back that they was because they were saying mean things about a girl in a wheelchair. The two of them said they wasn't talking about me, they were talking about a girl who was in the special education class. I then told them, "If I hear or see either of you guys pick or point at any of those kids again, I'll turn you in." They said "Whatever" and made the comment of me being a "Bitch." I might have been one at that moment in their opinion, but there isn't any reason to put someone down because they are different than them. Especially those kids. Maybe those two guys should have spent one whole day with those kids and find out how amazing those students really were.

In November of 2004, Nathaniel and I found a house to rent in town. Living in town was based on Katie's wish alone. She was quite persistent in asking that we live in town so she could continue to walk with her friends to school and quite adamant about not wanting to ride a school bus. The house was about five blocks away from school and Katie was fine with the walking distance, so we moved in.

A definite fixer upper, but the little house had a lot of potential. The owner was looking to sell the house and we were interested in buying. The downside of this particular home was the fact that it only had one bedroom, but did have an enclosed porch where we turned it into a bedroom for Katie and Heather, when Heather visited.

We began looking into getting pre-approved for a loan to buy the house. Since there was concern over Nathaniel's credit rating and how it might jeopardize our chances of getting financed, it was decided that I apply for the financing alone. I wasn't really sure that financing a home was possible for me because I had just financed a car earlier in the summer. Financing the home turned out to be easier than expected. By early March of 2005, we finalized the sell of the house; it was when we called it home. It felt like home. I had everything, outside of Heather living with me that I dreamed of. A wonderful man to share life with and a sense that I would never again struggle as I had for so many years prior.

During Heather's visits, I begun to notice how she was having more difficulty walking. She would still wall surf (using the wall and other objects to balance herself), but fell more often. Her left leg was becoming a hindrance and tripping her up. What concerned me even more was the appearance of her toes and the bottoms of her feet. Several of her toes had dark purple and black spots on them. The presence of these spots always occurred during the cold season where her feet would never feel warm. No matter how many layers of socks she wore. I made an appointment to a podiatrist.

After examining Heather's feet, he stated that her condition was common among those who have Raynaud's disease, but advised us to watch closely for any ulcers that form. Once ulcers appear and rupture, gangrene can easily set in. He also ordered an ultrasound to be performed on the circulation flow in her legs. The results of the ultrasound showed relatively good flow in both her legs and feet.

Heather's condition of her toes and feet was serious. If her condition worsened, she was at the risk of losing some of her toes. It was beginning to seem like whenever Heather made progress in one area in her life, there was always a set back of some sort in another area with her. Was she ever going to have a period in life when nothing more was added to her list of challenges?

While talking with the podiatrist, I brought up how Heather's scissoring was becoming worse and asked if he had any suggestions. He spoke of surgeries that could help correct the scissoring and make walking easier, but we needed to have a specialist take a look at Heather's spine to evaluate whether or not her back would be strong enough to support her walking. By this time, Heather's scoliosis was plainly visible. She never had an x-ray taken of her back, so the actual severity of the scoliosis was unknown to us at that time.

CHAPTER THIRTY-ONE

"Some people come into our lives and quickly go.
Some stay a while and leave footprints on our
hearts and we are never ever the same."
Author Unknown

HEATHER'S WORDS

*W*HENEVER SOMEONE COMES INTO YOUR life, even if it is for a brief period of time, I truly believe the person is there to impact your life in some way. A way, in which no other person would. My friend Zachariah was one such person. He wasn't popular or the type whom needed to feel like he fitted in. He was friendly with everyone no matter their status.

Many of the girls I knew in Middle and High school would say how cute they thought he was and wished they were his girlfriend. I didn't see anything special about Zachariah until I became a Sophomore and him a Junior. I felt drawn to him, as if we were supposed to get to know one another. Whatever was drawing me to him, there was a sense of being safe. Even though I didn't know him, I would take the time to say "Hi" and asked how he was doing. The first few times I approached him, he seemed friendly and would respond back with a "Hi," smiling all the while.

As a result from my decision of writing him a letter, saying it would be nice to get to know him, the two of us became pen pals. Zachariah had a steady girlfriend, so I clearly stated in my first letter to him that my intention was based on friendship. His girlfriend, or other half as I called her and Zachariah made the cutest couple.

Their relationship had its ups and downs like most, but he was deeply in love with her. He told me there wasn't anything he wouldn't do for her. I was excited and anxious to get to know him. There was something unexplainable in his eyes, that seemed to be asking for someone to notice that he needed a friend to connect with on a deeper level than his casual friendships at school.

In his letters to me, he wrote about his life and what he wanted to do with it. I would always make a point of telling him how he could be and do whatever he wanted; I had faith in him. When I said this or anything positive about him, he would smile. In that smile and in his sparkling eyes, I knew he was an angel. My angel, that I kept and cherished.

We didn't talk much during school, but if him or I needed someone to confide in a letter would be written. It was an unspoken knowing that we were there for each other. As Zachariah was opening up to me, I began to realize he was indeed helping me tear down my wall. He was the first guy whom I opened myself to since the assault. I revealed all my personal thoughts and feelings with him. Why him? Again, there was such an incredible sense that something important was in store for me, as well for Zachariah.

One evening Zachariah called me at Dads and we talked about life, our family and our favorite things to do. He told me that his sister, who was in my grade, and him lived with their Uncle and Aunt. I don't remember why, or what he said about his parents. Boxing was Zachariah's passion. He said that he wasn't boxing anymore and wished he could start up again. When I asked him why he stopped, he said one of his knees was bad which prevented him to continue. I wanted to tell him that I knew how he felt, having something taken away from you. Our situations were different. I already had years to accept and adjust to what was taken away from me. Whereas, Zachariah, still hadn't accepted and adjusted to boxing not being a part of his life.

We talked about him coming over sometime to hang out. I told him the two of us could sit in the basement, sip on hot cocoa since the basement was so cold and play the one hundred question game. He just laughed at this, but did say that he wanted to take me out to see a movie. I thought that would be wonderful. It never happened.

A few days before ending my Sophomore year, Zachariah handed me two letters. One for me and the other was written to his "Other

Half." He told me to give it to her when the time was right. I gave him a puzzled look, then nodded in agreement. He bent down and gave me a hug before walking away. As he was walking away from me, I opened my letter. Only to notice that he had written on a letter that I had wrote to him earlier. In this letter he handed me, he said he was sorry for writing me on a letter that I had written to him. Looking at the letter more closely, I realized this letter, he had just handed me, was written on the very first letter I ever wrote to him.

Zachariah had written about his drug usage in the letter and how drugs could seriously mess up your life. I knew he was into drugs, but didn't know what all he was using and I never asked. I sincerely felt it wasn't my business. If he wanted to share this, he would have. Maybe the letter was a sign that he was ready to talk about his habit. I did tell him at one time, that it didn't matter if he used drugs as long as he didn't abuse our friendship because of the drugs; "Might have to beat him." He knew I was there for him and wouldn't judge him.

Until I received a call from him during the summer break, I thought his life was going perfect. Before answering the ringing phone, I noticed the caller ID displayed "Unavailable or Private" number. My first thought was telemarketers calling to sell something and I was ready to have some fun with them. It was Zachariah.

I never told this to anyone besides my mom, because I didn't want to be blame for not helping Zachariah. I was excited to hear from Zachariah, but when he started talking, the sadness in his voice revealed how depressed he was feeling. I wanted to go through the phone to give him a shoulder, but I couldn't. The first thing he said to me was how he loved me. He thanked me for noticing him and for being a great friend. Not to worry because everything was going to be alright. He then asked me if I still had the note for his other half. I said that I did. The two of us talked for a while and I blew him a kiss through the phone as we hung up. I knew, I don't know how, but really sensed what he was planning to do because when someone says "I love you and everything is going to be alright" in such a way as Zachariah had, it means goodbye. Zachariah was saying goodbye to me and his life.

I put the phone down and just sat there trying to figure out why he was telling me this. We only had written to one another and talked for over the past year. Was I that important to him? Was I the only one who took the time to ask him personal questions about his life? Was I that great of a friend in which he trusted the most, to share his inner most feelings and dreams, along with the demons he battled against? Maybe, he knew that I would accept his decision to end his life without intervening or becoming mad at him, by understanding the depth of his sorrow.

My cousin Morgan came over to Dad's house to spend the night with me a couple of days after talking to Zachariah. I hadn't received any calls from anyone about him and beginning to think his call wasn't intended to be a call saying goodbye. That maybe his call was a way for him to vent. Later that night the phone rang. No one came downstairs to hand me the phone, but I instinctively knew what the call was for. A sudden sense of loss swept through me. Zachariah had taken his life. His beautiful smile was gone.

Laying there in the quietness of my room, while Morgan slept, the sense of loss faded and was replaced by a deep feeling of appreciation. I felt so honored that Zachariah had allowed me the chance to know him. When I finally drifted off to sleep, I had a dream. The dream was about Zachariah. I have a gift which that allows me to talk to spirits. Sometimes, spirits appear in my dreams as a way to communicate. Some people believe it's a curse, while others don't believe it's possible to talk to those whom have passed away. Mom often had said that maybe since I was so close to death myself when I was younger, the veil between this life and the afterlife was lifted, giving me the ability to communicate with those who have passed on.

In the dream, I was standing in a corner of a room. The room wasn't familiar to me. I didn't know where I was until Zachariah walked in. I tried to reach out to him, but couldn't. I stood there waiting to see what he was going to show me. Without warning, he took his life. I suddenly woke from the dream and there he was sitting on my bed, like Great Grandma White had. Zachariah placed his hand on my cheek and said he was happy now. I felt the sensation of his touch and went to place my hand over his, but he began to slowly disappear. I will never forget that moment.

I believe the dream was his way of allowing me to witness his final moments and feel how miserable he was in life. I often wandered what if I had alerted his family or friends. Would they have believed me? Would he be in more pain because of what would be expected of him?

Like going into rehab and facing his drug and other personal issues. Would he feel betrayed by me and attempt suicide again without nobody knowing?

I went to his memorial service. It was an open casket. Zachariah was dressed in everyday clothes; jeans, sweatshirt and a baseball cap. I thought the choice of clothing was neat. I placed a white rose along side the body; to surround the body with positive energy. I looked up from the casket and there he was. Zachariah was standing at the end of the casket looking down at himself. He looked into my eyes and like always, gave me a smile.

I wasn't able to go to Zachariah's funeral, so when I felt up to it I asked Mom if we could drive to the cemetery where he was buried. I wanted to place a white rose by his headstone. I remember it being a Saturday when Mom, Mikey and I, went looking for Zachariah's grave. I didn't know where the cemetery was, but his obituary in the news paper mentioned Spencer Township cemetery. Mom said the cemetery had to be near Gowen, since Gowen was in Spencer township and this was where Zachariah's relatives, whom he was staying with lived. So Gowen was our starting Point.

We drove around Gowen and didn't find the cemetery. Mom decided to stop at the gas station in Gowen and ask if anyone knew where the cemetery was. The clerk did not know. We then headed for Greenville. Mom said that we were going to the funeral home where Zachariah's funeral was held. If anyone would know where the cemetery was, they would know there. Mom went inside the funeral home and returned back to the car without any information. She said there wasn't anyone in the funeral home, but not to give up hope. We would simply go to the police station and ask there. Off to the police station we went. The station was locked and there wasn't anyone who came to the door when mom rang the bell.

If all else fails, go to the gas stations and ask directions. That's what Mom always does. We stopped at one station and was given directions to a cemetery on the other side of Greenville, which happened to be the wrong one. Stopped again at another station, and again, it turned out to be the wrong cemetery. We ended up stopping at most of the gas stations in Greenville. Most of the workers hadn't even heard of Spencer Township cemetery.

We were becoming tired of driving around. Mom kept saying the cemetery had to be near Gowen. My mom, she even went speeding through town, thinking after she was pulled over and given a ticket, she would then ask the officer for directions. That is how desperate we were becoming. No luck in getting pulled over. We wasn't speeding real fast, only ten miles over the speed limit. Mom said that she would stop at one last gas station and ask for directions. If no one knew where the cemetery was, we were going to call it quits. We had been on the hunt for the cemetery for one and a half hours.

I told Mom that I bet Zachariah was sitting in a lazy boy, eating popcorn and enjoying the show. It would have been nice if he gave me a sign or something. We stopped at Meijer's gas station before going home. Mom went in and came out smiling. The worker inside, not only knew where the cemetery was, but he also said he went to the funeral. Where were we then heading? Gowen. The three of us were laughing so hard, because we had past the road to the cemetery on our way to Greenville and didn't even notice the cemetery nor the sign. Only us.

All we had to do now was find Zachariah's grave site. We spotted what looked like a fairly new grave and Mom and I walked over to it. It was Zachariah's'. When I placed the white rose on his headstone, I started to laugh because of what I saw. There were two cigarettes placed there as well. Only his friends would do something like that. Zachariah was loved by many. I was really going to miss his smile.

Mom and I visited his grave one more time before I didn't need to anymore. I'm not sure why I felt the need to even visit his grave. I felt his presence around me so often. My belief about life and death had begun to change. No longer did I believe in a Heaven or a Hell. I now believed that once a body has died, the spirit lives on and watches over loved ones. I think the spirit continues on a new journey. It may be in another physical life or may become someone's Guardian Angel; as I had felt Zachariah was a Guardian over me. I don't know exactly what is waiting for each of us, after our death. I do know the spirit lives on. I have had too many visits from loved ones who have passed, to believe anything else.

The letter Zachariah wrote to his love didn't make it to her because it felt like he was stopping me from giving it to her. Maybe, he wanted her to move on and live life. Occasionally I see Zachariah, not just in my dream state, but his form while I am awake. I am not making this up and know for certain that Zachariah is one of my guardian angels.

I feel his energy all around me. " I love you, Zachariah."

Thomas Joiner, Florida State University's Bright-Burton professor of Psychology, who has devoted many years on the study of suicide made this comment:*"Tomorrow there are 80 families in the United States alone, who will lose someone to suicide."* That tomorrow, for our family happened during Memorial weekend 2010, when my sister Shirley, took her life. The shock we all felt that day rippled through the very core of our souls, leaving us with the most unbelievable sorrow we had ever experienced.

The call reached me at home while writing. I was told to go to my sister's home at once. When I asked why, no reason was given, but by the tone of the caller's voice, it had to be bad. As I was nearing Shirley's home, the sight of the police car and EMS vehicle confirmed it. Something tragic must of had happened, because everywhere I looked, before getting out of my car, there were people grieving. I took a face count of all those who were standing and sitting in the front yard. No where among the people, was Shirley to be found.

The announcement of Shirley's suicide left me stunned. My first impulse was to find Mom, because not only did she lose a daughter, she had just lost her best friend. When Mom approached me, I hugged her as hard as I could, while telling her, in between my crying, "I'm so sorry, Mom." The rest of the day and well into the night, the family gathered and together we shared memories that later initiated the process of our own personal mourning.

After I had returned home, I sat for the longest time contemplating the topic of suicide. I pushed aside as many "What if" and "If only" scenarios I possibly could, in order to focus on "What was." Why? What was her reasoning for choosing to end her life? I can honestly say, trying to guess her reason(s), caused me more anguish than any sense of acceptance. In doing so, my thoughts went back to the "What if" and "If only."

In the end, there was nothing to do but acknowledged the fact that Shirley took whatever reason, for taking her own life, with her the day of her death. If I hadn't completely allowed myself to do that, I would have remained stuck, in the belief that I "Could have" or "Should have" done something to prevent her death.

In time, I have discovered that I really didn't need to know the reason(s). For me, closure came in the form of accepting that Shirley had made a personal choice. If I was ever going to fully honor her life, I would have to honor her death as well. There seemed to be something wrong about *needing* to honor her choice to die. I know I wouldn't feel any need to honor the way by which she died, if her death was caused by an accident or terminal disease. Then again, no other form of death has a stigma placed on it, as suicide has.

Out of my personal experience, of being a survivor of a loved one whom committed suicide, I arrived at the understanding that death is death. No matter, the way by which it occurs. So, after many months of contemplating my sister's suicide, the final question left to ask myself was this: "What do I want to carry with me from this experience? Do I wish to remain attached to the way Shirley had died, or do I wish to celebrate her life and cherish my memories I carry of her?" I wholeheartedly chose to carry with me, those cherished memories.

CHAPTER THIRTY-TWO

HEATHER'S WORDS

ONE DAY WHILE MOM AND I were sitting at the kitchen table, I told her that I was having trouble breathing. Taking deep breaths was causing me some discomfort. It felt as though my right lung was being squeezed. My discomfort wasn't real bad, but I was concerned. Maybe, the breathing difficulty was caused by not sitting up straight. Over the years, I noticed that I sat more sideways in my wheelchair. Sitting up straight made my back ache. Leaning to one side didn't cause my back to hurt, so I kept on sitting in that position. I don't know why this was starting to bother me now. I guess life was about to take me on another journey.

Mom said she would make an appointment with my family doctor; Dr. Ausiello. I agreed. I knew he would know what was happening to me. Dr. Ausiello was Great Grandma White's doctor and also my dad's family physician. He became my doctor when I moved in with dad, back when I was in the first grade. Dr. Ausiello took me under his wing and thought of me as a daughter. He was always straight forward with his thoughts; I liked that. What I liked about Dr. Ausiello the most, is that he talked to me as a real person, not talked about me like I wasn't in the room. His daughter, is the same age as I. We never hung out together, but talked in school. She was always very kind to me.

After examining my spine, Dr. Ausiello recommended that I be seen by a specialist. He was convinced my breathing trouble was caused from scoliosis. It had appeared that the scoliosis had advanced since he had seen me last. The amount of curvature of my spine may be causing my rib cage to press against my lung. If this was the case, he said that I had better address the issue right away and not wait.

Mom and I then talked to him about our visit with Stacy, the family member who is the podiatrist, and what Stacy had said about my toes, along with having an ultrasound done on my legs. Mom and I then asked his opinion on the surgeries. Stacy mentioned, that might make it possible to correct my scissoring. We asked if he, Dr. Ausiello, thought there was a possibility of me walking and not having to be in a wheelchair. Dr. Ausiello agreed with Stacy's prognosis, but added that a specialist would be better at determining whether or not my back could withstand the weight of walking.

He then went on to inform mom and I that walking would not happen overnight. The entire process could take up to three years. There would be several surgeries involved and a lot of therapy. I was surprised when he said I might very well have a 75% chance of getting out of my wheelchair and walk. I even may be able to dance at my senior prom. I was excited! I thought my dream of being able to walk would be coming true. As a little girl, I dream that one day I would be walking and not stuck in a wheelchair for the rest of my life.

If I could walk, I might be able to drive. Well, I wasn't completely sure about driving. My reflexes are really quite slow. But, walking. Finally, I would be able to do things with my friends. Maybe if they didn't have to worry about transferring me in and out of a vehicle, I might be asked to hang out with them. There would also be no more hassles of loading and unloading my wheelchair into the trunk of a car. The first thing I would do when I started walking, would be just that; walking. I couldn't imagine walking without falling or without using those bulky crutches I used. It wouldn't matter if I had to use a cane as long as I was walking.

Mom mentioned to Dr. Ausiello that her and I had already been discussing looking into the surgeries and what hospitals we were considering. Mom believed Shirner's Children Hospital in Chicago, or Cleveland Clinic Childrens Hospital in Ohio, would be the best. I wanted to go to Advanced Care Hospital near Detroit. Dr. Ausiello said all three hospitals had an excellent reputation and either one would provide me with the best of care. He told us to let him know our decision and he would gladly set up an appointment with one of their Orthopedic surgeons.

Shortly after our visit with Dr. Ausiello, Mom said since it was me, going through the surgeries, I should have final say where I wanted to go. Mom called Dr. Ausiello with the choice. Just as he had said, he arranged an appointment with Holly, an Orthopedic surgeon, for September 11th, 2006, at Advanced Care.

In every form of education, there are certain requirements one has to achieve in order to graduate. Throughout K-12 grades, certain achievements have to be reached in order to advance to the higher grade. During High school and if one attends college, teachers and professors hand out a syllabus, outlining topics that will be covered and their expectation of the student. But, in life, the most challenging and learning experience every human is born into, no syllabus is provided.

Wouldn't it be nice to receive a syllabus of some sort that outlines the topics each one of us will be addressing throughout our life span? Included in the life syllabus, a check list so one could keep track of one's progress. In all fairness, I think when one reaches a certain age, a syllabus should magically appear.

Would a life syllabus take away surprises, lessen the learning experiences, or change the course of ones decision making? Perhaps to some extent, but how often does an individual really pay attention to guidelines and requirements without trying to sidestep any unpleasantness in some way? No, I believe life would still bring about surprises and lessons, even if a life syllabus was given. However, with the existence of a life syllabus, Heather and I would have had at least some type of warning of how the two of us were about to embark on the most challenging experience of our lifetime thus far.

Over a three year period of time, Heather and myself would endure challenges that made whatever we experienced in the past, seem like a walk in the park. Every ounce of our personal strength to cope, along with Heather's and my faith in doctors would be challenged, including the wisdom of a select few at Advanced Care Hospital. Before our journey was all said and done with, perhaps the most agonizing question we would be faced with: "Would we ever find the help that would make it possible for Heather to regain her independence and move on with her life?"

191

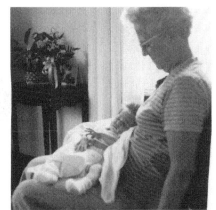

Heather and Great Grandma White

The Lid Drawer

Heather Getting Into Mischief

Heather and Laddie

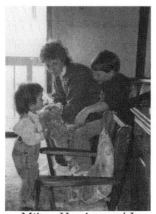

Mikey, Heather, and I

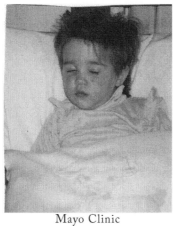

Mayo Clinic

193

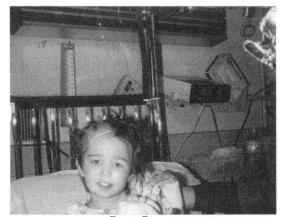

Brain Biopsy

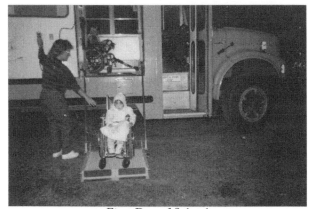

First Day of School

Graduation at Little People Land

Heather and Sebastian fixed

Prom Night

Heather and Her Boys

High School Graduation

Wedding Photo

Heather and O'Brien

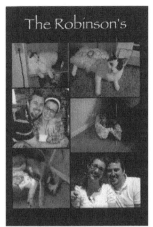

The Robinsons

Katie

Mikey and Family

Part Three

"Anyone can give up, it's the easiest thing in the world to do. But to hold it together when everyone else would understand if you fell apart, that's true strength."

Author Unknown

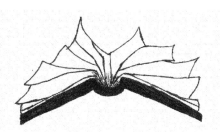

CHAPTER THIRTY-THREE

HEATHER'S WORDS

*W*OW! I COULD NOT BELIEVE that I was about to begin my Junior year in high school and how in a few weeks, I would be turning seventeen. I was happy that most of my classes were going to be easy. However, there was one class I knew of that was going to be hard. I was taking Chemistry that year and knew the class would require a lot of studying.

Even before school started, I knew the school was going to feel empty without seeing Zachariah's beautiful smile, along with Antwone. A friend told me that Antwone had moved away from Greenville during the summer. I wished I had known he was moving, at least I could have said goodbye. I still carried the memory of my first kiss with Antwone. I guess I always will.

During lunch, Elizabeth and I still ate together like we always had, but after I was done eating, I usually left the cafeteria in order to talk to other students in the halls. Some days I would get out of my wheelchair and sit on the bench in Common Hall, where many of the students gathered during lunch period. If there wasn't anyone I knew in that area, I would just watch and listen to the other students talking amongst themselves.

What a sad feeling I felt back then, when I listened to what the students did with their friends during the weekend, or when they made plans to hang out on the upcoming weekend. Except for going over to Elizabeth's house and a couple of birthday parties, I didn't have that type of experience those students were talking about. I never went shopping with a group of friends, nor to a football game or to a movie with a group of friends. Every time I saw a circle of friends together having a great time, I wished I was in that group. I always wondered what it would be like to have that special bond which is shared by the group. I think many students overlooked the possibility that I was just like them, wanting to hangout without parents around. I guess my disabilities hid that part of me from them.

It wasn't like I wanted to be popular or anything, I just wanted to experience one time of being invited out to do something by a group of friends. One time driving to the mall. One time going to the football game, while dressed in our school colors and afterward going to a bonfire. One time seeing a movie with friends. Whenever I did anything such as shopping or going to a movie, it was always with family.

I imagine that every young person with disabilities, at one time or another, has asked them self, "What if?" What if I wasn't handicapped? Would I be invited by others to do things with them? Would I be asked or be the one asking someone to a dance and have them accept? I often wondered how I would be if I didn't get sick when I was younger and could walk. For the longest time, I thought that maybe I wasn't asked to do things with others was because I would slow them down or that they may be uncomfortable being seen with someone in a wheelchair. I began to think that maybe after the upcoming surgery, when I regained the ability to walk, I would then be asked to do things with others. Deep down I didn't believe things would change, because it shouldn't matter if one is in a wheelchair or not, true friends would have asked all along.

One weekend, I wanted to see the movie *"Invincible,"* which was playing at the cinema in Greenville. I called up some of my friends to see if they wanted to go. Elizabeth couldn't and the others were either busy or didn't want to. My brother, Kaleb, and our cousin, wanted to watch *"Snakes on the Plane."* Both movies started at the same time, so there would be no problem if we went to the cinema together, then went our separate ways in the theater. This would be the first time I went to watch a movie without supervision. On the day we went to the theater, Momma Denise dropped the three of us off in front of the cinema and gave us money for the tickets, popcorn and pop. I couldn't get any popcorn or pop because I had no way to carry them into the theater. I was using my crutches that day to walk.

Once I purchased my ticket, I walked into the dimly lit theater and chose a seat near the front. Sitting in front of me were a group of kids near my age. I watched them as they were laughing and having a lot of fun being there together. Even though I wished some friends came with me, watching those kids in front of me didn't make me feel bad. I felt happy anyway, because today people in the cinema had seen that I was independent. It was an amazing feeling to be on my own. After the movie, I waited for everyone to leave before I walked out. A good feeling swept over me that day because I did what I wanted. For a brief period of time, a part of me forgot that I was handicapped.

At school, I was telling everyone that I had an appointment with an Orthopedic specialist. I talked about how Dr. Ausiello had felt there was a good possibility of me getting out of my wheelchair and walking on my own. That was why I was going to see the specialist. Everyone I talked to wished me luck. I was so anxious to hear what the specialist had to say and if there really was a way for me to walk on my own.

The day before the appointment, I stayed the night with Mom. Mikey was coming with us which made me so happy. Mikey had always been a huge part of my life. Watching over me and protecting me. I knew he had missed out on a lot of attention from Mom when I was younger, but he never showed any dislike toward me for that. He was more than a big brother to me. He had been my playmate, my caregiver at times and even acted as a parent when Mom was at work during the summer.

Mom said that it would take us close to three hours to get to the hospital. Since we didn't know our way around the area where it was located, she believed that we had better include some lost time. Adding that factor in, Mom figured the trip there would take us about four hours.

We left about 6 am the following morning. I was glad that I had brought a book with me to read on our way there to busy myself. When we reached the city, we became lost as expected, but it was fun to get back on track. I was glad Mom wasn't one of those people who gets upset whenever she gets lost.

When we drove by the hospital, I couldn't believe how big it was. There were medical doctors, along with medical students walking everywhere on the sidewalks. We had some trouble finding the entrance, but after calling for help, we managed to locate the right road. The hospital was huge inside and there were many people coming and going. We stopped at the front desk and asked how to get to the specialist's office. All I could think of as we made our way there, was what the specialist had to say.

The moment I saw Holly, the orthopedic specialist whom was taking on my case, I thought she looked too young to be a doctor; to be my doctor. However, as soon as Holly begun to speak to me, I just knew we were going to get along great. The energy I felt around her was so positive and she actually addressed me while talking, instead of talking to Mom about me. Mom and I would never refer to Holly as Dr. Thomas. We addressed her as Holly right from the moment we meet her. I guess she instantly became family right from the start.

Holly sent us to x-ray shortly after our introduction to one another. It would be the first time I had an x-ray taken of my back. While getting the x-rays, the radiology technician told me to sit this way and that way, then asked me to lay down for a couple of more x-rays. I guess Holly wanted every angle of my back and hips. As soon as the x-rays were taken, Mom, Mikey and I, headed back to Holly's office.

Holly then showed Mom and I the images of my spine. My spine looked like a big "S." Holly pointed out that I had at least a 65 degree curve in my spine. She showed us how my lower ribs on my right side were resting on the top of my hip. No wonder why I couldn't breathe that well, my right lung was being squeezed by my ribs. By the way the x-ray looked, I really did need surgery. Not only for helping me get out of my wheelchair, but to live a long life.

I couldn't believe what the images were showing. I sat there wondering why my parents didn't have x-rays taken of my spine while I was growing up, instead of waiting until I was this old. If they had, I probably would not have had breathing problems to begin with. I kept those thoughts to myself and did not say anything to Mom or Dad.

Holly began talking about the surgery that was needed to correct my spine. Once the curve in my spine was corrected and if I could bare the weight of standing, she said that there possibly could be a 75 percent chance of walking on my own. There it was. The words I was waiting for all day. Holly said almost the same things as Dr. Ausiello.

Reaching that goal was going to take time and physical therapy. Tons of physical therapy. As much as I hated doing therapy, this time

I was going to push and push myself. I was ready to walk. Holly set a date for the surgery and told Mom and I to let her know if we wanted to go through with it. If we did, October 4, 2006, would be the day. Of course, Mom and I chose to have the surgery. We would meet one more time with Holly to go over the procedure and to ask questions, if we had any. From October 4th, 2006, and throughout the following two and one half years, I had no idea that my life was going to turn into a nightmare. A nightmare, I thought would never end.

The morning of September 11th, 2006, Mikey, Heather and I traveled to Advanced Care Hospital. The hospital's reputation was outstanding and the pediatric ward, where Heather would be staying if surgery was decided upon, was ranked as being one of the best pediatric care unit in the nation. It seemed reasonable to assume that Heather would receive the best medical attention and patient care offered at that facility.

The drive seemed like an eternity. I imagine this was due to the fact that I was so anxious to hear what the specialist was going to say. Stopping at Burger King in Ionia that morning for breakfast, marked the beginning of a ritual we would carry out throughout Heather's ordeal. Funny how little the things, such as stopping for breakfast, quickly formed into a tradition and how that tradition seemed to complete each trip we made.

Mikey was the appointed navigator. He would warn me when we were about to reach our exit off the interstate. He was chosen as the appointed navigator because getting lost is only to be expected whenever I am behind the wheel. I either become lost in thought or distracted by the surroundings. Many times, I manage to be in the wrong lane when exiting is needed. Navigator or not, it's best to add lost time to any traveling when I am driving somewhere unfamiliar.

The first question that popped into my mind when we exited off I-94 and entered the unfamiliar city was, "Is hospital signs so costly that only a few can be placed along route to the hospital complex itself?" There was one hospital sign pointing us in the direction of the hospital just off of I-94. Other than that, we were left clueless. Following the step by step directions, sent to me by Holly's secretary was not exactly possible. The reason in two words: "*road construction.*"

Side roads had to be taken as a result, with no hospital signs along the way for guidance.

When we did come across the hospital, I could not locate the road to the entrance. Finally, I pulled into a parking lot and called Holly's office for help. With all the side roads we had taken, plus going in circles around the hospital, for what seemed like hours, I managed to pick a parking lot right across from the entrance we were searching for. Go figure.

Advanced Care was so impressing, enormous, and extremely busy. I had never seen so many patients and physicians gathered in one place before. Locating the orthopedic lounge, as I called it, was not that hard to find. I referred to the waiting area as a lounge because comfortable seating was provided and not those hard chairs commonly used in waiting areas at hospitals.

Once I finished signing Heather in, the three of us waited in anticipation to meet Holly. As Heather mentioned, Holly looked way too young to be a orthopedic surgeon. I guess, I automatically assumed she would be an older woman. Holly was such a small framed woman, but when it came time to lift Heather on the table for observation, she lifted Heather up with such ease. Once on the table, Holly immediately began stretching Heather's legs, while checking the tightness in each. After which, Holly had Heather stand to get a better view of her posture and gait as Heather took a few steps.

I was instantly impressed by Holly's demeanor. When talking to Heather and I, Holly took the time and shown a lot patience as Heather answered all of Holly's questions. This approach she had taken with Heather was what established a trusting bond between the three of us. Heather was being viewed as competent and not considered incapable of understanding what was being discussed. I had witnessed time and time again, when dealing with other doctors, Heather was treated as if she had a mental impairment. All because she was in a wheelchair.

After that brief interaction with Holly, Heather was sent to x-ray. On our way to have x-rays, we passed what would become a source of breaking the bank, so to speak; the gift shop. I am a stuff bear collector and by the amount of bears in the gift shop that appeared in desperate need of a home, I knew it would be hard to leave the hospital without buying one; or two.

After finishing with the x-rays, I began to feel nervous as the three of us were making our way back to Holly's office. I was anxious to view the x-rays, but I was also afraid to look at the consequences of not paying more attention to Heather's physical development. Maybe it wasn't a nervous feeling after all, but a sense of guilt that I was feeling.

Viewing the image of Heather's spine was such a shock. The reality of how Alex and I failed Heather could not have had been more evident. I literally felt myself slumping in disgrace. All I could think of was how the severity of Heather's scoliosis was the direct result of our failure of being aware of how Heather's posture would be effected by sitting in her wheelchair throughout the years she had.

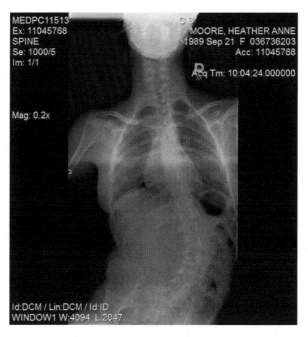

The thought of Heather developing scoliosis over time never crossed my mind. I always imagined scoliosis was a birth defect. That goes to show how little I was educated on the issues that may arise during Heather's life.

The results of Heather's physical exam was as follows:

She had marked increased lordosis of her lumbar spine. In layman's terms, Heather was swayed backed. Her lower spine curved inward more then usual, making her buttocks protrude more than what is considered normal. Heather internally rotated her left leg approximately 45 degrees, whereas, her right leg appeared to be rather straight. Holly commented on Heather being flat footed and how tight her hip flexors and hamstrings felt.

The results of Heather's x-rays revealed a 65 degree Levo-Convex curve. Levo-Convex curve is a curve of the lower spine twisting to the left. Adding to that, Heather's right hip was about three inches higher than her left hip. Her rib cage was impinging on her right hip and there was rib cage torsion noted. Heather's ribs were widely separated on her left side, and were narrowed spaced on her right side.

Holly recommended posterior spinal fusion. Meaning, Heather's spine would be fused together from the middle of her shoulder blades down to her pelvis. Surgery for adolescents with scoliosis is only recommended when curves are greater than 40 to 45 degrees. Heather exceeded that range. Without a lot of options available for correcting, or at least decreasing Heather's scoliosis, surgery seemed to be the way to go.

Holly said to expect 4-6 weeks off from school and that Heather should return to normal activities within a short period of time, but with some limitations. Holly also informed us of several risks involved with an invasive surgery such as this. Infection was always a possibility and there was a slight risk of Heather becoming paralyzed. We were also informed that there would be some blood loss during the procedure and we might want to contact family members for donating blood; two pints worth.

Before leaving her office, Holly told Heather and me to call her secretary with our decision. Heather and I spent a lot of time discussing the surgery and how it would affect her school year. Was this the best time to pursue the surgery, or would it be best to wait? The two of us believed the sooner the better. Home bound school would be needed and I was certain that Heather's school do it's best to accommodate her.

So without further researching the surgery or getting another opinion, Heather decided to have the surgery and I backed her decision. Like many other individuals, Heather and I entrusted our hopes and Heather's health into a medical specialist, expecting only positive results. This actually places a huge amount of responsibility on the part of the specialist. Kinda unfair, but it is done none the less. October 4th, 2006 would be the day Heather was to undergo the surgery. It would also mark the day her and I begun one hell of nightmare.

CHAPTER THIRTY-FOUR

HEATHER'S WORDS

*T*HE REASON I WASN'T MAD at my parents for not taking me to see a specialist or even having a back x-ray taken when I was younger, because I believe that everything in life happens when it is time for it to happen. So, September 11th, 2006, was the exact day that life planned for me to have my x-rays taken. Instead of being upset by the unbelievable images of my x-rays that day, I just begun counting down the days till October 4th. I was ready for the surgery.

Mr. Gates was going to become the principal at Greenville High school that same year. By this time, I called him Gates instead of Mr. Gates. He was more than my principal, he had become my friend. I felt comfortable enough around him to talk about anything. He was the first person I talked to about the surgery. I knew he would be excited for me and also knew he had a good idea of what I went through being in a wheelchair. His wife was in a wheelchair as well, so he understood the frustrations I felt at times.

The two of us talked about the reason for having the surgery and how this was the first step in maybe getting out of my wheelchair for good. I told him about the x-rays and how my right lung was being crushed from my ribs. We also discussed home school and my worry about being able to continue at Greenville since I would be staying with Mom during my recovery and perhaps throughout the school year. Gates told me not to worry. He would make arrangements with the ISD bus garage about transporting me back and forth when the time arrived. He would also arrange for a teacher to come over to Mom's for home bound school. Gates just wanted me to focus on recovery.

The day before the surgery, Mom came to pick me up at Dads. Since I wasn't allowed to eat anything after midnight that night, we stopped at Burger King before going to her house and I pigged out on a triple stacker and a large order of onion rings. This would be the last time I ate that much for months to come.

Mom thought we should drive to the city that night and get a room near the hospital, since I was scheduled to be at the hospital at six in the morning. This would save us a lot of time driving in the morning. Family members pitched in for gas and hotel money. I thought that was very thoughtful. After packing Mom's clothes and personal belongings at her house, her and I took off for the city.

We stayed at a Motel 6 that night. It wasn't far from the hospital so I could sleep in a little. Before going to bed, I took a bath as Mom was getting things ready for the next morning. After my bath, Mom brought a container for a urine sample I needed to bring in with me for the required pregnancy test. It was a great idea doing this at the hotel, because it would have taken me a long time to go pee at the hospital. With my shy bladder, I might have missed my surgery all because they needed a urine sample before surgery.

Morning came fast and the next thing I knew, I was staring out the car window at the entrance going into the hospital, while Mom was taking my wheelchair out of the trunk of the car. My heart was beating fast as Mom and I walked into the hospital. I was so nervous and excited at the same time. One step closer to my dream of walking was all I thought about. I wasn't that worried about having surgery.

Not surprising, Mom forgot the way to the prep-operating area, so yes, we asked for directions. Once there, I handed the receptionist my pee as Mom grabbed the paper work that need to be filled out. Even before Mom had a chance to finish filling out the paper work, a nurse came over to where Mom and I were sitting and asked if I was Heather Moore. Mom and I both said yes. The two of us were escorted into the prep-operative room. The nurse asked me what my birth date was, to make certain I was Heather Moore. This question would be asked over and over throughout my stay, as a means of identification. Birth date or social security number.

I noticed four other people waiting for surgery as the nurse took

Mom and I to the stall I would be placed in. It looked like a stall, because it was a small space with a bed and some medical equipment, closed off by curtains. I was then asked to change into a hospital gown. At that time, I cared about being naked in front of strangers, so I asked the nurse to leave while Mom helped me into the gown. The nurse stepped out and returned moments later with warm blankets for me. I was glad because the room was really cold.

The nurse then said that she needed to put an IV in my hand. In the past, nurses never had much luck with inserting IVs in my hand. I asked her if she could put the IV higher on my arm instead, while telling her straight off, "I hate needles!" I asked the nurse if she could count out loud to three before sticking me, this always seemed to prepare me for the prick and I didn't flinch as much. She did such a good job, I didn't feel much of anything as she hooked up the IV.

There were so many doctors, nurses and technicians coming in and out of my stall after that. Mom and I met everyone who was going to assist Holly in the operating room. They all seemed really nice and I felt safe knowing they were going to be watching over me. When it was time to go into surgery, the nurse wanted to give me some medication to relax me. I asked to be awake while they pushed me into the operating room. I wanted to see what it looked liked. She said it wasn't a problem and that I could be given something in the operating room instead. Mom gave me one last kiss and told me that she would see my face when I woke up.

The operating room was really big and *COLD*. Above me were maybe three huge lights. Instruments were laid out and there were machines everywhere. I thought it was amazing that I saw the operating room before being sedated. One of the assisting doctors asked me if I was ready and I said "yes."

The anesthesiologist put a mask over my face and told me to count back from ten. The smell of it made me sick so he grab a syringe and put some medicine in my IV to make me sleepy. I had no idea why they tell you to count back from ten. I barely made it to seven. I think they should tell you to count to three. Anyway, the next thing I remember was my name being called out.

When I was trying to open my eyes, I heard the voices of Grandma Sandy and Dad. I wanted to cry because I was so happy that they came. When I opened my eyes I saw a doctor instead. He was asking if I felt okay. The only thing I could do was shake my head yes. I then whispered Dad. The doctor didn't hear me and bent closer to me as I repeated what I had said. I said Dad, Mom. He told me that they were there and eager to see me. Dad was the first person I saw before Mom and Grandma Sandy peeked around my bedside.

I instantly begun crying. The nurse told them that I probably would because the Anesthesia makes everyone more emotional. Dad held my hand and told me he loved me, then Grandma Sandy gave me a kiss. The two of them left shortly afterward. Mom approached me last and gave me a slight hug and kiss. I drifted in and out for a while. Next thing I knew, I was waking up in a different room altogether. It was my hospital room and I noticed Mom was there sitting in a chair with her eyes closed; napping.

As soon as I moved in my bed a tiny bit, Mom immediately opened her eyes. She stood up and came to my bedside and asked if I needed anything. I shook my head yes. While being still very sleepy, I managed to whisper *"water."* I think I was only allowed ice. I don't remember much of that afternoon expect for being examined by so many different doctors.

As I said before, I hated being naked in front of people. I'll tell you one thing, before my stay at Advanced Care was over, any embarrassment I felt before vanished. So many different doctors, nurses, and even medical students had an up close and personal look at my naked behind. Whenever any doctor came in to examine my back, I would automatically throw back the covers myself, giving them a good look at my backside.

I was in some pain, but it wasn't bad at first. If I needed some medicine for pain, I hit the little black button that was hook up to a morphine machine. I was the only one who could push the button. A nurse came into the room about every hour or so to roll me over so I would not get bad sores. The nurses showed Mom how to roll me over as well because she would have to do the same when we returned home. I was beginning to wonder when I would be able to roll myself over. The rolling from one side to the other went on even during the night. It was so hard to get any rest. For weeks that followed, I would have to have pillows tucked behind me supporting my back and in between my legs to help make me comfortable.

Sitting up was difficult for me. My back felt like there was a piece of board strapped to it preventing me from bending or twisting. My back felt really stiff, but I noticed right off that my breathing was back to normal. The pressure I felt before the surgery was gone and I was glad.

During my week at the hospital, I called Gates. I wanted to let him know how I was doing and asked him how he liked being principal. I could tell from his tone of voice that my call meant a lot to him. I had a few visitors during the week, but mostly it was just Mom and me. The physical therapist came around every day. I began to sit on the edge of my bed and before mid week, I was starting to use the commode which meant getting that catheter out of me. I was encouraged to take a few steps, but I couldn't withstand the pain it caused me. The pain seemed to be coming from my lower back and hips.

A few days after surgery, Dad, Momma Denise and the rest of the family came to visit, along with my Aunt Karmen. Mom left the room shortly after their arrival to grab a coffee or a smoke. It was the first time for Mom to have some free time. I remember my Aunt Karmen walking in, shaking her head and saying "your father!" I started laughing at her expression because I knew what she meant by "*your father.*"

Dad is not a pleasant man to ride with in a vehicle. When he is driving, he would say rude comments about others drivers. I knew it must of been a long three hours for Aunt Karmen on their trip to the hospital that day. Whenever I rode with Dad I would always laugh by the way he became angered or frustrated over nothing.

One evening during my recovery week at the hospital, I heard some voices in my room that I didn't recognize. I slowly opened my eyes and saw some guys talking to Mom. I thought maybe they were doctors checking up on me. With being on several different pain meds, I was drifting in and out of sleep. I remember turning my head to face them because my back was facing them. I glanced at the guys and rolled my head back. I was too tired to talk. I do remember feeling that familiar sensation of my behind being exposed. Mom didn't even notice until she saw one of those guys look in that direction. I guess we were so used to this sort of thing happening to me.

Later I asked Mom who the doctors were that she was talking to. She said they wasn't doctors, they were some players from a football team. They came up to the childrens ward to meet the kids and handed out some hats to the kids. I guess, every week members of different sports teams would visit the children in the hospital as a way to lift the childrens spirits. I thought this was a great idea. It also gave the athletes a chance to make a child smile. Mom handed me a hat that was signed by the players who were in my room.

As I looked at the names, I recognized all the names and was surprised that the players actually had been there. I imagine they all had a look at my back side. Good thing I was drowsy. I didn't keep the hat. I gave it to Jordan, one of my friends at school, when I returned back to school. Didn't see the point in keeping it, because to me, it was just a hat with names on it. Just knowing that those guys were in my room meant more to me. I am not a person who goes crazy about those things. Like if I saw a celebrity walking down the street, I would just wave and smile as I went by. That's how I am.

At the end of my stay Mom was becoming sick. You think the hospital would be the last place you would become sick. WRONG! With nurses and doctors going from patient to patient and plus the amount of sickness patients had, there is a huge chance of getting sick. I felt so bad for Mom because she was trying to fight off whatever she was catching, watching over me and dealing with the nurses and doctors. By that time, she was the one who was turning me over every two hours. She didn't get a lot of rest either. I too started coming down with signs of a cold. I was getting fevers. Holly was worried that maybe an infection was setting in, but it didn't. It was nothing serious. All I needed to do was sweat the fever out which I did in a couple of days. After that, I was back to my normal self. Mom wasn't that fortunate.

The last day of my stay at the hospital, I was given a different wheelchair to use while I recovered at home. It was so uncomfortable and oversized. It had no padding whatsoever and I looked so tiny sitting in it. The wheelchair had a high back. This would help support my back while it was healing. I was ready to go home and see our dog Sebastian, along with the rest of the family. What I didn't realize when Mom was driving home was, the night before my surgery at the hotel, would be my last time taking a regular bath, last time crawling, wall surfing, climbing up and down the stairs and even using those ungodly crutches I walked with. I never imagined that I would also be stricken with such unbearable pain. If I knew these things were going to happen, I would not of had gone through with the surgery.

Before Heather's surgery, Heather and I met with Holly to go over the procedure and ask questions or voice any concerns that we may have had. Surprisingly, there were few of each. It seemed as if Heather and I heard what we wanted to hear without considering the slightest possibility of something going wrong.

The details of the surgical procedure didn't raise any concern. It would have appeared that Heather and I was more concerned with the amount of time it would take Heather to resume her daily activities and return back to school. There didn't seem to be the need to worry about risk factors associated with the surgery. Most likely, because Holly assured us that none of her patients had experienced any real serious complications. Looking back on this, I can't believe we were that naïve.

Holly described to us that when Heather was safely sedated, an incision would be made from above her shoulder blades down to her pelvis. The muscles would be stripped up off the spine to allow access to the backs of the vertebra's that lie along her curve. Screws would then be inserted into the spine and Harrington Rods would be placed on both sides of Heather's spine, secured with hooks, in order to reduce the amount of curvature. To fuse her spine, bone would then be added in between the vertebra's (either Heather's own, taken from her hip, or cadaver bone from a bone bank). In Heather's surgery both was used. This procedure would incite a reaction that would result in the spine fusing together.

Holly informed us that the fusion process usually took about 3-6 months, but could continue up to one year. The rods would help prevent the chance of disruption in the bone fusing, that could be caused by twisting or bending of the spine. We were told to expect a 4-7 day hospital stay. Heather and I spent 7 days altogether in the hospital before she was discharged. If Heather had no complications, she may be able to return back to school in 2-4 weeks after surgery. As for Heather returning back to daily living and mobility, there was no set time frame.

Recovery after this type of surgery varied among patients. A lot depended on how Heather's body adjusted to the limitations the surgery would present her with. Holly emphasized the importance of Heather sitting up often and making continuous efforts at standing and taking steps. She also recommended in home physical therapy when Heather was discharged, where the therapist could assist Heather in learning new ways of regaining her independence. There was a lot of information presented to Heather and I during that visit. Most of which I had forgotten before the visit was finished. All I know is that Heather and I left the hospital with such a sense of "*all would be okay.*"

Taking on the role of caregiver for Heather following her surgery, is what I chose to do. I strongly felt that she needed to be with me during her recovery. However, I knew far to well how a relationship could easily dissolve, when challenged with an experience that demands ones attention to shift from the partner and placed on another individual. Nathaniel and I discussed this thoroughly and he assured me his intention of growing old with me would not waiver. More than anything, I needed his reassurance.

So much of my strength and well being rested in him. We seemed to give one another that sense of security in knowing that when life seems to crumble around one, the other will be there to lift you up. Nathaniel said he had the home front covered and not to worry about nothing. The only real worry for the two of us would be the financial scope of things.

For the time being, I would use whatever vacation time I had left, before relying on a family leave of absence. The problem with taking a family leave of absence, is that there would be no income coming in on my part. Thank goodness Nathaniel was great at budgeting money. He had already drawn up a budget that included my loss of income. Things would be tight, but not impossible. This was a huge worry lifted from my shoulders.

Driving to the city and staying at Motel 6, the night before Heather's surgery was a great idea. I'm glad we did this. Not only did it save an early morning commute, but it gave Heather and I alone time. Throughout the night I caught myself staring at Heather in amazement. She had been through so much growing up and yet remained unaffected. Her acceptance, of what ever challenges life presented her with was inspiring. Heather was another source of strength for me. The mother/daughter relationship had grown incredibly close. In the end, this closeness between her and me is what would sustain us in the darkest moments we would soon encounter.

In the prep-operative waiting area, Heather showed no signs of nervousness. I, on the other hand, was beginning to feel apprehensive. The two of us joked around and found it astonishing by the amount of individuals that were going to be involved with her surgery. All those involved with Heather's surgery, whom came and introduced him/her self to Heather, she cheerfully greeted each individual, as if they had been long time friends.

On our last visit with Holly, we were told Heather's surgery could take up to ten hours. Heather and I didn't think nothing about it then, but waiting in the prep-operative room, I was beginning to grasp just how intricate Heather's surgery really was. I could feel the worry begin to stir in the pit of my stomach. Before Heather was taken to the operating room, she underwent a preoperative evaluation. Her vitals, weight, height were recorded along with a brief medical history relating to any medications she may have experienced any negative side effects; namely undergoing anesthesia and the use of pain meds.

They also made a notation of how Heather was able to stand quite easily and being able to walk short distances. Crawling and the use of wall surfing was Heather's method of moving throughout the house. She was, for the most part, independent with her daily activities, but needed some assistance with dressing (mostly pulling up and fashioning her jeans) on occasions. It was also noted during the evaluation, Heather had Cerebral Palsy and attended regular school. She had *NO* chronic pain and her current pain score was *ZERO/NONE*.

CHAPTER THIRTY-FIVE

*J*UST AS HOLLY HAD MENTIONED, Heather's surgery, along with waking up from the anesthetic totaled ten hours. I waited alone in the waiting area for the first few hours before Alex and Grandma Sandy arrived. Passing the time by reading, napping and sneaking out to have a smoke every now and then. Like all hospitals today, Advanced Care Hospital was a smoke free facility. Meaning, to smoke, one must walk across the street from the hospital. In spite of the hospital's policy on smoking, I, like many other parents and family members of patients, chose to chance my luck with smoking in the parking ramp area. While I was out and about, I also spent some time seeking out different locations throughout the parking area for later smoking. For I knew there would be an urgency for a late night cigarette during the week stay with Heather. Only those who smoke can grasp the importance of such strategic planning.

The waiting area I was sitting in, filled to capacity shortly before noon. Talk about feeling boxed in. There was little room to move about with the amount of people occupying the small area. The flow of people coming and going seemed never ending. I was lucky enough to sit next to a window in the waiting area. My view of the outside world may not have been the greatest, but it did serve as a kind of distraction.

It was hard to believe, that what had started out as being an attempt to get Heather walking and out of her wheelchair, actually ended up revealing a serious health issue. I found myself wondering to what extent Heather's home care would require of me. If what Holly had described to Heather and I regarding Heather's recovery, she should be back to being independent in no time. I strongly felt I needed to be Heather's caregiver during her recovery. For the most part, Heather and I journeyed alone throughout her ordeal resulting from the vaccine reaction. It seemed only fitting that her and I would journey together again.

Updates on the progress of Heather's surgery was given every two hours. So far, Heather was tolerating the surgery well with no reported complications. After what seemed like days of waiting, a nurse's aid approached Alex, Grandma Sandy and myself. She announced that Heather was out of surgery and asked us to follow her to a room where Holly was waiting to brief us on Heather's condition.

Holly said she was pleased with the surgery and that Heather experienced no complications. We would be allowed to see Heather in the recovery room once Heather was stable enough for visitors. After our conversation with Holly, we went back to the waiting room, feeling relieved that the surgery was finally over. When Heather regained consciousness and her vitals stable, the three of us were escorted to the recovery room. Seeing Heather for the first time since that morning was some what of a shock to me. Holly had warned us to expect some swelling to occur in Heather's face from lying on her stomach for that amount of time. There was a lot of swelling in her face. She was almost unrecognizable to me.

As Heather was trying to focus on Alex, I automatically headed for the other side of her hospital bed to inspect the incision. All I was able to see, was what appeared to be one continuous bandage, starting above her shoulder blades extending down past her hips. I stared at her bandage wondering how it was even possible to recover as soon as Holly had predicted. Heather's overall appearance was very overwhelming, as she lay there looking so tiny and vulnerable. I suddenly felt that familiar sense of being helpless in comforting her. I wanted to trade places with Heather and take on whatever pain and discomfort that I imagined she was feeling. In reality, Heather wasn't feeling much of anything at that time.

It meant the world to Heather seeing her dad standing next to the bed when she was alert enough to recognize him. He was the first person Heather wanted to see when she woke up. After a short visit, the three of us left recovery and grabbed a bite to eat, while waiting for Heather to be transferred to the pediatric ward. In the cafeteria, we ate in the Wendy's section. I heard of McDonald's being in some hospitals, but never a Wendy's.

Once Heather was transferred to pediatric ward, Alex and

Grandma Sandy stayed a while longer before saying their goodbyes to Heather and leaving for home. Heather's room, where I would call home for the next seven days, was cluttered and small. We shared the room with another patient and the patient's mother. My sleeping quarters, so to speak, resembled a full size truck seat that was positioned under a huge window overlooking a rooftop. At least I could see sky which gave me some type of comfort. As anyone who has stayed with a family member in the hospital, knows there is no such thing as privacy. However, I was quite fortunate to have a curtain that could be drawn at night, encasing me between the walls of my truck seat bed.

Heather drifted in and out of sleep throughout the remainder of the day of her surgery and the next day. Nurses and doctors were coming in all hours of the night checking on either Heather or her room mate. I slept little. To pass some time during the night when I wasn't sleeping, I walked the halls of the hospital trying to familiarize myself with my temporary home. At first, I ended up getting lost on every outing and had to ask for directions back to Heather's floor. It wasn't until toward the end of our stay, when I was able to find my way back without help.

My mornings begun early. I would go down to the main lobby, grab a coffee, couple of doughnuts and head outside to where my car was parked. I would sit on the hood of my car and watch the sun rise while drinking coffee, eating doughnuts and sneaking a smoke while peering out across the surrounding area. I would then go back to Heather's room to attend to her. During the day, more trips were taken outside where I explored the hospital grounds just to busy myself. On the warm days, I would take Heather outside to soak up some sun if she felt up to it.

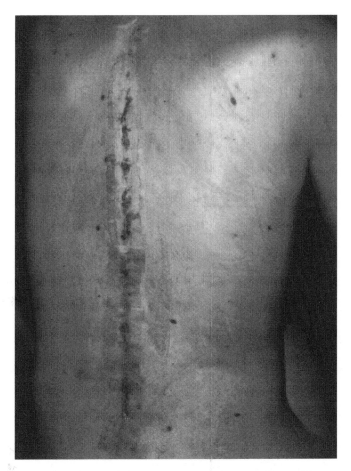

By the end of day three, I begun to feel as if a cold was coming on. My body was achy and I started having intermediate fevers. What didn't help matters any was the inconsistent room temperature during the night. One minute the room was extremely warm, the next it felt as though the air conditioner was on.

Right from day one, I was feeling nauseated from the ungodly stench of hand sanitizer that filled the air in the hospital. Bottles upon bottles of hand sanitizer were placed everywhere. By every room and at each nurse's station, the bathrooms....everywhere. I bet the manufacturing company of the brand used by the hospital, must have loved this particular hospital.

In the days that followed, I learned how to properly turn Heather from side to side in her bed. I soon took over that role and didn't have to rely on the nurse any longer. I also was shown a completely new technique of transferring Heather from the bed to her wheelchair and commode.

The transfers required a lot of upper body strength and it didn't take long before my back muscles begun to ache from lifting Heather in this new position. Stands to reason, Heather's body weight and my own was close to being the same.

The first time I saw Heather sit upright was amazing to say the least. Her back appeared to be completely straight. One would not have ever guessed she had scoliosis. There wasn't the slightest evidence of a curve. The day her bandage was changed was another story. I almost gasped out loud from the sight of the incision. Up until then, it still didn't register that Heather actually underwent a surgery of such magnitude.

Along with the Morphine Heather was on, she was given Diazepam; a drug to treat anxiety, insomnia and also effective on muscles spasms. Oxycodone, which is used to treat moderate to severe pain, along with Acetaminophen, which basically is like Tylenol. These were given to Heather throughout the course of each day and evening. No wonder Heather remained quite drowsy during our stay. By the third day, she was taken off the Morphine pump.

Heather and I met the physical therapist assigned to her on day two. His objective was to get Heather standing and taking steps before her discharge. Unfortunately, Heather's progress in achieving those goals would become a source of disappointment for her therapist.

Standing and attempting to take steps caused a lot of pain in Heather's lower back/hips region. Before the scheduled sessions with the physical therapist, Heather was given pain medicine to help relax the tightness in her legs and pain in her hips. Right off, I could see that this approach defeated the purpose it was intended for. For the obvious reason, the pain medicine made Heather sleepy and somewhat limp.

Following her surgery, I notice that every time Heather sat upright, either on the edge of the bed or on the commode, her legs instantly began to quiver. More so, when she stood up. Her legs did not do this before the surgery and when I questioned the therapist about this, he believed the quivering stemmed from not being mobile since her surgery. In the back of my mind, his reply made no sense. It didn't seem possible that within two days Heather's legs could become that weak. No, something else had to be causing the quivering. In order to stop the quivering, Heather's legs had to be held downward with quite a bit of force.

I watched as the therapist grew inpatient a little more each day with Heather. Apparently, she wasn't making the kind effort he expected from her. Heather also picked up on this as well. Her willingness to comply with the therapists requests dwindled with each session. To make matters worse for Heather, on one occasion, I noticed that I sided with the therapist. Demanding that Heather put forth more effort. I felt so bad when I became aware of my remark. I knew she was giving her all, but there was a part of me that wanted Heather to meet the therapists' expectations. I had it all wrong.

It wasn't Heather's responsibility to live up to the therapists' expectations, it was the therapist whom had the responsibility of discovering the best approach that worked for Heather. Unless the therapist had tried everything in his power to approach Heather with activities she could tolerate, he had no grounds on which to criticize her. The day when the therapist remarked that he was more or less wasting his time if Heather wasn't going to try harder, was the day Heather gave up trying altogether.

By day five, we both wanted to go home. My cold symptoms seemed to worsen each day. Now 1 was dealing with upper chest congestion which made sleeping even more harder. My coughing was becoming non-stop. By then, Heather and 1 were both fighting fevers. It was feared that Heather's fevers may be a sign that an infection may be setting in. Thank goodness it wasn't an infection, we both were just fighting off a cold. Heather broke her fevers without much effort, but I would carry mine home with me.

On the evening the football players visited the children in the hospital, three young men entered our room. I had no clue as to who they were. Heather's roommate knew the instant they walked in. Her voice echoed with excitement as she called out the name of one of the players. Heather was so drowsy at that time, it didn't registered who was in our room. Before I even noticed Heather's bare butt exposed to the world, two of the players peeked around the curtain and whispered "Hi." I quickly covered Heather's rear end, but not before they noticed.

They introduced themselves to me as the two made their way

around the curtain. We exchanged some small talk before I asked if they knew another player from the team. The only reason I knew of this player was through Heather. He played high school football on the East Grand Rapids team, which played against Greenville High school.

The two players quickly remarked that they knew who I was asking about and commented on what a cheat, he was when playing Monopoly. From that point on it was like talking with ordinary young men, not well known football players. Their presence in the childrens ward meant a lot to the kids. It also brightened my night as well.

October 10th, was the day Heather was going to be discharged from the hospital. With the number of times I would be rolling Heather side to side, I knew there was no way I would manage turning Heather, without causing some type of head injury to myself, if she were to lay in the lower bunk bed at home. Using a hospital bed would be perfect for Heather. I began to ask family members if they knew of anyone whom may have access to one. Thankfully, Alex knew of a hospital bed we could use during Heather's recovery. I immediately called home and told Nathaniel to expect Alex with the bed.

The only available space to set up the bed in our small house was in the kitchen/dining area. With a bit of rearranging the dining table and chairs, Nathaniel said the bed fit perfectly, but left little room to move about. He also built a couple of wooden stands to hang sheets across, giving Heather some privacy when she needed to use the commode. Quite unusual, but the set up would prove to work out well. The advantage of this setup was Heather's visitors did not have to walk far when they came over. After entering the front door, they only had twenty feet to walk before reaching Heather's bedside.

Heather and I were up bright and early on the morning of the tenth. I planned for the two of us to be on the road at least by 9:00am or before noon. I had the car packed and ready before 7:00am. I was that anxious to leave. Every morning since her surgery, doctors began coming in the room to examine Heather around 7:00am. Not that morning. Heather and I began to think she had been forgotten, because there was no sign of any doctors until after 8:00am.

The only concern Holly had on the day of Heather's discharge, was the lack of progress Heather made with standing and walking.

Otherwise, Holly felt that Heather was ready to return home. She assured us that Heather's discharge papers were being drawn up, listing the recommendations for Heather's home care and activities Heather would be allowed to do. The moment Holly left the room, time just seemed to have stopped.

Heather and I waited and waited for our freedom. It wasn't until late afternoon when Heather's discharge papers finally materialized. Before allowing Heather to leave the hospital, the nurse requested that Heather leave a urine sample. Simple fact is, Heather can not go to the bathroom on demand. I had explained to the nurse that Heather's issue with having a shy bladder was recorded in her file. Once the nurse spoke to Holly and Holly waiving the need for a urine sample, I signed Heather out and wheeled her out of the pediatric ward. We pulled into our driveway close to 9:00pm that evening. Exhausted, but so very happy to be home.

CHAPTER THIRTY-SIX

HEATHER'S WORDS

*B*EFORE MOM AND I COULD leave the hospital, my nurse told us that I had to pee. Something to do with hospital procedure, wanting to make sure I could go without any problems. I didn't have any trouble going throughout the week so I couldn't believe I had to do this. Mom and I just looked at each other confused. I didn't have to go and Mom reminded the nurse that I couldn't go on demand because of my shy bladder. Mom and I both wanted to get out of there and start for home and didn't want to spend one more minute there. Finally, Mom told the nurse to contact Holly and see if this was really necessary. About a half hour later, Mom was pushing me to the exit doors.

Once we reached the main lobby, Mom ask the receptionist if he would wait with me as Mom went to bring the car to the entrance. When Mom walked through the automatic doors leading to the outside, cold air blew in. The smell of the fresh air was wonderful. It seemed like months since I had smelled the freshness of the outdoors.

After I lost sight of Mom as she made her way to the car, I just sat in silence. The receptionist and I didn't talk. I was still tired from the medication I was given before we left the hospital room. Even with taking the pain medication, my back felt very stiff and sore. I couldn't wait until the medication kicked in and took away the pain. We hadn't even begun our trip home and all I wanted to do was lay down.

When I spotted Mom pulling up, I felt a rush of excitement. Mom's car was easy to spot. The windshield wipers, when they are turned off, always stop pointed straight up instead of laying down. This has become the car's trademark and we always know it's Mom. When the receptionist saw Mom getting out of the car, he pushed me through the doors toward her. He offered his help, but Mom said she didn't need any. I said good-bye and thanked him for staying with me. As Mom carefully lifted me out of the wheelchair, I felt so weak. Once she had me situated in the car we were off. I dreaded the long and bumpy ride ahead of us. I just hoped I could maybe sleep most of the way and not have to feel any pain.

I was so happy to be leaving and seeing the outside world. The season was changing. Fall leaves were beginning to fall from the trees and I noticed several flocks of birds and geese looked as if they were flying southward. Mom thought it might be a sign of an early winter. I was glad I had a chance to see the trees and birds because I would be laid up in bed recovering, without being able to go outside when we reached Mom's house.

On the highway, I could feel every little bump. No matter how slow Mom drove over them. We had to stop often on our way home, so Mom could move me in a different position. It seemed as if we wasn't making any progress getting home. I just couldn't get comfortable. It was hard to take a nap. My legs would not stop shaking and my lower back/hips were in pain because of sitting up.

At the hospital, I didn't sit up for very long. I couldn't without feeling a lot of pain and pulling in my back and hips. I really wasn't prepared mentally to be in this amount of pain. The pain medication didn't seem to work during the trip home. I just wanted to get home and lay down, see the family and our dog Sebastian.

Sebastian was the greatest dog. I remember when Mom called me at Dad's to tell me she had brought home a puppy. I was never fond of dogs, but thought I could at least try to like him. Cats are my favorite pets because they are easy to care for and independent animals. Dogs are more needy. You have to take them out every time they need to go bathroom.

When I first saw Sebastian I fell in love with him. He had the biggest brown eyes and a tubby body. He was a rottweiler and black lab mix. Mom said that Sebastian was going to grow into a big dog because he had such big paws. The only area Sebastian grew big was his stomach. Otherwise, he grew into an average size dog. Right from the start, I didn't want to share him with anyone.

Sebastian must have sensed that I wasn't as strong as others in the family. He was very gentle around me and stayed close to my side. He was the perfect family dog. Never aggressive or hyper. We called him our Eeyore dog with seal eyes. His loyalty was with Mom. When ever Mom was present, he followed her every where. Otherwise, his best friend was anyone who had food.

When Mom and Katie moved into the apartment in Lakeview, no large pets were allowed. Mom asked Aunt Shirley and Uncle Kurt to keep Sebastian at their house. Aunt Shirley loved Sebastian as much as we did and said yes. I wanted to go to her house every time I went to Mom's house for the weekend to see him. Aunt Shirley took such good care of Sebastian. Even when he helped himself to the ten pounds of hamburger she had on her kitchen table thawing out one evening.

One thing was for sure,Sebastian could not be trusted at night. He was a trash dog. Loved to go through the trash looking for snacks. Well, the night he helped himself to the hamburg, Aunt Shirley didn't have to worry about waking up to the trash being scattered, if she forgot to put it up. It wouldn't be until Mom and Nathaniel bought the house in town when Sebastian was reunited with us for good.

I remember Mom could hardly push me through the door when we finally arrived home after leaving the hospital. Sebastian was so excited to see us that he just stood in the doorway. She had to nudge him with the wheelchair to get him to move. I was never so happy to be home. I could finally lay down and relax. My lower back and hips were throbbing in pain. The first thing I noticed about the house was the hospital bed that was set up in the corner of the kitchen. I couldn't believe how small the kitchen looked with a hospital bed, table and chairs, my walker and commode. This was going to be one crowded recovery. The hospital bed was borrowed from Grandma Cole. Grandpa Cole used it up until his death from battling lung cancer. Love you Grandpa!

My entire body was stiff and in pain as mom laid me on the hospital bed. Instantly, Sebastian came over and sat next to me. I reached over to pet him. I looked into his eyes and could feel that he knew I was in pain and that I wasn't able to sit next to him as I usually did. I felt a strong energy coming from him and knew he was going to have a huge impact with my recovery. No matter how tough my recovery was going to be, I knew Sebastian would be at my side and offering companionship. That is what I felt while peering into his eyes.

At one end of the hospital bed, curtains hung to give me a sense of privacy. I felt nothing of the sort. I would ask the family to go into a different room when I had to go to the bathroom. Even going into another room, they still were close to the kitchen. That is how small our house was. I listened to my iPOD and would try to forget I was in the kitchen going bathroom. It was awful trying to go bathroom without a lot of privacy.

Since the surgery, I wasn't able to wipe my butt after going bathroom. I was embarrassed that Mom had to help me. She didn't complain, but it made me feel like a baby. I guess I had to wait until my back healed more before I could wipe again. I was not allowed to take a bath or shower either. Mom had to give me sponge baths. For those who has had sponge baths, they are not that great. While Mom washed me, I found myself wishing I could sink into a warm tub of water. I was always cold after Mom finished washing me. My body would stiffen from being cold which made dressing me a chore.

Good thing at that time, I was wearing a hospital gown we took from the hospital. This made dressing me easier. Mom also had to wash my hair in the kitchen sink. To do this, she place me in that oversized wheelchair and tilted the back downward so I could lean back into the sink. At that time, I had long hair but not for long. I soon had it cut since I couldn't take care of it myself.

Mom had two more weeks off from work which I was glad. What ever she caught in the hospital was becoming worse. Plus, I needed her to help me become strong again. I couldn't wait to get back to being independent again and start walking. Walking was still my number one wish and I was ready to do anything to make it happen.

Mom and I never seemed to get any real sleep. Mom slept on the couch because I needed to be turned often. I would wake her every two hours or so to move me. She was coughing a lot throughout the night which didn't help in getting any sleep. Then there was Sebastian who snored so loud. Another reason I had a hard time with falling asleep, was the constant pain I was in. The pain medication didn't seem to relieve the pain for very long and I didn't want to take more than I was told to take. I didn't like how the pain medication made me feel. I felt somewhat relaxed, but still could feel a dull ache in my back and hips. I also was getting mild spasms in my legs and back as well.

By the time I did fall asleep, Nathaniel was getting up for work and Katie for school. I would be so mad because I had just found a comfortable position right before the two of them were up and making noise. After Nathaniel and Katie left the house, Mom would take Sebastian out and the two of us would try to fall back to sleep again.

During the day, Mom would sit me up in the wheelchair for a few minutes. Every time I sat up, my lower back/hips felt like the muscles were pulling and ripping. I thought this was normal and believed it would pass as my back healed. A home therapist started coming by two or three times a week to stretch me out and begin working on standing and walking.

The first therapist was a male therapist, but he thought it would be best if I worked with a female instead. I think he felt uncomfortable around me because I still was wearing a hospital gown at that time, so my body wasn't always covered. The next therapist was fun to be around. She worked at stretching my legs and getting me to stand. The longest I was able to stand lasted under five seconds. I felt so disappointed with myself. Before the surgery I could stand close to an hour before my legs weakened and my feet hurt. How was it possible not to be able to stand longer than five seconds now?

I never knew what each day was going to bring me. One minute I was in zero pain then it would suddenly turn into a ten on a pain scale. Some days I was getting spasms in my back and legs that was unbearable to the point, where tears would be running down my cheeks. But, I kept my hopes up and constantly told myself *"I'm going to walk."*

Just like the therapist I had in the hospital, the home therapist gradually grew disappointed with me because she felt that I wasn't putting in a lot of effort. Not only did I hear this remark from the therapist, other family members had begun making similar comments about the lack of progress I was making. I knew right then I needed to fight the pain and the spasms. I needed to be strong.

A home bound teacher began coming to our house soon after returning home from the hospital as well. I was glad because I didn't want to fall behind in my studies. I was taking six classes at that time. Most of them were required. The home bound teacher was so patience with me. Some days I had to lay down in the middle of our time together because the pain became to much to bear while sitting up. She took this all in stride. I thought we barely made any progress with my school work, but I managed to keep up with the majority of the work.

Every time she came over or when I saw Katie going to school, it made me miss school even more. I couldn't wait to get back to see my friends and teachers. I especially missed Gates and the office staff. I always made sure that I stopped in to say "*Hello*" and hangout for a while. I really enjoyed their company. I wanted to hang out with friends like before. I really missed school. I didn't know then, but many students and teachers were going to have a huge impact on my life. It wouldn't take place until my senior year, but I would be given a wonderful gift from others without them even realizing it.

On the days when no therapist or home bound teacher came over, I would catch up on my rest. There wasn't a whole lot I was capable of doing. Mikey sat with me on his days off while Mom worked. Grandma Ski would sit with me on the days Mikey worked. There was always someone with me, at some point in the day. If I needed Mom for anything, I could call her at work and she would come right home. When Grandma Ski sat with me, her and I played games or watched television. Visitors came by now and then to see how I was doing and Dad started visiting once a week. Even with the company, I began to get restless and wished I recovered enough to go back to school. I wanted so much to leave the house. I wanted more than anything for the pain and spasms to stop. I was tired of being in bed more often than out of bed. I wanted my independence back.

I did go outside of the house one time shortly after returning home from the hospital. Dad called and told me that the family was gathering for a family portrait. All my Aunts, Uncle and cousins were expected to show up. This was going to be a gift for Grandma Sandy and Grandpa Tom. I didn't want to go because the setting for the picture was in a park. Being outside made my muscles stiff. I knew that would bring on spasms and cause me a lot of pain, but I couldn't say no.

The day of the pictures, the sun may have been shining, but the wind cut right through me. Mom drove me to the park where all my relatives were gathered. Even my Aunt Sue and her family drove over from Wisconsin. I was excited to see them all. The location was perfect and beautiful. Once Dad spotted Mom and I, he came and stood by the car as Mom transferred me into my wheelchair. Once I was seated in my chair, Dad begun to take my winter coat off. I looked at him like he was insane. I wanted to keep it on, but he said that no one else was going to wear their coat. I thought to myself "*good for them.*"

As soon as Dad took off my coat, a huge spasm hit. The way I had to bend for Dad, to make it easy for him to remove my coat was painful. I almost cried, but I kept telling myself "*don't cry.*" I was becoming so cold while waiting for the photographer to finish. My legs would not stop shaking and I needed to lay down. I was never so happy to hear the words "last picture" coming from the photographer. I wanted so much to get back into Moms car where it was warm. I didn't stay around to talk with the family. Mom and I left as soon as I was put back in the car.

With missing school, my friends, not being allowed to shower, being in constant pain and perhaps the most disappointing aspect of recovery, not being able to wipe my own butt, I felt that life may have thrown too much at me. I wasn't prepared to be laid up like I was. I could slowly feel myself losing my positive outlook. I wondered what Holly was going to say when I went in for my first check up. I surely hoped she would say "*You can take a shower.*" That sentence alone would add some much needed joy in my life at that time. So until my appointment I kept my fingers crossed.

CHAPTER THIRTY-SEVEN

*U*PON OUR ARRIVAL HOME FROM the hospital, a sense of well being rose within me. Before shutting the car engine off, I turned to Heather and made the remark: "*We did it. We made it.*" The statement not only referred to arriving home safe, but was also acknowledging how the two of us endured the hospital stay, along with Heather coming out of surgery without any immediate complications.

Our drive home did involve many stops along the way, in order to reposition Heather in her seat. The pain medication given to Heather before leaving the hospital made her drowsy, but didn't relieve her pain to where she was able to nap comfortably. The two of us didn't talk much during the trip home, which left me with hours to just think. My thoughts mostly revolved around Heather's pain. I wondered when or if the pain would soon begin to subside, to where the strength of her pain medication could be lessened.

The effects of the medication left Heather feeling tired, quite limp and her appetite was declining as a result. With her energy level lowered from fatigue, depression could easily set in and this was a major concern of mine. By nature, Heather has always been a fighter, with a strong determination to achieve whatever she set her mind to. I feared that her inner strength would slowly weaken if she didn't regain her independence soon. The independence that seemed to have been taken away after her surgery.

The pain Heather was experiencing did not seem to be a significant concern to Holly or her assistants. Maybe, there was little reason for concern at that time, since it had only been little over a week since Heather's surgery. Considering how Holly didn't seem overly troubled by the amount of pain and lack of mobility, Heather and I believed it was all part of the healing process. However, there was one nagging thought I couldn't seem to shake. How it was possible for other patients, whom underwent a similar surgery as Heather's, to be up and moving about within days following surgery, while Heather could not even sit up for very long before her pain became unbearable?

One can only imagine the extent at which Heather's muscle structure was being pulled to accommodate the new position of her spine. After years of being in a certain position, then suddenly forced in another unfamiliar to her body, no wonder Heather was in that amount of pain.

I began wondering if Heather's lack of progress in standing and taking steps during her hospital stay, was more of a repercussion from the surgery itself, rather than the notion of Heather's own lack of effort. Before leaving the hospital, I should have asked Holly if any of her other patients, past or present, experienced similar pain issues or delayed mobility following surgery. If so, Holly could have assured Heather that all was going to be fine, or prepare Heather for what may be expected in the future. Either way, any such input would have been beneficial to Heather. It may have even lessened the amount of disappointment Heather felt for not being able to do what the physical therapist expected of her.

When we arrived home that night, Heather's morale was instantly lifted from the sight of Sebastian and the hospital bed in which she desperately needed to lay down on. Mine was lifted just by being home. All Heather and I wanted, once inside the house, was to lay down and sleep. I was fighting off yet another fever and felt completely physically and emotionally drained.

The instant I walked into the house, I was greeted by both Katie and Nathaniel eagerly awaiting to fill me in regarding their week away from me. As much as I wanted to give them my attention, I had to focus on getting Heather settled into bed. Katie soon sensed my lack of interest at that time and went off to bed. It wasn't until I had Heather settled in, did I go into Katie's bedroom to apologize and tried to explain how I needed to get Heather into bed.

This was not the kind of homecoming I had in mind. In just a short period of time, I had already managed to hurt Katie's feelings by not being more attentive. Katie would not be the only one who felt over looked by me, Nathaniel also acted disappointed from my apparent lack of attention. He wasn't at all pleased when I informed him that I would be sleeping on the couch for the time being, because Heather would need my help during the night. Upon hearing this, he instantly walked away from me without saying a word and went up to bed. I guess all of us dealt with feelings of frustration that night. Sometimes, there just isn't enough of one person to meet everyone needs.

There wasn't much sleep for me during our first night home or the following nights, for that matter. Every two hours or so, Heather would be calling out to me. I would slowly crawl out from under my cozy blankets in order to turn her over, then return back to the couch and attempt to fall back asleep. Some nights, Heather and I would be up for hours after turning her just talking because neither one of us could sleep. Then, when we finally felt sleepy enough to sleep, it wasn't long before we were awakened by Katie and Nathaniel. Katie getting up for school and Nathaniel for work.

Heather's mobility was not improving any as the days went by. She continued to remain in a lot of pain and the spasms in her back and hips seemed to be increasing. Neither of the in home physical therapists made much progress with Heather's mobility. This was when I really began to worry about the possibility of some type of permanent damage being caused from the surgery. Where others may have felt that Heather was not doing her best to get back on her feet, I knew different. Beyond a shadow of a doubt, I knew Heather wasn't being lazy or defiant. Something was clearly wrong.

Heather and I both were becoming discouraged from hearing how she should be sitting up more or walking. There were so many comments of *"Heather should be doing this and that,"* that we started to dread family visitors or their calls. It seemed the first question always being asked was *"Is Heather walking yet?"* Instead of surrounding Heather with positive energy, she was more often than not, smothered with negativity. The impact of these so called comments only created a deepened sense of despair in Heather.

Heather's first follow up with Holly was two weeks after her discharge from the hospital. The appointment couldn't arrive fast enough for me. Deep down, I was hoping that Holly would find a valid medical reason why Heather was failing to regain mobility. Heather on the other hand, was more concerned about getting permission to shower. Sponge baths were not enjoyable for Heather.

Her muscles would stiffen in her back which would trigger spasms. Sometimes the spasms would be so strong that tears could be seen in Heather's eyes, but she always managed to hold them in. I would often tell her to allow herself to cry. It would help release a lot of the pent up frustration she was feeling.

The first two weeks after coming home was indeed challenging for all of us. Katie remained distant from me and Heather. Nathaniel, also wasn't very accepting of the amount of care Heather needed. There definitely was a feeling of resentment surfacing. As a result, he began to spend more time away from us.

Now that I think about it, I don't believe the resentment was directly caused from Heather's dependency on me. He mentioned early on, when we first began seeing one another, how his mother's attention was solely focused on his stepfather, when his stepfather was battling cancer. Nathaniel commented on how he felt pushed aside by his mother. Maybe, this experience with Heather, was bringing to the surface some past hurt that he had not completely dealt with. Life seems to have a way of making us revisit past hurts in the most unusual ways.

CHAPTER THIRTY-EIGHT

HEATHER'S WORDS

OCTOBER 23RD, 2006, WAS MY first check up with Holly since the surgery. Nineteen days had passed and I didn't seem to be recovering very well. Again, Mikey rode along to the hospital with Mom and I.

During our drive to the city, I kept thinking of how interesting my check-up with Holly was going to be. Before seeing Holly, I would be having x-rays taken of my back and hips. Maybe the x-rays would reveal the reason for my pain and explain why I wasn't regaining any mobility. I wanted the pain to go away and get on with my life.

I would never again take for granted going up and down stairs, dressing on my own and walking as I had done before the surgery. I was growing so tired of laying in bed as much as I was. There were days when the pain in my back and hips never stopped. Other days, the pain seemed to just come and go. Those were the days I would be able to sit up more often and sleep without much trouble.

I also wondered what Holly would say about my legs; especially my left leg. The shaking of my legs was driving me insane. Every time I sat up, my legs would begin shaking. They would begin bouncing up and down really fast. Non-stop. The only way to stop my legs from doing this was to hold down on them until the shaking stopped or when I was laid back down. Before the surgery, my legs did have a tendency to shake a little in the mornings when I got up, but never shook to this extreme. In the past, the shaking only lasted a few seconds and didn't occur any other time during the day.

The drive to the hospital didn't seem as long as the drive home

HEATHER ROBINSON and BARB JOHNSON

after my discharge. The bumps and dips in the highway did not bother me and Mom didn't have to stop as often to rearrange me in my seat. Maybe I was healing more than I thought. I couldn't wait to ask Holly my two questions: "*Can I take a shower?*" and "*Why am I experiencing this amount of pain?*" The pain mostly felt like a pulling and ripping sensation. I also was feeling a slight pinch in between my shoulder blades when I moved a certain way.

Once inside the hospital, I still could not believe how many people were in the hospital. It was like being at the mall in a way. Instead of different shops along the hallway, there are different types of medical offices that treat different types of medical conditions. But, like the mall, people were always always coming and going.

The first thing Mom, Mikey and I did was go to x-rays. Holly had already faxed a request for my x-rays to the radiology department. The radiologist took a lot of x-rays. The ones I had to lay down for hurt the most. The muscles in my lower back and hip area, once again, felt like they were pulling and ripping. X-rays were also taken of my spine while I sat up in a chair. Once the radiologist was satisfied with the x-rays, she said that Mom and I could go to the Orthopedic waiting area. While the three of us waited to see Holly, I began to wonder if my x-rays turned out good. I was also worrying about the rods. Had they moved out of place somehow? Maybe they had and this was causing the pain. I figured the pain was happening because my muscles were so used to being one way and now they were being pulled to a different position.

I was really hoping Holly would find a way to remove the pain I was having. I also wanted to get off the medication I was taking. I hated how the pills made me feel and I was afraid of becoming addicted to them. If Holly could take away the pain, I would be able to get back to school or better yet, be out of bed for an entire day. Laying down in bed as much as I was, was boring. I wanted to move around again.

The three of us didn't wait long before for my name was called. Mikey stayed in the waiting area as Mom and I were taken to a small room to wait for Holly. Holly came walking in shortly with my x-rays in her arms. She handed Mom and I copies of the x-rays to take home with us. She then put an x-ray up on the lighted screen for us to look at. I took a double look and was amazed by what I saw.

My back and hip area were full of hardware. I saw the rods along my spine and the screws. I was shocked by the length of the screws that were in my lower back. I wondered how Holly and her team put every piece of hardware in without touching or messing up the nerves in my back. Maybe they did and that could be why my spasticity was becoming worse and the reason for my legs shaking as much as they were. Or not.

Holly took away my worry I had about the rods moving when she said that the x-rays looked good and my back was healing great. She was impressed at how well the incision was healing. Next came the words I was waiting to hear: "*You can take a shower.*" I instantly felt the biggest smile sweep across my face. The first real smile I had in a while. Right then I couldn't wait to get back home. I wasn't sure what my choice was going to be. A hot bath or enjoy feeling the warmth of the water spraying down on me in the shower. What I did know was: "No more sponge baths!"

I told Holly that I was having a lot of pain in my lower back and hips. She wasn't worried at that point because it was only a couple of weeks after the surgery. Holly told me not to push it and do what ever I could tolerate. That's what I was doing all along, but there were those who believed I wasn't putting in enough effort. They didn't seem to believe that I was doing the best I could. I knew they were concerned about my progress.

Yes, I did become mad and frustrated. I questioned myself over and over, as to why my body was giving me so much trouble. Why couldn't I be one of those people who could get up the next day following surgery and begin taking steps? I thought maybe I was going to be a late starter and have to recover longer. Plus, I needed to get the pain under control. I knew I would be able to do more once the pain was under control.

The visit with Holly did not last very long. I guess there wasn't a lot she had to say. Mom and I asked a few questions about the pain and how long it might take to get me back on my feet again. Holly couldn't answer that one. She said that every patient is different. Before leaving the hospital, another appointment was scheduled with Holly. The next appointment would be in 4-6 weeks. Maybe, I would be living without any pain. I might even be taking steps by then.

Mom, Mikey and I made it back home safe. I was so ready to take a bath. There wasn't anything that sounded better than soaking in a tub full of hot water. Nothing seemed to come easy for me or for Mom. Getting me into the tub was hard work. Being tired out from the trip didn't help matters any. Mom brought a kitchen chair into the bathroom and sat it next to the tub. I would have to stand while Mom pulled down my pants. If I couldn't stand that long, I would just sit on the chair until I felt enough energy to try standing again. Every time I stood up, a sharp pain hit my left hip and made me lose my balance.

Mom had a hard time trying to pull down my pants plus making sure I didn't fall forward to the floor. From then on, Katie would be called in the bathroom to pull down my pants while Mom helped me stand. This made it a lot easier for everyone. Maybe not Katie, she didn't like the job of pulling down my pants.

Once my clothes were off, I began to get chilled which made my body stiffen. This made it hard for Mom to swing my legs over the tub. She didn't want to just lift me and put me into the tub because she might bend me to far and this would have caused a lot of pain. When my legs were finally in the water, my feet felt like they were on fire. My feet get cold really fast and the water felt like it was boiling, instead of being warm. Mom then picked the rest of my body up from the chair and twisted me slowly into the tub. She lowered me into the water. The tub felt so hard when I sat down in it, but the warm water felt good on my hips and back. I didn't stay in long because I couldn't hold my balance while sitting there.

When Mom lifted me out of the tub, I felt the worst pain I had ever felt. I thought a rod or screw came out of my hip. A huge spasm in my lower back suddenly hit so hard, it took my breath away. Tears were falling from my eyes. I did all I could not to scream out loud. I asked Mom "*Why. Why all this pain and no progress?*" Mom didn't know what was happening to my body. We both was feeling discouraged at not hearing anything encouraging from Holly. Day after day I was getting worse and I felt my will power to fight begin to slip away.

I began thinking that maybe I needed to go back to the familiar surroundings at Dad's. I would be close to school and maybe my friends would come and see me. I thought that Mom could use a break from taking care of me and could then spend more time with Katie and Nathaniel. She still was fighting what ever she caught from the hospital and had not gone to the doctor. Mom and I talked about my moving back to Dads and she asked me if I really wanted to do it. I shook my head *"yes."*

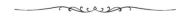

What I failed to take under consideration when Heather chose to have her surgery at that hospital, was the number of returning trips we would be making for Heather's check-ups. Heather's first check-up with Holly was before 10:00 am. This meant leaving home by 6:00 am. The drive there and back totaled close to seven hours. The time we spent at the hospital was less than one hour. The actual visit with Holly; less than twenty minutes.

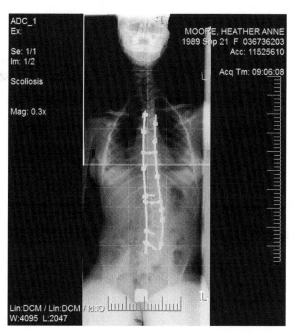

When Holly put two images of Heather's spine and pelvis up on the screen, both Heather and I could not believe what we were seeing. The curvature of Heather's spine was barely noticeable. The transformation from Heather sitting sideways before the surgery, to sitting perfectly straight was unbelievable. However, with the pain Heather was experiencing, I wondered if the procedure was too sudden for her body. Maybe if her spine was gradually corrected, her muscles would have had time to adjust. Would her pain have been less? I never asked Holly about this.

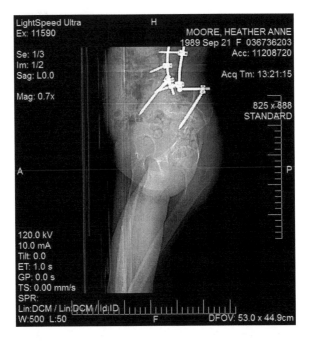

The most frightening sight of Heather's x-rays were the length of the screws placed in her pelvis. I didn't even want to think of the depth at which those screws went into Heather's bone. There wasn't any sign of protrusion of any of the hardware along her spine, but internally, her body must have been shocked. No wonder so much of Heather's pain resided in her lower back. Holly didn't notice anything out of place in the x-rays that would cause Heather to be in the pain she was in. She did mention that maybe the tension between Heather's hips was set too tight, which may be the cause of Heather's pain.

As Holly stated, Heather's incision was in fact healing nicely. The length of the incision still was astounding to me. If nothing else, we had to be thankful of Heather's ability to fight off infection and how quickly her wounds heal. Holly commented on how well Heather's sitting balance was, but did notice the tightness in her hip region. When Heather mentioned the amount of pain she was having, Holly had no valid explanation regarding a direct cause. Holly told Heather not to over do it. Only do what she was able to tolerate with the in home physical therapist. After writing a prescription for pain medicine, Holly told Heather she wanted to see her back again in 4-6 weeks.

Since Holly didn't seem too concerned over Heather's lack of progress. I told Heather that maybe when the family heard this, those who expected Heather to be up and walking would back off on the comments they made. Holly never hinted around to or implied that Heather wasn't trying to regain her mobility. To Heather and I, Holly seemed to be giving Heather the needed reassurance that Heather needed to let recovery take its course and not to rush anything.

About a week after Heather's first check-up, she said she wanted to move back to her Dads'. I knew she wanted to be close to him, but felt it was a huge mistake doing so. No matter how things were going at our house, I knew this was the best place for her. I was worried about the quality of care Heather would be given there. I realize that this may have sound prejudice, but at that time, Heather needed a lot of assistance. At our home, someone was always there to meet her needs. I wasn't sure if her dad and the rest of the family comprehended this. Knowing Heather as well as I did, once she makes up her mind about something there's little that can be done to change it.

Looking back, I can understand Heather's decision to move back. Tension was beginning to grow between Nathaniel and me. He was having a hard time dealing with the visitors coming and going at our house. Nathaniel, a private sort of person saw it as an invasion of his privacy. We were beginning to see very little of Nathaniel. When he was home, his resentment was clearly brought across to us by his sarcastic remarks and his distance. This worried me.

I had hoped that he would have been able to step aside from his need to have my sole attention and support me in the effort of taking care of Heather. At the time when he assured me he understood and accepted my decision to care for Heather, I don't believe he really planned for things to be the way they were turning out. Katie was also beginning to spend less and less time with Heather and I and spent more time alone in her room. Being 11 years old, no doubt she was feeling left out.

The cold I caught was not going away. When I returned back to work my friends said I sounded and looked awful. They said that more than likely I had pneumonia. I still refused to see a doctor. It wouldn't be until I heard gurgling in my lungs did I go. My condition turned out to be walking pneumonia. No wonder I was always so exhausted.

The doctor ordered a chest x-ray on me and it revealed a spot which caused the doctor to become concerned. My lungs revealed some scaring in them and early stages of COPD (chronic obstructive pulmonary disease,) but the spot the doctor showed concern over may be lung cancer. The doctor insisted that I return back in a couple of months for another x-ray. She advised me that the image on the x-ray wasn't clear enough to out rule cancer. My God, could anything else be added to the hectic life I was living?

I walked out of the medical clinic more angered than scared. If the spot on the x-ray could not be positively identified as being cancerous, then why assume it was cancer? Maybe, it was her way of preparing me for what the next x-ray would reveal. All I knew was I didn't have the time nor the energy to be worrying. My main concern was Heather and getting her well again.

This is not what I imagined Heather's recovery would be like. What I visioned was what Holly had told us before the surgery. Expect six weeks or so off recovering before Heather would return back to normal activity and school. Three weeks had barely passed and nothing close to what she had said was in sight.

CHAPTER THIRTY-NINE

HEATHER'S WORDS

I CALLED DAD A FEW DAYS after my check up with Holly and asked him if I could come back home. Without hesitation, he said yes. I'm not saying that I didn't want to be with Mom, but by this time, I was feeling homesick. I missed Sasha Kitty, school and my friends. A month had passed since my surgery and none of my friends from school had come to see me at Moms. I thought maybe if I were back at dad's house, a few would visit.

It was beginning to feel like a lifetime ago since I could walk and was independent. I felt more and more each day like I was imprisoned in bed. The pain was always there and the spasms in my lower back and legs occurred more often. I placed a lot of faith into believing my recovery would go more smoothly if I was back in my comfort zone; which was at dads. I wasn't used to being away from home as long as I was. I guess, I thought moving back would bring Dad and I close as well.

I was seventeen years old, but still wanted to feel like his "*baby girl.*" I needed his nurturing nature and moral support more than I ever let on. Maybe if he spent time with me, he would see that the pain was real and understand how difficult it really was for me to meet his expectations. Not being able to meet the expectations of those who mattered the most to me was constantly on my mind. Add that to the pain I was in, plus how physically weak I was becoming, one might understand how depression and self-pity was beginning to take over my emotions. These feelings were not common for me. I have never felt sorry for myself in the past. I needed to feel like my old self again and home at dads was where I truly believed it would happen.

What would become clear soon after moving back in with Dad, was how mistaken I was to even imagine that moving back would lift my spirits and that my recovery would somehow be more productive. The move was going to be a heart breaking experience. The day arrived when Dad came to pick up my belongings at Mom's house. I was excited to go back home. Just the thought of sleeping in my own bed lifted my spirits. At Dads, I would at least have some privacy. There wasn't any at Moms, where felt so exposed in my kitchen bedroom. I figured sleeping in my bed would help me rest better. The hospital bed wasn't very comfortable and somewhat lumpy.

Leaving Mom was going to be hard. I didn't like to be apart from her because we are so much alike. If I ever had a question or needed advice, she was the first person I went to. I felt so close to her. Maybe because we had been through so much already and have shared a special bond. Mom knew me better than anyone else. I was going to miss our late night talks when I left, but, I wanted Mom to get back to her own life. She spent most of her time caring for me, which left little time for herself, along with Nathaniel and Katie. She could finally get some much needed rest and maybe start feeling better. I was also hoping she would go to the doctor.

Once Dad's truck was loaded with my things, Mom and I followed him to his house in Mom's car. Mom was going because she needed to show Momma Denise and Grandma Sandy how to transfer me from my bed to my wheelchair. Mom also needed to show them the best way to get me in and out of the shower. On the way to Dads, Mom and I talked about everything. The surgery, my pain and how we were not prepared for my recovery to be this disappointing.

At Dads, I couldn't wait to be laid down. The muscles in my lower back and hips felt as though they were ripping apart. I could have screamed when Dad lifted me out of Mom's car and carried me down to my room. The pain was that bad. I was glad I took some pain medication before leaving Moms, because the pain would have been much worse. Dad didn't realize how the slightest twist or turn of my body would trigger such pain. So, he had a hard time believing I could be in so much pain. Since it was late in the afternoon, Momma Denise and Grandma Sandy thought it was best to get me into the bath tub as soon as I got there. The medication made me too weak to balance myself in the tub. We used a shower chair so Momma Denise was holding me while Grandma Sandy washed my body. Before getting out of the tub, I looked over to the doorway and saw Mom standing there. I was wondering what she was thinking because there was a sadness in her eyes.

Momma Denise and Grandma Sandy handled me with such tenderness, as they took me out of the tub just as Mom instructed them to. They dried me off and clothed me. I felt completely helpless. I hated being so dependent on others. All I wanted to do after being dressed was to lay down and sleep. I felt so tired and weak. Mom saw how tired I was and decided that it was time for her to go home. We kissed and hugged. Said "*I love you*" to one another and she left.

That night, sleeping in my own bed was miserable. For one thing, I was sleeping in a full size bed. There wasn't anything to hold onto to help me roll over if I needed to. When I did try to turn over, my lower back muscles felt like they were ripping apart. Tears filled my eyes and I wanted to scream. I never tried rolling over by myself at Moms, something I should have worked on before coming home, because it would have helped me now.

During the night, my side began hurting bad. The muscles along my rib cage felt like they we now pulling. I desperately needed to roll over. I tried yelling as loud as I could to Dad and Momma Denise. After ten minutes or so, I gave up. No one could hear me since I was downstairs. There was no way to let them know I needed help. Maybe, we should have used a baby monitor as a way to communicate during the night, but we didn't think of it.

So there I was trapped in one spot. There had to be a way to roll over on my own. I was thinking and trying everything, but nothing seemed to work. This went on for over an hour before I realized that my efforts were useless. I almost gave up, but something inside me urged me to try one more time. I held my breath, gritted my teeth and gave it everything I had.

The pain from twisting my body, in order to roll over caused me to cry out loud. I managed to roll over, but laid there crying as the pain ripped through my shaking body. At least now I could reach my water and pain medication. Even with the amount of pain I was in, a great feeling of accomplishment began to fill me which seemed to help drown out everything else.

One thing was for certain, I wasn't able to sleep in my own bed. I would have to talk to Dad about setting up the hospital bed. At least that bed had side rails to grab onto to help me roll over. I was bound and determined to learn how roll over on my own. If I could manage that, it would be a step toward becoming independent once again.

I finally fell asleep after taking some pain medication. I was taking Oxycodone and Valium at that time. It didn't take long before I felt my muscles relax. Morning came too soon. It felt I had just fallen asleep when I was awakened by Dad, asking if I was ready to get up. I barely had time to nod yes before he sat me up on the edge of my bed. A sharp pain swept throughout my body. It took my breath away. Dad didn't realize that I had to be moved slowly and couldn't handle any sudden jolts. I wanted to cry, but I held in my tears. I didn't want to show any weakness around Dad.

Dad carried me upstairs and sat me in his chair. His chair was the most comfortable chair in our house. Once I found a comfortable position in his chair, I started telling Dad and Momma Denise how I had trouble rolling over in my own bed and asked if the hospital bed could be set up. They both agreed that the side rails on the hospital bed would make it easier for me to roll over. Dad said he would set it up downstairs. I asked if there was room upstairs for the bed. I knew there wasn't enough room, but at least I would be around the family more. Dad said there wasn't any place to set the bed up upstairs. So I guess, I was going back downstairs. Even though we were living in the same house, I knew I wouldn't be seeing the family much. I know I said I wanted more privacy, but I didn't want to feel isolated either. Why couldn't they make room for the bed upstairs? The couch could have been moved downstairs for a while. Couldn't it? I guess the living room wouldn't have looked good when people visited.

This came as no surprise, because when I was younger, I remember asking Dad if he wouldn't mind putting a railing up along the stairs leading downstairs. I could then walk up and down the stairs instead of crawling. He said the rails wouldn't look good and most likely, the rails would pull away from the wall when I put my weight on them. "So what?" That was my thought about that. I thought he could find a way to secure the railing to the wall in order to hold my weight. I never got the railing to make going up and down the stairs easier.

By the time Dad set up the bed, I was so ready to lay back down. I hadn't been sitting in his chair very long before the pain began to set in. Laying down seemed to relieve some of the pain; but finding a comfortable position was almost impossible.

In the basement, there are two bedrooms, the laundry room, one bathroom and at the far end, and a type of living room. The hospital bed was set up in a corner of the living room. Dad placed a card table beside the bed, along with my commode and walker. The furniture in that room was moved far enough away to give me plenty of room, but also facing me so when visitors came, I could see them.

When Dad went back upstairs after laying me in the bed, this is when I felt living with him was not going to work. The vision of how I imagined it would be like when I moved back to Dads, was fading. This was heartbreaking. I was left feeling alone and right back where I was before the surgery, away from everyone.

During that week I spent at Dads, Momma Denise, Kaleb and Nibbles left early in the mornings. Momma Denise went to work, and Kaleb and Nibbles went off to school. This gave Dad and I some time to spend with one another before he too had to leave for work. If he wasn't busy around the house, we would eat lunch together and play a couple games of Cribbage. I enjoyed my time with him. We didn't talk much and really we didn't need to.

Before leaving for work, Dad helped me in and out of the bathroom and made sure I had everything I needed; such as snacks and water to last until Momma Denise came home. He also put a phone by my side in case I needed to call someone for assistance, because I would be home alone unless Grandma Cole came over before the kids came home from school, which she did a few days that week. However, she would not have been able to help me get out of bed since she had back surgeries herself. She was limited on what she could do.

The house became so quiet after Dad left. I welcomed the quiet on the days I was really tired. I could then easily fall asleep. But, on the days when I was feeling more energetic, being alone was so boring. I had the option of watching TV or reading, but I was just too restless to focus. Even my school work didn't interest me. I just wanted to get out of bed and move around. Recovery would have been more tolerable if I were able to move about instead of being bedridden.

One afternoon after Dad had left for work, I heard Shadow, the family dog, barking outside. Since I couldn't see out of the windows above my head, I yelled out loud to her. Telling her I knew how she must be feeling. In a way, we both were living in bondage. Her being the dog kennel she was kept in, mine being my body. I also shouted out of how one day the two of us would be freed from our loneliness and happily live life. There just had to be something good in store for my life. How I wished whatever it was, would happen soon because I felt myself feeling more and more discouraged.

When Momma Denise came home from work, she would come downstairs and take me to the bathroom and help me back into bed. She would then go upstairs to help the kids with their homework before making dinner. I felt utterly alone when I heard the family upstairs laughing and talking. I wanted so badly to be up there with them. I couldn't understand why making room for me upstairs wasn't possible. I wondered how they would have felt if they were me, being alone and downstairs all the time. I wondered if it ever crossed their minds how I felt. I remember eating dinner alone every night. Well, I wasn't completely alone, Sasha Kitty would sit on my lap while I was eating, begging for a handout.

Pets can be the greatest gift in a family. They make you laugh, play with you, sleep with you and keep you company without asking much in return. Some people may not believe that pets can pick up on how their owners feel, but I believe pets can. Just as Sebastian did at Moms, Sasha always seemed to sense when I needed her company the most. She would spend a lot of time laying with me. She was my greatest source of comfort for the most part. At night, Sasha would jump up on the bed and lay with me until she heard Dad's truck pulling into the garage. She would jump off the bed before he entered the house, because she knew Dad would kick her off the bed when he came down to check on me.

At least once a day, Kaleb and Nibbles would come down to visit me, but it wasn't for very long. They would sit on the bed with me and talk about their day at school. I enjoyed every single moment with them. I still didn't have any friends come to visit me yet. I was beginning to feel forgotten by them by that time.

I made sure I called Mom every day. Hearing her voice always had a way of comforting me. Everything seemed better after talking to her. She was always reassuring me that all was well. The pain and recovery would be over soon and I would then go on with my life. "You are being treated by the best," Mom would say. "It's one of the most prestigious hospitals around. Holly will surely find the cause and the help you need." I held onto those words as long as I could, before I slowly stopped believing in them and myself.

Mom and I talked about the family and of course, life in general. Katie was beginning to talk and hang out with Mom more. Nathaniel and Mom were getting reacquainted once again and Mom finally went to the doctor. Mikey and Sebastian were doing great, but Mom said Sebastian acted a bit mopey ever since I had left. I guess he was missing me.

After we talked about everyone, Mom would ask how I was doing and if I needed anything. I described the spasms, I was getting and how they seemed to be getting worse. I was experiencing spasms every ten minutes or so in my lower back, hips and legs. The spasms in my legs happened more at night. It actually felt like I was having one continuous charlie horse in my hamstrings, moving upward into my lower back. My hips ached so much. The pain reached the point where I began taking more pain medication than I was supposed to. Mom sounded worried when I told her this, but she understood how much I needed the relief form the pain.

My home bound teacher came three times that week while I was at Dads. She stayed close to two hours each time, but it didn't seem that long to me. It was good to have the company. The hours we spent together was devoted to six classes worth of work. So much information and material was being thrown at me, that I had a hard time grasping the context of the material. I tried my best to get most of my work done before she left. After finishing what we worked on, I would forget it. I was having a great deal of trouble concentrating and remembering more and more. I'm sure the medication had much to do with this.

When it came time to take a test, I didn't have a clue what the questions were about. I didn't purposely do bad on those tests, I just couldn't remember the material we had covered. I'm surprised I did as well on the test as I had. I had too much other stuff on my mind, like getting better. Plus, the lack of sleep from all the pain I was in, really left me emotionally and physically drained.

My in home therapist came in the mornings at Dads. Each session would begin with her stretching my legs. She started on my right leg first because it was more relaxed than my left leg. Now, my left leg was a whole different story. My leg would automatically jerk and turn inward every time she moved it. It was hard for her to control the leg. The hamstrings in my left leg were so tight. The muscle relaxer I was taking didn't seem to work. My hips would also begin to act up while she was working on my legs. Sharp pains shot through my lower back and down my legs. Sometimes, the pain would take my breath away.

After finishing with my stretches, the therapist helped me sit on the edge of the bed. I wished she taught me how to sit up in that position on my own. If I could have sat up on my own, I thought I may have been able to transfer myself from the bed to the commode, without doing a lot of standing. But, I guess showing me wasn't important at that time. Standing hurt the most because the muscles in my lower back and hips were now being stretched. Spasms instantly began in my back and legs, making my legs shake uncontrollably. My hips would also give out on me, which caused me to lose my balance. I believe the longest I managed to stand was about ten seconds before having to sit. One day when the pain was at its worse, I came right out and told the therapist that I was done trying to stand.

She became somewhat upset and asked what she was doing there if I wasn't going to try. I looked at her puzzled and didn't answer. I had reached my breaking point. Maybe, I just needed her to message my hips and stretch my legs more than working on standing. Yes, I know how important it was to for me to be up and about, but the pain was too strong to bare. I wished she and everyone else could have felt how I was feeling.

One day Dad was watching me struggle with sitting and trying to stand. I didn't want him watching because I knew he would become upset and impatient with my limitations. Well, I was right. Both him and the therapist spoke of their disappointment in my efforts. Dad should have noticed that I was trying and should have questioned why I was regressing during my recovery, instead of getting stronger, but he didn't. He just told me that I needed to try harder and tough it out. To me, Dad's words not only made me feel like a failure, but also it sounded as if I was lying about the pain I was in. I wasn't looking for Dad to baby me, I just needed him to stand up for me. What hurt the most was both Dad and the therapist didn't ask how I was doing or even seemed concerned about the pain. I wondered if they ever experienced pain like I was in?

At this point, it was becoming obvious that depression was setting in. I was very upset with the results of the surgery. Without a way to release my frustration, I slowly began not to care about anything. Trying harder or toughing it out, would never be an option if my pain didn't ease up. How could those around me not see this?

It was nearing the end of the week, when Dad came downstairs to check on me one afternoon, before going to work. I remember him waking me up and asking if I needed to go to the bathroom. Not fully awake, I said no and fell right back to sleep. When I woke up again, I really had to go to the bathroom. I turned on the TV in order to check the time. I remember I had an hour to wait before Momma Denise arrived home. With no one at home, I had better hurry and think of someone to call, who could help me go to the bathroom. Laying there, I looked at my commode and wished I could get out of bed on my own. In my mind, I felt like I could just get up, but in reality I couldn't. The pain was a constant reminder.

I didn't want to call Dad at work because I felt he would become a little upset; having to leave work after he had already asked me earlier. The only person I thought of was Mom. I called her and she said she would be right over. Mom lived about thirty minutes away. I knew after calling her I couldn't hold it for that long. Then I thought of Elizabeth. She lived closer and could get to me sooner. Elizabeth eagerly said yes. While waiting for Elizabeth to rescue me, I began thinking that I should have had a nurse or someone to stay with me. Not only would I have some company when everyone was away, but I would have help in case of an emergency, like this one.

Elizabeth arrived only minutes after talking with her and was so happy to see her when she came downstairs. Not only because I could now go to the bathroom, but also seeing her there, really shown how deep rooted our friendship was. Elizabeth was always there for me all the while I was growing up, as I was for her. Of course we fought at times, but always made up. Don't all sisters do that? I have, and always will, think of Elizabeth as being my sister. I can only hope she knows this, even though we rarely see one another now.

Elizabeth was unsure of how to help me out of bed, so I explained what she had to do. When she pulled my legs off the bed, in order to sit me upright, a huge spasm took place in my left hip. The intensity of the spasm was so great that I began to cry. Elizabeth had such a look of shock and sadness when she noticed my tears. I told her not to feel bad because she didn't do anything wrong. Every time my body is moved in certain positions, I always get those spasms. By the way she was looking at me, I could tell she was having a hard time seeing me in the condition I was in. The last time she had seen me was before my surgery.

When the pain from sitting eased somewhat, Elizabeth helped me transfer to my commode. I was of little help as Elizabeth tried to pull my pants down. She helped me stand, but when she let go of her grip on me, my hips would give out and I immediately went down. Her and I tried so many times to get my pants down. What a pair we made.

Elizabeth helped me to stand back up again and this time she tried to hold me up with one arm. while attempting to pull my pants down with the other. Finally, after many attempts, she managed to pull my pants low enough for me to go. Mom walked into the room just in time to help Elizabeth put me back in bed. Shortly after I was in bed, Momma Denise came home. So, I guess I didn't need to call anyone after all. I could have waited for Momma Denise. But, this gave Elizabeth and I a chance to see one another and catch up on things.

Elizabeth, Mom and I talked for the longest time that night before Elizabeth had to leave. Mom stuck around a little longer. Her and I talked about how I wasn't getting better and how weak I was feeling. I told her how my days were filled with pain and that I was not sleeping a lot. I also mentioned I was becoming depressed and didn't want to deal with all the shit anymore. I wanted this all to end. I also asked Mom if she thought I would ever be able to go back to school and see my friends. Mom just shagged her shoulders and said that hopefully Holly would have an answer for us at our next appointment.

With the pain not going away, being bed ridden, listening to Dad's remarks, along with several family members saying how I wasn't trying hard enough with therapy, plus feeling isolated, depression finally got the best of me. I was a little depressed after the surgery, but not to the extent I was now. I thought for sure I would be up and around shortly after the surgery. I never imagined I would be in the condition I was in.

Again, what hunt the most were Dad's remarks. I was getting weaker and the pain was so overwhelming. Dad, whom I looked up to, seemed to look at me as a failure. His remarks hurt me when he was telling me how I wasn't going to be able to live on my own if I didn't become tougher. I would be living in bed for the rest of my life. Then his remarks about how I wasn't going to graduate from high school. I heard that one a lot. I couldn't understand why he was so obsessed about me graduating at a time when I was suffering. I realize I was falling behind in my classes, but I had another year ahead of me to catch up.

Dad should have been worrying about why I was having the amount of pain I had and about the spasms that occurred every day. He should have been concerned about why his *"baby girl"* couldn't sit up for very long or even stand. Maybe, he could have questioned how it was possible for me to undergo surgery and come out of it sad and miserable? It could be that Dad didn't know how to come across without sounding critical. Maybe, he thought by sounding stern, I would become more determined.

There were times during the week where Dad and I talked and laughed. I enjoyed those days the most because we weren't fighting. I began to miss Mom and everyone at her house more and more each day. I finally told her I wanted to come back and live with her. This time, I wouldn't leave until I was better or could live on my own. Mom said it was the best place for me to be, but I would have to be the one telling Dad.

Telling Dad about moving back to Mom's house didn't go very well. He bluntly said no without hearing me out. He went on to say that the reason I wanted to go back was because Mom would baby me. He then lectured how life isn't easy and that is why I needed to tough it out. If I did go back to Moms', he said for sure I wouldn't graduate.

I began to cry at that point and said that I didn't care if I wasn't going to graduate or if I wasn't going to be able to live on my own. I don't think he could see how lonely I was living with him or how real my pain was. I don't believe he could accept that it was the pain that was keeping me from making progress. He didn't even seem to consider that the medication I was taking, left me feeling so tired and weak.

I knew beyond any doubt, I needed Mom to help me get through recovery and help me deal with my pain. She knew I was trying my best. Perhaps, she was the only one that did. Mom wasn't worried about the future or if I graduated on time. She repeatedly said that I would graduate. After Dad had his say, he said he didn't want to talk about my moving anymore that night. For the rest of my week there, I begged Dad every day to allow me to move back. I was bound and determined to get my way.

The last night I stayed with Dad, all the disappointments I felt throughout the week came crashing down on me. For starters, I wasn't sleeping well because of the pain. The fighting with Dad about moving back to Moms, along with feeling isolated and not able to do much of anything, I laid there in bed hating my life. So, when Dad went upstairs to bed after he checked on me that night, I took ten or more Oxycodone pills. I really wanted to sleep, but at the same time, I didn't care if I woke up. If I didn't wake up, at least I would finally be pain free.

After taking the pills, my body began to relax and I must have fallen asleep because I remember nothing more of that night. The next thing I remember was Dad nudging me the following morning, in an attempt to wake me up. I was mad because when I awoke, the pain was there. I was so drowsy and feeling very weak. I had a hard time talking because I was slurring my words and I broke out crying. As weak as I was, I begged Dad again. This was going to be the last time I would beg and if he didn't let me go back to Moms', I guess I would remain stuck in bed forever and continue to feel alone.

I don't remember what exactly took place between Dad and I when I begged, but Mom came and got me soon after. I was very happy to see her, but yet, felt sad as well, because I couldn't or Dad would not let me get close to him. I said goodbye to everyone and gave Dad a kiss, even though I was angry at him for not letting me go to Moms' the first time I asked. On the drive back to Moms, I was in and out of sleep. I didn't tell Mom or anyone about taking the pills until months later.

On my way home after saying goodbye to Heather the first night she stayed at her dads', it dawned on me how alone I suddenly felt. The closer I was nearing home, the more anxious I was beginning to feel. Just as Heather's world had instantly changed after her surgery, mine did as well. Life as I knew it would no longer be as it was. The anxious feelings I felt was a reaction to what I sensed would be waiting at home for me. The consequences of taking care of Heather.

When I stepped inside my home that night, my presence was not acknowledged by neither Nathaniel nor Katie. Even when I spoke to each of them, they both acted cold and distant. Their reaction was the consequence I feared the most. Katie, as young as she was, reacted as any child most likely would, she felt left out and invisible. Not because I completely ignored her while taking care of Heather, but because the amount of attention she was accustomed to before Heather's surgery, wasn't given when Heather and I came home from the hospital. Nathaniel, on the other hand, chose to distant himself. Instead of stepping aside from his own need for attention and becoming supportive, he gradually grew resentful.

This is a very common reaction many caregivers face from those in the household. Especially, those in the household who can not understand and accept how impossible it is for the caregiver to meet the needs of everyone. It seemed unfair to me to be placed in such a predicament. There should be no price or consequence one has to pay when caring for another in need.

I didn't know what to do with myself when I returned home, without Heather being there. Since Nathaniel and Katie gave no indication of wanting to communicate with me, I went from room to room in search anything that needed to be done. When I was finished cleaning, I went upstairs to my bedroom where I sat in the stillness of the darkened room. It seemed so odd to be in the room. Quite frankly, I felt out of place. I had not slept in my own bed since Heather's surgery over a month and a half ago.

Being alone in the bedroom allowed me to reflect on what was happening to Heather and myself. I couldn't imagine what her body was going through, but I did know that she was becoming very discouraged with life. I also knew if others did not let up on the negative comments, she would give up and give into depression. This worried me the most. Her physical condition had me less worried, only because I believed Holly could fix Heather.

During the week Heather stayed at her dads', I slowly readjusted to my life. Work became my place of refuge. At work, I could lose myself in my job and escape the reality of my home life. Many of my co-workers would often stop by and ask about Heather and how I was doing. So many times in the days that followed, they allowed me to vent my frustrations and cry if I needed. It was their act of kindness where I drew a lot of my strength from during that time and it really gave me a sense of not being alone. Truthfully, there were many days when I did feel as if Heather and I were up against the world alone.

Every day after talking with Heather, I grew angrier and angrier. I knew how important it was to Heather reconnecting with her dad. Feeding my anger was how blind Alex seemed to be when it came to Heather's need for his approval. As angry as I became when Heather spoke of her days there, it did not even come close to the anger I felt when she said Alex would not allow her to move back with me and how she resorted to begging.

There wasn't much I could do to bring Heather home with me. Alex had legal custody over Heather. This is the reason I told Heather she had to be the one talking to her dad. Going to court was an option, but I didn't want to start a long drawn out battle. There seemed to be many different obstacles being thrown at Heather and I all at once and we both were feeling the strain of it all.

The day Heather called with the news she could move back was indeed a good day, for Heather and I anyway. There was such a look of disappointment on Nathaniel's face when I told him. Katie wasn't too pleased with the news either. At a time such as this, I felt it wasn't my responsibility to please either one of them. Heather needed to be back with me and if Nathaniel saw it as an inconvenience, then I guess he would either walk away or see the opportunity that was being presented; to become more loving rather than remaining self absorbed as he had been in the past. When it came to Katie, I urged her to do her best in thinking how she would feel if she were Heather. I told her that what I did for Heather, I would do the same for her. With that said, Katie seemed to better understand why Heather was the center of my attention at that time.

I couldn't wait to bring Heather home. When I arrived at her dad's house and saw her laying in bed, my heart sank. Her condition seemed to have deteriorated since I last seen her, three days before.

She looked pale and extremely weak. Her speech was slurred more than usual. For the life of me, I could not figure out why she was in that condition. I was so flustered by then, all I could think about was getting Heather home and fast. At that time, I had no idea the amount of pills she had taken the night before. Looking back on the week Heather spent at her dads', an amazing thought came to mind. *Perhaps God, Life, or whatever name is used to honor a Higher power, purposely places a child with special needs within a family whom is in need of being reminded, how important it is to be tolerant, accepting and loving toward others.*

CHAPTER FORTY

HEATHER'S WORDS

*M*AYBE THE WORD "HOME" IS not where you grew up at, but the place where you actually feel you belong. As much as I wanted to believe I belonged at Dads, my week there opened my eyes to the possibility that maybe Dad, Momma Denise and the family were not really prepared to care for me in the condition I was in. Up until then, I didn't need a lot of help from them in caring for me. I was able to take care of myself for the most part.

I was happy to be going back to Moms house. Although, it did seem strange to think that her house was going to become my new home. I felt comfortable at Moms because she was laid back. Not too many things upset her. One thing was for sure, as Mom parked the car in the driveway, I was more than ready to be laid down. I felt sick from taking so many pills the night before. I couldn't understand how I could still be feeling so much pain. Didn't make sense to me. With all the medication in my body, it would seem like I would be in no pain at all. But, instead of being pain free, I felt sick to my stomach and dizzy. I was having a really hard time focusing and staying awake.

As Mom unloaded my wheelchair from the trunk of the car, I automatically turned my head toward Sebastian's dog house. Sebastian was just sitting there doing his usual reminder barks. He had this habit of barking once or twice in a row, whenever we got out of the car. I guess it was to remind us he was ready to come into the house. He should have known by now that we wouldn't forget about him, but being old as he was, he seemed to forget this at times.

After Mom put me into my wheelchair, she went over and unchained Sebastian. He came running over toward me to say "*hello.*" Afterward, he took off running a lap around the house. One lap was his limit before he had to take a rest. He was then ready to go inside the house. When Mom opened the door, Sebastian plowed through Mom and I in order to get inside first. Once in, he went straight to the couch and rubbed his body along the couch before plopping to the floor. He would then roll on his back and twist and turn as he tried to scratch his back. He had dry skin and was always looking for someone to scratch his body. After rolling around on the carpet, Sebastian just laid there not caring if he was in the way of Mom and I. Sebastian's greatest joy in life was eating and it was obvious because he was quite fat. That dog could be in a dead sleep, but if Mom threw a chunk of dog food in his bowl, he would race into the kitchen to eat it. This always made us laugh a lot.

As Mom wheeled me into the house, I didn't feel at all welcomed by Nathaniel. When I said hi to him while passing him in the living room, he said "Hi" back, but not in a friendly tone. He quickly walked out of the house without saying anything else to anyone. I didn't know what his problem was and chose to ignore him. We used to get along really good, but after my surgery he seemed to have changed. He didn't talk to me as much and acted mad at me. Katie seemed unhappy to have me there as well. Maybe because I would be getting a lot of attention again. I was hoping she would become involved in my recovery and not feel isolated from Mom.

This time, I would be sleeping on the bottom bunk in Katie's room and not in the hospital bed like I did before. I was happy because there was more privacy in Katie's room. The only problem with sleeping on the bottom bunk was getting used to Mom hitting my head on the top bunk bed frame whenever she sat me up. Never failed.

To help me roll over, Mom tied clothes line rope along each side of the bunk bed. I would grab onto the rope and roll over. At first it was difficult, but after a while, I found a way to twist my body that didn't cause me to be in a lot of pain. Rolling over was a great way to strengthen my arms. It was a good feeling to be able to roll over on my own and not have to rely on Mom all the time. However, there were nights when I was too weak or when the pain was really bad, that I needed Mom to help me.

Some nights, Sebastian would jump up on the bed and sleep with me. Those nights I didn't get a lot of sleep with him hogging the bed and him snoring. Mom usually tied him up in the room, since he could not be trusted at night. He would sneak into the garbage or into the bathroom trash in the house. If he was tied up, he would crawl under my bed and sleep there. It was a good place for him because it was cooler for him. Even there, his snoring echoed throughout the room.

Katie and I slept in a room just off from the kitchen. It was actually a porch, but Mom and Nathaniel made it into a bedroom. The room was small and had no door. To give Katie and I some privacy, Mom hung a sheet across the doorway. Every morning during the week, I was awaken by Nathaniel as he made his breakfast in the kitchen. He was always up before Mom and left for work before Mom did. Mom would come downstairs later and wake Katie up for school. She would ask me if I needed to go to the bathroom, which I always did. Mom would sit me up on the edge of the bunk then waited a minute before transferring me to my commode. This was to give me time for my pain to ease a little in my hips and back. Some mornings, I would stay up while Mom was getting ready for work to eat breakfast before being laid back down.

Mom would leave her cell phone by my bedside in case I needed to call her at work. Mom had spoken to her boss about me and my situation. They allowed her to leave when I needed her to come home; which was often. Every Wednesday, Mikey came to the house and sat with me. This was his day off from work. He would stay until Mom came home. When Mikey came over, the first thing he did was carry me out into the living room and lay me down on the couch, then we would watch movies. I enjoyed this time with him. These were a lot of days where I would fall asleep when he was there, but he didn't seem to mind. Mikey would also come over during the week when he was on his lunch break and we would eat lunch together; usually Subway subs. Normally, I stayed in bed on those days because he couldn't stay very long, plus sitting still caused me to be in a lot of pain. My bed was really the only place I could get comfortable in. I was getting so used of being in my bed so much, I didn't like getting out of it.

Two or three times each week, Grandma Ski would come down to visit. On those days, Mom would lay me on the couch before she left for work, so Grandma didn't have to get me out of bed. I would watch TV with Katie before she left for school. I would then take a nap until Grandma showed up. Grandma Ski usually came around noon or shortly after. She would help me into my wheelchair and wheel me to the kitchen table. She would fix me a glass of Carnation Instant.

I didn't have much of an appetite for food, so Mom insisted that I drink the breakfast drink in order to get some nutrition in my body during the day. Grandma and I would spent our time together playing Yahtzee and watching TV. I cherished those days with her. I always had a great time. I'm not sure that Grandma Ski really knows how much her visits help me during my recovery. Even though she had a lot going on in her life, she took the time to sit with me. This meant a lot to me.

A couple of weeks after moving in with Mom, Dad started coming over on Thursdays to eat lunch with me. He would bring doughnuts and chocolate milk and we always played Cribbage before he had to leave. The visits were great. He was still worried about my health and school, but I always told him "*Everything will work out*." Even though I didn't know what was going to happen next or if I would be able to go on dealing with the pain I was in. I felt myself becoming more depressed and weaker as the days passed. Couldn't life give me a break or something? Maybe one day.

During the hours when I was home alone, I slept a lot. There wasn't much else I could do. Those were also the days I had to call Mom home from work, so she could help me on the commode. If the medication I was taking didn't make my mouth so dry, I wouldn't have to drink as much as I was and not have to go to the bathroom as often.

On one occasion while Mom was at work, I called Mikey's Dad who lived just three houses down from ours and asked if he could help me on the commode. I didn't want to call Mom away from work. Daddy Al said he wouldn't mind helping me and came right down. I wasn't embarrassed anymore about others seeing my naked behind. After being exposed so often while in the hospital and sleeping in the kitchen. I could tell that Daddy Al was a bit uncomfortable while he was helping me. I looked at him as a father figure as well. He would always buy Katie and I Christmas gifts. Plus, the family took me underneath their wings. So happy that I have them as my family as well.

My school work was going good and the in home therapist had stopped seeing me. The therapy wasn't doing anything for me. I just needed to get the pain under control. My next check up with Holly was coming up soon. Maybe, she would have an answer for the pain.

The day of my appointment, Mom, Mikey and I left for the hospital at 6:30 in the morning. We always made the appointments early in the morning because we had such a long way to drive. When we arrived at the hospital, I first went to x-rays. I always had x-rays taken before seeing Holly. I was hoping Holly found the reason for the pain in my back and hips or maybe had an idea of what to do to get the pain under control. I wanted to be pain free so I could do more things; like sitting up longer. If I could sit up longer, I might be allowed to go to school.

I don't remember much of the visit with Holly, only that the x-rays looked fine and my incision was healing good. What surprised me was Holly didn't know why I was having so much pain. Holly thought it would be a good idea that I receive some Botox injections to help relax the muscles in my legs and hips. She also wanted me to come in for inpatient rehab after the injections. I was excited to get into rehab. Maybe there, the therapists would know what they were doing. Hopefully, more than my in home therapists did.

Perhaps, I could learn how to do daily things, like getting up from bed on my own, standing and perhaps walking again. I knew there was going to be a lot of exercising to help me become stronger again, but maybe with the Botox injections, the pain would not be an issue. Holly said she would be checking up on me while I was in rehab. This sounded good because she could be informed about any problems I was having and do something about it. An appointment with Holly and to with meet Dr. Snyder, whom would set up the date for the injections and rehab was made for November 27th, 2006.

On the 27th, Mom and I met Dr. Snyder. She seemed really nice and concerned with the tightness of my legs. After examining me, she said the Botox injections would help me out a lot. Going into rehab following the injections was planned as well. The date for the injections and being admitted into the hospital was set for December 4th. The plan was to be in rehab for two weeks.

Even though it was only eight days before I would be going into the hospital, I never thought the day would ever arrive. I was so excited when it did. Maybe this time when I get the Botox injections, it will take some of the pain away. It had been two months since my surgery and everyday I have been in pain. Nothing seemed to make it go away.

Once again, Mom, Mikey and I, headed to the hospital. I was beginning to think I should have just lived at the hospital, since we were always going there. I asked myself why did I even choose a hospital that was so far away. I guess because I heard how good the doctors were.

While waiting at for my injections, I was thinking how I was going to be put to sleep, so I didn't have to feel the needles going into my muscles. I still wondered why Mary Free Bed didn't do this for me when I was younger instead of just putting on numbing cream that didn't seem to do anything because I still felt the needles pricking me. I was also thinking about rehab and how I was going to have therapists who knew how to work with patients like myself.

The therapists at the hospital worked with a lot of younger children whom had the same type of surgery as I had, along with having Cerebral Palsy. I believe the in home therapists I had, wasn't as skilled in that area. I was ready to become strong. My goals were to be able to stand, wipe my own behind, and sit up longer than five minutes at a time. What I looked forward to the most was Holly finding the reason for my pain.

I don't remember how long I was asleep for the injections, but when I woke up, Mom and Mikey were at my bedside. Mom said they couldn't stay very long because it was snowing quite hard and they had a long drive ahead of them. Mikey let me borrow his cell phone so I didn't have to use the hospital phone. This way, I wouldn't have to call for the nurse to hand me the phone every time I wanted to call someone. During my stay, I called Dad once in a while, when I wasn't in therapy to keep him posted on how I was doing and also Gates. I called Mom everyday.

After Mom and Mikey left for home, it hit me that I was on my own. It felt good being out of the house, but I wasn't too sure about being away from Mom for two weeks. I could only hope that I was going to be in good hands while in rehab.

My mornings in the hospital started early. My nurse would wake me each morning and take my vitals before I ate my breakfast. After eating, the nurse handed me my medication and the schedule for my therapies. I went to Physical and Occupational therapy twice each day. Once in the morning and then again in the afternoon. I also had sessions with Adam, the hospitals psychologist, who taught pain management by using breathing techniques. Later, Mom and I gave him the nick name of "Adam, the Breather Man."

During PT, the therapist would begin each session stretching my legs. Then I was asked to try to stand and encouraged to take a couple of steps. It didn't matter that I took a pain pill just before therapy. The pain I felt after the therapist stretched my legs was strong. My legs would be shaking so hard, which made it difficult for me to stand. We practiced transferring from my wheelchair to the mat. I needed a lot of assistance with the transfers, because my legs were so weak. I was having trouble sitting during therapy because of the pain. I didn't see where the Botox injections made any difference. I still had the same amount of pain I had before. Maybe there would be some relief in a couple of days.

I knew the therapies were going to be hard for me, but I was willing to do what ever I had to do, in order to get stronger. I wanted to walk so bad. Life would be a lot easier for me if I could walk and be out of my wheelchair. I just didn't think I would have to go though so much pain in the meantime. Holly made it sound so easy, when we talked about getting out of my wheelchair and being able to walk. She did say there would be a lot of therapy I would have to do, but the pain I was in prevented me from making any progress.

I don't remember what all I did in OT, but do remember working on techniques for daily activities; such as dressing, showering and other personal hygiene tasks. This is when I realized how much muscle tone I had lost since my surgery. I wasn't that muscular before my surgery, but I could do more than I was able to do now. Every movement I made caused me pain. The most discouraging thing was how no one seemed to know the reason why; not even Holly.

After my therapy sessions, I went back to my room. The nurse would help me back into bed. It felt good every time I was laid down because the muscles in my back and hips would begin to relax. That was pretty much my days while in the hospital. I rarely was out of bed, outside of going to therapy.

For the first four or five days after being in rehab, I called Mom everyday when she came home from work to tell her about my day.

I would tell her that I was doing my best and how happy I was to be there to get stronger, but missing everyone back home. Then as the days went by, my enthusiasm begun to die away. I know part of the reason was being homesick, but the main reason was because the pain wasn't giving in. I didn't feel any less pain now than I did at home. The Botox injections hadn't made any difference in the pain or helped with relaxing my muscles. My muscles and tendons still felt extremely tight. I began to feel that it was a mistake going into rehab. I was getting to the point of not wanting to get out of bed in order to go to therapy. The pain was still constant and I was taking medication whenever I could get it. I felt myself becoming weaker and weaker. I wanted to go home.

I started calling Mom more often each day. I would start crying each and every time I called. I told her I wanted to come home and felt that nothing was being done to take away my pain. I explained how I was feeling weaker and couldn't do much in therapy. Mom told me to give it a couple more days and see how things go. We got into a little fight over the phone because it felt like Mom thought I was giving up and wanted an easy way out of rehab. I was so mad at her, but I did as she told me to do because I believed she knew what was best for me.

Day after day I called Mom and told her I wanted to come home, but she didn't give in. I was not doing good. I was tired all the time because of the medication I was given to control the pain. I wasn't eating well and always wanted to stay in bed. This wasn't the plan I had when I entered rehab. The plan was to learn how to transfer and for Holly to take away my pain or at least find the reason for having the pain. I needed to be able to sit longer. I couldn't reach that goal if the pain wasn't controlled. If I couldn't sit up longer, then I wouldn't be able to return back to school. Oh, how I missed school. Seeing friends, teachers, the office staff and especially Gates. I missed getting out of class to go down to the office to relax and chat with everyone. This was my favorite thing to do when I was at school.

It was at the beginning my second week in rehab, when I really began to hate being there. No one came to see me during the weekend. I felt alone and spent most of each day in bed. The following week would turn out to be the worst. One day while in my room, a nurse came in with my pain medication. I looked at her disappointingly. Was this the only way they knew how to lessen my pain? What I needed more than medication was for Holly to look for the reason I was having so much pain, not just keep issuing me drugs. So far, I had only seen Holly twice during all the time I was there. I was so upset by this time, because I felt as though no one was trying to help me.

I grabbed the container of pills from the nurse and threw it across the room. I knew the nurse was only doing her job, but come on. Couldn't anyone see what the medication was doing to me? It was affecting my ability to do therapy and my appetite. I was always feeling so tired and worn out. I knew I was losing weight because of not eating much, but didn't expect to find that I had lost close to twelve pounds during my stay there. Couldn't those in charge of my care see this?

I guess not, because within minutes after throwing the container across the room, the nurse called the social worker up to talk with me. My attitude was being questioned. Not what caused my attitude. I felt as though they believed there had to be something emotionally wrong with me to be acting out like I did. Soon after talking with the social worker, I was given a series of tests by Adam. I wasn't sure why I was being tested. The test dealt with my ability to problem solve and memory. I was feeling so drugged while being tested. I couldn't even count back from ten when I was asked to.

It was getting close to the date I was supposed to be discharged. Mom said she was coming to a team meeting to discuss my case. Everyone involved in my case was going to be there. I couldn't wait to see Mom. That morning while having PT, I remember sitting on the edge of the mat. A therapist was holding my walker in front of me and encouraging me to stand and to try taking a few steps. There was another therapist sitting behind me on the mat holding my body and head up, because I was too weak to do it myself. I slowly turned my head toward the door of the room and started to cry so hard, because an angel was walking toward me; Mom.

I was so happy to see her. Somehow I knew this met that I was going home. I could tell from the look on Moms face, she was furious. Mom walked up to the therapists and told them that she was taking me back to my room. I had an appointment to meet with Adam, the Breather Man, right after PT, so Mom and I went to see him before going up to my room. From then on, I have little memory of what happened at the hospital. I just remember Mom waking me up and telling me we were home.

CHAPTER FORTY-ONE

AFTER MEETING WITH HOLLY AND Dr. Snyder, I felt confident Heather would finally receive the help she needed. By this time, my major concern was getting Heather physically stronger. She had lost a good amount of muscle tone and her weight loss had me worried. Heather was showing signs of depression, but I believed if the medical staff involved in Heather's case could pin point what was causing her pain and address that issue, then she would at least be able to fully participate in rehab. If Heather was able to actually feel as if she was making progress in regaining mobility and able to perform more daily activities, I believed her depression would lessen.

I felt the major contributor to her depression was the side effects of the pain medication she was taking. Fatigue, loss of appetite and weakness were commonly associated with those meds. It seemed as though Heather's situation was tuning out like a "catch 22" scenario. Heather's pain was a direct result from her surgery. Physical therapy was required to regain the mobility which she lost following the surgery. Pain medication was prescribed to relieve or lessen the pain in order to tolerate physical therapy, but the medication made Heather physically weak and very emotional. Even with taking the medication, Heather was plagued with pain, which in turn, limited the amount of therapy she was able to withstand. So, where did this leave Heather? How much progress was possible if she remained taking the medication that wasn't solving her pain issues, but only adding to her continuous regression?

The pain Heather was experiencing was mainly in her lower back and hips. Not from the incision itself. She kept saying that it felt as though her muscles were ripping and pulling with movement; any movement. Then on top of that, she began to experience spasms in her back and legs. My stance on Heather's condition was this: "*Since her present condition was created at Advanced Care Hospital, then it was the responsibility of those in charge of Heather's care, to do what ever was needed in order for Heather to regain mobility, independence and relieve her of the continuous pain she was in.*"

Heather and I were told that she would be admitted into the hospital for intense rehab following the Botox injections. The areas targeted for the injections would include Heather's hip flexor muscles, hamstrings, and the muscles going from her pelvis to her thighs. A total of four hundred units of Botox, at the cost of fifty six hundred dollars, would be injected into Heather.

I was under the impression that after receiving the injections, Heather's muscles and tendons would relax fairly quickly. With her muscles relaxed, the pain medication could possibly be lowered in strength. Lowering the dosage would have a huge impact on Heather. Her appetite would definitely improve, allowing her to gain some much needed weight. She would also begin to feel more energetic. The feeling of being tired all the time was really wearing Heather down emotionally. Hoping to get Heather off or lessen the amount of medication was my rationale for placing such high hopes on the Botox injections taking effect fight away. My lesson to be learn from this? "*Never place a lot of faith on assumptions.*"

I really believed the best place for Heather was inpatient rehab. With Heather in the hospital, Holly would have an opportunity to keep a watchful eye over her. The physical therapists, working with Heather would be in a position to observe what movements triggered Heather's pain and spasms. Their findings could provide the most useful information in assisting Holly, as she determined what course of action should be pursued. Why else was Heather going to be admitted, if not to work as a team to improve her overall condition? The date set for Heather's injections and admittance into rehab was scheduled for December 4th, 2006.

It was a snowy morning as Mikey, I and Heather left for the hospital on the fourth. We always made early appointments whenever Heather went to the hospital. Leaving early and arriving back home in the late afternoon. The trips were usually uneventful, but during the winter months, we always seemed to managed traveling on the days when it was either snowing, sleeting or during a blizzard.

Mikey and I stayed at the hospital until Heather woke from the anesthetic after receiving the Botox and was settled into her room. By that time, the weather was becoming quite nasty and I wanted to head home before the roads became really bad. We left Heather in the hands of her team at Advanced Care.

If there was going to be a time for Heather and I to regain our strength, it was during her stay. It was so obvious that Heather and I were both in need of healing. I had been neglecting my health for far too long and it showed. I too had lost quite a bit of weight and was tired all the time as well. Days before Heather went into the hospital, we discussed how often I would visit her. We decided I would not visit unless she absolutely needed me there. In order to stay connected, we planned to talk on the phone everyday. There was no way Heather and I could go more than a day without talking to one another. That was the type of close relationship we shared.

For the first few days, Heather sounded cheerful over the phone. Then her demeanor over the phone began to change. She became very emotional during our conversations. Heather sounded quite homesick, but what was most disturbing, Heather felt like she wasn't getting better. This is not what I imagined Heather would experience. Becoming a little homesick was understandable, but not getting healthier was confusing to me. When I asked how therapy was going, Heather said she wasn't making a lot of progress. She said she tired out so easily and by the end of each session, needed total assistance from the therapist. She wasn't sleeping good, the pain was still there and the nurses kept giving her drugs.

Heather said the injections didn't seem to have worked. She then informed me that she spent most of her time in bed. I told her to give it a few more days. Maybe the Botox would begin to work by that time. I didn't know then, but later learned the effects of Botox usually takes around 3-10 days to work. Around the second week after receiving the injections, the muscles tend to relax the most and this can last up to three months or longer. If I had been more familiar with Botox, I would have questioned why Heather was admitted for intense rehab at that time, instead of waiting until the effects of the injections had relaxed her muscle tone. At this rate I knew there was little chance of Heather making any progress and understood why she felt therapy wasn't helping her.

When Heather said she wanted to come home, my first instinct was to go and bring her home. I was torn between acting on parental instinct or going along with the opinions of family members. Several family members, including Nathaniel, felt Heather should stay in the hospital and continue with therapy.

"If I went and brought her home, I would only be causing her further delay in her recovery. Heather needed to start working harder with therapy and not expect me to rescue her when things became too hard for her." That statement, when said to me by others, made sense, but also upset me as well. Perhaps, I was too involved with Heather, because I had a hard time accepting their perspective as being true for me. Unfortunately, instead of acting on my gut instinct, I went along with the opinion of the family, just to stop their comments. By doing this, I placed Heather in a position of feeling abandoned by me. I told Heather I wasn't coming to the hospital until the following week, when I attend the team meeting.

Heather became angry over the phone when I told her this. I grew angry at myself for not just jumping into the car and bringing her home. This ate at me for days. What bothered me the most was that I knew Heather wasn't looking for an easy way out. I knew how badly she wanted to get back to her old self. My decision, not to go and bring her home still bothers me today, because Heather went through her own little private *Hell* alone.

Heather kept calling everyday. Sometimes three to four times throughout the night. By the way she sounded on the phone, I knew what needed to be done and didn't care how others were going to respond. My mind was made up. If Heather was as bad off as she sounded on the phone the day I attended the meeting, I was bringing her home! Didn't matter if her two weeks of rehab were up or not.

On the day of the team meeting, I arrived early in order to spend some time alone with Heather. As luck would have it, Heather wasn't in her room when I walked in. I went to the nurse's desk and asked the where abouts of Heather and was told she was having physical therapy. I went to where therapy was taking place and entered without being noticed. I stood there in the corner and watched in disbelief as the therapists working with Heather, were encouraging her to stand.

One therapist was standing in front of Heather holding onto the walker. Another therapist was positioned behind Heather holding her upright on the mat, since Heather could not balance herself. Hell, she couldn't even hold her head up without the assistance of the therapist behind her! I stood there frozen, growing angrier by the second and not believing what I was seeing. I then started to walk slowly toward the mat. Heather caught sight of me and began crying. I walked up to her, gave her a kiss and looked directly into the eyes of each the therapists and told them; *"Heather's session is over."* I bent down, scooped Heather off the mat and placed her into her wheelchair and wheeled her out of the room.

Once Heather and I were out in the lobby, she said we had to meet with Adam, the Breather Man. This would be my first time meeting him. To help assist Heather in managing her pain, Adam was bought in to teach Heather breathing techniques. He also was the one who conducted the cognitive testing, in order to have a better understanding on how well Heather is able to problem solve, along with her present state of mind. After the episode of Heather's seeming aggressive action of throwing the pill container across the room, there was concern among the staff about Heather's emotional state of mind.

When Heather told me about the incident, I knew the reason behind her action. By throwing the container, Heather was actually making a statement, otherwise overlooked by those whom were in charge of her care. Heather wanted relief from the pain, without the feeling of being in a stupor. Sadly, it was only her and I that apparently knew this. Those new to her situation, including the nurse, social worker, along with Adam, viewed Heather's action as being somewhat defiant and acted accordingly, by testing and analyzing her cognitive skills and personality. I was about to be informed of these findings while meeting with Adam. After what just took place in the therapy room, listening to Adam analyze Heather, without fully knowing her, was not a good place for me to be. I was ready to lash out at anyone by that time.

When Heather and I knocked at Adam's door, he greeted us with a smile and invited us in. His office was tiny and cluttered, with files and documents scattered everywhere. Not a lot of room to move about. Adam introduced himself to me and spoke of his involvement with Heather. He said working with Heather was a pleasure, but there was some concerns he had over her test scores. Her scores on the cognitive tests ranked average to below average against those of her peers. She was having issues with memory, difficulty in problem solving and appeared to be overly compliant. As soon as Adam mentioned something on the lines of Heather showing signs of a boarder line personality disorder, I went off. If he thought Heather had a personality disorder, before leaving his office, he would definitely believe it stemmed from me.

When one grows up in an environment with others choosing what one can and can not do, the likelihood of becoming overly compliant or submissive is pretty much a given. I agreed with Adam on this. Heather was quite limited on things she was allowed to do. She must have felt like she had no voice on many occasions. I admit that I had done my share of telling Heather what was best for her, without giving her much say.

I failed to recognized that Heather was very capable of making good choices as she was becoming older. As life would have it, I would soon have to face and deal with letting go of my control over Heather before this journey of ours was over. In the process of letting go, I was about to become amazed by her ability to make good choices. But, until that time, I still saw her as my little girl who needed protection.

The notion of personality disorder was what got my blood boiling. Because of the pill incident, Adam felt as though Heather was displaying signs of an anti-social personality disorder. When I questioned him if he had taken the time to discuss with Heather the reason behind why she had thrown the container across the room, he said he had, but was concerned by her display of anger. Adam felt it would have been more appropriate if Heather had talked about her frustrations, regarding taking the medication, instead of throwing the container.

"Talk about her frustrations to whom?" I asked in a sharp tone. "To the nurse whom was only carrying out what Holly prescribed? To the social worker, who had no previous knowledge of Heather? After the both of you discussed her reasoning, what did you do? Did you contact Holly and notify her about Heather's dissatisfaction of the drugs given to her, or did you just write it off as being anti-social."

Like the professional that he was, Adam advised me that becoming upset wasn't helping the matter out any. He was correct at pointing that out, but at that time I was beyond mad and remaining calm and rational was nearly impossible. I strongly felt labeling Heather was unacceptable. Not once was there any mentioned of how the side effects of her medication could have played a part in the low test scores and on Heather's present mental condition. It wasn't until I confronted him on this, did he admit that the test results might not be conclusive.

Heather was in the hospital to be treated for chronic pain and undergo intense rehabilitation, not for the purpose of being evaluated for any psychological disorder. The Heather being evaluated was not the well adjusted, average to above average student whom inspired many, but was being looked upon as being a young woman with multiple learning and coping deficits. I couldn't help, but think how it was possible that Adam, or anyone for that matter, did not consider that maybe the medication, Heather was taking was causing more harm than good. Adam's over all opinion on Heather's state of mind was meaningless to me. He did not know the real Heather, whom was sitting before him.

Since Heather was often teary eyed throughout her stay thus far and showing signs of depression, she was prescribed 20mg of Celexa twice daily. Celexa was the newest anti-depressant to be approved by the FDA. When I was informed of this I grew even more angrier. Instead of exploring the idea that maybe the drugs Heather was taking may not be suitable for her, they went and prescribed yet another drug with side effects that included dizziness, drowsiness, dry mouth, loss of appetite and suicidal thoughts. Add Celexa to her other pain medication she was taking, I had a hard time of believing what possible benefit the drug would be offering Heather.

After meeting with Adam, Heather and I went up to her room. She needed to use the bathroom before laying down. Things were about to get even more unsettling for me.

There is a breaking point when self control goes out the window and one is left with hostility. I reached this point while in the bathroom with Heather. On Heather's backside, there appeared to be what looked like a bed sore. I immediately called the nurse to the bathroom and questioned her. In all the time Heather was in my care, there was never any signs of bed sores. I made sure she was moved often for that reason alone.

"What the hell is this on Heather's backside?" I yelled out to the nurse. "Is this a bed sore? Because to me, it looks like a bed sore." The nurse was hesitant to even come near Heather and I in order to look at the spot I was pointing out to her. It was indeed a bed sore and became apparent that Heather spent the majority of her time in bed without being rolled over often as she should have. There wasn't a doubt in my mind that I was going to take Heather home with me. I told the nurse to contact Holly and have her begin the process of discharging Heather.

The nurse looked shocked by my request. I am really surprised that she didn't call the social worker up to the room, to help deal with Heather's out of control mother. Instead, the nurse remarkably remained poised and mentioned that I could request Heather's discharge at the team meeting. There would be no requesting a discharge in the meeting, there would be a demand for it.

All those, with the exception of Holly, involved with Heather's care, were seated around a conference table when Heather and I entered the room for the team meeting. The therapists, social worker, Adam, Dr. Snyder's assistant, along with Holly's assistant, were waiting to brief me on Heather's progress. Right off, I announced that I planned to take Heather home with me after the meeting. There were quite a few disappointed and confused faces staring at Heather and I after I had said that. When I was questioned why I insisted upon Heather being discharged, I began my attack. I criticized the care in which Heather received, the lack of progress in Heather's condition, the psychological testing and evaluation and the lack of discovering the cause of Heather's pain.

When one is surrounded by a room full of professionals, it's not really a good idea to criticize. They all listened to me rant and rave, but I wasn't heard. That was the impression I was feeling. Because after I was finished, every individual in that room took their turn on reporting Heather's status, as if I never said anything.

A lot of information and different approaches each staff member wanted to on work with Heather was bought out in our discussion. My reply to them was this; "All of you had time with Heather to work with her. Each one of you had seen that she wasn't making progress. You watched her becoming weaker and apparently chose to do nothing about her condition. Could someone explain, what I witnessed in physical therapy this morning, was in any way helping Heather?"

There wasn't a word muttered by anyone on the team. They all just sat looking at me and casually glancing at Heather as I continued to question and criticize their care of Heather. Dr. Snyder's assistant finally shut me up by informing me that Holly was considering removing the pelvic fixation and re-mobilize the pelvis. The hardware in her pelvis may be too restrictive when combined with her hip muscle tightness. However, before resorting to surgery, Holly would like Heather to undergo another series of Botox injections, this time using CT guidance. By using the CAT Scan, the injections can be precisely targeted. The injections were scheduled to take place in a few days.

I looked over at Heather and noticed her looking at me. God, she looked frail and tired. Then I looked around the room at everyone waiting for my response. I was so angry at everyone in that room, because in my eyes, they all had failed Heather. My decision to take Heather home that day stood. I was then asked if the Botox injections could be administered the following morning, would I consider staying the night. Heather could then be discharged the following day if I still wanted to take her home. When I didn't come back with an answer right away, someone in the room asked Heather if she want to go home or continue with therapy.

In a soft tone of voice Heather replied, "Look at me. I was able to do so many things before my surgery and now I can't even wipe my own ass." Heather's words made everyone in that room look down. "How am I suppose to do therapy when I am too weak to even hold myself up? I want to go home." With that said, Heather began to cry.

Nothing much was said by anyone after Heather had her say. I then told them that if the procedure was arranged for the following morning we would stay, but after that, Heather and I were out of the hospital. Heather and I ended up spending the night and she underwent another series of the injections. We left the hospital as soon as Heather was cleared to go. If there was no improvement in Heather's condition within a week or so, then we were to contact Holly and she would schedule a date to remove the hardware in Heather's pelvis.

I can't help but wonder if anyone in that room felt as though he/she could have done more for Heather during her stay. Each one of them had the opportunity to do something when he/she had seen how

Heather was becoming weaker. It wasn't all caused by Heather being homesick or any psychological disorder as they might like to have believed. Heather left Advanced Care Hospital in worse condition than when she went in. She had lost close to twelve pounds and was more depressed than ever.

Heather and I placed high expectations on Holly in finding and correcting whatever was causing Heather's pain. We also believed Heather would be leaving the hospital stronger and more mobile. Even as Heather and I began to doubt the reputation of the hospital, we still believed in Holly. There was a sincerity about her that captured our hearts. We believed Holly would not give up on Heather, so we did not give up on her. That was our basis for continuing treatment at that hospital.

CHAPTER FORTY-TWO

Before Heather and I begun writing, Heather requested a copy of her medical records to help us accurately recall the events and procedures in detail. The both of us did not think to keep a journal of the experiences she had gone through during her treatment at Advanced Care Hospital. In fact, the thought of writing a book had not even occurred to us as of yet.

As with all patients being admitted into the hospital, a patient history is taken. It is noted that Heather, a seventeen year old female with spastic quadripartite Cerebral Palsy, was being admitted directly from home for intense therapy to restore mobility, activities for daily living and optimize pain control. Botulinum toxin (Botox) injections would be administered soon after her admission.

Prior to her surgery, Heather was near independent or independent in all activities of daily living and ambulated using crutches, holding onto walls, or crawled around the house. For longer distances outside the house she required a wheelchair. After her surgery, she continues to be plagued with pain and had not returned to her baseline function. She has impaired mobility having greater difficulty with stand pivot transfers, standing and ambulating, than before her surgery. Heather is a eleventh grade student, receives average to above average grades. Mainstream curriculum. A-B student. Parents are divorced. Heather is negative for neurological or other neuron muscular disorders. Anticipated stay; two weeks.

The day after being admitted, Heather was seen by the hospitals psychologist for an inpatient consultation. Once again, it was mentioned that Heather was an average to above average student. She has a history of a learning disability in reading and writing. She is in special education class for English only. She also receives one hour of resource room for catching up in her classes. Heather receives counseling through the school social worker. (The counseling with the school social worker, was not individual counseling, but as a group setting.) For needed support, Heather talks with her mother and keeps journals.

Cognitively, since her surgery in October, Heather has reported having difficulties with her memory and mild difficulties in problem solving. At this time, Heather denies difficulties with her emotions. However, her interpersonal demeanor was significant for a tendency to possibly be overly complaint. Given that one of her good friend recently committed suicide, it is warranted to follow up with Heather to monitor her emotional in addition to cognitive functioning.

Physical and Occupational therapy evaluations were also held on the second day. The Occupational therapist noted that Heather is able to upper extremity dressing with minimal assistance. She fastens and unfastens her bra in the front because she is unable to extend her arms high enough to fasten the bra from behind. Grooming is minimal assistance. Lower extremity dressing maximum assistance is needed. Recreational activity is minimal assistance. Nursing reports Heather pain is well controlled and sleep is adequate. No skin breakdown. In other words: no signs of any bedsores.

During Heather's physical therapy evaluation, she was able to transfer to her wheelchair without becoming tired. Although, she did require assistance with second transfer and appeared more fatigued at the end of the session. Her tone in lower extremities was noted to be tight, thus limiting her range of motion. Before the evaluation ended, goals for Heather's therapy were set. The only goal Heather set for herself was to be able to walk eight feet without assistance in and out of the bathroom. The discharge goals set up by the therapist were:

Goal 1: Heather will be modified independent with bed mobility.

Goal 2: Heather will be able to transfer with stand pivot by assistance using appropriate assist device (walker).

Goal 3: Heather will be able to ambulate for household distances with walker and stand by assistance.

Goal 4: Heather will participate in wheelchair evaluation for manual chair to increase independence in mobility.

Short term goals were also established during the evaluation.

Goal 1: Heather will be able to perform bed mobility with min assistance using correct motor plan.

Goal 2: Heather will be able to perform transfer with minimal assistance consistently for full treatment session.

Goal 3: Heather will be able to walk five feet with minimal assistance using walker

Goal 4: Heather will be able to tolerate three lower extremity exercises in supine (laying on her back) utilizing pain management strategies.

During Heather's nutrition assessment, according to the hospital's criteria, she was considered as being a patient with malnutrition. Starting immediately, Heather's intake of calories was set at 1800-2250 calories daily. It was noted that Heather's inadequate food and beverage intake was related to decreased appetite and fatigue.

On the morning of Heather's second day in the hospital, the morning nurse noted that she had trouble sleeping the night before and her back pain was rated as being 9 out of 10. Heather's physical therapy did not go well. Her mornings session was basically stretching her legs and ankles. The afternoon session was worse. Heather still rated her pain as being a nine. The physical therapist reported Heather was experiencing heightened anxiety with mobility. She was crying often during the session and needed maximum dues to console and calm her. Anti spasticity agents should be considered, as Heather's tone is limiting her mobility. In the meantime, the hospitals psychologist will begin counseling for anxiety and begin assisting with coping and pain management skills. At the present time, Heather was being given ATC acetaminophen (Tylenol) and Oxycodone for break through pain. Heather was given Oxycodone prior to her PT sessions to optimize pain.

In Heather's PT session, she was having pain in her left leg along with spasms. Heather worked on upper body strengthening by using two pounds weights and batting a beach ball with a cane for endurance. She was fatigued at the end of her fifteen minute session and needed maximum assistance for transfers, unsafe with less assistance. Heather needed maximum assistance for calming her when she was put in her wheelchair along with maximum assistance to maintain her balance while sitting in the chair. Heather was noted to have been leaning heavily forward and unable to support herself upright due to crying and pain.

December 7th, Heather's third day in the hospital, she was still having severe pain in her lower back and thighs. The pain was worse on her left side. It was believed that the Botox should begin to take effect now and hopefully bring some relief from her pain. This also was the day Heather was prescribed Celexa for her anxiety and depression. Because according to recent medical notes, Heather had been tearful and very anxious with other medical staff. (It was just after the pill container incident.)

In her physical therapy session that day, Heather rated her pain as being an eight. It was noted that she often bursts into tears and told the therapist her crying was due to pain and spasms in her quadriceps (muscles on the front of the thigh), abductor (muscle originating on the pelvic bone and attached at intervals along the length of the femur), and hamstrings. Once again after her session, Heather needed maximum assistance to transfer from the mat to her chair due to fatigue and pain.

The following day, Heather rated her pain at nine. She was crying less during her PT session, but was unable to bear weight without severe pain in her left leg; when she attempted to stand. Sitting was also becoming more difficult due to pain. In her quest to become more independent with bed mobility, Heather wanted to learn how to sit up right from a laying down position in bed. Because of her muscle tone and spinal fusion, she was unable to balance herself and required maximum assistance to complete the process.

Sunday, the sixth day of her stay, Heather still remained in pain. The Botox injections had not yet taken effect. She spoke of how Oxycodone didn't seem to help and oddly enough, the pain seemed to have intensified since she had her injections. Again, the pain seemed to worsen with movement of her legs. Heather's muscles and tendons in her legs were noted as being somewhat tight. Heather was given 250mg of Naproxen (a drug used to reduce inflammation and relieve pain) twice daily, in addition to Oxycodone, Diazepam (Valium), Tylenol, and Citalopam (an off Brand of Celexa). These drugs were not given to Heather all at once, but given at different times and different strengths throughout the day.

On that Sunday, Heather was reported to be upset and saying that she wanted to go straight home because she was sick and coming there was a mistake. She had not been out of bed since Friday and was now using a bedpan. Heather was noted as being very emotional and refusing to go to therapies. At present, Heather required total assistance for transfers, for wheelchair use and is unable to walk.

The day before I was to attend the team meeting, Heather was reported as appearing pale and required maximum encouragement to engage in conversation and therapy session. Her pain was rated a ten with difficulty sitting in her chair. She needed maximum assistance for every activity. This also was the day Heather was given yet another Anti spasticity drug added to her daily meds; Baclofen.

The physical therapist reported that Heather arrived to her session (the morning I attended the team meeting) unable to support her head secondary to fatigue. Heather appeared pale and somnolent (drowsy) and required maximum clues to engage in activities. Heather needed total assistance from wheelchair to mat. Heather's, Mom, arrived at the end of the session and transferred Heather back to chair.

In the team meeting, the physical therapist presented us with Heather's overall assessment. Heather's progress was limited by her increased pain, increased sedation secondary to pain medication and spasms of her lower extremities. As for the goals that were set at the beginning of Heather's stay, two of the discharge goals were met. Heather was able to roll over on her own in bed and participate in stretching. Being able to transfer with moderate assistance; goal was met but inconsistent. The short term goal not met by Heather was transferring with minimal assistance. The goal for walking the household distance with walker before being discharged was not met.

Walking the household distance with her walker, was never a realistic goal in my eyes to begin with. It sounded good, but Heather's muscle tone in her legs had weaken so much by the time she entered rehab. All along, I had spoken of how Heather's tolerance to her pain medication was holding her back from making any progress in her recovery. Everyone involved in Heather's care during her stay must have noticed this as well, shouldn't they of had?

Heather's lack of progress was not due to being homesick. Not due to the lack of effort on her part. But, in my unprofessional opinion, her lack of progress was hampered by the side effects of all the pain medication she was being given. This was why I was so angry at those involved in Heather's care during her stay. Each one watched as Heather weakened during her time there and apparently disregarded any coalition between the two.

CHAPTER FORTY-THREE

HEATHER'S WORDS

ONCE AGAIN, I WAS HAPPY to be home. Having family around me means a lot to me, even though some of the family members did not seem to be behind me a hundred percent. There was a feeling I sensed when they were around me, that I in some way had let them down. I'm not sure how I could have. I did my best at rehab, but I guess that wasn't enough.

I was also glad to be back with my room mates; Katie and Sebastian. Sebastian was my sleeping buddy. When he wasn't hogging the bed, he could be found underneath the bed snoring away. Even though his snoring was loud it was comforting to me.

Mom and I fell back into our routine again. Mikey, Grandma Ski and Dad began coming on their usual days as well. Even Grandma Sandy and Grandpa Tom came to visit. Always arriving with extra food for us. Grandma Sandy is like that. Bringing my favorite foods, along with a dog treat for Sebastian. She is such a caring person. If the two of them didn't know how thankful we were, I hope they do now. We were always so grateful.

Mom's cousin, Jimmy Gigowski and his wife Nancy, along with their two daughters Amanda and Megan, would pop in to see us from time to time. Jimmy along with my Great Aunt Phyllis, donated blood for me when I had my first surgery at the hospital. Out of anyone in the family, Jimmy and Nancy had a good idea of what I was going through. Their daughter Amanda had rods placed along her spine as well, but she didn't have her surgery at the same hospital.

Mom and I loved their visits. The visits were always filled with laughter and support. With them, I didn't feel as if I disappointed them with my lack of progress. They were over to visit with Mom and I. Not to question why I wasn't walking or telling me I should be trying harder. I really want all the people reading this to know how important it is to be supportive, instead of expecting someone to be doing things he/she may not be capable of doing, at the time when others think he/she should be. It bothered me so much when I was expected to do things I couldn't do.

I still remained in pain, even after those second Botox injections. I told Mom one day that maybe we should send a copy of my medical files and x-rays to John Hopkins hospital. They would know what was wrong. Mom said she believed Holly knew what she was doing and just needed more time. I was upset by her words because I thought Holly already had enough time. I wondered if Holly had talked to other specialists about me and if they had given her any advice. Maybe with the help of others, a solution would be found.

I just wanted to move on with my life. I still couldn't do much of anything. I felt really weak and wasn't eating much. Laying in bed most of the day was getting boring and my depression was getting worse. I didn't give it a thought how many other cases Holly was working on besides mine. I figured since I wasn't dying, I could wait until she found something. As I look back on it now, in a way I was dying inside. I found it harder to believe life was worth living and I felt myself losing my will power to remain positive.

After a week and a half had passed since my discharge from rehab, Mom called Holly and told her how I wasn't doing any better. Holly said that she wanted me to have another surgery. I didn't want another surgery, but I told myself I had a 50/50 chance for the pain to go away. I wasn't excited about surgery, but I said "*Okay*."

Even before calling Holly, Mom and I both agreed that we were only staying at the hospital for three days and no longer. Mom was getting to the point of hating hospital stays like I. Holly was okay with our request, as long as nothing happened to me during surgery or showing any signs of infection or any complications after the surgery. Holly called Mom back later on and said that I was scheduled for surgery December 28th, three days after Christmas.

That year, would be my first Christmas away from Dad and the family. It seemed really strange to me. I always spent Christmas Eve with Dad and the whole family, including my Uncles, Aunts and Cousins, along with Grandma Sandy and Grandpa Tom. Then on Christmas morning, the Grandparents, on both sides of the family would come over to watch us kids open our gifts from Dad and Momma Denise. There was also a gift or two from Santa as well. It was tradition to have a big breakfast afterward before Mom came to pick me up for Christmas with her side of the family.

All that changed after my surgery. Dad, Momma Denise and the kids came to Mom's house for a while that Christmas. I was so happy that they decided to bring my Christmas gifts for me to open in front of them. My favorite gift I received that Christmas was spending time with them in Mom's living room.

I don't remember very much of our stay in the hospital after my surgery, but do remember Mom got food poisoning. Poor Mom. The first surgery she ended up getting very sick. Now, she was sick after eating a hamburg from Wendy's. Mom and I did get to go home in three days. We left the hospital in the afternoon and didn't make it home until it was dark outside. When we left the hospital, Mom and I did not know that waiting for us at home was some unexpected bad news.

The drive home from the hospital was peaceful. I was in and out of sleep, but when I was awake, Mom and I talked and laughed. When we pulled into the driveway and went into the house, there was such a strong sense of negative energy coming from Nathaniel. He said something about going fishing, but later told Mom that he was leaving and already had an apartment. What a wonderful welcome home gift. "Hi, I know you had a long trip and probably stressed and tired, but let me add some more on top of that." I wondered how long he was planning this and how he could do this in that moment.

Before Nathaniel left, Mom put me in bed. She was trying to hold back her tears, but I saw the tears. I had tears also, but was mad at the same time. I kept thinking to myself; how could he do this to Mom? In a way, I was happy he was moving out. He didn't want to hangout with us kids. He wanted only Mom's attention and if he didn't get it, he would become upset and spend most of his time out in the garage or else go somewhere.

After Nathaniel moved out, Katie moved upstairs into the big bedroom. Mom didn't want to sleep in it anymore. Mom slept in a small room at the top of the stairs. If I needed Mom during the night, I would call Katie on her cell phone and she would get Mom. We tried using walkies-talkies, but the batteries didn't last very long. I had a bedroom to myself, well Sebastian still slept with me. It wasn't long after Nathaniel had left, Mom and Katie brought home a kitten. We named her Snitsky. Later on, I gave her the nickname "*Dumb Dumb*." It didn't matter how much she bit and terrorized Sebastian, he never hurt her. He was always so gentle with her.

Within a week after coming home from surgery, the pain in my lower back and hips returned. I was pissed. This was getting so old. I started hating my life. I needed to go back to school. At that point, I didn't care how much pain I was in or how weak I was. Mom and I talked about it and she decided that if I really felt ready, I could try going back to school when my incision healed and if Holly said it was okay.

I called Holly when there was no noticeable change in Heather's condition after a week and a half of being home from rehab. This is when she suggested surgery. The hardware in Heather's pelvis was going to be removed along with shortening the length of one of the Harrington rods in her lower left side. Hopefully, this would bring Heather relief from her pain.

Holly predicted a three day hospital stay would be sufficient, as long as Heather did not experience any complications. Heather and I were both happy to hear this, because we did not want to spend any more time than needed at the hospital. The surgery was set for December 28th, 2006.

Surgery went well and no complications were reported. After waking up in recovery, Heather was taken up to the pediatrics ward where she ended up staying in the same room as she had after her first surgery. Since I would be staying with her, the familiar "*truck seat*" would once again serve as my bed. Just as I did during Heather's first hospital stay, I roamed the halls and hospital grounds to busy myself.

On one of my excursions the second night there, I decided to go have a hamburg at Wendy's, which was located in the hospital near the cafeteria. A few hours later, I started feeling nauseated and spent the majority of the night in the bathroom being sick. I knew it had to be from eating that hamburg, because I felt fine earlier. Staying with Heather at the hospital started to seem hazardous to my health. First stay, I ended up with walking pneumonia, which I was still battling with. This stay, food poisoning. I didn't even want to think what another stay would bring about.

The following morning I wasn't feeling much better than the night before, but it didn't matter because Heather and I were going home. Knowing that alone, made life seem more tolerable for me. I'm not sure if others had a bad experience with Wendy's food as I had, but it wasn't long after my incident, Wendy's was no longer at the hospital.

The drive home was quite relaxing. The roads were nice and clear. Unusual for that time of year in Michigan. Heather slept on and off during the ride. When she was awake, we talked about how this surgery might just take away her pain. We laughed and joked like usual, which always seemed to bring the two of us some escape from dwelling on the negative aspects of our journey thus far.

We pulled into our driveway a bit after nine at night. Like always, I turned to Heather and said; *"We did it. We made it."* As soon as I wheeled Heather into the house and saw Nathaniel, I could feel something was up. He was sitting on the couch with his coat in hand. There was no welcome home greeting from him. Instead, he stood up and informed me he was going up north fishing with his boss. Right off, I knew he was lying. Number one, he wasn't dressed to go fishing and second, it was New Year's Eve weekend. No way would his boss choose to leave his family and go fishing that weekend.

As I stood looking into Nathaniel's eyes, I saw nothing resembling compassion or even a connection to me. His eyes were completely empty. I had a strong feeling of what was about to happen if I were to question him on what was really going on. Questioning him, I feared would mean hearing what I wasn't ready to hear. Not questioning him, would just prolong the inevitable; him saying how things were not working out like he hoped they would have

Being a need to know type of person I questioned him. Never did I imagined the kind of response I was about to hear. Without the slightest hesitation, he said he was leaving us and already had an apartment rented in town. Which meant, that while I was in the hospital with Heather, he was busy moving out without ever saying a word about it. He had cleaned out the garage and all his belongings in the house except for his clothes and personal items.

He went on to say that he planned to move back to Colorado as soon as he could afford it. No real explanation was given by him as to why he was leaving, but being in a state of shock as I was in, I would not have had heard it anyway. In a matter of minutes after I had laid Heather in bed, he packed up his clothes and was gone. I felt so betrayed by him. All along, he was playing out the role of being somewhat supportive, but in reality, he was just biding his time until he found an apartment to move into. With things going the way they were with Heather and me being so focused with that, wanting to leave was understandable. The way he went about it was just wrong, in my opinion.

That weekend, as millions of people were celebrating the coming of a new year, my world came crashing down around me. It was just too much for me. Suddenly, nothing in life made sense to me, as I sunk into a depression unlike I had ever felt before. Actually, I felt paralyzed from life itself. I was little help to anyone, let alone trying to deal with my own issues. There for a while, Mikey and Katie stepped in and helped out with Heather whenever they were needed. Heather tried her best not to request help as often. We were all struggling to keep it together during that time.

Without the help of Mikey, Katie, Heather and my Aunt Marge, I seriously believe I would not have had bounced back as well as I did. My Aunt Marge, whom lived in Oregon at the time, was/is my closest trusted friend. During the course of a few weeks of talking on the phone for hours on end with her, I slowly began to feel life flow inside of me again.

Out of her willingness to allow me to express my emotions, while coming to grips with all that was happening, she managed to challenge my perspective in a way that seemed to bring about letting go of a lot of self pity, while helping me notice how destructive holding on to it was. Not an easy thing to do. It seems as though the mind loves to cling onto negativity more so than searching for the seeds, in which a sense of well being can grow upon.

The biggest worry I had after Nathaniel left was losing the house. There was no way I could manage paying the bills that I owed. Everything, the house, car and all the other monthly bills were in my name. Nathaniel had me believing that his credit was too poor for him to apply for any type of loan. Therefore, it was decided the loans for the house and car would only be in my name. By doing this, Nathaniel was free to walk away without any financial obligations.

Without that second income and often missing work, due to doctor appointments and staying home to care for Heather, basically there was very little income coming in. Mom, Shirley and Grandma Sandy bought food over to us, which helped out a great deal. Otherwise, we lived off of pancakes, Ramen noodles, saltine crackers, cereal and stoganoff. I never would have believed that we would be poverty stricken again. Especially, at a time when we were already dealing with a lot of set backs with Heather.

In those difficult times like we were experiencing, we desperately needed something to look forward to. Something inspiring in which we could use to draw positive energy from. What did we choose for inspiration? We chose to run away. I talked to Marge about going to Oregon for a visit. She encouraged us to come and spend a week. Since I was going to be facing financial ruin in a very short time, we might as well go down doing something totally absurd. Instead of saving my tax refund and using it to pay bills, I purchased plane tickets to Oregon for Katie, Heather, and myself. It wouldn't be until August when we planned to go, but knowing that we were going gave us that "*something*" to look forward to.

Heather continued to be in pain after her surgery. Although, Heather did feel some relief in her hips, it wasn't what Holly nor us had hoped for. It seemed reasonable to believe that since her pelvis was not as restricted as it had been the pulling and ripping sensation would ease up or end. That wasn't the case. Even the muscle tone in her legs remained tight. After the amount of Botox injected into her legs and hip region, one would think Heather would be feeling the effects of Botox by then. There wasn't much going in Heather's favor.

She still experienced pain all along her spine, as well as, spasms in her back and legs. Sitting up was still limited. Standing was almost impossible, because her hips would give out causing her to fall back down. On occasion, Heather said it felt as though the rods were pinching some nerves in between he shoulder blades. Then, out of the blue Heather began having bouts with pleurisy. She said it felt like her chest muscles were ripping away from her ribs. The pain would come on suddenly and last for a week or so before she was able to breathe without bursting into tears. Throughout the year, we made several trips to the ER for this condition.

The cause of Heather's pleurisy was never found. Usually, pleurisy can be triggered by a viral infection of fluid build up in the lungs. Heather did have small amounts of fluid in her lungs, but the doctors, whom treated her, didn't believe it was the cause. One possibility which made the most sense to me, was maybe the strain placed on her chest muscles after straightening her spine was the cause. Whatever the cause, Heather was in an extreme amount of pain during every episode of pleurisy she had.

With every visit to the ER, Heather was given some strong pain medication to help ease her discomfort. Pain medication and muscle relaxers were becoming Heather's primary substance being ingested into her body, over riding food and drink. And it showed. The spark in her eyes was fading and she was falling deeper into depression. Heather and I talked about her returning back to school. Heather believed that school would give her a sense of being somewhat of her old self again. Something she hadn't felt since her first surgery.

Whether or not Heather was strong enough to even return back to school had to be considered. She would have to be watched over very closely and be allowed to lay down when the pain from sitting became too much for her. I wasn't sure if the school would allow Heather to return in her condition. Plus, allow her to take the pain medication she was on. Heather had her mind set on going back. In all honesty, she basically had no life to speak of, or any other aspect that brought her a sense of purpose. School was the answer and I sensed it as much as Heather.

As soon as Holly gave Heather the go ahead to return back to school, I contacted the school along with the ISD bus garage. Because Heather was placed in a resource room, she was eligible for pick up by the ISD bus. Otherwise, she would not have had transportation to and from school. This was such a blessing for Heather. What wasn't expected by her and I, was how early she would be picked up and how long the bus ride was going to be.

Chapter Forty-Four

Heather's Words

I was so excited the day Holly told me I could go back to school. Not only would I be seeing my teachers and friends, it meant getting out of the house. It was so boring doing the same thing everyday; laying in bed and sleeping. But, the big question I was asking myself, "Was I really ready? Could I possibly sit up a whole school day?" Ten minutes or so was my limit before having to be laid back down at home. Mentally, I was ready to go back to school. Physically, I knew I would be pushing it. I was so determined to return back to school that it didn't matter how much pain I would be in. A week before going back to school, I called Gates to let him know. He told me not to rush into coming back if I wasn't ready, but I told him I would be seeing him the following Monday.

Mom called the bus garage and made arrangements for me to be picked up. Since I was going to be picked up in Lakeview instead of Greenville, we were told the bus would be arriving around 5:20 am or so. The bus I was going to ride, was kept at the Lakeview bus garage, which meant I would be the first to be picked up and be riding the bus for almost two hours just to go to school.

It would have made more sense to go back to Lakeview High School, since the school was just around the corner from Moms. But, Greenville school was where all my friends were at. The teachers at Greenville understood my situation and allowed me to take my time on assignments and make up work. Besides, Greenville school is all I know. The school was home and everyone in school was family to me.

It felt like I was going back to school after summer break, after being absent for such a long time. I was very anxious to see everyone. I didn't get to much sleep the night before starting school. Getting comfortable enough to fall asleep that night was hard. Not only was my left hip giving me problems, Sebastian was hogging the bed. I finally ended up taking an extra Valium to help my body relax and then I managed to fall sleep for a few hours.

Mom had to wake me up at four in the morning in order to get me ready for school. Since I was returning back to school in the winter, Mom would have to get up at three just in case if the driveway needed shoveling before the bus came. I always felt bad when Mom had to shovel so early in the mornings.

There were mornings when the ISD bus didn't come because of the snow. Since Mom and I had to get up so early, we never knew until later if school was canceled or not. I hated those days because I got up for no reason. If school was canceled or when the ISD buses were not running, I had to take down my hair and remove my make-up; plus Mom would have to undress me and put my pj's back on, then lay me back into bed. What a pain that was.

Anyone who knows me well, knows that I am not a morning person. However, that first morning of school, I had a smile on my face and was ready to get out of bed. Just as Mom helped me sit up on the edge of my bed, a huge spasm instantly began in my left hip. I sat there tensing my body until the spasm eased and I was able to transfer to my commode. Mom was concerned about me going back to school while I was still in so much pain, because once at school, there would be no way for me to come back home during the day unless I called Mom at work to come get me. I told Mom not to worry and that I would be fine. If I needed to lay down during the day, I knew I would be allowed to go to the office and lay down there. I did my best to convince Mom that I would be well taken care of at school.

When I was finished using the commode, Mom grabbed a pair of jeans I picked out to wear that day and helped me put them on. I still remember how loose those jeans fit, because of all the weight I had lost since my first surgery. I weighed 105 pounds before going into surgery in October. In just over five months, my weight dropped to 87 pounds. I didn't care how big my jeans were, I was going to wear them. I just tightened my belt up. My T-shirt I chose to wear that morning was big on me as well.

After wearing mostly PJ's since my first surgery, I was so ready to begin dressing in my regular clothes. Of course, there were days when I wore PJ's to school. Those were the days when I didn't feel very good and didn't care about what clothing I wore. Gates recommended that I stay home at least one day each week, because he knew I tired out so easily. So, I stayed home every Wednesday. His idea was great because, by Wednesday, I was totally exhausted. I also stayed home when I was on my period. I didn't want my aid dealing with that. Sometimes, I stayed home because I just didn't feel good and did not want to risk getting sick. It would be so easy to become sick since my immune system was run down. Other than that, I was in school and enjoyed being there.

After getting dressed in the mornings, Mom would wheel me up to the kitchen table in order to finish getting ready. There wasn't enough room in the bathroom at Mom's for me to sit in front of the sink while sitting in my wheelchair. I wouldn't be able to see myself in the mirror anyways, because the mirror was hung too high on the wall. The kitchen table became the bathroom counter, where Mom set out my hair stuff, make-up, a little mirror, along with my tooth brush, tooth paste and a cup of water. While I was busy getting ready, Mom would turn on the radio, then begin getting herself ready for work.

The first morning while waiting for the bus to arrive, Mom and I were like little kids waiting for their bus to come on their first day of school. Any noise we heard that sounded like something coming down the street, we would be looking out the door. When I finally saw a bus stopping at the end of our driveway, my heart begun racing with excitement. It felt like forever since I even rode on a bus.

While driving my wheelchair down the driveway, I couldn't believe I was actually going to school. Once my wheelchair was inside and strapped down in the bus, I waved goodbye to Sebastian and Mom. I felt so free as the bus began pulling away from the house; I could have cried. With all that had happened to me since my first surgery, I was beginning to give up hope of ever returning back to school. I had been so bound to my bed since October and isolated from friends. I love my family very much, but I needed to socialize with others outside of them.

Wouldn't it be great to see into the future? I wish I could have.

The reason why I say this is because I would know what the bus ride was going to be like. I swear, I felt every crack, dip, and the tinniest pebble the bus drove over on our way to school. If I thought the car rides were painful, I was wrong. Whenever any spasms flared up or the pain started to become more severe, I would turn up the volume on my iPod and try to focus on the music, instead of giving into the pain.

The moment I caught sight of the school, it was as if I had no pain. The excitement I felt at that time is unexplainable. After being on the bus for that amount of time, the bus aid and driver couldn't unbuckle the straps off my wheelchair fast enough. I was so anxious to get off the bus and into the school. When I finally entered the school, I just stopped and stared. I couldn't stop smiling. I was so happy to be there and seeing familiar faces coming to greet me, it just overwhelmed me.

I soon began looking for my aid whom was going to be helping me during the day. I didn't have to look long because he was just down the hall walking toward me. The two of us went to my locker where he helped me take off my coat. I noticed right off, he had a worried look on his face. I knew what he must have been thinking *"What are you doing here?"*

I looked so pale, thin and very weak. I didn't want him to think I needed him to do everything for me, so when he asked if I needed anymore help, I told him no. After he left me at my locker, I reached up to grab my textbooks, notebook and folders. Reaching upward was so painful. I couldn't even lift my textbook off the shelf with one hand anymore. I couldn't believe how I had lost so much muscle tone in my arms and legs. Not wanting to ask for help from anyone, I repositioned my wheelchair to where I could grab everything I needed with both hands. Doing so made it easier to get what I needed, but set off spasms in my back.

The first place I headed for after getting everything I needed from my locker, was to find Gates. I spotted him in his usual spot, greeting students as he had done every morning. He looked happy to see me, but yet I could see a look of concern on his face.

Going through the halls and common hallway at school, it felt like all eyes were on me. Many friends greeted me or called me over to them to ask how I was doing. I told them I was fine, but at the same time, I was dealing with a lot of pain. Sharp pains in my lower back and hips were beginning to become more intense, The pain I felt was hard to hide from others, but I did the best I could. I didn't want anyone to feel sorry for me.

On my way to my first class, I passed the bench where Zachariah had sat every morning and during lunch. It was empty. How strange it was going to be not seeing him sitting there, smiling at me as he had done every time I passed him by. However, I honestly felt his presence around me at all times.

Before returning back to school, I chose to drop French and Chemistry. Both of those classes were too hard for me to keep up with, without actually being in class where the teacher could help me. The home bound teacher did her best, but our time together was too limited to go over everything needed for each class.

My sister, Cori, came to the house several times to help me with Chemistry, but there was just too much material to learn and memorize. I dropped my Child Development class a day or two after going back to school, because I didn't have enough time to make up the late work before the semester ended. All I had during the remainder of my first semester were three classes; English, Math and Study Skills. Surprisingly, I finished first semester with a 2.56 Grade Point Average.

The classes I would be taking when second semester started were, English, Study Skills, Critical Issues, Contemporary U.S. History, Earth Science and Math. Math and Earth Science gave me the most trouble. Maybe because the two were my least favorite subjects. I was already behind everyone in math because I didn't fully understand what was being taught during home bound. Moving to the next level of math without being prepared, left me struggling even more in keeping up with the class.

Mr. Fortino, my math teacher, kept telling me everyday that I was doing great and not to get discouraged. When I was home bound, Mr. Fortino gave my home bound teacher a printed picture of himself smiling to give to me. On the picture, he wrote "Get Well Soon" along with his signature. I laughed when I received it and felt so honored. I still have that picture.

The worst time I had during the day at school was sitting in the class room. Sitting without moving about gave my mind plenty of time to focus on the amount of pain I was in. Sometimes, if the pain became too much for me, I would raise my hand and excuse myself from class and go to the office. The office became a sort of escape from my pain. I was allowed to lay down if needed or just hang out with the office staff. If Gates wasn't busy, I would bug him. He always had a stash of candy or cookies on hand to share with me. I felt so supported by the office staff and Gates. Being in their company, made each day at school so wonderful.

The look on the face of my physical therapist, the first time she saw me at school, was the same look I seen on everyone; a look of concern for my health. Becky could not believe how thin, pale and weak I was. I told her how I was laying in bed most of the time at home because of the pain. I described the pain I was having and had since my first surgery. She asked if I was able to walk or take a few steps. I just shook my head "*NO.*" I told her how standing was very painful and transferring was impossible without assistance. Becky and I talked about the week I spent in rehab and the amount of weight I had lost. She didn't say too much, but I bet she was thinking how it was that I went into surgery independent and came out being in so much pain and having to start from stretch.

During lunch, I often sat with Elizabeth if I wasn't sitting with other friends. Sadly, Elizabeth and I were growing apart. I really missed our time together; spending nights at one another house and our phone calls. She did come to visit me a couple of times when I moved back to Moms, after that week I spent at Dads. Life seemed to be taking each of us in a separate direction.

Dad would visit me during lunch hour on Thursdays, bringing with him food from Burger King. I missed him and the family, but I needed Mom the most to help me get through this journey I was on. That year , I wanted to surprise Dad with a special birthday gift. I heard that Kenny Chesney was going to be in concert at Van Andel. Both Dad and I liked Kenny Chesney and I thought Dad would enjoy seeing him. One of my teachers at school helped me get tickets and when Dad's birthday came, I gave Dad his. He was both shocked and happy when I handed him his ticket. It was going to be a perfect night for just the two of us.

The night of the concert, Dad picked me up after school. I felt like "*daddy's Little Girl*" again and loved every minute of our time together. Before the concert began, Dad and I bought T-Shirts. Even though we sat in the handicapped section with the stage far below us, we still enjoyed the concert. Thanks to those huge screens at Van Andel Arena, it was possible to see everything going on up on the stage.

By the end of the concert, I was ready to lay down. My back and hips were hurting so bad. I had been sitting up all day at school and way late that night. Once I was back at Moms, I went straight to bed and told Mom not to bother getting up early the next morning, because I was not going to school. I made sure I got all my assignments from the teachers before leaving school just in case I didn't make it to school the following day. Thinking ahead helped a lot.

May 18th, 2007, I had an appointment with Holly. I still wasn't making the kind of progress she had hoped I would. Holly suggested it might be time to consider straightening my left femur and lengthening a tendon which would help relax my left hip. With my left leg straightened, I would trip less when I did begin walking. Walking was still my dream I had and I would do anything to get it. Even after all I had gone through so far, I believed whatever Holly suggested was in my best interest. Both Holly and Dr. Ausiello, had said right from the start, that this procedure would require more than one surgery and take up to three years before I was finished. I accepted and understood what all was needed to be done to get me walking and out of my wheelchair, but I wasn't prepared for all the set backs and pain I was in.

The way Holly explained what she intended to do made sense to Mom and I. Anything that would loosen the tightness in my hips sounded good. I imagined what it was going to be like laying in bed, standing or sitting without the pulling and ripping sensation I experienced everyday. Mom and I agreed to go ahead with yet another surgery, on one condition. Yep, you might have already guessed it. The condition was, only if I was able to go home in three days following the surgery if nothing went wrong. I didn't want to miss any more school, so the date of my third surgery was set for June 5th, 2007 .

I talked to Gates and my teachers about being able to take my final exams early and finish the school year before school was officially over. By then, I was all caught up in every class and was going to pass eleventh grade. Gates and my teachers said I could. While *Swing*

Out week was going on at school for the Seniors, I was in the office studying and taking my final exams. With a lot of hard work and determination, I managed to end semester with a 2.73 GPA. Passing eleventh grade seemed like a miracle, because I fell so behind in my school work before returning back to school. Not a day went by that my teachers didn't tell me I was doing a great job. They all knew I was going through hell all the while I was attending school. Their encouragement really did boost my morale and inspired me.

Before leaving the school for summer vacation, I said goodbye to my teachers and friends. I told them, Hopefully, when I see them again next school year, I would be feeling better and my pain would be gone. While many of my friends were making plans for a fun summer, I was about to undergo another surgery. All I could think of before Mom and I arrived at the hospital the day of my surgery was: *"Here I go again."*

CHAPTER FORTY-FIVE

*W*HEN HEATHER WENT BACK TO school, I was rising, but not shining, at three in the morning. Up until then, I was sleeping in until 5:00am before having to crawl out of bed. Since Heather was returning to school during the last months of winter, the first thing I did each morning was check the driveway to see if I needed to shovel. If so, I was out shoveling before waking Heather.

With the bus arriving around 5:20 AM, I usually had Heather up around 4 AM or there abouts. I would help Heather out of bed, on and off her commode and dress her before wheeling her out into the kitchen. Heather would finish getting ready on her own. While she was busy with that, I went back outside to inspect the end of the driveway.

By this time, the snowplow had usually gone by and filled the end of the driveway back in with snow, which needed to be shoveled away. Shoveling was beginning to seem like a never ending ritual, because as soon as I came home from work, I would be once again shoveling before Heather returned home on the bus. Rarely did she get stuck in the snow with her wheelchair. It was the ice in the driveway which would cause Heather's chair to spin out.

Then came the winter thaw. Driving through the mud was a completely different story. Heather's powered wheelchair weighed so much that it would easily get stuck in the mud. Most times, I managed to push the chair out of the mud. Other times, I ended up carrying Heather into the house and leaving the chair for Mikey to push out.

During spring, tracking mud into the house was unavoidable. There were tire tracks from Heather's chair leading from the front door, straight into the kitchen. Maybe, that was the reason behind someone inventing that rusty semi-shagged multicolored brown carpet, which we had. To help hide all kinds of messes; like mud. Needless to say we vacuumed quite often in spring.

With Heather back in school, being at work was less stressful. I worried less when she was at school than when she was at home. There were days when Heather was home alone for a few hours before someone came to care for her. During the hours I knew she was alone, many different scenarios would pop into my mind as to what could happen to her. Like someone breaking in our home, fire, Heather needing help and not being able to call me. Things like that. Thankfully, none of those occurred, but could have. OKAY, I take that back.

There was one incident where Heather called me home from work, because she had fallen out of her wheelchair and couldn't get off the floor. As bad as that sounds, Heather wasn't hurt by the fall. When I walked into the house that day, there was no sign of Heather. I saw her wheelchair, but not her. I called out to her only to discover she was laying under the kitchen table laughing.

When she fell out of her chair, Heather said that our faithful watch dog and companion, Sebastian, high tailed it upstairs and left her to fend for herself. Perhaps, he thought he would be in some sort of trouble? Hard to say, but if Heather were able to reach his dog treats, chances were very good he would have never left her side. Heather wasn't completely abandoned as she laid on the floor. Snitsky, our cat, stayed by her side. However, there was a motive to her loyalty. Snitsky, most likely figured since Heather was down by the drawer where we kept her fluff balls, the least Heather could do was open it so Snitsky could snatch one out and play with it.

Making light of Heather's fall was how we dealt with the situation. Over reacting would have only caused Heather to become overly cautious whenever trying anything new on her own. This would not be the last time Heather took a spill. With every failed attempt at doing a certain task, Heather was adjusting to and applying new methods at accomplishing what she wanted to do. She didn't give up trying and that in itself was the greatest accomplishment.

Going back to school was indeed the best medicine for Heather. She was smiling more and the sparkle in her eyes shined. She arrived home each day with stories about her day and how she loved being back among her teachers and friends. It made getting up as early as we did and the shoveling all worth it. Except on the days when school was canceled because of the weather. Since Heather and I had to get up so early, we never knew if school was going to be canceled or not until later.

Our daily life throughout Heather's journey was based on whatever routine that worked out for her in that moment. Returning back to school was no exception for us. By the time Heather returned home from school, she was experiencing a great deal of pain and very tired. Before Heather did anything, I would put her into the shower. The warmth of the water help relax the tightness in her lower back and hips. Many times after she was home, she would break down crying because of the spasms she was getting in her back, hips and legs.

After showering, Heather did homework while eating dinner, before laying down for the night. Both her and I went to bed early because we both were exhausted from our day. This left very little time for Katie and I. Because of the amount of care Heather needed, I missed many of Katie's soccer games and school events. Amazingly, Katie never demanded special attention nor acted out in any way to get attention. In a way, she was experiencing a similar childhood as Mikey had. Growing up in a broken home, filled with uncertainty and adversity.

By the time Heather returned back to school, the pain in her left hip and lower back had significantly improved. Removing the hardware in her pelvis seemed to be working in Heather's advantage. The Botox injections she received before her discharge from rehab, had also kicked in. The improved flexibility in her legs and hips was a promising sign that Heather may just be on her way to regaining her mobility and independence.

During one of Heather's follow up visits with Holly, we discussed the next step in the process of getting Heather walking and out of her wheelchair. Walking was still Heather's dream. She had her heart set on walking up to receive her high school diploma on graduation day. Nothing concrete was decided at that appointment. Holly scheduled another appointment in two months, to determine if Heather's hip flexors still gave Heather problems once the Botox had worn off. If so, Holly would then decide if surgery was needed.

One month after our initial visit with Holly, Heather began experiencing the same type of pain in her right hip as she had in her left hip before the surgery in December. The pain was becoming increasingly worse with sitting and standing. Laying down was the only way to relieve the pulling sensation Heather was feeling. So we made an appointment with Holly to get her opinion.

At that appointment, Holly noticed that Heather's range of motion in her hips was considerably impaired, due to the tight hamstrings and hip flexors. Before rushing into another surgery so soon, Holly prescribed an anti-inflammatory along with physical therapy. Heather was also give an implant card, which would allow her to board the airplane for our trip to Oregon. With the metal in her body, Heather would trigger the metal detectors at the airport. The card would show cause for the detectors going off. Heather was then scheduled to see Holly in three months.

Heather started physical therapy, but did not continue after a few sessions. Going to therapy in the winter was pretty much a waste of our time, not to mention the therapist's time. Heather's muscles would be so tight because of the exposure to the cold, that it would take the majority of her session just to warm up enough to get a few minutes of stretches done. We thought about bring in an in home therapist, but with the luck we had before we decided against it. Plus, the insurance wasn't being very cooperative at that time as well. We ended up canceling future appointment with the therapist. I began stretching Heather's legs every night before bedtime.

In early May, Heather returned for another followup with Holly. At this time, Heather was having more difficulty standing than before and sitting was becoming even more painful. The pain in her left hip was beginning to come back in full force and the tightness in both her hips and legs had increased. This was probably due to the Botox wearing off about that time.

Holly was pleased with how well Heather's spine incision had healed since her surgery in December and remarked that Heather's pelvis appeared level. There was concern when it came to Heather's hip flexors. Her left hip flexors were extremely tight and straightening her leg while laying down was difficult to do. Holly also noted Heather had a femoral ante-version measuring about eighty degrees.

Femoral ante-version is the medical term used to describe the way in which Heather's left knee and foot turned inward because how her femur itself had rotated inward. Normally, a child is born with forty degrees of femoral ante-version, which gradually decreases to ten to fifteen degrees by adolescence. Because Heather's femur rotation had not been addressed while growing up, the rotation only worsened over time. Surgery would be needed to correct it and is only advised if the ante-version is over fifty degrees. Heather exceeded that amount by thirty degrees.

The only surgical procedure to correct the rotated femur is called "Femoral Denotation Osteotomy." This is what Holly suggested for Heather next surgery, along with tendon lengthening. Once Holly explained the roles each muscle plays in Heather's legs and hips, it was making sense to Heather and I as to why she had the pulling and ripping sensations in her lower back and hips.

To Heather and I, rotating her femur and the lengthening made perfect sense. Her left leg was a hindrance as she walked because of the way it tripped her up. Lengthening the muscles would relieve a great deal of tightness in her hip flexors. Maybe the spasms in her lower back, hips and legs would end if the tendon was lengthened as well. Heather was ready to do anything that might take away her pain and the spasms.

In addition to that, if the surgery took away the consent pain Heather was in, then maybe she would not have to take so much pain medication. Heather's intake of Valium, Baclofen, and Motrin was becoming a concern with me. Her body seemed to be growing immune to the drugs and she wasn't benefiting from the amount prescribed. As a result, Heather started taking higher doses and that had me worried.

In our calculations, if Heather underwent surgery in early June, she would be ready to travel to Oregon in August well healed. Because it did make sense pursuing the surgery, Heather and I agreed to it. The only result I expected afterward was seeing Heather living without pain. It had been seven months of dealing with one set back after another. Not only for Heather, but for all of us.

The surgery Heather was scheduled for, involved intentionally cutting her left femur, rotating and plating it in a more correct position. Then Holly would perform the tendon lengthening before closing. Surgery number three was planned for June 5, 2007. Holly was confident Heather was physically capable of handling surgery. I had no reservations as well. What wasn't taken into account was Heather's frame of mind. This was a huge oversight and the consequences of not doing so, would soon make itself known.

CHAPTER FORTY-SIX

EATHER'S SURGERY WENT SO WELL, she was discharged from the hospital a day earlier than we anticipated. Better yet, no unexpected illness or mishap happened to me during my stay. Before leaving the hospital, Heather was given several prescriptions for pain. A postoperative followup was also scheduled as well. Holly also seen patients in her office located in a city closer than where the hospital was. From then on, any follow up visits with Holly would be at that location. This would save us about thirty minutes of extra driving.

Heather and I left the hospital that day filled with high hopes of her recovering completely from all three surgeries and finally regaining her mobility and independence. Each time we left the hospital following a surgery, we always had high hopes. Maybe this time, what we thought of as being high hopes was merely wishful thinking.

Heather returned for her followup in less pain than what she had been in before the surgery. The x-rays taken of Heather's spine, pelvis, and femur looked good. While examining Heather, Holly was pleased to see that Heather's range of motion in her left hip, had slightly improved during the past two weeks.

Holly informed us that while in the operating room, Heather's femur was derotated about thirty degrees. Right after the fixation of her femur, Holly tested Heather's range of motion in her left hip before lengthening the tendon. Already, there was a great deal of improvement in her range of motion.

When I first seen Heather's leg, I was absolutely amazed by the appearance. The leg looked completely straight to me. If one didn't know any better, one would have never guessed her leg had rotated inward the way it had. Seeing that Heather was healing well and in less pain, the plan was for Heather to return back in four weeks for another series of x-rays. Holly encouraged Heather to begin weight bearing on her left leg as much as she could tolerate.

Two weeks hadn't past since our latest visit and here I was scheduling an appointment to bring Heather in to see Holly. It seemed as though Heather's body rejected the notion of recovery. In a matter of days following our last visit with Holly, Heather began having a throbbing pain in her lower back and left butt cheek. The spasms, that had eased, returned as well in her back and legs. Once again, sitting and standing caused that familiar ripping sensation to resurface. We had hoped all this would have quit after this last surgery.

Heather would be able to see Holly July 9th, if we wanted to drive to the hospital. Didn't matter where we had to drive at that time, something had to be done. In the back of my mind, I seriously began to consider contacting Mary Free Bed and having Heather examined by a specialist there. However, that is as far as I went with that notion. The belief that *Doctors knew best and it wasn't my place to challenge them,* was so ingrained in my mind. All the while Heather was depending on me in knowing what to do, I was depending on Holly to know what to do.

When Holly was examining Heather on July 9th, she did notice some tenderness over Heather's sacroiliac region (left pelvis) and extending down into her buttock. Holly wasn't sure why Heather was experiencing this sort of pain. There was no sign of an infection and everything in the x-ray looked intact. Holly asked if there was a chance of Heather overdoing it at home, which could have resulted in tearing or straining a ligament she had lengthened. We told Holly that Heather barely begun weight bearing on her leg before the pain returned.

It was obvious that Heather was not doing well at home. She was back to laying in bed the majority of the day; sleeping more and eating less. Holly stressed how valuable physical therapy was at this time and how Heather needed to be stretched by a skilled therapist. We then discussed inpatient versus outpatient therapy. We told Holly about our lack of confidence in the local therapist and how tiring it would be for Heather to travel outside of Lakeview for physical therapy. Holly suggested returning back to the hospital for another inpatient stay for rehab. This time, she assured us that the focus would be on stretching out Heather's muscles only. Then, if possible, move forward with weight bearing and walking.

Heather and I both cringed at that suggestion, but given our circumstances, we didn't see any other option. We agreed to inpatient rehab if Holly gave us her word, Heather would not end up like she did during her first stay in rehab. We knew Holly was just as concerned with Heather's well being as we were. The concern showed in her eyes and was spoken in her words. As long as Heather and I sensed her sincerity, we would continue to believe in her. Before leaving her office, Heather was given a new prescription for Valium since she had run out just prior to her appointment. Heather declined Holly's offer for additional medication. Until we heard back from Holly regarding rehab, Heather had little to look forward to. Her daily life reverted back to the way it was before she returned school. With the latest setback, there was no doubt about her depression returning again as well.

The following night, July 10th, 2007, I went to check on Heather before going up to bed. Something I had done every night. Usually, the two of us would talk a while before calling it a night. However, that night Heather wasn't talkative and sounded as if she was on the brink of sleep. Or so I thought. Before leaving her room, she asked me to roll her over on her side. I noticed her speech was slurred and her body was very limber. That was quite unusual. After rolling her over, I accidentally knocked over her bottle of Valium, we kept on the nightstand by her bedside. It sounded empty. My first thought was the pills must have scattered when I knocked the bottle over. Finding no pills anywhere, when I turned on the light, I knew what Heather had done.

Not being aware of Heather's overdose of Oxycodone while staying with her Dads, I had no reason to believe there was any risk of her deliberately over medicating. Which is why I allowed Heather's medication to be within her reach. Just in case she needed it for pain throughout the night.

Heather openly admitted to taking all the Valium that was in the bottle. In such a matter of fact tone, she told me:"Mom, I just wanted to go to sleep. If I didn't wake up, that would be okay." I stood there looking at her and feeling absolutely nothing. It wasn't as if I didn't hear what she had said, it was if my mind rejected the reality of it all.

Normally when faced with a crisis, the mind and body will automatically jump into immediate action in an attempt to resolve the crisis. In my case, that mechanism which triggers the mind and body to respond, must have had been temporary out of order. Something as obvious as rushing Heather to the ER, or calling 911 didn't even occur to me. I just calmly walked out of Heather's room.

It wasn't until I was halfway upstairs when it began to register, that Heather had overdosed. Still it didn't seem real. Somehow, in the midst of the bombardment of thoughts rushing through my mind, there was one thought that dominated all others. It was as if there was someone right next to me yelling in my ear, "*Call Deb!*" Could it be, by calling a friend and confiding in her, the overdose would become real to me? Did I actually need an outsider to confirm what was happening in my own home? I guess that is exactly what was needed. Because, as soon as I heard the intensity in Deb's voice, while telling me to get Heather to the ER, something clicked. I instantly jumped into action.

I rushed into the bedroom where Katie slept, woke her up and told her to get dressed because we were taking Heather to the emergency room. As Katie was getting around, I went back to Heather. I pulled back her blankets, lifted her out of bed and carried her out to the car. Heather asked where we were going. I replied, "I'm taking you to the hospital." Heather said nothing to dispute my authority. There was no fight left in her at that time. Once I had Heather secured in the car, I went back into the house to retrieve both Katie and Heather's wheelchair. Thank goodness the hospital was less than a mile away. I wasn't aware what time Heather took the Valium or if the effects of the overdose had the advantage over any effective intervention. In other words, I was deathly afraid that Heather was going to die. All because I didn't react sooner

When asked by the receptionist why Heather was brought into the ER. I announced that Heather had taken 25 Valium pills. The receptionist immediately contacted the nurse on duty, whom rushed in and took Heather to the examining room where the attending physician was presently being paged to. Katie and I followed behind and stayed with Heather until we were asked to leave.

We went back to the waiting area where I begun the process of filling out paperwork. Not even ten minutes had past since our arrival, when my friend Deb and her daughter, Mckenzie walked in. After making certain that I was alright, Deb offered to take Katie home with her so I could go be with Heather. The hospital was no place for Katie to be at that time. She was already feeling bad from Heather yelling at her to leave the examining room, because Heather didn't want Katie seeing her in that condition. I took Deb up on her offer and told Katie I would call if anything happened.

Aside from the receptionist, I was alone in the waiting area after Deb, Mckenzie and Katie left. Looking around the room, I found myself trying to recall how many times I had taken Heather to an ER throughout her life. Countless of times. First time when she was 22 months old. Several times throughout the course of that experience. Couple of times after she had taken some mighty spills. The episodes she had with pleurisy and now this; an overdose. If everything has a purpose, which seems to be the general agreement among us, what was the purpose of Heather's continuous ordeal? Before I even started to ponder on it, I was asked to accompany the nurse back to where Heather was.

When I walked into the room where Heather was, she was alert and in the process of answering questions. As soon as I took a seat, the questioning was then directed to me. "In your opinion," the doctor began asking, "Why do you think Heather took the Valium?"

Right off, that question struck a nerve. It was so hard for me to hold my tongue and not become sarcastic. To me, the answer was so obvious. However, I reminded myself that this doctor had no clue as to what Heather had been through. Plus, my annoyance wasn't with him. It was located over three hours away. So, I answered his question respectfully.

"In my opinion, Heather wasn't attempting suicide. I believe she did want to get rid of the pain in order to sleep."

"How long has Heather been depressed?"

"Shortly after her first surgery back in October of last year," I replied. "She was placed on anti-depressants, but quit taking them because of the side effects. I didn't notice her becoming real depressed until a week or so ago."

"Do you have any idea of what might have triggered her depression?"

Could he not see her condition beyond the effects of the Valium? "She recently had a setback in her recovery and now that school is out, she has nothing to take her mind away from the pain."

"Was counseling sought after for Heather's depression?"

"No. She did receive some counseling at the hospital while in rehab, but not afterward."

"Had Heather mentioned anything suggesting suicide?"

"No."

I was beginning to feel very uncomfortable. There was so much I was dealing with in addition to Heather. Maybe, I did miss the warning signs. "If Heather really wanted to end her life, she had plenty of medication at her disposal to do so. That is why I am convinced that this wasn't a suicide attempt."

"Has Heather attempted suicide prior to this overdose," The doctor asked.

"No."

The last question to be asked, was by far, the one I would revisit for a long time to come.

"If you noticed Heather's depression was becoming heightened, why was the Valium kept on her nightstand?"

I told him exactly what I had imagined to be true. "I never imagined Heather would deliberately over medicate." What I really wanted to do after my interrogation, was shift the questioning back at him. Why was Heather and I being drilled? Why wasn't the surgery that brought all this about, in question? Better yet, why isn't the hospital being held accountable for Heather's condition?"

Those questions were not his to answer. I knew this, but the cause of Heather's overdose seemed to be viewed as being solely of our own doing, without any other factors involved. There were other factors involved and Heather was about to fill the doctor in on them.

Heather then began to tell her story. The surgeries she had gone through, the pain she was constantly in, rehab at the hospital, and how she was slowly giving up all hope of ever getting better. Silence filled the room after Heather was finished. There was a moment when it seemed all of us felt Heather's desperation. I don't know what the nurse and doctor assumed at the start, but I could clearly see the two of them were moved by Heather.

Poison Control and Mental Health were contacted shortly after Heather arrived at the ER. Poison Control didn't recommend any invasive action taken at that time, since Heather's vitals were stable. However, Heather was admitted to the hospital for detox and placed under suicide precaution. A representative from Mental Health was expected to visit with Heather the following day to help determine what the next step for Heather was to be. So, for the time being, Heather would be staying at Kelsey Campus, in Lakeview.

I stayed with Heather while she was being settled into her room and watched as she drifted off to sleep. For the first time, in such a long time, she looked so peaceful as she lay sleeping. It's saddened me to think what it took for her to be at peace. When I began dozing off while sitting next to her, I decided to go home.

Once home, I called Alex to inform him of what had happened and that Heather was expected to be in the hospital for at least three days before being moved elsewhere. To my surprised, there was no quarreling between Alex and myself while on the phone. The news about Heather's overdose surely must have shocked the hell out of him. How could it not have.

When I hung up the phone, I turn the phone completely off. I sat alone with Sebastian and my thoughts. Even though I was physically exhausted, I didn't make any attempt in going to bed. It would have been useless to try and sleep, for my mind would not quiet itself. I remained sitting at the kitchen table with Sebastian laying at my feet.

Ever notice how when left to its own accord, the mind automatically creates all sorts of self-defeating thoughts? Especially, when one is normally feeling unsure of oneself? Before long, I was so engrossed in recalling every conceivable flaw and fault I saw in myself. Over the course of a few minutes, all the pride I had taken to heart, for my great parenting skills, was being shattered to pieces. "If I was such a great parent, as I had imagined myself being, how is it that Heather was laying in the hospital because of an overdose?"

There was no answer, only the sense of being a complete failure at protecting Heather from self harm. Here I was, barely able to manage my own state of affairs. How could I have possibly imagined being capable of caring for Heather on top of that? Again, I had no answer which would stop the self criticizing thoughts. The last thought I remember having that created a sense of fear, was one in which we all seem to be conditioned to indulge in,"What will people think, when they hear about Heather's overdose." I never did get up from the kitchen table that night. I ended up folding my arms on the table, laying my head down and cried till I fell asleep.

Sebastian woke me up early the next morning, wanting to go

outside. Its a good thing he did because I needed to call work and let my supervisor know I wasn't going to work that day. There were many spur of the moment calls I, along with Heather, made to my workplace during the course of Heather's journey. Despite all the days I missed and my leaving early, management was always supportive and accommodating.

Their tolerance of my frequent absences played a huge part in lessening stress, while I attempted to hold it all together under the strain of everything that was happening. I couldn't imagine myself trying to cope with worrying about job security on top of, dealing with the set backs of Heather's recovery, along with the real possibility of foreclosure, struggling with paying monthly bills and putting food on the table. Not excluding, all the emotional anxiety I was still experiencing following the breakup with Nathaniel.

Before I went to see Heather, I made sure the swelling around my eyes had gone down. She needed to focus on her own well being and didn't need me visiting her looking pitiful, which would have only created a deeper sense of guilt than she was already dealing with.

When I walked into Heather's room, a social worker from the Mental Health Department, was already visiting with Heather. In spite of appearing sleepy, Heather seemed to be in good spirits and instantly smiled when she saw me. I smiled back as I made my way over to her bed. I leaned over and kissed her on the forehead, then asked how she was feeling, before I even acknowledged the social worker. Once we introduced our self to one another, we began the business of discussing the overdose and future plans for Heather.

Heather had told the social worker her motive for taking the Valium. It was the same statement she had told me, as well as, the doctor. The social worker then asked if I was doubtful of Heather's motive. I never questioned her motive. Why? Because I saw how she struggled with the pain and was aware of how difficult it was for her to get comfortable enough to fall asleep. I told the social worker that in my opinion, Heather overdosed hoping to ease the pain she was in, not to intentionally kill herself. "Heather is a strong willed young woman, a fighter. I know she would have mentioned any thoughts of suicide to me. We have such a close relationship."

I believed this wholeheartedly. However, in the near future, I would be confronted with the realism of being mistaken. The first mistake I made was taking for granted the amount of fight Heather had within her. The second being, no matter how close the two of us were, Heather did in fact keep many feelings to herself.

When asked about future plans for Heather, I informed the social worker that we were waiting to hear back from Holly, Heather's surgeon, regarding inpatient rehab. The social worker offered to contact Holly and fill her in on what happened, that is, if I didn't have any objections. She also advised us of Heather's need for counseling as well. My first thought was, not Adam, the Breather Man, again.

With the help of the social worker, Heather's admittance into Advanced Care Hospital was arranged, following her discharge from Kelsey Campus. We either could have Heather taken there by ambulance or I could drive her myself. I chose to drive her. There didn't seem to be any need for Heather to be transported by ambulance.

Once Heather and I arrived at Advanced Care Hospital, we learned that Heather wasn't going to be admitted into rehab at that time. Instead, she was going to be admitted into the Psych Unit for the time being. There, Heather would receive one on one counseling group therapy, as well as, physical and occupational therapy. The plan sounded perfect to me. Heather didn't have much say in the matter. I decided for her, mainly out of my concern for her well being.

CHAPTER FORTY-SEVEN

HEATHER'S WORDS

THE NIGHT BEFORE MY NEXT surgery, I watched as Mom packed my bag for the stay at the hospital. There wasn't much to pack for me. My phone, Ipod, personal items and a change of clothes for our trip home. No sense in packing extra clothing since I would be wearing one of those great looking hospital gowns during my stay. As for Katie, she was going to her dad's house and Mikey, well, he had the chore of babysitting our beloved pets. Sebastian wasn't any trouble, just give him food and he was content. It was Snitsky (Dumb Dumb) who terrorized the neighborhood.

After Mom finished packing our bags, she sat on my bed and looked at me. With that familiar look in her eyes. I knew what was coming next; the "*pep talk.*" "Maybe, Holly has finally found the answer in relieving the pain this time." Mom said. "Straightening your leg and lengthening the muscles or tendons makes sense."

Maybe Mom was right. If nothing else, I was hoping the surgery would help me to be able to stand long enough in order for Mom to dress and undress me without the worry of me falling while she was doing so. Maybe, I might even be able to sit up longer without feeling any strain on my lower back and hips. I hoped for the best, but the word "*Maybe*" was getting so old. I wished Holly knew the cause and wasn't just guessing at it. Once again I thought, "Well, I have a 50/50 chance of this surgery being successful." I wasn't sure if Mom even believed in what she had told me, but I guess it gave her hope.

Before Mom went up to bed, she tied Sebastian to the leg of my bed and then kissed me on the forehead. I listened to her footsteps gradually disappearing as she went upstairs, then I fell asleep to the sound of Sebastian's snores. The night flew by and before I knew it, Mom and I were at the hospital.

By now, Mom and I had the routine down at the hospital. Go in, check in, hand the receptionist my pee, undress and put on a hospital grown. Next, we were visited be the team of doctors, nurses, and anesthesiologist whom would be in the operating room with me. Each one describing their job and asking me if I had any questions. Oh, can't forget getting the IV placed in my upper arm before surgery.

What I liked most before going into the operating room, was being awake while being wheeled down the long hall leading to the operating room. By now, I wasn't nervous about going into surgery. I liked looking around the operating room and seeing the instruments and machines. I felt comfortable as the nurse told me to count back from ten. I never made it to one before I was out, only to be awaken afterward by the sound of someone calling out my name.

The only thing I remember about this surgery was that Mom and I only stayed at the hospital two days because I was doing so well. No, two things I remember. The other was waking up one morning to find that Mom had bought me a stuffed animal and had placed it at the head of my head. It was the first thing I saw when I opened my eyes; it made me smile. It was a stuffed dog that looked so much like Sebastian. The "*fatness*" any ways. I decided to call the dog "Sebastian the Second."

The trip home wasn't bad. I think it was because there wasn't any pressure placed on my leg. With my back surgeries, I had to lean back in the car seat causing my back to rub against the seat; plus we had to stop a million times to move me. Maybe not a million, but it seemed like it. I think Mom and I stop a couple of times on our way home to move me and for coffee. Mom can not go without her coffee. It's her life.

I was so happy when I saw our house. I missed Katie, Mikey, Dumb Dumb, and of course; Sebastian. Home is always better than staying in the hospital. The first thing I wanted to do was lay down in bed. Before I was able to relax from the ride home, Sebastian jumped on my leg right after Mom laid me down. I started to yell at him to get down. Mom hurried over and simply snap her fingers at Sebastian and pointed to the floor. He automatically jumped off the bed and scooted under it. We never had to yell at Sebastian, he knew what to do when Mom snap her fingers. As much as my leg was hurting, I was happy to receive a big "welcome home" from him. Mom looked to see if the incision had torn open. Nothing appeared to have happened. Later, when Katie came home, she came into my room and we chatted for a while before I began falling asleep on her. I wouldn't be seeing Mikey until the next day. He was going to be watching me while Mom went back to work. Watching me, more like babysitting me. That's what I felt like on most days, a helpless baby that needed to be cared for. Mom looked so tired. She never slept good when she stay with me in the hospital. To bad Mom couldn't take another day off from work to rest up.

My bedroom at Moms used to be a porch. There were windows all the way around the room. To help keep the room warmer in the winter, Mom had someone take out the windows, all the windows, and board up the walls. No windows in a room, during the month of June, meant sweating. Sebastian and I only had a fan on us when I was laying in bed. It wasn't bad in the mornings, but when it was about four o'clock in the afternoon, I remember it getting so hot in there. Mom would put me on the couch when she came home, where it was a little cooler.

I was beginning to think that this surgery I had was a good idea after all. The pain in my lower back, hips and left leg was going away. I was taking hardly any pain medication and feeling more energetic. I still wasn't sitting up anymore than I was before or standing a lot. I spent the first two weeks after the surgery, just resting and healing.

When Holly saw me for the first time since going home from the hospital, she was happy to hear that I was doing better. She told me that I could start standing more and to try putting weight on my left leg. This was good news. To me, it meant I was ready to take steps. The tightness in my hips and hamstrings had relaxed also. I was doing so good that Holly said I didn't need to see her again for a month or so. Holly asked me to stand for her. When I did she said my leg looked good. Every time I stood, I was amazed be see how straight my left leg was. There was actually a gap between my knees. Something I hadn't had since I was a little girl walking, before I had my DPT shot.

It was a couple of weeks after the appointment with Holly

when the pain in my hips and lower back started up again. I didn't know why it couldn't have just stayed away. I began taking more medications then I was before the surgery. Mom called Holly and made an appointment to take me in.

I told Holly that all my pain was back and I was hurting so bad. She asked me what pain medication worked best for my pain. I thought to myself; "*That's all I need, more medication.*" Wasn't there anything else instead of medication for my ongoing pain? I guess not. Since I had plenty of other pain killers at home and only needed a prescription for Valium, I asked for Valium. Valium worked the best in helping to relax me so I could sleep.

With every inch that I moved, my muscles felt like they were pulling and ripping. Once again, I was drugged up and tired all the time. I was becoming depressed and really started feeling sorry for myself. Why me? Why can't I just get better? Why can't Holly find something for this pain instead of upping the dosage of my medication, or just writing more prescriptions?

How I envied Katie. Going to her friends houses and doing whatever she wanted. Here I was in bed and suffering. Three of my classmates came by, but it was only one time. I felt so alone even though I had family around me, I was getting to the point of not wanting to leave my bedroom. What was the sense of doing that? Just to lay on the couch? Couldn't sit up longer than a few minutes before I needed to lay down again.

In the back of my mind, I began to think that it would be easier on everyone if I just die. I was tired of living like I was, immobile and being in so much pain. No one would have to worry about me graduating or not trying hard enough to walk. Mom wouldn't have to take me to appointments, no more hospital stays and she wouldn't have to miss so much work. Her and Katie could spend time together. I hated knowing that I was taking up all of Mom's time. Most of all, Mom wouldn't have to watch me struggle or see me crying everyday. She could sleep through the night without having to get up several times just to roll me over or put me on the commode. If I took my life, she could have her life back.

I knew Mikey would miss our time together, but he would somehow understand. Katie would be sad, but she would have Mom back. Dad and the family would definitely blame Mom, but maybe accept my decision later on. Days went by with the thought of killing myself. In a weird sort of way, I felt content, which made it easy to hide how depressed I felt from Mom.

At night, is when I talked to Sebastian. I would tell him about my thoughts of death. I talked about how I felt about everything. I added, "I seem to be getting worse everyday." Sebastian would just stare at me if he wasn't sleeping while I was talking. I let go of a lot of hidden feelings with him. There were just somethings I could not talk over with Mom. She had so much to deal with already and I knew she would only feel like she had failed. I remember one night I was having massive spasms while Sebastian was laying in bed with me. I bet he could feel my pain, because without telling him to do so, he jumped off my bed and laid on the floor.

Going back into rehab at the hospital was more of Mom's decision than mine. I didn't ever want to go back there, but didn't feel like I had any say in the matter. Hearing Holly say she would watch over me while in rehab meant a lot, but would she really? The day after Mom and I saw Holly, I remember saying goodnight to Katie and Mom kissing me on the forehead. I laid there staring up at the ceiling in my room. Sebastian was already sleeping so peacefully. As I lay there, I was thinking now is the time.

I knew I was going to hurt my family, but I wanted to leave my body. I would be watching over my loved ones. I knew some family members would be in fear of me going to Hell, because I killed myself. But, what they didn't know is how happy I would once again be and would always be around them. I don't believe in a Heaven or Hell. I think you make your own Heaven and Hell here on Earth.

I turned over on my side and stared at the bottle of Valium. I was ready. When you get to this point and your mind is set, there is no turning back. That is how I felt. I was at peace and felt happy with my decision. I reached for the pill bottle and took two handfuls. It didn't take long before I begun to feel my pain going away and felt sleepy. Then, I remember hearing footsteps coming down the stairs and heading toward my room. It was Mom coming to check on me. I thought, "Why? Why did she come down now? She had just went upstairs."

Mom came into my room and asked if I needed anything. I asked her to roll me over. When Mom rolled me over, she tipped over the pill bottle. I barely remember her turning on the light, then asking me if I had taken the pills. At that time, I was slipping in and out of sleep. I told her that I did take the pills and made up the excuse of wanting to get rid of the pain so I could sleep. The next thing I knew, I was being carried out to the car and going to the ER, in Lakeview.

I remember going into a room where I pushed Katie away from me. I didn't want her to be there and see me like that. I was crying when I pushed her away. I was crying all night. I was so tired, but wasn't allowed to sleep. I was asked so many questions by the doctor and nurse. Was I sorry about what I did? No, because I wanted it all to end. I wanted to leave my body. Mom stayed with me until the doctor felt I was out of danger and was transported to a different room. It was her and I in my room, when I finally fell asleep. Mom wasn't mad at me, but I could tell she was really sad.

The next day when Mom came to see me, she said that she had called Dad and told him what happened. Did he make time to visit me? I was only thirty minutes away. Was his hands broken, making it hard for him to dial a phone to call me and see how I was doing? Was he even concerned about his *baby girl*? I guess not, because I never seen or heard from Dad, while I stayed at the hospital in Lakeview. I really needed my dad at that time. To hold me and tell me that he loved me. I needed him so much and he never even called. My heart was so broken and I became very angry at him.

On the last day at Kelsey, a social worker told Mom and I that I was going to be admitted into Advanced Care Hospital for rehab. The hospital offered to drive me there by ambulance, but Mom said she would drive me. When Mom and I arrived at the hospital, we discovered that I was going to be admitted into the Psych Unit for therapy. When we reached the floor of the Psych Unit, the door leading into the unit was locked. In order to get inside, you had to talked through an intercom to get someone to open the door. Right off, I felt like I was going to be caged until I was better. I guess they had to keep the doors locked at all times so no one would try to escape. We were let in and taken to the main desk. I remember being stared at by other patients in the unit as we were walking. Some of them looked younger than me. I wondered what their stories were. I would be finding out later.

While Mom was filling out the paper work and checking me in, a nurse was looking through my bag of clothes and things. Things that looked dangerous or what I might use to inflict harm to myself was taken away and locked in a cabinet. The nurse took my hair spray, bobby pins, nail clippers and my iPod charger. I wasn't allowed to have my cell phone. I would have to use the hall phone to call anyone. If I wanted to use anything that was taken, I had to ask for it and then be watched by someone while I used it.

Mom and I met with the psychiatrist whom would be working with me. We met most of the staff and answered tons of questions before being shown to my room. It looked like a ordinary hospital room. Surprisingly, there was no bars on the windows like you see in the movies. When I was all settled in, Mom said her goodbye. I just stayed in my room until the next day.

In the morning, a nurse came in and helped me get ready for my first day there. I felt tired and had a headache. They felt that I was still detoxing from the Valium. My body hurt from the same old pain that never went away. I wasn't given any strong medication, only Motrin. I was already missing home. Missing the snoring of Sebastian underneath my bed. I miss seeing Mom, Katie and Mikey.

My daily routine started with breakfast, group therapy, one on one therapy, lunch, and school, that last for an hour each day. To me, school was a waste of time, but it did give me something to keep my mind occupied. I had Physical and Occupational therapy later in the afternoon. Most times I had it when others were enjoying free time in the unit. Free time was a chance to do whatever you wanted. Watch TV in the lobby room, play card games, color and do puzzle books.

When I didn't have PT or OT, I went into the lobby room. It was a gathering place for all of us. I asked Mom if she could bring some movies from home for us to watch, because the movie selection there was slim. We had a lot of movies at home. Mom was always picking up movies from the five dollar movie bin at Walmart. Mom brought down a whole bag of movies for us to watch. There was always something to do and I felt very comfortable being there and among the other kids. I thought I would have to stay in my room all the time. I was glad that I was wrong.

In group therapy, I talked about the overdose, but mostly listened to the stories told by the other kids. There was only a few of us in the Unit. Each one was troubled in his/her own way. The kids there were dealing with drugs, self-mutilation, anorexia and we all suffered some sort of depression. One day during group therapy, a girl talked about her rape experience. She looked so terrified telling her story and in her eyes I could tell she felt so alone.

In my one on one sessions with the Psychiatrist, the focus was on my relationship with my Dad and my depression. I revealed how much I wanted to be close to my dad. How important it was to know that he was proud of me and that he would always be there for me. The therapist asked if I ever told Dad how I felt. I shook my head "*Yes.*" It seemed like I had tried my whole life to make him appreciate me. I needed to be showed by Dad, that he loved me more than hearing him say he loved me.

Mom and I talked on the phone almost every night. Every time we talked, I asked if Dad or his side of the family had called her to ask how I was doing or to get the number, so they could call me. She always said,"They hadn't called yet." I broke down crying every time she said that.

Mom, Katie, Mikey and Grandma Ski came to visit me during my first week in the Psych Unit. It was so nice to have visitors. I remember being allowed to leave the unit with them, so we all went out to the garden. They stayed closed to two hours. I will never forget how much laughing I did that day. Other than that visit and a few other visits from Mom, no one else came to see me.

I stayed in the Psych Unit one week before I was moved to the pediatric floor for rehab. I hated being there. I hated being in bed all day until it was time for my therapies, I hated every second I was there. Therapy wasn't just about stretching like Mom and I were told. They were back trying to get me to walk.

My body wasn't ready yet. The pain ready begun to get worse. Since they didn't want to give me too much pain medication, they decided to give me Botox injections. Didn't make sense to me. The Botox never kicked in until two weeks after being injected. There was no way I planned to stay in that place that long. Soon I was crying more and didn't want to do rehab. I started talking about having suicidal thoughts. They arranged for me to have sitters stay with me during the night because they feared I would attempt suicide.

After a week on the pediatric ward, I was once again admitted back into the Psych unit. Mom had to come to the hospital to fill out the paperwork once again to get me in. I told Mom I never wanted to go into rehab here in the first place. I never want to go back to the pediatric ward or stay for inpatient rehab. All I wanted was for the pain to go away. It didn't matter to me anymore if I ever walked again. I just want the pain to go away.

Holly came to visit me one time during my stay. She didn't keep her word about watching over me. I hated everything about that hospital at that point. Mom knew I was serious. She didn't try to talk me into staying and continuing with rehab. Mom told me she would take me home when I was discharged from the psych unit. I never did go back to that hospital for any kind of inpatient rehab.

Once I was back in the psych unit, the Psychiatrist worked on helping me deal with my emotions. He taught me how to become aware of certain signs that may lead to depression. I agreed to tell Mom if I ever had any thoughts of suicide or when I was feeling depressed. There was a lot of emotions pouring out of me during rest of my stay in the unit. There was more anger hidden inside of me that I was aware of. I let it all out. I had to if I was ever going to get better and go home.

The psychiatrist wanted to have a family meeting with Dad, Mom, myself and him. He wanted to discuss what was planned for me when I was discharged. Plus, talk about my depression. The therapist insisted that I call Dad and ask him to join us at the meeting. It would be our first conversation we had since before I overdosed. I told the therapist, "If Dad didn't visit or call me during my stay here, he won't come." Why the therapist still insisted that I call Dad, I don't know. I called and asked. I will never forget what Dad said to me that day.

He told me, "It wasn't a family emergency and he couldn't take off work." It was so hurtful hearing him say that. I needed my "*daddy*." With a broken heart, I turned to the therapist and said, "*Thanks*" as the tears were pouring down my cheeks. Maybe now the therapist finally knew my frustration when it came to Dad. I felt like money met more to Dad than I did.

Here was my mother, who took me to all of my appointments, stayed with me in the hospital after every surgery, while trying to make it in life with so little. She couldn't afford missing work all the time, but she did it. Why couldn't my father take one day off of work to come to the meeting? I guess I really wasn't important to him.

The therapist and I worked through my emotions I had toward Dad once again until I was discharged. He helped me release a lot of hurt. In the end, I was able to accept Dad's decision not to come without feeling like Dad rejected me. If the therapist hadn't helped me with this, I would have continued to believe that Dad didn't love me enough to be there for me, I know different now.

At the meeting the three of us, Mom, the therapist and I, sat and talked in his office. The first thing he said was that if I was going to be discharged, I had to show proof that I would be seeing a psychologist on a regular basis. Mom had a few days to set up an appointment with one and bring in proof that I was going to see him/her. There was no way I was going home without it. Mom found a therapist, who accepted her insurance in Grand Rapids. She scheduled an appointment and brought in a paper from that office as proof.

On August 7th, 2007, I was finally discharged from the Psych Unit. I had spent a total of twenty-six days at the hospital. I couldn't wait to sleep in my own bed again and be around family. I promised myself that I would never go back to that place again. But, if I wasn't taken there and had help dealing with my depression, I would have attempted suicide until I did succeed. I know this for a fact.

I went home feeling emotionally better, but still in pain. Nothing was accomplished in PT nor OT. For the time being, I had a new look on life and was able to endure the pain more. Besides, we were going to be flying out to Oregon in a week. I was so excited. I wasn't going to let the pain get the best of me and keep me from going.

CHAPTER FORTY-EIGHT

IGHT AFTER I HAD LEFT Heather at the Psych Unit, July 13th, she had a consultation with pediatric physical medicine and rehabilitation team. It was decided that Heather would begin her physical and occupational therapy while in the Psych Unit. The therapists would either go up to Heather's room, or if Heather was up to it, she would be transported to the therapy room.

An inpatient rehab stay was still in the works, once Heather was believed to be medically and emotionally stable. Medically stable. Did that mean getting Heather's pain under control before rehab, or just allowing Heather's body to detox before admission into rehab? The plan was to get a jump start on intensive therapies to increase Heather's functional mobility while she was in the Psych unit. Would it not be somewhat accurate to assume that intensive therapies might be too much for Heather to withstand when her spasticity, pain and painful spasms was at such a high level?

Pain management, coping strategies, and to increase ability for ADL's (Activities for Daily Living) were also listed in the recommendations the consultant wrote out. Each one of those was implemented during her first inpatient stay with little success. Did the team of therapists, medical staff, and psychologist actually believe, what wasn't successful in the past was magically going to work this time around?

If Heather's pain, due to her tightness/tone throughout her lower extremities was not addressed first, there wasn't any sense of creating a list of goals to work at and be expected to reach in such a short period of time. The majority of the goals, at the end of her stay would most likely be defined in two words:"*Not Met.*"

Heather had dealt with spasticity since she was young. She

managed to walk and was independent with all her Activities of Daily Living. She woke up every morning with her legs twisted and tight, but worked out the tightness and went about her day. How was she able to do that then and not now? This was the million dollar question, in which no one seemed to have an answer for.

Bottom line, how was it possible to even assume progress could be made, if the underlying cause that prevented progress, wasn't solved first and foremost. And that would be the pain. Take away the pain then focus on goal setting. No amount of pain management or coping strategies was going to give the therapists the results they were hoping for. How was it that I knew this and they didn't?

Heather seemed to thrive during her first week in the psych unit. We talked over the phone every night. In her voice, I heard the old Heather beginning to re-emerge. I wish I could say the same thing was happening with me. My old self was buried under a tangled web of emotions left unattended. The benefit of being so busy with Heather while she was home, it gave me an outlet. I didn't have to acknowledge all the suppressed emotions, that were now screaming for some type of closure. In all honesty, I should have been in a bed next to Heather in the psych unit receiving counseling.

With Heather away, I didn't even know what to do with myself. Anyone whom has cared for a loved one in a similar way, will fully understand what I mean. You loose yourself in the process. Then once the caring for the loved one is no longer needed, all you see when you look in the mirror is a stranger.

Heather underwent an occupational evaluation, the third day after arriving at Psych Unit. Her performance areas during the evaluation is as follows:

Eating: independent.

Bathing: moderate assist for transfers, Maximum assist for bathing tasks. Although Heather did in fact wash her face, arms, chest, and stomach. Maximum assist for underarms and her lower extremities. Heather sat on a shower chair using a hand held shower head.

Upper Body Dressing: Min assist with shirt. Max assist with fastening bra. Lower extremities.

Lower Body Dressing: Max assist with underwear, pants, socks and shoes. Required assistance for sit to stand, in order to pull up pants as well.

Grooming: independent with tasks at sink edge while sitting in her wheelchair.

Functional Mobility: Min-Mod assist for stand pivot transfers from wheelchair to/from bed.

Sensory; including pain: Heather was limited at times during evaluation with transferring due to increased pain in lower left leg and hip.

Coordination: Heather demonstrated decreased reaction time.

Endurance: Limited by pain at times and fatigues quickly.

Pain management Issues: Weight bearing and limited by pain with lower extremities.

Goal Setting and Treatment Plan. Upon discharge from OT, Heather will be able to:

1) Demonstrate lower extremity dressing with mod assist.

2) Demonstrate upper body dressing with Min assist. Including bra.

3) Demonstrate shower using. shower bench with Min assist.

4) Demonstrate toileting with Min assist.

5) Will tolerate age appropriate activity thirty minutes while in unsupported short sitting.

Following her occupational evaluation, she was then evaluated by the physical therapist. This is how she performed during the evaluation.

Transfers: Heather required Mod assist with maximum cues and encouragement to complete task.

Mobility: Propelled wheelchair ten feet. Heather was also able to take 1-2 steps with Max assist to support her.

Endurance: Fatigues during session quickly. Decreased strength through Heather's bilateral upper body, increased muscle tone in lower extremities.

Knee Range of motion: Right knee lacked approximately 10-15 degrees from full extension. Left knee lacks approximately fifteen degrees from full extension.

Discharge Patient Goals:

1) Heather will walk 200 feet with rolling walker with stand by assist.

2) Will complete bed to wheelchair transfer with stand by assist.

3) Will propel wheelchair 800 feet with stand by assist for steering.

4) Will complete wheelchair to toilet transfer with stand by assist.

5) Will ascend/descend one stair with Min assist.

6) Caregiver will be independent in assisting Heather with mobility and transfers.

As much as goal number six sounded encouraging, achieving such a goal was highly unlikely and should have never made it on the list. The goal just wasn't realistic, given the limited time Heather was allowed to stay in rehab, which was solely determined by the insurance company she was covered under.

How did the insurance companies obtain the power it has over medical care for patients? I remember when Heather was younger and going to outpatient rehab. The insurance company would only cover 30-60 days of rehab at one time. Then, there was a waiting period before Heather was once again eligible to receive therapies, in which the insurance company would pay for. For the majority of us, affording continuing services when insurance companies chooses not to cover the treatment, is far too expensive to manage.

Unless Heather miraculously became more agile and pain free before her allotted time expired under her insurance coverage, any success of reaching the goals set by the therapists was in doubt. The therapies were limited by Heather's spasticity, level of pain and endurance. The therapists were limited by the amount of time allowed to work with Heather. As for Heather, she was just limited altogether.

My concern in all this was where Heather's overall well being fit into the equation. It seemed more necessary to dive into intensive therapies than focusing on a more subtle approach, where the attention was centered on improving Heather's muscle tone, by gently stretching out her lower extremities. Better yet, why not utilize the time Heather was three by establishing the cause and resolving what ever was creating her debilitating pain?

On July 20th, one week into her stay, the psychiatrist felt Heather was stable enough to be admitted into pediatric ward for rehab. Heather was still considered as being mildly depressed, but she denied any thoughts of suicide. I went to the hospital to fill out the paperwork for her admission. Heather and I spent the morning and afternoon together.

I met with the psychiatrist and was brought up to date on Heather's progress. He did have some concern about the limited family involvement with Heather during her stay. Limited was an understatement outside of myself or the day Grandma Ski, Mikey,

Katie and I went to visit Heather, family involvement was non-existent. This weighed heavily on Heather's heart.

Again I stayed with Heather until she was settled in her room on the pediatric ward. Holly visited Heather for the first and last time, the day after Heather was transferred on that floor. Holly believed Heather was already benefiting from the therapies she was receiving thus far. I wasn't present when she visited, but if I were there, I would have had to ask what improvements she saw that I didn't see the day before?

Later in the day, Heather reported having a headache, dizziness and nausea. Seemingly, brought about by some type of adverse reaction to the Oxycodone she was given earlier. Within three days of her admission into the pediatric ward, Heather began showing signs of increased depression. A rehabilitation psychologist was called upon to evaluate Heather's emotional state.

In the psychologist's opinion, Heather was reporting symptoms consistent with a depressive episode, including suicidal thoughts. Heather indicated that she believed she was at risk of self-harm. She wished she were dead and wished she had been successful in her recent suicide attempt. Heather then was reported to have said, "I wish I could put an end to my physical and emotional pain."

The psychologist's concern at this point, was Heather's inner restlessness, combined with her depression, suicidal thoughts, and chronic pain, did in fact place Heather at high risk for self-harm. The psychologist did not feel this was an effort to gain attention or manipulation of any kind. As a result, Heather was placed under the watch of a sitter and Psychiatry was consulted. The following day, July 24th, Heather continued to be under constant supervision when not in therapies. Heather reported that she wasn't having suicidal thoughts, but tends to become more emotionally overwhelmed as the day progressed.

Because of the increased spasticity and pain in Heather's hips, left leg and knees, physical therapy was showing no advancement in her mobility. Instead of administering more oral medication to help relax her muscle tone, it was decided that Botox injections to the hamstrings, hips, and Iliopsoas (the muscles Heather had lengthened), would be most beneficial. Oral medication had more mood effects than Botox.

The following day, Heather was injected with 600 units of Botox. If the Botox had an immediate effect on Heather, then having the injections would have definitely been beneficial during rehab. It had always taken at least two weeks before Heather experienced any improvement in her muscle tone, following the injections. As it stood, the therapists would still be fighting against Heather's spasticity and pain without much success.

Another concern regarding Heather while she was in the pediatric ward, came from the nursing staff. The concern revolved around their ability or inability to provide constant supervision in a normal setting without completely disrupting normal routines/schedules. It was then recommended that Heather be admitted back into the psychiatry unit with rehab therapies brought there.

On July 27th, one week after being admitted to the pediatric ward, Heather was discharged and transferred back to the psych unit. I went back to the hospital to meet with the psychologist, psychiatrist, and the team of therapists working with Heather. Once again, I filled out the necessary paperwork for Heather's admission back into the psych unit. Together with the psychologist and psychiatrist, Heather fragile state of mind and overdose was explored more in depth.

Being absolutely convinced Heather did not deliberately intend to kill herself with the overdose of Valium, I found myself rejecting any notion of a possible personality disorder, the psychologist and psychiatrist was insisting Heather may have had, or that it actually was a suicide attempt. I was *"Hell Bent"* on convincing them that Heather's overdose was to ease her pain so she could get some sleep. I was then asked if I was aware that Heather had attempted suicide a year to the day Zachariah had shot himself. "Did I believe that was a motivating factor?"

"Wait!" I blurted out. "Number one, it wasn't a suicide attempt. Heather's overdose was intended to relax her, in order to get some sleep". Why were the two of them so convinced that it was a suicide attempt? What did they know that I didn't? "What was Heather's response when asked about Zachariah?" I asked.

Heather denied any connection between the two. However, Heather did confess to each of them that it was indeed a suicide attempt. The reason Heather gave them included, not wanting to live in pain anymore and wanting her Dad to take her seriously and stop pressuring her. When I looked over at Heather after hearing what was just said to me, she sat there focused on the floor and did not move. Heather didn't have to say anything. Her body language said it all. I just wandered if she confessed truthfully or was swayed into believing her overdose was, in fact, a suicide attempt. I'm not sure if this was an effort to avoid what I didn't want to accept or because I knew how easy Heather could be manipulated into believing what others wanted her to believe.

Heather had already told three different reasons she overdosed that night. Could it be that she didn't know the reason behind it herself? Was this an indication that it was a suicide attempt after all? I didn't believe it was. I stood firm in believing Heather's first reason for taking the Valium. If by chance the overdose was an suicide attempt, maybe, there wasn't just one motivating factor, but a combination of several factors leading Heather to believe suicide was her only option to escape.

I couldn't say whether or not Zachariah's suicide was a motivating factor. I wasn't even aware a year had already passed since his death. None the less, it did make me stop and think. What is interesting, Heather had felt Zachariah's presence around her ever since his death. She had commented on this often. Heather showed no signs of being grief stricken following Zachariah's death. In fact, Heather's reaction to his death was complete acceptance.

Many questions were asked during the session, some of those already addressed in the ER. While I thought others were clearly questioning my ability/inability to care for Heather. It was all very overwhelming, to say the least.

"Did I feel Heather was receiving adequate care at home?"

"Yes."

I did believe this. Even though Heather did spend time alone, I actually believed the family and myself was providing adequate care. The word "*believed*," justified every course of action I took, because I knew no other action to take at that time.

"Did I ever consider contacting an agency, regarding home care for Heather?"

"No." The thought of bringing in outside help, when I believed we were managing just fine, didn't come up.

"What best describes Heather's living environment, regarding decision making and family relating? Would I describe it as being functional or dysfunctional?"

"Not intending to make light of your question," I said, "I have always told my kids that each of us are somewhat dysfunctional, but together we always seem to function just fine."

I suddenly felt myself feeling afraid. Was I being investigated for negligence? It was beginning to feel that way. Were the two therapists going to recommend Heather be taken away from me? Did I actually cause Heather more harm than good while in my care? I'm not exaggerating one bit, when I say I thought for sure Heather would never be allowed to come back home.

During the session, Heather remained silent. Maybe Heather herself said she didn't want to return to my house. My mind was racing from one thought to another. Each thought creating more fear. Surprisingly, the last few questions asked were not focused on me or Heather's care. The therapists asked about the relationship between Heather and her Dad. The only word which I thought best described their relationship was "*estranged.*"

They also wanted my opinion on Heather's relapse while in rehab. Before even giving my opinion I had to ask, "Did you really believe Heather was stable enough to be transferred over to the pediatric ward? She was here only one week and then was transferred to the place that cause her so much grief in the past." The psychiatrist assured me that he felt confident Heather was mentally stable at the time of her admission into rehab. He noted that Heather never expressed any anxiety about entering into rehab.

My intention by asking a question as such, was not to imply that he rushed into his decision to release Heather. I wasn't sure if he had taken into account her past experience while in rehab. The opinion I gave to the therapists may not have been well thought out, but I thought it was direct enough for each of them to consider the possibility that even though Heather may have expressed excitement about rehab, under the surface she was feeling anxious.

My opinion, I gave to the therapists was this: "Heather was taken out of an environment that provided activities, therapies and best of all socializing. She was placed into an environment where socializing and activities were limited to her PT and OT sessions. She spent the rest of her time where? In bed. There was nothing to keep her mind off her pain or to prevent her from becoming depressed again. The visits from the psychologist was helpful, but only for a short while. Plus, without feeling supported or visited by other family members, what else could be expected to happen, but fall back into depression."

Neither of the two offered any insight on my opinion. Maybe, our time together was running out, because right after I had quit talking, Heather was asked if she had anything to say before ending our meeting. Heather had little to add. She did however, say that she needed to lay down. The pain in her hips and lower back was beginning to fare up, from sitting for that length of time.

Before leaving the office, the psychologist and psychiatrist both thanked me for coming in. They also commented on how Heather viewed me as being her best friend and it was oblivious that the two of us were indeed close. This made my day. To hear that Heather hadn't lost faith in me was heart warming. We were best friends. How could we not be, with everything we had been through together so far? It may to not have been the healthiest way to interact, but I depended on Heather as much as she depended on me.

As expected, I stayed with Heather until she was settled into her room, before taking off for home. It was an exhausting day for the both of us. Before I left to go home, Heather begged me not to have her return back to the pediatric ward for rehab. She just wanted to come home. Heather and I were at a crossroad. Whereby, neither direction looked promising in leading us to our destination.

As much as rehabilitation was needed, Heather was clearly against re-entering therapy at that hospital. By this time, Heather's mental state became my primary concern. Risking another relapse is all I would be doing if I gave my consent to another inpatient stay. It may have been wrong to think, but I could not allow Heather to be placed at the mercy of those whom assumed she would progress well in rehab. Given Heather's past history along with her recent backslide, I couldn't imagine how the therapists figured Heather would achieve significant gains if she were to re-enter rehab.

Heather remained in the psych unit for another eleven days. I received a call from Heather's psychiatrist, informing me that he was arranging a family meeting to discuss Heather's discharge and future counseling. He had insisted that I show. Heather's Dad was also contacted and asked to participate as well, which he declined.

Having knowledge of Heather's relationship with her Dad, it made little sense to me, that Heather was asked to call her Dad and invite him to the meeting. Maybe in an odd way, it was an opportunity for the therapist to witness how Heather dealt with rejection offhand.

There were only the three of us discussing Heather's fate, in the meeting that afternoon, Heather, myself and the psychiatrist. I was told, in no uncertain terms, the only way he would discharge Heather was if I made arrangements for professional counseling for Heather and present proof of doing so. There was no compromising what-so-ever. Actually, it was the best course of action the psychiatrist could have taken.

Knowing how bad I am at procrastinating, getting around to seeking counseling for Heather, would have been put off until we returned home from Oregon. Even though I had to scurry around like a mad woman, in order to meet the conditions of Heather's discharge, I found a psychologist in Grand Rapids who was willing to work with Heather and our insurance. I walked into the hospital on August 7th, 2007, with proof in hand and walked out pushing Heather shortly after. As far as making any significant gains with therapies or being any closer to becoming pain free, Heather remained just as immobile and in pain as she was before.

Counseling was the greatest form of therapy Heather could have received. She was able to come to grips and finally release a lot of buried emotions. Heather was by no means, out of the woods, so to speak. She still was considered mildly depressed and the risk of self-harm was still a possibility if suicide precautions were not followed through with. This meant, Heather had to alert me when she was feeling suicidal or when her depression was becoming to much for her to deal with. This also meant that I had better become more attentive to Heather's moods.

The trip to Oregon couldn't have come at a better time for us. Running away seemed even more urgent, than what it was at the time I purchased the tickets. Something was waiting for me in Oregon. I could feel it in my bones. Ever have a feeling like that? Where you intuitively know something is going to happen, but can't put your finger on what it is?

CHAPTER FORTY-NINE

*"Vacation is what you take when you can't take
what you've been taking any longer."*

Unknown

HE ARRANGEMENTS FOR OUR TRIP to Oregon were all in order. Rather than having one connecting flight in between Michigan and our destination, we were scheduled for two. For some reason, the bigger airlines were not equipped to accommodate Heather. One might think the bigger airlines would have been more capable of accommodating than the smaller airlines, but that wasn't the case. Maybe, because Heather needed assistance boarding and exiting the plane. As a rule, anyone whom needed assistance with a wheelchair, boarded the airplane first and exited last. Could it be, it was more of an inconvenience for the bigger airlines, rather than a matter of being capable of accommodating Heather?

Our first stop, after taking off in Grand Rapids, was St Paul, Minnesota. Second stop, Portland, Oregon. Then a short flight to Eugene, Oregon, where Marge and Peter planned to meet us. Following our arrival in Eugene, another three hours would be spent driving to Ashland, where Marge and Peter lived. We could have flown from Portland to Medford, only thirteen miles from Ashland, but Marge suggested driving to Ashland from Eugene, because the scenery would be absolutely breath taking and she wanted us to experience it. Estimated travel time from home to Ashland, Oregon, close to thirteen hours.

Our trip to Oregon may have met the criteria as being a planned vacation, but in the truest sense, we were just plain running away. Heather and I were both beaten-down, worn-out, drained, exhausted and discouraged. We were not seeking any kind of an adventure. We needed to escape from confinement and negativity hovering over us at home. It may be true that you can't leave your troubles behind you, but I sure was hoping it would be possible to acquire a new perspective and re-group in a different environment, free from what was resonating within our own home.

If given some serious thought, it can be said the every aspect of one's emotional well being, determination and view of what is happening around him/her, is a product of his/her own inward perspective. Argue this statement, if you will, only to find the argument itself is based entirely on a perspective. Interesting, isn't it?

I have found that there is a strength within, that can prevail any hardship if one can manage staying connected to that inner strength. But, once that connection becomes clouded over with layers of negative perspectives, it becomes difficult to hold on to even a sliver of strength or will power. In order to regain any feeling of strength, I had to physically remove myself from the despair that filled our home. This is what was calling me to Oregon all along. Oregon was where I would regain a renewed sense of inner strength, needed to continued on with our journey, without giving up hope or the will to fight against the odds of Heather regaining mobility and independence, along with ever restoring some type of normalcy back into my own life.

For spending money, Mom and my sister Shirley, gave me one hundred fifty dollars. Heather's dad had given her some money and Katie's dad also supplied Katie with a few dollars to spend while in Oregon. Our flight out of Grand Rapids was scheduled to take off at 6:30 am, August 18th. Grandma Ski arrived at our house at four in the morning to drive us to the airport. An early start to a very long day ahead of us.

Heather and I had each flown in a single engine plane before. Heather went flying with her Dad and Denise. Mikey and I flew around our area when the fall colors were at its peak. This would be Katie's first experience with flying and she was very excited. I reserved a window seat on each flight so all three of us would have a turn at sitting by the window. Katie would be first to sit by the window.

Our luggage was taken at Grand Rapids and would be waiting for us in Eugene. Which was nice, because this would make traveling easier for us. We each took a carry on bag filled with essentials that occupied us during our travels. Katie's excitement from sitting by the window, quickly turned to fear as the plane began its take off. Once in the sky, she relaxed and really enjoyed the view. I think Heather said it best, "Isn't it amazing that we can travel this way, it's like we're flying with the birds."

Word to the wise, wear running shoes if you expect to catch a connecting flight at the airport in Minneapolis. Our plane landed at the opposite end of the airport to where we needed to catch our connecting flight to Portland. Without the luxury of a lay over, Katie and I had to make a mad dash across the terminal. Katie was in charge of our carry on bags, while I attempted to maneuver Heather through the crowded airport.

On the way to the plane, our names were called over the intercom in the airport. "Hey, that's us!" I called out, as we went rushing past other travelers. Luck was on our side that morning, because the flight did not leave without us. The passengers were already seated when the girls and I were helped to our seats. This was the first and last time we would be the last to board a plane. I can understand why the airlines insist that those in wheelchairs board the plane first. It becomes quite difficult to move about freely, without bumping into seated passengers while seating Heather.

Somewhere, somehow, we managed to fall behind schedule while flying from Minnesota to Portland. After landing in Portland, the stewardess asked those whom were not catching a connecting flight out of Portland, to remain in their seats and allow those who had a plane to catch to exit the plane first. We fell in that category, but the stewardess would not allow us to exit the plane until all the passengers were off. Even those whom were staying in Portland.

Heather, Katie and I were seated one row from the exit door. It would have been a simple procedure getting Heather off the plane without taking up a lot of time. I suggested we ask the remaining passengers if they minded if we exited the plane before them. By the look I received from the stewardess, there was no chance of that ever happening. "I have to abide by the airline policies," she remarked in a smug tone. "Well, if we are to wait until everyone is off this plane, we will miss our flight to Eugene," I argued back to her.

The tension mounted between her and I when I suggested that

she call someone who had the authority to let us off the plane and not have to wait until the plane was emptied. Well, we ended up exiting the plane last and missed our connecting flight to Eugene. The next available flight to Eugene was in three hours.

As the girls and I were settling in for the three hour wait, the stewardess just happened to be walking by. I waved to her and graciously asked if she would like to join us as we waited three hours for another flight. She happily declined and went on her way. Maybe, there was another airline policy that prevented her from interacting with passengers outside of the plane?

We called Marge to inform her of our situation and not to expect us until much later. Good thing we had each packed a carry on bag, with books, iPod, along with Heather's medication, and thank goodness; my smokes. By then, I was really craving for a cigarette. The waiting was torture for Heather. She ached all over and needed to lay down, but all there was in the airport were single chairs. No benches or couches were available.

Katie and I ended up laying on the floor toward the end of our wait. Three hours never passed so slowly as it did in that airport. Finally, the announcement we were waiting for came across the intercom. We could now board our plane to Eugene. The plane we were about to board was a smaller aircraft. The kind of plane with a giant propeller attached to each wing.

Katie and I found it amusing that it just happened to be Heather's turn at sitting in the window seat. The only view Heather saw, when looking out the window, was a huge propeller spinning ever so closely to her. That and some city lights during take off, because by this time, it was quite dark outside. Even before the plane had stopped rolling on the runway in Eugene, Heather had her seat belt off and was more then ready to exit the plane.

There were only seven other people on the plane with us, so it didn't take long to empty the plane of passengers. Once we were off the plane, our first mission was to locate Marge and Peter. The airport was small, nothing compared to the other two airports we had been in earlier that day. As we headed to the baggage claim area, one woman in particular caught our eye right off. She was dressed in some type of black and red leopard print robe, white shorts over black tights and had this red and black hair color thing going on.

Marge had made the comment about how diversified Oregon was in one of our conversations over the phone. By the looks of the woman in the airport, Oregon would have to be diversified. Being from a conservative small town, dressing in such a way would only be seen on Halloween.

We walked right passed Peter in the airport and didn't even realize it. I hadn't seen Peter since he was a small boy. When he approached us, it was shocking to see the small boy, I remembered him as, had grown into a young man. Peter said Marge was off somewhere in the airport looking for our flight. He then escorted us to luggage claim.

Claiming our luggage was not as successful as we planned for it to be. Apparently, since we missed our flight in Portland, our luggage was sent back to Portland after it had arrived in Eugene. Go figure. As the clerk at the baggage area was explaining the mishap, I was suddenly bumped aside unexpectedly. I turned thinking it was Marge, but discovered the shove came from that peculiar looking woman dressed in black and red. When I looked closely at the woman I burst out laughing. The woman was Marge in disguise.

I should have guessed right off that the oddly dressed woman was Marge. Marge was famous for pulling pranks on others. At last, Heather and Katie had finally met their Great Aunt Marge. The woman, which whom I had spent so many hours talking on the phone with. Marge, along with Peter had become a tremendous source of inspiration to us, during a time when we needed it the most.

Katie was so fascinated by Marge's outgoing personality, she wanted to bring Marge back home with us and take her to show and tell. The family reunion was short lived at the airport, since we had a long drive ahead of us. So much for the scenic drive to Ashland. It was way past nightfall when we landed in Eugene. Midnight when we reached Ashland.

Marge had previously offered to house sit for a friend before our arrival to Oregon. Instead of staying at Marge's home while Marge house sat elsewhere, we were invited to stay along with Marge at Catherine's estate. Nestled on the hillside overlooking Ashland, was what appeared to us as being more like a mansion than a typical home.

My first impression of Ashland when I crawled out of the car was how the town with its shimmering lights, reminded me of a Thomas Kinkade painting. Heather said it looked as though the sky had fallen, because the town looked like a million stars were shining in the tiny valley. The view, overlooking Ashland was even more spectacular in the morning. Ashland is seated in a valley and surrounded by mountains and hills. The town itself is only six square miles in size. All this beauty, no wonder Marge decided to make Ashland her home.

Time seemed to cease in existence while in Oregon. I guess this happens when one has no agenda or schedule to keep. The time or even what day became irrelevant. I woke up early each morning just to sit out on the deck and soak up the amazing view. Marge joined me most mornings, where together we would indulge in philosophical discussions about life. Everyone has at least one passion in life, mine is philosophy and the meaning of life.

To many, life's meaning isn't the least bit appealing. Others may ponder over life's mysteries, but tend to lose interest. Then there are those, like myself, who become fully engaged in seeking what the purpose of life really is. Explains why, my viewpoints throughout the book, may come across as being some what perplexing at times.

On the mornings when Marge and Katie were busy else where, I would sit and read, drink coffee and smoke. Everything I needed to restore a sense of well being was provided for me. Nature provided me with a vast imagery of beauty, with background music performed by the perching birds in the nearby trees. Marge provided me with a sanctuary, where I was able to quite my mind from the racing thoughts, causing me so much chaos and anxiety. The entire atmosphere there created such a blissful feeling. I felt as though I would break down crying, without needing a cause to cry. It was that overwhelming for me.

It took Heather a couple of days to bonce back from traveling. When she felt up to it, we all took a tour of Ashland. The character of Ashland was nothing short of charming. The majority of citizens in Ashland appeared pleasant and extremely accepting of others. There didn't seem to be a separation among the residents as one would expect. In other words, status in the community did not seem to influence the importance of an individual. From what I noticed during our time in Ashland, the homeless and poor were treated with just as much respect as all others.

As we made our way through the business district, people from all walks of life greeted us with hellos and smiles; especially Heather. There wasn't the amount of staring or peculiar gazes by others directed at Heather, like what we've grown accustomed to whenever we were out and about around home. Only once during that outing, did we encounter the familiar feeling of being looked upon as indifferent.

While we were making our way to an outdoor cafe, I noticed three young men, in single file, walking toward us. Looked to me, they were in their late teens. Right off, I could tell by the expression on the leader's face and by his appearance, they wasn't the sociable type. It was apparent these young men belonged to a different type of society. A type of society, teaching racism and hatred toward the indifference's of others.

As the first two young men walked by, I instantly felt a wave of intimidation sweep through me. The look in their eyes, as each one glanced down at Heather, then up to me, was a look of contempt. When the last teen approached Heather and I, he also glanced down at Heather, then made eye contact with me. I smiled and greeted him with a *hello*. In his eyes, a hint of compassion shone through, as did an inkling of a smile. The encounter, although lasting a micro second, remains ingrained in my heart. In that precise moment, he had let his guard down and allowed himself to reveal that tiny piece of his true nature still alive within him. It meant that the teachings of the racist community he belonged to, had not yet fully engulf him. I think of him from time to time and am sadden when I think of how the young teen's life may now be filled with anger and hatred.

Marge and Peter made arrangements for us to visit a Buddhist temple just outside of Ashland. The visit to the temple is one of Heather's fondest memories of our trip. Heather was at that time, researching many different beliefs in spirituality.

It was at the temple where Heather met a young man, whom also was living with Cerebral Palsy. The only difference was, Brandon, was born with CP, while Heather's CP was an outcome from her DPT vaccination. Brandon was fun to be around and he took to Heather right off. He even took Heather to the movies one night. Being around Brandon made Heather a little nervous. There were many emotions Heather was still dealing with from her rape experience, which made her leary of being alone with young men. Following the night they went to the movies, Heather chose not to spend time alone with Brandon. However, the two of them did exchange phone numbers and promised to keep in touch when Heather left.

Our week in Oregon went by so quickly. Why is it that some days seem to be as long as one week, while a week can seem like only a day had passed? It was unfair we had to leave so soon. Marge had planned a "perfect last day outing" for us. The five of us, Peter, Heather, Katie, Marge and I would spend our last day traveling and sightseeing. No, our travels did not include the scenic drive to Eugene. We never did get to experience it. While Marge and I rode together in one car, Peter and the girls followed behind in his car. Ashland is about fifteen miles or so from the California border. Northern California, *here we come!*

Our first stop was at the Redwood National Forest. The redwood trees in the forest, may not have been as massive as the Sequoias in other parts of California, but to me, the redwoods were magnificent. Definitely a "must see" for anyone who loves being among nature and trees. I had seen photos of redwoods in magazines and books, but it wasn't until I actually stood next to one did I fully appreciate their beauty.

Cresent City, California, was where we stopped and walked along the shoreline of the Pacific Ocean. The surrounding area looked more like the landscape one would see in the region of New England. Instead of driving back to Ashland and staying the night, only to wake up extremely early for the three hour drive to airport in Eugene, we drove up to Eugene by way of Highway 101 and numerous side roads. Highway 101 has to be one of Americans most beautiful scenic drive along the coast. Nature displayed so much beauty along the way. From the mountain cliffs towering along the side of the highway, to the sporadic rocks formations rising above the ocean floor. We were then presented with the most incredible sunset I had ever seen. It was indeed a "perfect last day outing."

The itinerary for the trip home was slightly different than our flight schedule to Oregon. We flew out of Eugene at 6:30 am, landed in Seattle, Washington, at 7:25 am. Flew from Tacoma International airport in Washington, at 8:00 am, and arrived in St Paul, Minn, four hours later. With time to catch our connecting flight, without having to rush, we boarded our plane in Minn, and landed in Grand Rapids, in just under two hours.

Was running away from home worth whatever consequences were coming our way? Consequences stemming from not saving our money and using it toward more practical things; such as food and bills? Most definitely! The trip brought me back to myself. I arrived back home feeling more energized than I had felt in such a long time. It also gave Heather and Katie an opportunity see places they may have never been able to see. It was a bonding experience for the three of us as well.

Katie had been pushed into the background, so to speak, ever since Heather's first surgery. The trip gave her a sense of being included. I had no regrets about running away. Whatever was going to happen to us, would just have to happen and I would deal with it then. This was my attitude I approached our situation with after our trip. If I were to begin worrying about all the things I had no control over, I would quickly grow as discouraged as before. I never wanted to feel like I had before going to Oregon. I wasn't sure if there would be anywhere we could runaway to, if things went back to how they were. Eleven months had nearly passed since Heather's first surgery. Considering what all we had been through, I figured it was enough and no further challenges were needed to test our strength of character.

CHAPTER FIFTY

HEATHER WORDS

I WAS SO GLAD KATIE, MOM and I went to Oregon. For one whole week, I was able to escape my roller coaster life. Everything that is except my pain. My pain followed me like an unwelcome guest. Traveling was exhausting. I sat up in my wheelchair the entire day until we reached Catherine's home. I ached all over from being lifted, twisted and jerked around in different positions while getting in and out of my seat on each flight. Once I had a couple of days to just relax and rest up, I was ready to get out and do things.

The pain wasn't nearly as bad during the day, it was at night when I felt it the most. I guess my mind was so preoccupied during the day that I didn't pay any attention to it. I slept in every morning and stayed up late most nights. Probably, why I slept in longer than everyone else.

I had the best time getting to know Aunt Marge, Peter, along with Peter's friends. Now, meeting Brandon, at the Buddhist Temple was something I didn't expect to happen. He was nice, but he seemed to be carrying a lot of anger and self-pity around with him because he had Cerebral Palsy. Maybe being angry at the world was his way of dealing with all the frustrations of being limited by his CP.

When we met, I think Brandon thought that since I also had CP, we would automatically become more than friends. I wasn't interested in anything more than friendship and knowing that he did, made me really nervous being around him. Before leaving Oregon, Brandon and I exchanged phone numbers. I thought it would be nice to keep in touch with one another, but I stopped talking and texting him shortly after school began. I just grew tired of listening to his self-pity attitude and reading the nasty comments he would text me. I didn't need his kind of negativity draining mine energy. I already had my own challenges I was dealing with.

As wonderful as our vacation was, I was excited to return back home, because home is "*home*" to me. I missed seeing family and really missed my sleeping buddy; Sebastian. On top of that, I was very excited about school beginning. I couldn't believe I was going to be a Senior and that the upcoming year would be my last year attending school with my classmates. I thought of my classmates as being family. In a way we were a family. We had all grow up together during our school years. Sometimes we even fought like we were siblings. Some of us knew more about the other than what our actual family knew about us.

Elizabeth and I had gone through a lot of changes together throughout school. By our Senior year, we had drifted apart. We rarely ate lunch together nor did we spend time together outside of school. The bond between us will always remain strong. If one of us needed the other for anything, Elizabeth and I both know, we would be there for one another; always.

Health wise, nothing had changed much since my Junior year. I already knew my Senior year was going to be like my Junior year where I would often be absent. I was going to try my best to attend school everyday and was determined not to let anything keep me from graduating along side my classmates. That determination is what kept me strong on the days when my pain was at its worst and when my depression seemed to be getting the better of me.

While at school, I always tried to hide my pain and depression from others. I didn't want anyone to feel sorry for me. No matter how hard I did try to hide my pain and depression, there were a few people who could see right through me. Gates was one who could tell right off if I was having a bad day. He watched over me like a concerned parent. Again, he actually ordered me to stay home at least one day each week to rest.

My physical therapist, Becky, was another who would check up on me, since I wasn't doing any physical therapy at school during my Senior year. Becky visited me because of her concern about my overall health, especially my weight. I still had not gained back any of the weight I had lost. I remained as frail looking as I did in my Junior year.

For the first couple of months after school had started, I went to counseling for my depression, at North Kent Guidance Services in Grand Rapids. My appointments with the therapist were on Saturdays, so I didn't have to miss school or go on a school night. Like in the Psych unit, my therapist and I talked about my feeling toward Dad and the lack of progress I was having in recovering after my first surgery at the hospital. My outlook on life was changing at this time. I wasn't feeling hopeless as I had been. Maybe because I was taking lower doses of pain medication and going to school.

School was a place where I felt the most alive. It was about this time when I actually gave up all hope of ever walking. When I let go of the idea of walking, a huge weight lifted from me. I realized that the importance of me walking was more for the family than for myself. If I were able to become independent once again and live life without pain, I would be more than satisfied with that, walking was optional.

Before the school year began, I received my class schedule for the first semester. A total of six classes was listed: English, Study Skills, Computer, Write Right, World History and Senior Government. The class that had me worried the most was Senior Government. There was going to be a lot of material I would have to memorize. I didn't know how I was going to manage, because I was having trouble remembering anything at that time. I wasn't sure if my overdose effected my ability to remember things or if the medication I was taking was causing the problem. I told Mom how worried I was passing Senior Government. Mom decided to write the teacher, explaining the trouble I might have in his class, along with asking him to keep on eye on me if he would. She wrote about my overdose and how I might seem withdrawn or overly tired from the medication I was on.

The Government teacher did more than just keep an eye on me. Mr. O'Brien, became a close friend and someone whom I looked up to as a father figure. Right off, I had this feeling that I had know him from somewhere. Ever get a feeling like that? When you first meet someone whom seems like an old friend?

It was easy to talk with Mr. O'Brien about anything. I started to hang out with him during lunch time and soon, it naturally developed into a routine. It wasn't long before I began calling him O'Brien. No more mister. I wasn't being rude by doing so, it just sounded better to me. His son was a Freshman and would sometimes stop by during lunch. O'Brien also had a daughter who was in the Middle school. She was the same age as Katie.

Talk about a busy guy, O'Brien was always on the go. He coached track in the spring and football in the fall. He also was at school early every morning. I was always telling him how he needed to slow down. I don't know where he ever found time to spend with his family. Good thing he has a supportive and understanding wife.

O'Brien told me a anniversary story that he did for his wife. I just shook my head. After he told me, the following day, I brought him in some books written by Nicholas Sparks to read. I informed him that he needed to become more romantic. I was always picking on him and he took it well.

O'Brien was/is very well liked by the students in his class over the years. In his desk drawer, he had a pile of photos from students that were once in his class. Plus, he made sure that he took a class photo at the end of every semester of his students. All those pictures were scattered every where. I asked him if I could make a photo album, arranging the pictures accordingly to the year they were taken. Surprisingly, he allowed me to do this for him. He loved his photo album when I was finished with it.

O'Brien friendship had such an impact on me during my senior year at Greenville. I may have had Government for only one semester, but I continued to eat lunch and hang out with him all year long. We still talk once in a while, to catch up on what is happening in our life. I am so thankful he came into my life. I love you, O'Brien.

Since I couldn't tolerate the cold without my muscles tightening and causing me to spasm, I wasn't able to attend any football games during my senior year. Going to home football games and choir concerts, was what Grandma Sandy and I used to do together. I hated not keeping that tradition going. Whenever I used to go to school activities, I felt like I was a part of the school. Not going to any school activities my senior year, I felt kinda out of place, like I was just disconnected from the main stream. There were a few times when a football player allowed me to wear his football jersey on game day. This made me feel good and some what important, but I still missed out on the feeling one gets when you're actually at a game.

My mornings, when I did go to school, was the same routine as my Junior year. Up at four o'clock in the morning and picked up at five twenty by the ISD bus. I had a different bus driver and aid during my senior year. The funniest two women, I loved spending time with. I already knew Joy, the bus aid. I met her when I used to visit the special education class in the middle school. She was an aid in that room. Kathy, the driver of the ISD bus was the best. She would always comment of my shoes I wore to school. Saying how I had too many pairs, because it seemed like I wore a different pair every day.

Kathy and I became good friends and she asked me if I wanted to go shopping along with her and her daughter. I was so excited that she asked me. The three of us went to a mall in Grand Rapids and had the greatest time. As soon as we reached the mall, Kathy told me jokingly, that I wasn't allowed to buy any shoes, since I already had too many. Her daughter and I were going through American Eagle and I spotted a pair of blue and brown flats that I had to have. So, before Kathy caught up with us, I bought the shoes. When she found out, she just stood there smiling, shaking her head and said, "*only you.*"

My first semester at school was tough. I missed a lot of days and keeping up with my school work was really hard. But, I did it and passed the semester with a 3.25 GPA. I was very surprised I did that good. With everything I was still dealing with. I don't think I would have done that good if it wasn't for the encouragement I received from O'Brien, Gates and the office staff, along with many of my classmates and teachers.

I received the greatest news before starting second semester. I only needed to take four required classes in order to graduate. What a relief it was to hear that. I didn't worry as much when I needed to miss a day of school, because I had less homework to do. I ended up spending more time during second semester, bugging the office staff. They never grew tired of seeing me. I wondered what they were going to do after I graduated and wasn't there visiting them anymore. I imagined my awesome face would be missed.

Mrs. Bell, my English teacher, invited a local author to come and speak to our class. Richard Baldwin, is a author of several mystery novel's, based in Michigan. In one of his books, he included the students in Mrs. Bell's classroom. The book was titled "The Lighthouse Murder." I wasn't in the book because he hadn't met me. I was absent from school that day he came in. On his next visit, I was there and I went up to him and asked if he could put me in another book, when he wrote one. He said yes. He made me a character in his novels, "Murder in Thin Air", and "Murder at the Ingham County Fair". It was the coolest thing to see my name in his book.

When Thanksgiving was approaching, Mom thought that we needed to so something which gave us a sense of purpose. Something that took our minds off our own struggles we were having. Mom volunteered all three of us to help serve dinner at the Mel Trotter Ministries Thanksgiving Banquet, held every year at Devos Place in Grand Rapids. The Thanksgiving dinner was offered to those in the community that were poor or homeless.

Katie, Mom and I were assigned a table to serve food. We had two families who chose to sit at our table for dinner. Mom and Katie brought the food to the table and refilled drinks. We talked with the families and became friends with each other before dinner ended. We could have ate dinner with the two families, but when Mom found out that the leftovers could be taken home by the families at our table, she said we would eat something when we went home. She wanted those at our table to take the food home with them. We had nothing much to eat at home ourselves, but it seemed good to give to others that day. It was an experience I will never forget. I love helping others. Seeing the smiles of those at the table we served at, made that Thanksgiving Day the best day I had in a long time.

There was one school event that nothing was going to keep me from attending and that was Senior Prom. I decided to make some posters and I had help to hang them up. I do remember I was the only one whom made posters. I wanted to be prom queen, so I made sure I put the words out.

I was watching as guys begun asking girls to go to the prom and how groups of students were planning to go together. Crossing my fingers, I was hoping I would be asked to go by someone. No one ask me. Maybe no guy wanted to deal with the hassle of my wheelchair or with helping me in and out of the car. I envied all the girls who were asked out. I wondered for so long what it would have been like to go on a real date. I wondered what love felt like or a meaningful kiss. Not like the kiss the eventually led to my rape.

I felt out of place when no one asked me to the prom. I guess I shouldn't have been that surprised that I wasn't asked. Well, I would just ask someone who wasn't uncomfortable going to the prom with me. That someone was my cousin, Peter, from Oregon. Peter was very excited and honored to fly to Michigan and escort me to the prom. It's funny, Mikey asked our cousin, Jaimee, to his prom and my cousin, Gus, also took Jaimee to his prom. I guess taking family members to the prom runs in my family.

For my prom dress, I wanted to wear a dress like the one in the movie, "*The First Daughter.*" I fell in love with the purple dress Katie Holmes wore. Mom and I went to a fabric store and found a pattern and the perfect material that match the dress from the movie. I asked Grandma Ski and Aunt Phyllis, if the two of them could team up and make the dress. They both felt honored to do this for me.

Peter was going to rent a white tux. So I wore white gloves to match his tux and I also had a white ribbon that wrapped around my dress and was tied in the back. To match my dress, Peter wore a purple vest with his tux. My dress turned out so beautiful, it looked exactly like the dress worn in the movie. Mom took me to a hair salon in Lakeview, the day of the prom. I'm not a dress wearing type of girl, so I wore a pair of rolled up jeans underneath my dress. No one could tell I was wearing jeans.

Peter and I went over to Dad's house before going to the prom. Dad, Momma Denise and the kids took Peter and I out to dinner. It was nice seeing the family and having them meet Peter. We then left the restaurant and headed to the High school, where prom was going to be held. Peter and I arrived quite early, but was allowed to enter. We picked out our table to sit at and waited for others to begin arriving. The theme for Senior prom was "*Phantom of the Opera,*" so the gym was decorated accordingly. Friends of mine would stop by our table to say hello and I would introduce Peter to everyone. After a while, our table became so crowded with my friends. It was so great being there and sharing the night with my classmates.

The moment arrived for the announcement of prom Queen and

King. I was excited and nervous at the same time. I'm not sure why it was so important to be named prom queen. Maybe, I just wanted something good happen to me for a change instead of setbacks. I was sitting with my fingers crossed as the announcement was made. I may not have been chosen to be prom queen, but a little later into the night, I was given one very special tribute from three of my guy friends.

Chris Reisner, Jordan Nester, and Lukus Anstett, all whom I called "my boys." They wheeled me onto the dance floor for a dance. Jordan grab one hand, Lukus grab the other, and Chris was in between of them. As I looked at my boys as we swing side to side in one place, I had a tear coming down my cheek. For me, that moment will forever be remembered. What a wonderful way of saying, "We are here for you." I felt so honored and after prom come to its end, I gave each of "my boys" a hug.

After prom, many of my classmates were heading over to the middle school to play games and hangout with one another before calling it a night. I was debating whether or not Peter and I should go, because by that time, I was in a lot of pain. Then I thought that this might be the last time I'll have to hang with my friends, before we go our separate ways after graduation. Peter had no problem with us going. In fact, Peter fit in with my friends like they had know him for years.

Peter and I didn't stay long at the middle school before I needed to leave. I needed to lay down, my lower back and hips were killing me. Peter, being a social butterfly like myself, ended up getting a friend of mine E-mail address and phone number before we left for home. Lucky guy. I wondered if I was ever going to meet my dream man. I guess. It wasn't my destiny to have a relationship yet. I always could hold onto that dream of someday when the perfect man shows up at my door? Right? Anyway, Peter gave me a wonderful night full of memories. He flew from Oregon just to be my prom date. That says a lot about what kind of man he is. I love you Peter for being there all through my journey and being the best date I could have ever asked for.

When I was a Freshman, I attended what is known in our school as "Swing Out." It's a day when the graduating seniors dress in their caps and gowns for everyone in the school to see. Family members were invited to join us at the assembly. Scholarships and Academic Awards were given to many of the Seniors, along with handing out the high honors and honor cords. Swing Out, marked the last day Seniors would be together as a class before their Graduation. After the assembly was over, the seniors went around and said their goodbyes to the teachers that had impacted their life and went on a "mystery trip", paid for by fund raisers, the seniors held throughout the school year. From that moment on, I couldn't wait for my own Swing Out.

During my senior year, Mom and I made a lot of trips to see Holly. Every time we went, we walked away knowing just as much as we did before going. Holly still didn't know what was causing my pain. She continued to insist that I receive physical therapy. Yeah, right. I began asking Mom why we even bothered going back to see Holly, if she wasn't finding anything to help me get better.

For pain relief, I was now being prescribed 350mg of Vicodin. At first I only took a tablet now and then. Mostly at night to help me sleep. Most of the time I took strong doses of Motrin to dull my pain while at school. As the school year progressed, so did my pain. Mainly because of the two hour bus ride to and from school. I felt every bump and dip in the roads the bus drove on, which caused my muscles to tighten and spasm. Sitting in my wheelchair from four in the morning until I went to bed, didn't help either. I was always in constant pain. Some days I could tolerate the pain well enough to concentrate on what was taught in class. Other days, I fought like hell to keep from crying or going home.

I began taking a Vicodin before school, after second semester started. This was so I could handle the bus ride. The effects of the medication usually wore off after four hours, but I still felt tired afterward. By the time I came home from school, I was ready for another Vicodin. Then after a while, I was taking more Vicodin than Motrin. My depression was an up and down thing. Some days I wouldn't talk or participate in class nor with my friends. Those were the days where I felt like giving up. Then there were days where I couldn't talk enough and felt like my old self. I feel bad for anyone who fights with depression. It's so hard to break out of that feeling of emptiness one feels and find the strength to go on with life.

The night before my Swing Out, I took a Vicodin and went to bed early. I was so excited and couldn't wait until it was morning. I even asked my Guardian Angels to "please take my miserable pain away for tomorrow." Something was going on with my rods that night, because when Mom laid me down in bed, I felt a pinching sensation between my shoulder blades. It hurt so bad. Sabastain jumped up on my bed like he normally did, but I didn't let him stay there very long before pushing him off. I needed all the room in my bed to try and stretch out my muscles, in hopes of stopping what ever was pinching in my back.

Four O'clock came too soon. I barely slept at all. When Mom helped me to sit up on the edge of my bed, my muscles felt as though they were ripping and pulling apart. I hadn't felt that much pain in a long time. I told Mom to lay me back down and give me a few minutes to stretch out my back.

"Why? Why was this happening on this day?" I once again tried to sit up, but the same thing happened. The pain was worse the second time I tried to sit. I was so mad that I couldn't get up for school and knew that I would be missing one of the most important events of the school year.

I called Kathy and told her not to pick me up for school. I waited a while before trying to call the school. When I did call the school, Mrs. Nester, a member of the office staff, answered the phone. I asked if it was alright to stay home. I usually didn't call the school if I wasn't going to be there. The office personal knew the reason why I didn't show up for school. Either I was in too much pain or had a doctor's appointment. Mrs. Nester said I wasn't required to be there for Swing Out, but I would be missed. I also called Dad to tell him not to show up for Swing Out because I wasn't going to school. Him and Grandma Sandy planned on going to the assembly. I was so devastated that morning. I asked Mom for more Vicodin before she went to get ready for work. To even feel any relief from the agonizing pain, I ended up taking two tablets.

By the time I woke up I knew Swing Out was over. I called Gates to find out how everything went. He told me it was great and wished I could have been there. "Yeah, me too," I said to myself. Then Gates told me that I was given an award called, "*The Principal's Special Recognition Award.*" He then read it to me:

Principal's Special Recognition Award

Over the last four years we have watched one of our seniors overcome tremendous hurdles. This senior hasn't been involved in many activities or sports. But, every day gets ready for school to be picked up at 5:20 in the morning for a challenging day often filled with pain. She comes to school as often as humanly possible and always with a smile on her face. Her smile is infectious and she is just happy to be here. She lights up a classroom with that smile of hers and an attitude of pure appreciation. Last Summer, she even called me from the hospital to see how I was doing on my new job. Mr. O'Brien, one of her teachers writes this about her:

What have I learned from Heather Moore? Never to complain or feel sorry for her, because she doesn't do either. Live life to the fullest and laugh. Thanks Heather, for getting me to laugh when I didn't feel like it. You have more courage than the most courageous. Take time to read and listen to people more often. Slow down. Pick on people if they have a good sense of humor, but you better expect it back. Thank you Heather for being my friend and teacher.

Tim O'Brien

After high school Heather will be at Mary Free Bed for rehabilitation and independent living training. She plans to attend college and become a counselor. Please join me and congratulate our recipient of the Principal's Special Recognition Award: Heather Anne Moore.

I was crying at the other end of the phone. Gates also told me that all the seniors gave me a standing ovation. I was so honored. This is why I have always thought of my class as being family. They were always there supporting and cheering me up. Isn't that what a family is? We may have had our share ups and downs throughout school, but when all said and done, we all still loved each other. I am proud to have called them family. Gates asked me to include the following paragraph in the book:

"I had tears in my eyes when the entire Senior Class gave Heather a

standing ovation for the Principal's Special Recognition Award and she could not be there. She was not feeling well on that special day. This was a new recognition that I was giving for the first time and Heather Moore set the standard for that award with her determination to graduate no matter what obstacles were put in her path."

Graduation Day was set for June 1, 2008. Our class motto: *Hakuna Matata,* color for gowns: purple and black. Class song: *Don't Blink,* by Kenny Chesney: Class Flower: *Venus Flytrap Blossom.*

I told myself that I didn't care how much pain I might be in, I wasn't going to miss graduation, like I missed Swing Out. Dad picked me up at Moms the morning of Graduation. He hauled a trailer behind his truck so I could use my power wheelchair at graduation. Dad took me to his house since it was too early to go to the High school. I visited with Sasha Kitty for a while at Dads, to pass the time away. I missed her a lot since moving in with Mom.

When it was time to leave for the school and as Dad and I pulled into the school's parking lot, I spotted Mom and Grandma Ski right off. Momma Denise and Grandma Sandy were on their way and would be there soon. I was only allowed five tickets to give out for the Gradation ceremony. There were 303 Seniors graduating that day; out of 303 students, I was ranked 183. I managed to pass second semester with a 3.25 GPA. I feel the only person, who was the most concerned about how well I did academically, was my dad. My grade point average didn't mean a whole lot to me, all I cared about was receiving a high enough grade to pass each class, in order to graduate.

There wouldn't have been enough room in the gym if everyone invited all their family members to the Graduation ceremony, so that is why we were given a limited amount of tickets. The first thing I did when I arrived at school was find Gates. I missed the practice walk two days prior to Graduation. Gates was going to show me when I was going in the gym and where I would be sitting. I found Gates and he walked me through what I needed to do. He said that my name will be first to be called to get my diploma. After he had done that, he told me to find him after the Graduation ceremony was over. He wanted to present me with my award. I then headed off to the other the gym where all my classmates were waiting. Before entering the room, I stopped in the doorway and just watched as my classmates were saying their "goodbyes" to one another and celebrating the fact that they were about to graduate.

I felt so honored to be a part of such a great class and sharing the amazing journey of growing up with them all. I didn't have a lot of time to visit with everyone, before we lined up. I was going to be following the class president which meant I would be entering the gym second. I hoped I would do okay with wheeling in and getting to my place without too much trouble. When I heard the band begin to play the Graduation song and seeing the class President taking her first steps, my heart began beating so fast. Not because I was nervous, I was just so happy to be there and getting my diploma.

It was very hot in the gym. Sweat was forming on my forehead. It seemed like forever before the last seniors walked in and took their seat. When all of the graduating seniors were seated, Gates gave a little speech, followed by others who gave speeches before the diplomas were handed out. My named was finally called out by Gates and I wheeled up the ramp, where he handed me my diploma. I proudly took it and wheeled back to my place and watched as my classmates received theirs.

After the ceremony, I went outside to meet my family. I had the greatest pleasure rubbing my diploma in Dad's face. After I did that, Dad gave me a hug and told me how proud he was of me. Friends came up to say hi and goodbye. I then told the family that I needed to find Gates. When I did, he told me to get on the stage.

Gates walked up the ramp with me and then presented me with the trophy with the award's title written on the base of the trophy. While Gates and I were having our picture taken together, Jordan Nester, one of "my boys" who I danced with at prom, came up behind me and gave me a hug. He said me was very proud of me.

After all the pictures were taken, I ask Gates if he still have the "Principal's special Recognition Award"speech. He shook his head yes, and the family and I followed him into his office. He handed me the speech and also a backpack full of stuff from the mystery trip. I looked inside and saw the CD's of Swing Out week. I couldn't wait to get home to watch them. There were other goodies inside.

I was going to miss school so much, but I didn't have the worry of "how am I going to catch up on any school work." I was going to miss everyone and the socializing I did with others. That day may have marked the end of going to school, but the memories of my classmates, the office staff, teachers, Gates and O'Brien will always be in my heart.

CHAPTER FIFTY-ONE

"Where ever we are, it's our friends that make our world."
Harry Drummond

THE HUMAN SPIRIT CAN BE inspired by many things. For instance, nothing seems to inspire the human spirit as much as the kinds acts bestowed upon us by family, friends, acquaintances, and even strangers. Heather was very fortunate to have the sort of friends whom cared about her enough to take the time to brighten her days at school, when she needed it the most. Few people actually knew just how difficult it was for Heather to attend school. If she had gone to school without the encouragement she received from her friends, teachers, and her bus driver along with the bus aid, I know for a fact, Heather would have given up on graduating altogether.

Her friendship with Mr. O'Brien was perhaps the most unique and rewarding friendship Heather has had with anyone outside of Elizabeth. "Her boys", as Heather referred to them, those young men were always a topic of our conversation everyday when Heather came home from school. Each one of them deserves so much credit for including Heather into their day. Whether they realize it, they helped Heather feel alive again and brought her out of many depressive moods. Mr. Gates and the office staff, provided Heather with a place to socialize and hangout. She adored everyone who worked in the office. These acts of kindness helped bring Heather back to all of us, and that is no exaggeration.

I guess, it was a year of reaping what we sowed. I too, would be on the receiving end of unexpected gifts and surprises throughout Heather's senior year. I am not sure if this applies to everyone who feels overwhelmed at times, but whenever I become overwhelmed by stress, there is a part of me that feels as if I am carrying the weight of the world on my shoulders all on my own. In all honesty, I was never alone. All I ever had to do was pick up the phone and let others know I needed their help. I'm not sure if it was pride that kept me from doing so or if I felt too ashamed for being in the situation I was in financially.

Living behind us was a very generous and caring man. Dan Rice was a kind of neighbor that would extend a helping hand to anyone in need. He would pop in from time to time, ever since Nathaniel left, to see how the girls and I was doing. He especially kept an watchful eye over Sebastian. Dan was also a youth group leader at a local church. He surprised us one day with the news that his youth group choose our house to paint as a community project. All the supplies would be supplied by the church if we allowed them to paint our house. If there was a home in need of being painted, it was ours. Every time the wind blew, one would swear it had just snowed around our home. That was how badly the original paint was flaking off the house.

Dan said that I could choose what color our house was to be painted. I chose a gray/blue tint for the main portion of our home and burgundy for the trim. When the painting was finished and dried, the house took on a distinctive look. The paint dried a bit lighter than what I had expected. Our home definitely stood out in the neighborhood. The gray/blue tint turned out more like a light lavender and the burgundy dried to a light mauve. No one had trouble finding our home again.

As Christmas neared, Dan must had known I wouldn't have any money for gifts, because he delivered several gifts for the girls and Sebastian. The gifts came from the youth group as well. Several times, food would also be dropped off at our home from the church. Their thoughtfulness help us get through some very difficult times.

Instead of joining my family for Thanksgiving, I volunteered Heather, Katie and I to help serve a Thanksgiving dinner put together by Mel Trotter's Ministries, in Grand Rapids. The dinner was for those whom were homeless, poor and those who were going through a rough period in their life. I guess I felt being in the company of others who were struggling in life, like the girls and I were was where we fit in best. Plus, no one there would be asking about my financial situation or questions about Heather.

There comes a time when one gets tired of answering questions, when there are no answers. The time spent with those whom, the girls and I served at our table, was an extraordinary experience. There were two families seated at our table. Each with a completely different cultural background. By the end of the dinner we all became friends. The girls and I were allowed to eat along with those at our table, but when I learned that the families at our table could take home the leftovers, I told Katie and Heather that we would eat back at home and not there. It was our way of giving to those who were in need, like we were being given to.

After helping with cleanup duty, the girls and I left Grand Rapids and headed for home. It was a very rewarding morning. One in which the girls and I are thankful we took part in. Little did I know, but waiting for us at home was a gift. As we were pulling into our driveway, I noticed there was a blue tote sitting up against our front door. When I brought it into the house and opened it. I found it stuffed with food. A lot of food. The person who left the tote made no attempt at taking any credit for showing should a wonderful act of kindness. But, she didn't have to. I knew who it was from. Thanks Jobi.

Heather and I continued to drive to the city on several occasions for routine checkups with Holly. I was becoming extremely dissatisfied with the care Heather was receiving, but still hadn't voice my feelings out loud to Holly. I'm not sure why I hadn't, I guess it just wasn't time to do so.

If one really takes the time to notice, everything happens according to life's plan, not always on our schedule. Heather and I already knew what to expect during each visit with Holly, but we still continued to go. In early November, Heather underwent another series of Botox injections to help relax Heather's muscle tone. She was also injected with a steroid to help ease the pain in her knee joint, since that was now causing Heather a lot of discomfort. Everything was addressed but her main issues, her lower back and hip pain. What was becoming clearer to me during that time, was how Heather was being treated for her symptoms and not for the cause of her symptoms. As far as I could tell, trying to pinpoint the underlying cause and correcting it, was no longer focused on. Heather, by all accounts, had fallen through the cracks. That may sound cynical, but after taking a long hard look at the way the medical staff approached Heather's treatment, there was little to prove me wrong. It would seem, Heather's condition would have sparked the interest, of such a renowned institution such as Advance Care, to want to solve and correct what ever was happening to Heather. Why it didn't, I will never know.

The highlight of our year was Heather graduating. She managed to rise above her pain and depression, to achieve what some felt was unattainable. To those who really knew Heather, Graduation day wasn't about receiving a diploma. It was much more than that. The ceremony was held in the gymnasium at Greenville High school, and boy was it hot in there. Families of the graduating seniors filled every seat available. Mom and I sat high enough in the bleachers to watch Heather enter the gym and also gave us a great view of seeing her receive her diploma.

The sight of Heather entering the gym was an incredibly moving experience. She just beamed as she slowly drove her wheelchair up the aisle to her designated area. Mom and I both fought back our tears, but to no avail. As I was wiping away a tear from my cheek, an older woman sitting next to me, asked if I was a parent of a graduating senior. I turned to face her and said "Yes, my daughter." She then remarked how I must be very proud of her. I just smiled and turned my focus back on Heather.

I sat there starring down at Heather, while thinking about what the woman next to me had said. You know, I wasn't feeling a sense of pride in Heather in that moment. I was overwhelmed by a feeling of being honored. Honored by being Heather's Mom. Honored at being present and actually watching Heather's dream come true. The dream of graduating along side her classmates. Being able to share in this last milestone that her and her classmates will finish together. This was Heather's driving force all along, to cross the finish line of school with those she spent so many years growing up with.

Heather's senior year should had been a year of fun and a time of deciding what she wanted to pursue in life following graduation. Heather didn't have the option of pursuing anything other than more doctor appointments following graduation. My concern following Heather's graduation, was if Heather would have the willpower to keep fighting and not give up the hope of getting better. Now that school had ended, there wasn't much to keep Heather from falling into a deep depression.

CHAPTER FIFTY-TWO

HEATHER'S WORDS

*M*OM TOOK ME TO SIGN up for SSI (Disability) benefits in the fall of 2007. Once I was signed up and receiving SSI, I was now able to help out with the bills and buy things for myself. I asked Mom if we could get the internet for my laptop if I paid for it. The internet would make it easy to stay connected to my friends and I would have something else to do, besides watching TV or just laying in bed on the days I didn't go to school or on the weekends.

Mom thought it was a good idea as well. Since we didn't have a home phone, Mom ended up getting wireless internet. My bedroom was the only spot in our house where the internet worked best, so that is where we kept the computer. In my room, right next to my bed.

I found a game website called Pogo.com. The website offered hundreds of games you could play for free. I started playing Yahtzee and it helped me to keep my mind off of my pain. It was funny, every time I rolled a Yahtzee, a voice would call out *"Yahtzee"* from the computer. Whenever Mikey was over, he would mimic the voice and laugh at me. MySpace was really popular then and so I created a MySpace page. A lot of friends at school had an account on MySpace, so I was able to chat with them. I also thought it would be cool to make new friends with others who were on MySpace as well.

It wasn't long before I began receiving all kinds of emails on my MySpace messenger, and when I was browsing through the profiles of others. Strangers would pop in and start chatting. Most of the emails were from guys I didn't know. Guys who lived all over the US and I even received emails from Europe, Middle East, and Africa. When filling out my profile for MySpace, I wrote that I was handicapped and was interested in friendship only. Many of the emails I received started out with *"Hey sexy"* or *"Baby."* I knew those emails were sent by guys who were looking for an easy lay. I guess it didn't matter what physical condition I was in. Maybe, they didn't even read my profile, but looked at the picture of me that I had posted.

What bothered me the most, was how some of the emails sent to me contained photos of naked guys who wanted to chat. I couldn't believe it. What was happening in this world of ours? What ever happened to old fashioned romance? Where the guy takes a girl out for a candle lit dinner, walks her to her door, perhaps giving her a kiss before going home. Secretly, that was the type of guy I dreamed of meeting online. After so many years of not being asked out by anyone at school, I believed the only way I was ever going to find a boyfriend would be online.

I began emailing back and forth with a few guys, before one in particular grabbed my attention. His name was Blake and he was from California. I think what attracted me to him, was his need to be cared for. I figured since I couldn't do anything for myself, maybe I would be able to help Blake by making him feel like a good person. We began emailing each other a lot. Then we started texting each other on our phones, which led to calling one another.

The two of us talked on the phone for hours. Every time we talked, we each told the other more about ourselves and how it would be nice if we met face to face. It wasn't long before we began saying "I *Love You.*" Our phone had limited minutes on it. So it didn't take long before Mom told me to start limiting the calls. One month, the phone bill was over four hundred dollars! I didn't care. Since I had money of my own, I paid the bill. It was worth it because I found a boyfriend who cared about me. Mom jokingly said that it probably would be cheaper to fly Blake out to Michigan than paying the phone bill. I mentioned it to Blake and offered to help pay for his ticket, even before I asked Mom if it was alright by her.

Mom wasn't very open to the idea of Blake coming to Michigan when I first asked. She warned me about believing everything Blake was telling me about himself. Of course, I knew Mom was concerned, but I didn't believe Blake would lie to me about anything. Mom and

I talked a lot about Blake coming to visit me. I told Mom that Blake had to come because he needed to get away from his family. Blake had told me that at any time, he was going to be kicked out of his parents house. If he was kicked out, he would have no place to go, except live back on the streets again. This was the way his family was, kicking him out, then getting him to move back in again. A very troubled family life is what he grew up in.

Blake and I talked steady for seven months. It was just after I graduated when Blake called one night and said that he was kicked out of the house. He didn't have anywhere to go and no money. I talked Mom into letting him come stay with us. Mom and I went online and bought Blake a one way plane ticket to Grand Rapids. I told Blake that Mom and I would pick him up there. Blake went to the airport in California and waited for his ticket. He slept inside the airport and asked strangers if they could spare any money to buy himself food. Two days after his call for help, he finally arrived in Grand Rapids.

Meeting someone online is scary. You always hear stories about young girls being abducted or conned into meeting the guy, just to find out the guy is a predator. A lot of times, the picture of the guy you are talking chatting with, isn't really him. That was my worst fear when Mom and I drove to the airport in Grand Rapids. I wanted to believe Blake was honest enough to post a real picture of himself, but one never knows. I was excited and scared at the same time as Mom wheeled me into the airport. Excited because I finally met someone who accepted that I was handicapped and didn't have a problem with it. Scared because even though the two of us talked a lot, I really didn't know him. I only know what he wanted me to know.

Blake spotted me at the airport before I did him. I was so relieved that he looked like his picture on his MySpace profile. All he had with him was a change of clothes, along with a few personal items and his cell phone. He said he wasn't allowed to take anything else when he was kicked out of his parents home. Blake and I hugged for the first time. It was great finally meeting him face to face. Another chapter in my life was about to be written, including a life lesson that needed to be learn.

Mikey and Katie did not like Blake at all. Blake was different from us, but I had hoped that they would have given him a chance before disliking him. Mom was nice to Blake and the two of them talked a lot at first, but after a couple of weeks Mom also began to question Blake's sincerity.

Blake and I spent a lot of time in my room. It felt like he didn't want me to be around my family. Basically, the only time him and I left my room was when no one was at home or when he took me outside for walks. I enjoyed the times him and I went on walks. For a while, Blake and I talked about getting an apartment together in Greenville. We were both getting SSI benefits and if we could get into a income based apartment, I knew we could make it on our own.

Blake then changed his mind about living in Michigan. He thought it would be better if the two of us found an apartment in California instead. The weather would be a lot warmer and there was more to do there. I didn't care where we lived as long as we were together. Mom wasn't happy about the idea, but said if I showed proof of finding a place to live, a nice place to live, and a good hospital that would take over my medical care, she would give her consent. I was eighteen years old, I couldn't understand why I needed her consent for anything.

As the weeks went by, I started noticing changes in Blake, which should havewarned me that he wasn't right for me. I chose to ignore his behavior and only saw what I wanted to see. He stopped helping around the house and spent a lot of time on the computer. He was starting to become really antsy. Instead of caring for me like he had been, he began asking Mom to step in and care for me. He would get mad at me whenever I took any pain medication. I guess he was scared that I might become addicted to the Vicodin. Actually, I felt like I already was.

By then, I was taking Vicodin like candy. I guess my body was becoming immune to it. Sometimes the Vicodin would take away my pain for a while. Other times I didn't feel any effect it had on my pain. The reason Blake became upset with me over the pain medication he was trying to get off drugs himself. Something I didn't tell Mom about until Blake came to Michigan. Another reason Blake would get mad at me was because I wouldn't have sex with him. I wanted to wait and get to know him better before I said yes. I still was afraid to have sex. I had already told Blake about my rape before he came to Michigan, so it's not like he wasn't aware of it. He couldn't understand what my rape had to do with us having sex. I should have known right then that having sex was more important to him then anything else.

Dad and Momma Denise held an open house for me after graduation. With the money I received from everyone at the open house, I planned to buy plane tickets for Blake and I to go to California. I was ready to meet his family; especially his Grandma. Blake's grandma and I talked on the phone whenever Blake called her. She was the only family member Blake was close to. She took him in several times whenever he was kicked out of his house. I liked her already and couldn't wait to meet her.

The thought of being out of Michigan and on my own sounded too good to be true. No one in my family would be around telling me what to do or what I couldn't do. Mom, Blake and I talked about me going to California a lot. Mom kept saying that I had better not end up on the streets and that Blake had better take good care of me. She said that I had better get in to see a specialist as soon as I arrived in California. Mom lectured Blake so much about taking good care of me.

I spent days on the computer looking for an apartment for Blake and I. The rent in California was so much higher than in Michigan. The only problem Blake and I had was that we didn't have enough money for a deposit on any apartment. Blake said we could stay with his grandmother until we had enough for a deposit. Which I thought it was a good idea; Mom didn't.

Mom suggested that Blake fly back to California ahead of me and work on finding an apartment. After getting one, I could fly out. I knew this wasn't going to make Blake happy. I told Mom that everything was going to work out for us. My mind was made up. I was determined to go and begin living my own life. Even though Mom said that I was making a big mistake, I went ahead and bought two plane tickets.

One week before Blake and I were supposed to leave for California, I suddenly began having problems with my rods. It felt as though my rods were pinching some nerves in between my shoulder blades. My right arm would twitch and fly into the air for no apparent reason. I couldn't control my arm from doing this. I called Mom into my room and showed her what was happening. All I remember, Mom was saying that I had better get dressed because she was taking me to the ER, at Advanced Care Hospital. This would be Blake's first and last time going to the hospital, I started hating with a passion. I remember while Mom was driving us to the hospital, Blake held my hand and told me that he wished he could take away my pain.

When we arrived in the ER three hours later, Mom asked the nurse to get a hold of Holly. Mom wanted me to be admitted and once and for all, do something to stop my pain. The nurse hooked me up to a IV and said that's he would try to get in touch with Holly. Mom, Blake and I waited four hours before I was seen by a doctor.

An assistant of Holly's came to the ER. He said that Holly was in surgery and would not be seeing me. The doctor in the ER started asking me questions about why I was there and began pressing against my spine. When she pressed a certain area between my shoulder blades my arm went flying into the air. I thought Mom was going to punch the doctor when she said: "Okay, if I pressed down here your arm jerks upward."

When asked about my pain, I said it was a ten. Soon after, I was injected with a pain killer. Mom kept asking about getting me admitted into the hospital. Holly's assistant said that I wasn't going to be admitted. Mom and I would have to make an appointment with Holly and at that time Holly would decide what she wanted to do.

The ER doctor said that she wanted an x-ray taken of my spine. Mom told the doctor that nothing was going to shows up in the x-ray. Whatever was causing my arm to fly into the air had to do with my nervous system. The x-ray wouldn't show anything like that. Having an x-ray taken would be a waste of time.

So, after the x-ray was taken, the doctor came back and said that everything looked good. The exact words that Mom had said. I was given another shot of pain killer before leaving the hospital and Holly's assistant wrote me a prescription for a stronger dosage of Vicodin. I don't ever remember seeing Mom as mad as she was that day. On our way home, Mom said that we had been through enough. The rods were coming out and we were done with Advanced Care Hospital. Mom finally reached her breaking point, something I had reached a long time ago.

The next day Mom made an appointment to see Holly. Blake didn't go with Mom and I on that day. Even before Mom said anything about having my rods removed, Holly said that it might be time to consider having my rods taken out. Mom and I just looked at one another and smiled. Holly said that my spinal fusion should have had enough time to fuse together and the curve in my spine should not get any worse. Removing the rods may relieve the pain in my back and hips as well.

If I was going to have my rods taken out, I wouldn't be able to go to California with Blake. I didn't want Blake to go back to California without me. I was scared that if he went back alone, he would go back to his old habits and I would never see him again. I think Mom knew this as well. I think Mom believed all along that Blake would go back to his old habits even if I went to California. I told Mom that maybe I could have my rods taken out in California.

Mom said that I was going to have my rods taken out at Advance Care and nowhere else. Mom had Holly schedule my surgery. The night before Blake's flight home, I called Mom into my room and asked her if Blake could stay with us until I was well enough to fly. Mom said absolutely *NO*! Blake was flying back to California no matter what. While I was healing, Mom said that this would give Blake enough time to get things settled in California and find a place for us to live. If the two of us were meant to be together, then it would turn out that way. Mom wouldn't listen to any more talk of Blake staying.

Like I have been saying throughout this book, "Everything happens for a reason." Life didn't want me to go with Blake. That is why my rods began pinching when they did. Blake did go back alone and returned back to his old habits and ex-girlfriend. It made me so mad because I really believed him when he said that he would wait for me to get better and together we would start our life together.

I often wondered what would have happened if I had gone to California with Blake. Would he have taken care of me, or after a while, leave me to fend for myself? After talking with Blake's grandmother, following my surgery, I got my answer. Blake's grandma said she was glad that I didn't come there, because Blake wasn't prepared to take care of me. However, if I did go there with Blake and things became bad for me, she would have taken care of me and saw to it that I came back home safe.

You know, even though Blake wasn't the right guy for me, I still enjoyed our walks together and our talks we had. Under his surface, he was a gentle man that very few people saw. He didn't show his true self to others. I know Mom saw this side of Blake as well. The life lesson I was meant to learn, was to accept that I would not ever be able to help save another, if that other was not willing to change on his/her own. I was also given the chance to see how gullible I really was.

Would I instantly believe what was said to me by other guys online? Well, sometimes one has to repeat mistakes more than one time, before the lesson is really learned. Blake and I still texted one another for a while, until he began to text me some really disturbing messages. It was then that I stop texting him altogether. I still believe he was a gift and I became a wiser person from knowing him.

I fell into a depression after Blake had left. I had my rods taken out at the end of July. The pain in my lower back and hips continued, but the pinching in between my shoulder blades had stopped and my arm didn't fly in the air anymore. Life was hell for me. I was back to laying in bed all the time. I felt like giving up and couldn't find one reason why I shouldn't.

Mom said that she was going to have me evaluated at Mary Free Bed. Something she said she regretted not doing earlier. She called my family doctor and asked if he would make the arrangements. He said that he would and give us a call when the appointment was made. Either that or we would get a call from Mary Free Bed. There was nothing else for Mom and I to do except wait, and wait we did.

Right after my rods were out, I started chatting again online with guys. It gave me something to do and plus I didn't feel so alone. It didn't matter that these people were strangers, I just needed to talk and have some type of connection with the outside world. I started chatting with two guys everyday. One was from Texas and the other from Morocco.

Mohammed was from Morocco and barely spoke English. I bought a web cam for the computer so I could actually see who I was chatting with. It was so cool to see Mohammed on the computer. We decided to call one another. I had to buy special minutes to talk with him since he lived overseas. I paid around forty dollars for one hour of phone minutes. To chat on the computer, it cost Mohammed thirty five dollars a day for internet.

We did more laughing on the phone than talking. He would have me talk to his Mom and sister, who spoke less English than Mohammed. He was always so full of positive energy. We talked about what it was like being Muslim and about the Holy Qur'an. I thought his beliefs were interesting and I soon bought a Holy Qur'an to read for myself. Not that I was going to become a Muslim, but I wanted to learn about different beliefs.

Mohammed said that I should come and visit him in Morocco. He would make sure that I would be safe and that Mom should come with me also. Mom talked, well laughed, with Mohammed every time I did. She liked him right off. Him and his family prayed for me everyday, hoping that I would soon get better. We stayed in touch for a few months, but things started to change. He was beginning to talk about marriage and being in love with me. I couldn't handle that type of talk so I ended it. To this day, I laugh out loud whenever Mom mentions him. Thanks Mohammed, for making me laugh and lifting up my spirits when I wasn't up for it. He was another gift Life had sent to me.

Brad, the guy I chatted with on MySpace, was from Texas. We text one another and he seemed nice. He invited me out to Texas. I had told him about my home life and how I wish I could move away. He understood how I felt and was willing to help me out. When he asked me to go to Texas, I said I would. Mom, on the other hand, had different plans for me.

Oh my God, I never had Mom yell at me like the way she did the day I told her I wanted to go to Texas. I think the whole neighborhood heard her screaming at me. Mom told me I wasn't going anywhere except Mary Free Bed. If she had to go to court and get some type of custody over me she would do so.

Mom and I fought back and forth. I wasn't really mad at her nor did I hate her. I just needed to let my anger out that was stewing deep inside of me. I was so angry at everything and everyone. In the end, I did like I always have done. I gave in to what others wanted me to do. Here I was eighteen and still was treated like a helpless child whom needed to be told what was best for me.

I was tired of being a crippled, being criticized for not walking or getting better. Tired of all the pain I was in and tired of waiting for a doctor to heal me. I was beginning to forget the days when I wasn't in pain. I missed walking and even missed falling down. I missed being able to crawl and wall surf. Didn't Mom know that I had been through enough hell? Guess not, because she made it clear that I was going to Mary Free Bed.

I bet it was going to be like that hospital, where no one would know what to do with me except prescribe pain medication. I didn't see what the point was in going to Mary Free Bed. I didn't see what the point was to life at all. Once again, I began thinking about suicide. Even though I promised Mom that I would let her know whenever I was beginning to have suicidal thoughts, I didn't see what the point would be.

I didn't want to hear how I had to be strong and patient. I had been patient and strong for almost two years, and what did I have to show for it? Nothing. Without letting on to how depressed I was, again I waited until I felt it was time. Over time, I worked hard at convincing Mom that I would never attempt suicide again. She was afraid of leaving any medication by my bedside. I kept telling her that she could trust me. Finally, she gave in and began allowing my medications to be within my reach. This time, I overdosed on Baclofen. I remember calling Mom down stairs and telling her. Everything after that is a blur.

Mom took me to the ER in Lakeview. Hours later, I was taken by ambulance to Grand Rapids. Mom came to the hospital after she went home and made a few calls; one to my dad. I stayed in the hospital for almost a week. A Social worker and Mom talked about what the plans were for me when I was discharged. It was suggested that I go to Pine Rest for a stay there. Pine rest is a place where counseling for mental health issues are offered. I didn't want to go to pine Rest, Mary Free Bed or anywhere. I wanted my life to be over. But, I guess Life had a reason for me to be still alive. Mom thought Pine Rest might be good place for me to be. I think Mom didn't know what to do for me at that time, but after Mom and I talked she agreed to take me back home.

Two months after my overdose, Mom received a call from Mary Free Bed. I was scheduled for an evaluation on November 11th, 2009. We only had to wait one week until we went. The doctor who would be evaluating me was none other than my childhood doctor; Andrea Kuldanek. Mom was so excited by hearing that. She kept saying that the help we needed was there. Mom also said that I would meet my soul mate at Mary Free Bed as well. She could feel it in her bones. "*Yeah right*," like I even cared. I was through with guys and all the games they played. I was through with believing help was even possible for me. Without having any say of what I wanted, I had no other choice, but to tag along with Mom to Mary Free Bed.

CHAPTER FIFTY-THREE

HEATHER ON THE INTERNET COULD easily be a story in itself. She has been and always will be a social butterfly. I truly love this quality about her. Once she finds a common link to another individual, she considers that person to be an instant friend. Heather rarely kept herself protected against being hurt or disappointed by others. She openly expresses her deepest emotions, dreams, and opinions to everyone. At times, her innocence even takes me off guard. I guess because I tend to hold back and not allow others into my world quite as easily.

I wasn't surprised at all when Heather said she had met someone online, whom she wanted to meet. Blake appeared to be a perfect "*cause*" for Heather to become involved with. He was a young man with a difficult family life. Blake was the same age as Heather and had been in and out of trouble with the law, had lived on and off the streets, and battled with drug addiction. Heather didn't care about what his past was or even the possibility of trouble following him anywhere he went. She was convinced that the two of them had to meet.

Allowing Blake to come and meet Heather was a decision made on the assumption that if I didn't, Heather would find a way to secretly fly out to California. If she convinced a friend to help her purchase the ticket and take her to the airport, Heather would have went. She was eighteen and legally, I had no say over her. I thought it better to have Blake come to Michigan than risk the chance of Heather going to California and not knowing what would become of her. Given enough time together, I was hoping Heather would discover that Blake was just a cause and not someone with whom she would choose to become seriously involved with.

In all fairness, I have to admit Blake did bring joy into Heather's life for a time. He was respectful toward Heather and cared for her in ways that few guys would. He helped her dress, shower, took Heather outside on walks. In return, Heather provided a safe haven for Blake to live without the hostility he faced at home. Blake was basically a good kid. He had dreams and goals like any of us. The only setback for him was that he couldn't seem to follow through on any of them.

Blake was also responsible for bringing out a side of Heather I had overlooked, on so many occasions. If it wasn't for his presence in our home, I most likely would have continued to pay little attention to how responsible Heather was capable of being. Blake began having a serious asthma attack late one night. Heather took matters into her own hands and told Blake that the two of them were going to the ER.

I was very proud of Heather for being so grown-up like. The incident had certainly opened my eyes. I was so used to being the one making all the decisions and taking charge. I did all the talking with the doctors, therapists, and nurses, when all along, Heather should have had been included more often. It was time to begin thinking about handing over the reins to Heather. The time had arrived for everyone, involved in Heather's care to start addressing Heather, instead of side stepping her and addressing me.

It was such a habit for me to do all the talking for Heather, the transition was not going to be as easy as one might think. The truth of the matter was, if Heather was ever going to be able to live on her own, I had better stop being so overly protective over her. If I didn't, how would Heather gain any experience of handling her own medical care? I'm not sure if other parents in a similar situation with their child felt this way, but I was scared that if I did stop being so protective over Heather, she wouldn't need me as much. My role in her life would lessen and where would that leave me?

Heather wanting to go with Blake to California scared the hell out of me. By the time Heather purchased the tickets, I knew Blake was not going to take good care of her, but Heather couldn't be convinced of it. As the date of their flight grew nearer, I grew more afraid. I thought for sure Heather would see Blake as he really was and not how she had imagined him to be. Ever hear of the saying: *"Let go and let God?"*

Being more of a spiritual person and seeing no other alternative, I let go of trying to convince Heather she was making a huge mistake and let Life decide Heather's fate. If Heather was not meant to go to California then something unexpected would occur, causing her to stay with me. Life has a way of doing that. In the meantime, all I could do was wait and watch what direction Heather's life was going to take her. The wait wasn't long before signs of Heather's fate began to unfold. Honestly, I was furious by the circumstances that kept Heather in Michigan, but what a relief it was in knowing that she would not be going to California.

As I had already mentioned, very few people knew how difficult it was for Heather to attend school during her senior year. Traveling by bus to and from school caused Heather to be in a lot of pain. The very pain that plagued her ever since her first surgery. The same pain which Heather and I had repeatedly questioned Holly about. 2008 started out as being a year more challenging for Heather than any other time, I can think of since her first surgery and it wasn't going to be getting any better.

In January of 2008, Heather and I saw Holly. The concern I was having then was of course, Heather's pain, but also I had noticed Heather had begun sitting on an angle in her wheelchair. Holly noticed Heather was sitting slightly tilted as well. She assumed Heather was transferring weight to the right side, in order to lessen the pressure placed on her left hip.

Holly didn't seem well concerned about this, since Heather's rods would prevent any further curvature. The x-rays taken that day did show Heather's hardware to be in place with good alignment. This was good to hear, because Heather didn't need another issue added to her condition. When Holly asked Heather if she was still experiencing a lot of pain and spasms in her lower back, hips and legs, Heather said; "the pain is always there, but it's getting worse now."

It seemed that the effects of the Botox, injected into Heather, two months prior had already worn off. I asked Holly what she planned to do about Heather's condition. A question I had been asking all along. A question Holly must have had asked herself all along as well. The plan was this, Heather was to come back to the office in three months, where Holly would try to make arrangements so Dr. Snyder could attend as well. Together the two of them would decide what the best course of action would be. Until that time, Heather was given a script for 350mg of Vicodin and a prescription for Baclofen. Oh, another script for physical therapy.

In March, Heather was experiencing numerous spasms in her back and legs, along with pain in her right knee. I took Heather to her family doctor, Dr. Ausiello. Heather asked for a refill of Vicodin since she had taken all that was prescribed by Holly. Dr. Ausiello wrote one out, but expressed his concern toward Heather's well being. We filled him in on our frustrations with the hospital's treatment of Heather. He suggested Heather be seen by a pain specialist in Grand Rapids.

Dr. Ausiello felt that his friend Ramin Rahimi, D.O., at West Michigan Rehab & Pain Center could help Heather with the pain. Dr. Ausiello felt that taking so many Vicodin, as Heather had been taking, was more harmful than good. Perhaps, with the help of pain management, Heather could be weaned off of Vicodin altogether. This was our first real step toward seeking help outside of Advance Care Hospital.

Heather and I met Ramin Rahimi in early April. The two of us liked him right off. He examined Heather thoroughly and agreed with us that Heather's pain had to be dealt with before physical therapy could be beneficial. This was the first time anyone had supported my theory. The area in which Rahimi felt needed to be addressed first was Heather's knee, since her knee caused her the most discomfort. For the next two months, Heather and I traveled to Grand Rapids, where Heather was injected with steroids into her knee. She did feel a lot of relief from the pain, but like the Botox injections, it was just a temporary fix.

April 16th, Heather was taken to the ER in Lakeview. The pleurisy had returned. Heather couldn't take a breath without breaking into tears. This is the period in which Heather missed a lot of school, because riding the bus and sitting up in her chair all day was too painful. May 4th, Heather went back to the ER for chest and lower rib pain. Even though Heather had taken the Prednisone, prescribed to her at her last visit, the pleurisy was not going away. Again, Heather was placed on Prednisone and more Vicodin. May 23rd, back to the ER we went. Every part of Heather's body ached. Heather was again given a script for Prednisone and Vicodin. This time the dosage for Vicodin was raised from 350mg to 500mg.

That was why I was so furious the day Heather called me into her room to look at the way her arm was uncontrollably jerking upward. All I could think of was, *"What now?"* Shaking my head in disbelief, I told Heather to get dressed, because I was taking her to the ER at the hospital where this all started. I was convinced that once Heather was seen in the ER, Holly would have no other choice but to admit Heather and *FINALLY* correct whatever went wrong to cause Heather to be in the condition she was in. We wasn't dealing with muscle pain and spasms this time. We were dealing with some type of nerve issue. Something I was sure Holly would want to deal with immediately.

The environment in the ER at the hospital was so chaotic. So many patients, so few staff. After Heather was injected with her first pain killer, the jerking motion in her arm ceased and Heather's body relaxed. I asked the nurse attending to Heather to contact Holly and tell her about Heather's condition. I also asked about having Heather admitted into the hospital. The nurse said that she would try and contact Holly.

We waited four hours in total before an physician came in to see Heather. Along with the attending physician, one of Holly's assistant's came in as well. He told me that Holly was in surgery and that she would not be seeing Heather. I made it clear that I wanted Heather admitted into the hospital. When asked why I wanted Heather admitted, I flat out said, while peering into Holly's assistant's eyes "Because it's time you guys fix what ever you did to make Heather in the condition that she is in."

There was no holding back my frustration and I was ready to take on the whole hospital if need be. I was to. However, anyone who has dealt with the power of control hospitals have, they call the shots not you. Holly's assistant remarkably remain poised as he informed us that Heather would not be admitted without being seen by Holly. Heather and I would have to make an appointment to see Holly and discuss the matter with her. It wasn't his, or the ER physician's decision to make. All this took place even before the physician examined Heather and questioned why she was brought in. I should have excused myself from Heather's room before I made matters worse for Heather. I should have just gone outside and smoked a few cigarettes while trying to gather my wits, so to speak. But, I didn't, which only resulted in me becoming more upset.

My breaking point was reached when the ER physician asked

why Heather was brought into the ER. I described the twitching Heather was experiencing in her arm and how the arm would flare upward uncontrollably. I said that her rods have to be pressing or pinching some nerve to make this happen. The attending physician began pressing areas around Heather's shoulder blade and touch on the spot where it caused Heather's arm to go flying into the air. To my absolute astonishment the physician sounded so amused as she said; "Okay, if I press here, her arm flares upward." I'm not kidding, my fist was clenched and I wanted to strike that physician. She pressed the spot again with the same results. Holly's assistant and the physician look at one another, before discussing with me about the possibility of Heather's rod pressing against a nerve. I stood there glaring into the physician's eyes. If looks could kill....Well, you probably know the rest of that saying.

The physician then ordered an x-ray to be taken on Heather's spine. This really set me off . "I can tell you right now what the x-ray will show." I spouted off ." The rods look good and nothing is out of place. Wouldn't it make more sense to do some type of nerve test instead?"

"It's all we can do here." The physician replied back.

I turned to Holly's assistant and told him to call Holly and ask if an x-ray is needed. He reminded me that Holly was in surgery and also recommended having an x-ray taken. I thought to myself; "Sure, let's waste all of our time here, just to look at perfect positioned rods." The physician said the x-ray would rule out any problems with her hardware. It truly was the most she could do for Heather. I knew this but I wanted more to be done for Heather.

As Heather was wheeled into x-ray, I went outside and had my smoke. Blake went along with me and together we sat without saying much to one another. I was so angry and talking wasn't something I wanted to do. After a while, Blake and I returned to Heather's room where she was waiting to hear back from the ER physician and Holly's assistant.

Hearing how Heather's rods looks good in the x-ray was no big surprise. There was no need to stay in the ER any longer. The trip was a complete disaster. Instead of achieving my goal of getting Heather admitted into the hospital and putting an end to her suffering, I managed to create a higher sense of hopelessness in Heather, as well in myself. Before leaving the ER, Heather was given another shot of pain killer and a prescription for Vicodin. The dosage this time was increased another 250mg. Raising the strength of Vicodin to 750mg.

On our way back home, I told Heather that the rods were coming out and we were through with that hospital. I had no plan as to what we were going to do after the rods were out. I kept on having this feeling that Mary Free Bed was where we needed to go. Maybe, it was time to act on that feeling, instead of brushing it aside.

July 11th, Heather and I met with Holly to discuss the removal of Heather's rods. I was through with waiting on Holly to find what was causing Heather to be in so much pain. I knew there was a lot at stake by removing the rods, but I figured the time had arrived for Heather and I to take control of Heather's medical care. For the past twenty-one months, Heather went through hell. There hadn't been any improvement in her condition. If anything, her condition worsened even after trying the suggestions given to us by Holly and her team, along with Dr. Snyder and her teams of therapists.

Why physical therapy was repeatedly advised, when Heather was plainly in no condition to participate in, is beyond me. As for the Botox injections, her muscle did become more relaxed, but only temporarily, and the Botox did nothing in stopping Heather's spasms. The Vicodin helped dull Heather's pain, but Heather was in fact, becoming addicted to the drug. Baclofen also helped relax Heather's muscles, but also effected her mental state and appetite, just as the Vicodin had. Basically, oral medication had proven to be more of a hindrance for Heather than beneficial.

Given the amount of time Heather was under their care, the medical team had to have sensed this as well. As far as I am aware of, no other specialist, outside of Dr. Snyder was brought in to examine Heather. Maybe, another specialist would had seen something Holly may have missed. Holly did mention consulting with her colleagues regarding Heather, but not actually having Heather examined by him/her.

Maybe, just maybe, the responsibility for helping Heather didn't fall on Holly. Could it be that Holly's only role in all this, was to surgically implant the rods and nothing more? Holly never said and I never asked. I just took it for granted that Holly's responsibility included being totally involved in Heather's recovery. The Harrington rods had always shown to be intact with good alignment, which would easily exclude Holly from any wrong doing. I am very confident that all of her patients would be in agreement with me when I say that Holly is one of the best at what she does. Heather and I believed this right from our first meeting with Holly.

I strongly felt that Holly would have found a solution to end Heather's suffering if one was to be found; even after Heather had given up on her. There was a lot I didn't know when it came to whose hands Heather's well being fell into, but I did know, Heather's care had been mishandled for far too long. I still believe the hospital could have done more, but the brutal truth is, I should have taken matters into my own hands sooner. Sometimes, learning that the finest hospital may not hold all the answers, is a hard lesson to learn.

Surprisingly, Holly was in agreement with removing Heather's rods. She was concerned with Heather losing some of the spinal correction, but hopefully the removal of Heather's hardware would improve Heather's symptoms. Holly sincerely apologized for the hardships Heather had endured and still wasn't certain why Heather had been plagued with so much pain.

The date for Heather's surgery was set for July 31st. By that time, Brake would be back living in California. Heather didn't want Blake to leave without her and asked if he could continue to stay with us until she was well enough to travel. No, Blake was leaving and that was that. I knew Heather would be crushed, but in the long run, I was hoping Heather would realize it was for the best. No matter how much Heather claimed to be in love with Blake, I knew it wasn't love at all, but the need to be cared for by another. As long as Blake confessed his love for her, she believed their relationship was genuine and there was no proving it any different in her eyes.

Heather's surgery lasted only three hours, unlike the ten hours it took to implant the rods. She experienced no complications and was discharged three days later. For the first time, I did not stay in the hospital with Heather following a surgery. Heather said that she could manage on her own and would call if she needed me for any reason. Another sign of how Heather was breaking away from her dependency on me, while becoming her own person.

Heather and I met with Holly on two more occasions before we stopped going altogether. Heather's surgery was successful in stopping the twitching in her back and the flaring of her arm. Even the pain in her left hip began to subside. The problem that was confronting Heather now, was her right hip and lower back. I took her to Dr. Ausiello and asked if there was any way he could arrange for Heather to be examined at Mary Free Bed. He looked over at Heather and asked her what she felt about going to Mary Free Bed.

I know that I had said that Heather should have more say in her own care, but I wasn't ready to allow her begin at that time. Heather made it clear that she didn't what to go, which led to Dr. Ausiello asking me why I wanted Heather in Mary Free Bed. I wondered if hewas looking at the same Heather as I was. It was so obvious that Heather needed help and soon. She was becoming increasingly weaker and still losing weight.

Before leaving his office Dr. Ausiello wrote Heather a script for Vicodin and Baclofen, at Heather's request. I wasn't concerned about Heather asking for the Vicodin. Heather and I had been working on weaning her off of Vicodin since her latest surgery. Heather was down to only taking a Vicodin a day, instead of the ten she had been taking. It took some doing, but Heather did it.

He also said that he would contact Mary Free Bed to set up an evaluation for Heather and would be in touch with us when a date was set, or to expect a call from Mary Free Bed. While Heather and I waited for the call, Heather grew more depressed and Blake didn't help matters out any. Heather and Blake were still in contact with one another. He starting sending her a lot of disturbing text messages. Then he would call to take back what he had written. After a while, Heather's self-esteem and will power plummeted, leading to Heather's second overdose.

This time Heather swallowed several Baclofen tablets. Enough to put her at a very high risk of death. Unlike Valium, the side effects of Baclofen can be extremely violent. Because Baclofen is also a muscle relaxant, heart failure was a very real possibility and one the ER physician kept a real close eye on. At times, Heather's heart rate and blood pressure dropped dangerously low, but the doctor always managed to stabilize her.

I watched in terror as Heather's body put up a fierce fight against the mild convulsions and intense vomiting. With each seizure like episode, Heather grew weaker. It would take hours before she was stable enough to be transported by ambulance to Spectrum hospital in Grand Rapids.

I went home as soon as Heather was loaded into the ambulance and on her way to Spectrum. I planned to drive to Spectrum right after I called work, to let them know I wasn't coming in, along with another call to Heather's dad. Following Heather's first suicide attempt, I felt such a deep sense of guilt and failure. Something had changed within me, because this time I wasn't consumed with guilt. There was only a strange feeling of total acceptance of Heather's overdose, without judgment, blame, nor guilt. I still can not explain how it was that I didn't fall apart emotionally. Maybe, I had come to accept more readily, that Life, really is in charge and all I am actually capable of doing, as a person, is to react to each circumstance I am faced with, the best way that I know how.

When I arrived at Spectrum hospital in Grand Rapids, I had no idea what floor or room Heather was taken to when she arrived at Spectrum. My first stop, in my search for Heather, began at the information desk. Heather had been admitted into the Intensive Care Unit. When I finally located her room, I was surprised by the amount of medical personnel gathered in her room. Once my presence was known, their attention immediately shifted toward me. At this time, I was able to get a glance of Heather for the first time since she had left the ER in Lakeview.

The Heather I was looking at, I barely recognized. She was laying motionless in her bed, while struggling to keep her eyes open. Even before any one in that room had a chance to speak, I blurted out, "What the hell happened to Heather's face?", as I made my way over to Heather's bedside, so she could see me. I kissed her gently on the forehead and told her that I loved her.

I then stepped back, only to see that she was tearing up, while trying to mumble something. I couldn't make out what she was trying to say. God, she looked so worn. A look I'll never forget. All I could think of was how everyone in that room were all in the presence of a fallen angel needing to be healed. I wanted so desperately to snatch her up in my arms and embrace her with all the love I had within me, but didn't dare, for she looked too fragile to even hold without hurting her.

I turned around to face the strangers whom were still gathered in Heather's room. There were two doctors, an older well dressed woman, two nurses, and a young man who was sitting in a chair off to one side. Ben, the young men, had been assigned the duty of being Heather's sitter. Just as precaution against further self-harm that Heather may try. By the looks of Heather as she laid in her bed, it would take a miracle for her to even move any part of her body. Ben was not allowed to leave Heather alone at any time, without bringing in a replacement. For the first twenty four hours of Heather's admittance, a sitter was present in her room at all times.

The first individual whom spoke to me was Dr. Cooper. He would become Heather's primary physician while Heather was in Spectrum. Soft spoken with a great deal of compassion, best describes my first impression of Dr. Cooper. He introduced me to his assistant, Dr. Graham, before sitting down with me and Heather. Once we began discussing Heather, the two nurses and older woman, whom I would later learn was a social worker, left Heather's room.

Again I ask what happened to Heather's face and if it was permanent. The last time I had seen Heather in Lakeview, she looked completely normal. Now, she had taken on the appearance of either a stroke patient or someone with Bell's Palsey. The left side of Heather's face was drooping. That is why I said I barely recognized her with my first glance. Dr. Cooper stated that the condition was a side effect of the overdose and couldn't say if it was permanent or temporary. The good news was, the worst was over and he felt that Heather was doing well considering the amount of Baclofen in her system.

Dr. Cooper and I talked for the longest time about Heather. He occasionally jotted down notes while asking many questions. He inquired about Heather's disabilities and medical history. I found this so interesting, because he showed more concern with Heather's physical ailments than the overdose.

After telling Dr. Cooper Heather's story, he simply shook his head and softly said, "Such a young lady, to have gone through so much. No wonder..." He didn't finish his sentence, but he really didn't need to. By the look on his face, I knew how the sentence would have ended. Before leaving Heather's room, Dr. Cooper and his assistant, examined Heather one last time. He then turned back to me and vowed to take good care of Heather, as long as she was under his care. I was deeply touched by his genuine concern and bedside manner.

Unlike the interactions Heather frequently encountered with

the doctors, therapists, and nurses at the other hospital, Dr. Cooper addressed Heather on a more personal level, rather than just a medical case. I guess because that hospital focused on professionalism more than personalizing patients. This is perhaps, the greatest attributes of a smaller hospital, where the doctor/patient relationship often extends beyond the medical condition. When faced with an illness, doesn't everyone tend to need a bit more human compassion? There just seems to be a healing element connected with a genuine affiliation between a doctor and his/her patient.

I was finally able to sit with Heather once Dr. Cooper and his assistant left Heather's room. I sat as close to Heather as I possibly could by her bedside. I cupped her hand into mine and watched as she slept. I too was on the verge of sleep before being summoned out of Heather's room by the hospital's social worker.

Mary Ann, the well dressed woman I had seen earlier, apologized for disturbing me, but she needed to get a statement and some medical history on Heather. The social worker and I took a seat in front of a large observational window, just outside of Heather's room. Mary Ann was quick to inquiry about Heather's overdose. Her sympathetic mannerism put me at ease. I never felt threatened nor interrogated by any of her questions.

When asked why I believed Heather overdosed, I found myself looking through the window, to where Heather was resting. A moment of silence had passed before I began telling Heather's story. I began with Heather's first surgery and continued on from there. We talked about Heather's setbacks, the drugs she was placed on, and the continuous pain she was in. I mentioned how Heather had overdosed over a year ago and battled with depression, on and off for nearly two years. Then I reached into my shirt pocket, in order to retrieve Heather's cell phone. I believed the text messages, Blake had sent to Heather earlier, would provide Mary Ann with a better understanding of Heather's mental state before she overdosed.

The text messages from Blake contained some very crude remarks degrading Heather. All along, Heather still had it in her head that Blake and her would be together again, once she recovered from her surgery and was able to travel to California. Heather could not see or admit to, how destructive her attachment to Blake actually was. Understandably so, because if she had acknowledged how destructive her attachment was and that Blake was in fact moving on without her, she would have had to face the truth that she was unwanted by him.

During the course of their texting back and forth, Heather began pleading with Blake not to break up with her. Blake, on the other hand, was saying their relationship was over and he wanted nothing more to do with her. Most likely, out of a desperate attempt to change his mind, Heather had written how she was having thoughts of suicide. Blake's text message, in response to Heather's text was this; *"I hope you do and die. You are a bitch who is nothing, but a cripple."*

Heather had to have been devastated by Blake's rude text. Maybe, this was the last blow, which contributed to Heather's overdose. If I had not taken Heather's cell phone away from her in the ER at Lakeview and opened the text messages from Blake, I would have never known what Heather was going through with Blake. There were more disturbing messages from Blake that followed. All of which contained some very despite words. Words, I know Heather would have taken to heart.

Mary Ann had a puzzled expression on her face, as I was handing her Heather's phone. When I told her the phone was Heather's and that I believed she should read the messages sent by Blake, she shook her head no. Mary Ann strongly felt that Heather's right to privacy should be honored. I openly disagreed and repeatedly insisted that she read the messages. Mary Ann finally gave in and began reading. Her reaction after reading the texts, was one of disgust and pity. "Poor child, she sure has been through a lot."

"Yes, she has." I replied back to her.

I soon asked Mary Ann if she planned to conduct any psychological tests on Heather. The puzzled expression returned on Mary Ann's face, as if to ask, "What gave you that idea?" I described how Heather was subjected to various testing during an stay in rehab, before and after her first overdose. I told Mary Ann how the psychologist at that facility, felt that Heather had shown signs of having an anti-social personality disorder, which I completely disagreed with.

Again, a look of pity formed on Mary Ann's face. "No, I have no intention of ordering any such tests. If Heather has been through all that you have described, what she really needs is a great deal of support and rest. I'll be checking in on her each day and will offer her the chance to talk out her feelings if she chooses to. That is the extent of my services, along with arranging for any special needs Heather may require when she is discharged."

Maybe, a similar approach would have had been more beneficial to Heather while in rehab, where the focus was targeted more on supportive measures, rather than jumping right into testing for personality disorders. Possibly, what the psychologist deemed as being a sign of an anti-social disorder, was actually the actions of an ordinary frustrated young woman. Sadly, once the psychologist wrote his personal opinion in Heather's medical file, his opinion became the format in how Heather seemed to be perceived by the medical staff.

Heather remained at Spectrum one week. During her stay, she managed to win the hearts of everyone who cared for her. Even Ben came to bid Heather farewell the day of her discharge. Dr. Cooper was true to his word. He visited with Heather each day and saw to it that she was well cared for. Amazing what a week of rest and socializing had on Heather. The spark in her eyes was back, along with her irresistible smile.

By the time Heather was discharged, her facial muscles returned back to normal. The only sign of any permanent side effect of the Baclofen, was detected in her speech and also included memory issues. Heather's speech became more noticeably slurred than before, but if she didn't rush her words, she still could be easily understood. Sometimes, memory issues can be a blessing in disguise. Everyone, at one time or another forgets things. Heather just does it more often.

CHAPTER FIFTY-FOUR

RINGING HEATHER HOME FROM SPECTRUM was not my intention. In fact, It was I, not Mary Ann, who initiated the discussion of getting Heather admitted into Pine Rest for counseling after her discharge. On the surface, Heather may have had appeared mentally sound to return home, but there were underlying issues that needed to be dealt with. MaryAnn understood my concern for Heather, but did not recommend a stay at Pine Rest. She was totally convinced Heather's overdose was directly related to Heather's pain and was not an attempt to kill herself. I believed otherwise.

Yes, Heather's pain was a factor, but not the only factor. What Heather needed, more than coming home, was to be in an environment where she was surrounded by people. I figured Pine Rest could offer her that type of environment, plus receive counseling at the same time. Back at home the only interactions awaiting Heather were limited to a few family members, Sebastian and those she chatted with online. Rarely, was Heather visited by others.

Heather refused to even consider going to Pine Rest or any other place, she only wanted to go back home. Since she was eighteen, she had the last word. If I wanted her to be admitted into Pine Rest, I would have to petition the court for some type of guardianship over her. If I had done so, given Heather's medical condition and history of reckless choices, I most likely would have been granted the request. However, by doing so, I would have ultimately taken away Heather's dignity in the process. Something I could not bring myself to do. Heather already had enough taken away from her and didn't deserve anything else stripped away.

I hated being in the position I was in and cursed Life for placing me there. It just seemed easier blaming someone or something, other than myself for my hardships. Only because it took the burden of accepting responsibility for my actions and choices. There was a lot taking place in my life besides coping with the situation Heather was in. I was struggling to keep our home and our car. Trying to feed my family, while attempting to meet all the other needs that come with having children.

Finally, after falling months behind on my mortgage payments, I had no other choice but to admit to myself that I was way over my head and made that dreaded call to the mortgage company. What is it about placing such importance on pride? It just makes failure that much harder to tolerate. If I did lose my home to foreclosure, I knew the entire community would read about it in the newspaper. Foreclosure should be a private matter between the financial institution and the buyer. The local newspaper listed every foreclosure and the individual whom was losing their home. What was so vital about announcing the name of the individual(s) whom were losing their home? There wasn't any write up in the newspaper, about me buying my home. Just a thought.

In 2008, Michigan alone had an estimated 145,365 foreclosures, ranking Michigan third highest in the United States for foreclosures. If there was no workable solution between the mortgage company and myself, I would be adding another digit to the estimation. Like many other families facing foreclosure, I had no idea what I was going to do if I lost my home. Quite frankly, I really didn't have the energy to even care. There was just too many other concerns taking place in my life, Heather being at the top of the list.

The mortgage company I financed my home through was surprisingly sympathetic to my situation. Instead of threatening me with foreclosure, I was offered the opportunity to have my loan modified, if my income and credit score met the requirements to qualify me. I flat out told the consultant, it probably would be a waste of their time. With the amount of time I miss work, along with having really bad credit, I saw no way of being qualified. On top of that, taxes on the home and property were due and I had no means to pay for them. Eventually, I asked the consultant what the time frame was until my home was foreclosed on.

I nervously waited for a response. The response I received was nothing like I had expected. "This company in not going to put you and your daughters out on the street. There is no plan, in the immediate future to foreclose on your home." Had I hear wrong? I had to ask the consultant to repeat herself, because this sounded to good to be true. Not only wasn't the mortgage company going to pursue foreclosure at that time, the consultant informed me that the taxes would be taken care of as well. Those nagging phone calls from the collectors were also going to stop. Until my case was reviewed and a decision was made, I was exempt from making future payments. Sometimes, when its least expected, life comes bearing gifts. I cried. After hanging up the phone, I literally sat in my room and cried.

It wasn't long after Heather returned home from Spectrum, when she was back online chatting with strangers. Had she not learned anything from her experience with Blake? I repeatedly warned Heather about the consequences of seeking out a guy online. Without taking the computer away from Heather, I knew of no other way of stopping her. I knew nothing about blocking certain web sites, or if that was even possible to do so. The question I was faced with was this,"How much trust and freedom do I gave to Heather?" Without actually considering Heather, I would have answered *"very little"*.

However, Heather had to be considered. She wasn't a little girl anymore, but she also hadn't grown up experiencing the world as her peers had done either. Because of this, her view of the world was so much more naive than the average eighteen year old. I chose not to intervene with Heather's use of the computer, but if there was ever a more perfect time to receive that call from Mary Free Bed it was now, before Heather got any notion of leaving or went searching for someone online to help her escape. Lord knows what type of guy Heather would end up attracting.

Everyday I waited to hear from Dr. Ausiello's office or Mary Free Bed. Weeks went by and still no call. I was beginning to believe that Heather had been forgotten. Heather had to get into Mary Free Bed. I had the strongest feeling something good was going to happen for Heather. I'm no psychic, but I also had the inclination that Heather would meet the love she was desperately in search of. I told her not to invest any time seeking online, because the love of her life would be found while she was in rehab.

Heather continued to fight me on the notion of going into rehab at Mary Free Bed. I would just keep saying to her that she might as well plan on going, because she was. I stood firm on this, allowing Heather absolutely no say whatsoever. Finally, two months following Heather's discharge from Spectrum, the call from Mary Free Bed came. I was so excited to say the least. I went into Heather's room immediately after hanging up the phone. "This is it, Heather!" I shouted out. "You're in!" Dr. Kuldanek wants to examine you next week. "This is it!" Its all I kept repeating; "This is it!" I knew, without even knowing how I knew, but I knew Mary Free Bed was where Heather would be healed.

My overly enthusiastic mood was brought to a sudden halt, when Heather announced she wasn't going to Mary Free Bed. She had other plans. Plans of traveling to Texas. Since all my family members either lived in Michigan, Indiana, or Pennsylvania, this only meant one thing, Heather must have had made plans to meet some guy she chatted with online. I was right, Heather openly admitted she intended to meet a guy whom was willing to help her get settled in Texas. Upon hearing this, I really began questioning Heather's ability to ever make it on her own. She seemed to lack the capacity to reason.

Perhaps, being as overly protective as Heather's Dad and myself had been, all the while Heather was growing up, robbed her of the experiences which may have help her develop the skills in thinking things through before acting or making irrational decisions. Basically, all of Heather decisions up to this point, was made for her. Maybe, I was just now witnessing one of the consequences of being so over protective.

Normally, with Heather, I tend to take time to ponder over an issue I have with her, before confronting her with my opinion. Unfortunately, When Heather made her announcement of going to Texas and not Mary Free Bed, there was no rational thinking on my behalf. Instant rage was all I felt. I unleashed a wave of parental fury that took on a life of its own and let Heather have it with both barrels, as the saying goes. Surprisingly, Heather unloaded her rage unto me as well. Rarely can Heather show anger without crying, but I have to admit, she stood her ground for quite some time before her emotions got the better of her.

Round one of our screaming match consisted of merely venting frustrations the two of us were feeling at the time. Feeling powerless over the entire circumstances we had been facing and continued to face, brought about the core of our anger. Any other anger we were feeling, actually stemmed from that one aspect of feeling powerless. There was so much yelling going on between Heather and I, after a while there was nothing in particular we were yelling at back and forth. This is when I grew so frustrated, I had to walk away.

After a cool down period, round two began. This time I was determined to remain focused on one objective; Heather realizing and accepting that she *WAS* going to Mary Free Bed. I approached Heather using parental dictatorship. With the sternness of my words, I felt confident Heather would surrender to my will. Again, Heather stood her ground. Try as I might, I just could not break through Heather's stubbornness. She did not surrender and kept insisting that "she was never going into another hospital just to please me." At that time, I didn't give the remark a second thought. However, later on, Heather's remark would bring about one hell of a self discovery.

Since my authoritative approach didn't give me the results I expected, my next strategy would aim at installing guilt. Guilt is a powerful emotion. It wasn't the fairest way to go about getting what I wanted, but fairness was omitted from the battle between Heather and myself right from the start. You know, I knew all along Heather would be going to Mary Free Bed, she never had any other options. She wasn't able to physically fight back or run away, while I was loading her into the car against her will. For some reason, I had to hear her say; *"I will go."* Just three simple words.

I proceeded with my strategy of installing guilt. I reminded Heather of all that I too had gone through on this journey with her. The final statement, I clearly remember saying before allowing Heather to respond was this: "I didn't go through all of this just to have you quit on me."

Heather remained silent. Prior to that remark, Heather was full of fight. Now she appeared completely despondent. I figured now was the time Heather chose to give me the *"silent treatment."* She continued to stare up at me from her bed, saying nothing. Heather may not have had verbally expressed her feelings, but her eyes sure had. Just as Heather began to tear up, there was an expression of insurmountable sorrow pouring out through her eyes. The degree of sorrow showing in Heather's eyes, was unlike anything I had been accustomed to seeing. To get an idea of the amount of sorrow

Heather's eyes expressed, imagine yourself being in the darkest, most oppressed conditions. That is the best description I can come up with.

At that precise moment, I became consumed with the most heart-rending sorrow myself. The strange thing about it, the sorrow wasn't mine. The reason I knew this, was because I was still too wrapped up in my own anger to feel otherwise. Something out of the ordinary was taking place in Heather's room and somehow forcing me to feel the rawness of Heather's emotional pain. The sensation I felt lasted only for a brief moment before it disappeared.

I believe the experience was one those which it is impossible to be explained on a human level. All around us, there are incidences that occur where one just knows the occurrence was created by some form of a Universal Life source, referred to by many as God, or what ever other name one gives to a Higher power.

As awkward as that moment was for me, I waited for Heather to speak. When she finally did, she spoke so softly, I could barely make out what she was saying. "Quit on you?" Heather began, as she fought against crying. "I'm quitting on me. I give up, Mom. I gave up a long time ago. You just don't want to hear it." Heather then turned away from me and began crying, ever so softly.

The argument between Heather and myself was clearly over the moment Heather turned away from me. Obviously, there was something more important in the works, rather than hearing Heather say, *"I will go."* I just didn't know what it was. However, what I did know, Heather needed to acknowledge that she wasn't going to magically heal on her own. She needed to accept that her condition required more medical treatment. Heather had to fully acknowledged this for herself, if she was ever going to get better. Otherwise any attempt to help her would end up failing. If what I had felt, while in Heather's room, was truly where Heather resided mentally, I had better take measures to help her "want" to climb out of that darkness she surrendered to.

For days, I pondered over the experience I had in Heather's room. I sensed there was something I had to face within myself, which would led me to a better understanding of Heather's sorrow. The depth of her sorrow clearly extended further than just being caused by her medical condition. Discovering how Heather felt or didn't feel, wasn't the lesson I had to learn. There was something else unfolding. I still couldn't grasp what it was.

While sitting alone in my room one night, Heather's remark about never going into another hospital just to please me, popped into my mind. Just like that, right out of the blue. I sat with that thought for the longest time, trying to dissect it's meaning. With brain storming and self inquiry, I arrived at the self-discovery which helped me better understand Heather's sorrow and what it was I had to face within myself.

From the very beginning Heather depended on me to take care of her. She had trusted me to make the right choices when it came to her medical care. I thought that I had. The truth is, I was so naive when it came to knowing what was in Heather's best interest medically wise. I placed all my trust into the medical staff, whom was in charge of Heather's care, to know what was best for Heather. Then, in my quest to have the medical staff be held accountable and correct what caused Heather's condition, I had not fully considered the toll it was taking on Heather.

I wish I wasn't required to acknowledge my role, I played in all this. Life would be so much easier. Unfortunately, becoming a better person involves one to be completely honest with him/her self. I too, had to be held accountable for Heather's present condition. I offered her little protection against the hardships she had faced, while in the care of those after her first surgery. I was just now becoming aware of this.

Prior to this moment of self inquiry, I blindly went along with the suggestions of the medical professionals. Now, I wasn't so naive. This time around, I was acting accordingly to my own instincts. Unfortunately, Heather's trust in me was gone for the most part. Explains why she was so determined to escape, by whatever means she had to.

Another discovery I found about myself, which I was unaware of beforehand, was how much I had assumed Heather owed it to me to go into Mary Free Bed. My remark: "I didn't go though all this, just to have you quit on me," exposed my unconscious belief . The fact of the matter was, Heather owed me nothing. She owned nobody anything right from the start, but sadly was made to feel as if she did.

How was I ever going to convince Heather, that she owed it to herself to go into Mary Free Bed. There had to be some type of incentive to offer her, which would spark a willingness to go. I just knew Mary Free Bed was where Heather's journey would end. Then it came to me.

The day before Heather's evaluation at Mary Free Bed, I approached her with a deal. Ever since our argument, Heather and I exchanged very few words. It wasn't as if we both were still angry, we just didn't have a lot to say. There wasn't any grudges held against the other, nor a lesser amount of love between the two of us. We completely allowed the argument to be what it was, just an argument without feeling the need to hold onto any bitterness.

I sat down with Heather and began detailing my proposal. If she agreed to go into Mary Free Bed and give rehab her all, I would back her up, with what ever she decided to do following her discharge. Yes, it was sort of a bribe, but a very effective bribe. Of course Heather doubted me at first, but after giving her my word that I would do everything in my power to help her live on her own, she agreed.

It's common to have certain conditions placed on any type of deals. The deal I made with Heather also had a condition she had to abide by. In order to gain her *freedom*, Heather had to showed me that she was capable of caring for herself on a daily basis. This included being mobile, completing transfers by herself, dressing and showering. If Heather could manage these activities, I knew she would have a better chance of living on her own.

Without having the argument I had with Heather, along with the experience I encountered in her room, I know I would have continued to dominate her. Sounds harsh when I phrase it that way, but in a way, by being overly protective of Heather, I was dominating her all along. The time had come, whether I liked it or not, to allow Heather the opportunity to become an adult. To grant her what we all seemingly strive for; the right to pursue our dreams and to be heard as a person.

CHAPTER FIFTY-FIVE

HEATHER'S WORDS

THE LAST TIME I WAS at Mary Free Bed Rehabilitation Hospital, I think I was in elementary school or barely into middle school. I was injected with Botox for the first time at Mary Free Bed. That was also the last time I had seen Dr. Kuldanek. I wondered if she would even remember who I was after so many years. Even though I agreed to go with Mom. I was not in the mood of seeing any more doctors. I just had enough, but Mom was positive Dr. Kuldanek could help me.

While waiting to see Dr. Kuldanek, Mom began telling me stories about my stay at Mary Free Bed when I was younger. I didn't remember since I was only twenty-three months old at that time. Mom told me that I was loved by all of the nursing staff and therapists. I wondered if the same therapists and nurses still worked there now. Wouldn't that be so cool if they were still there? I bet they will be surprised at seeing that I was grown up now.

Mom and I didn't wait long before my name was called out. We were taken into the examination room and told that Dr. Kuldanek would be in shortly. After sitting in the room for a while, Dr. Kuldanek and a team of therapists came in. Once we were reacquainted with Dr. Kuldanek, Mom and I talked about what was going on with me and how Mom thought I should be admitted in to rehab. Dr. Kuldanek asked why we came to Mary Free Bed instead of going back to my surgeon. Mom and I both looked at one another and shook our heads before telling her how we felt about my experience while under her care.

My examination began with Dr. Kuldanek stretching out my legs and feet. She took a look at my back and had me stand, we then talked about the pain I was in. The therapists in the room were asking a lot of questions about the kind of therapies I had while in rehab. When I told them about my experience, none of them seemed real happy with what I had said.

Before Dr. Kuldanek even said anything about going into rehab, I came right out and asked the therapists in the room, "Do you guys know what you are doing?" The look on their faces told me that the question I had asked caught them by surprise. Maybe, no one has ever asked them that type of question before. I didn't asked it to be mean. I just didn't want to experience the same crap I dealt with at before.

Each therapist told me that if I did begin rehab at Mary Free Bed, they would do their best to help me. I believed them, because their eyes showed real concern. Dr. Kuldanek said that before I was able to be admitted into rehab, my pain had to be under control. She mentioned something about Baclofen. Mom didn't like the sounds of that and told Dr. Kuldanek about my overdose of Baclofen. She also described how tired and depressed I became when I took pain medication and muscle relaxants.

Dr. Kuldanek said she didn't mean oral Baclofen, she was considering a Baclofen pump implant. I had no idea of what that even was. With a Baclofen pump, the medication would be released directly into my spine. Dr. Kuldanek believed the pump would be the best way to go about controlling my pain. She only had one concern about the implant. Since my spine had been fused together, she wasn't sure if there was space where a catheter could be inserted. I would have to have an x-ray taken of my spine to find out.

Dr. Kuldanek gave Mom and I a pamphlet to read with information about the pump. There was little else she could do for me that day. Before Mom and I went home, I was scheduled for an x-ray to be taken on a different day. If there was enough space in between my vertebrates, Dr. Kuldanek would move ahead with setting up an appointment with the surgeon who implants the pump.

After I went back to Mary Free Bed and had the x-ray taken, Dr. Kuldanek said that there was room to insert the catheter into my spine. She then showed Mom and I the pump. There was a small version of the pump and a bigger one. To me, they both looked like hockey pucks. Dr. Kuldanek said that after the pump had been inserted and I was released from the hospital, I would go straight into rehab. This way, she could keep an eye on me and make adjustments to the dosage while I was in rehab. I couldn't understand how it was that Holly didn't mention anything about this to me. I wondered if she even knew about a pump like this. They should have, if they were one of the top hospitals in Michigan.

I told Dr. Kuldanek that I wanted to get the pump. Maybe, the pump would actually take away my pain. I doubted that it would, but I had nothing to lose by trying it out. Dr. Kuldanek set up an appointment for Mom and I to meet the surgeon. One week later we met him.

He was so nice and made me feel safe. I knew he would take good care of me. He explained how he was going to implant the pump and said that I would like the pump a lot. On January 23rd, 2009, I went into surgery.

I will tell you one thing, I know how women must feel after a C-Section. A cut into the stomach muscle is not a pleasant feeling. Moving around, coughing, laughing and even breathing hurts so much. I couldn't wait for the incision to be healed. The greatest part was, the pain from the incision kept me from thinking about the pain in my lower back and left hip.

My surgery was done at Spectrum hospital and of course Mom was there with me. I was glad I had her by my side for every surgery I had. She didn't spend the night with me, but came back the following day. I stayed in Spectrum only for one day before being transported to Mary Free Bed by ambulance. I was excited about riding in the ambulance. Unlike the last time I rode in an ambulance, this time I was more awake and aware of what was going on around me.

When I arrived at Mary Free Bed, I was taken up to the Pediatric floor and admitted. The atmosphere at Mary Free bed was different from the hospital I went to before. When ever I pushed the nurse button, a nurse came right in. There was no waiting like there was at that other hospital. Maybe, because Mary Free Bed is a smaller hospital. Some of the nurses remembered me from my first stay when I was younger. They said that I made them feel old. One of the nurse's I had back then, brought in a picture of me when I was in rehab. I looked so young in that picture. The nursing staff kept a picture of every child ever admitted into rehab.

Dr. Kuldanek came to visit me the first day I was admitted. I asked her if I could do my therapies in my room for the next couple of days. She didn't have a problem with that. I was allowed one more day to just rest before my therapies began.

Mom brought me our computer from home to help pass away time. I could keep in touch with friends on Facebook and play the games I liked on Pogo. I also had my pre-paid cell phone and my IPOD. I didn't have a room mate so these things helped me keep busy. Mom stayed with me until I was settled in my room the first day at Mary Free Bed. She said that she wouldn't be coming back to Grand Rapids until the weekend. Mom gave me a kiss before she left the hospital. I was once again, on my own.

My mornings at Mary Free Bed started early. My therapist would come in my room just after I finished with my breakfast. For the first couple of days, the physical therapist did a lot of stretching on my legs and we worked on balancing myself on the edge of the bed. The sessions with my therapist were short for the first couple of days. I couldn't wait until the pain went away in my stomach, so I could push myself to do more.

The next step my therapist and I worked on was getting me up in my wheelchair. We also began working on dressing. She taught me how to put on my underwear, socks and pants. In order to dress myself, I had to use a reacher grabber. I had one at home, but never had to use it. I could dress myself without it. Then after my first surgery , I was in to much pain to even begin thinking about dressing myself. Mom and Katie helped me dress. This was going to be my first experience with using the device.

I was given a sock aid to help me put on my socks. I also had one of these at home, but never used it as well. The problem with using a sock aid, is that the device stretches out your socks really fast. I managed to work the sock aid with little trouble. Pulling up my pants with the reacher grabber was a different story. I couldn't stand up long enough without my legs giving out, for me to even pull my pants up. I never thought I would have to relearn how to dress myself .

After a week of receiving therapy in my room, the therapist felt I was ready to begin more intense therapy. About this time, I notice the pain in my lower back and left hip had gone away. The pain was completely gone! I was amazed that this hockey puck pump was the answer. After being in constant pain for over two years, I was now free of that pain. Free of pain without feeling drugged up was the most amazing feeling.

The pump triggered a dosage of Baclofen every four hours. I could feel my body relax and for a short period of time I felt a little weak, but the effects did not last long. The Baclofen pump did not effect my mental state and not my appetite like oral medication had. For the first time, I felt like I was being taken good care of by everyone and that was a really good feeling.

I would be transported to the gym in my wheelchair each morning. The person who wheeled me down into the gym, would place me along the wall and there I would wait for my therapist. The therapy room wasn't as crowed like the one at the other hospital. It seemed like I always had to share a mat with another, which made it harder for the therapist to work with me.

As I waited I would talk to others who were waiting for their session to begin. It really is a small world we live in. One of the patients I talked to knew my sister Cori. They both attended the same church. There was a young man in his late teens who was in a car accident. His Mom was always by his side. I talked to her about her son. She said that her son was driving one night and he hit a patch of ice. He lost both of his legs as a result of the accident and for some reason, he couldn't speak. Up until his accident, he was very active. I bet he will have a really hard time accepting his condition. You never know what life is going to bring you. One day you are walking and playing sports, then all of a sudden you are wheelchair bound. Your whole world changes.

I met a little girl, whom I fell in love with. She became sick after receiving a flu shot, which left her physically handicapped. Now she walks with a walker and wears leg braces. This little girl was a happy child; always smiling. She reminded me of myself and what I had went through. Born healthy, then becoming sick from a shot. She will adjust to her new life like I did. To me, if something happens to you when your young, you adjust and accept life. If something happens that leaves you handicapped, like the young man who hit the patch of ice, you become angry at the world for a long time before you adjust and accept your condition.

For the first couple of weeks, I lifted weights to strengthen my upper body and did a lot of standing while letting go of my walker. My legs were still very weak from all those months I had laid in bed. You know what was the most amazing thing about my therapist at Mary Free Bed? She never showed any disappointment or said that I wasn't trying, unlike what I experienced at the other hospital. If something I tried wasn't working for me, she would have me try a different way of doing it until we found a way that worked best for me.

I felt myself growing physically stronger. I knew if I could regain my strength, I would be capable of taking care of myself. I had lost a lot of muscle tone during the past two years and I knew that it would take a lot of time to get it back. So, I wasn't worried about it too much.

I knew that my therapist would eventually encourage me to walk. The first steps I took, when I did try to walk, were difficult. My legs felt like they were going to collapse underneath me. I didn't understand what was so important about walking. Why was everyone pushing me to walk? My family, and now my therapist at Mary Free Bed. The only one who didn't push me was Mom. Mom and I talked a lot about me walking or not walking.

Mom said the choice to walk or not walk was mine alone. If I was comfortable with being in a wheelchair, than so be it. Being able to walk or not walk, did not define who I really was as a person. I'll remember what Mom had said for the rest of my life.

By that time, I did accept that the wheels on my wheelchair were going to be my legs. I just wished that others would have accepted that. You know what was more important to me than walking ever could have been at that time? Wiping myself, dressing, transferring, and standing. Those were my goals, not walking.

Since I was closer to home, I had a lot of visitors during my stay. It was only a forty five minute to an hour drive to Mary Free Bed. Grandma Sandy and Grandpa Tom came to check up on me. I loved spending time with them. They are always there for me and willing to help me out when ever I need help. Dad would try to visit on the weekend. Each visit he had the cribbage board in his arms, ready to play a game with me. While playing, we never seem to have a disagreement. It's just father and daughter bonding time and I loved every minute of it. Mom would also come down on the weekends. We talked about everything, even if we had just talked on the phone the night before. We just have to be in each others presence. We can not be apart for very long.

I also had a couple of surprise visits from people whom I never expected would take the time to come see me. My cousin Chuck, his wife Sherri, and their daughter Kelly drove all the way from Indiana, just to spend a couple of hours with me. I felt so honored. The other surprise visit I had was from two of my *"boys"* Jordan and Lukus. I was so excited to see them and to know that I was not forgotten by them. They visited me shortly after getting my pump implanted. Every time they made me laugh, I wanted to hit them. Laughing was so painful. Just as they did during my senior year, they made me feel as if I mattered.

One of my old classmates, Jeff Hendricks, emailed me and told me add him on Tagged. Tagged was a website similar to MySpace and Facebook. I didn't understand why he wanted me to add him on a website I never used. I already had him as a friend on my Facebook account. But, like I have been saying all along. Everything happens for a reason.

I created a profile on Tagged and added Jeff. Not even a full day had passed when I started receiving messages from other guys saying, *"Hey sexy."* I looked up at my ceiling and told my Guardian Angels that I was done with guys and tired of being hit on. After I had said that, two days later a guy wrote me who said that he just wanted to chat. In his message, he didn't he didn't write*"Baby or Sexy"*in his message.

I spent that night debating on if I should write him back. I looked at his profile picture and wondered if the picture was even his actual picture or not. In his profile, he said his name was Ricky. His eyes looked so kind and honest. He stated that he lived in Grand Rapids and was twenty six.

The following day, on my lunch break, I wrote him back. Ricky mentioned that his grandfather was in the hospital part at Mary Free Bed. There are two sections to Mary Free Bed. One section is known as St. Mary's and is for medical care and the other portion of the hospital is called Mary Free Bed for rehabilitation. Ricky wrote that he planned to see his grandfather in the hospital, before his grandfather was discharged. I offered to go along with him if he would like me to. Ricky wrote back saying he would like that.

I hoped that Ricky wasn't going to turn out to be like Blake who put me down or just wanted to talk about sex. One thing was for sure, I was glad that I was around people just in case he turned out to be one of those types of guys. I guess I would be finding out in a couple of days after saying I would go with him to visit his grandfather. I knew I had to stop looking for my prince to magically appear and focus on rehab, but it was a hard thing to do. More than anything, I wanted to experience love. Real love.

I asked my Guardian Angels to please, please, don't let Ricky be one of those guys who will hurt me. Since I shared just about everything with Mom, I called and told her about Ricky. The first thing Mom asked me was,"Good God Heather, what kind of trouble is he in?" I don't think she believed me when I told her that he didn't sound like the other type of guys I chatted with online. "You said that I was going to meet someone while I was here," I reminded Mom.

I was so nervous and excited the day that I was going to meet Ricky. My heart skipped a beat every time I heard a knock on my door. I think if I could have walked, I would have been pacing back and forth. I remember tapping my finger on the arm rest of my wheelchair and glancing toward the doorway every second. Finally, I heard a knock and there Ricky stood in the doorway. A huge wave of positive energy hit me. At that moment, I knew I didn't have to look anymore for my prince. Have you ever felt that feeling? You hear about love at first sight, but only in my dreams did I think it would happen to me.

Ricky introduced himself in the most gentleman fashion. His eyes caught me off guard just as they had in his picture. I invited him to sit on my bed and the two of us chatted a while before heading out to visit his grandfather. Ricky pushed me in my wheelchair over to St. Mary's. Once there we found that his grandfather had already been discharged. I invited Ricky to come back to a small waiting room back in Mary Free Bed, in order to chat some more.

We talked about everything. Life, our families, what we liked and disliked, plus how I ended up in a wheelchair. Ricky had known before coming to see me that I was in a wheelchair, but he wanted to know more. I told him the whole story up to being admitted into Mary Free Bed. I felt so comfortable around Ricky. It was as if we had known each other for a long time.

Ricky told me that sex wasn't everything and he would never

pressure me into having sex until I was ready. I had a smile on my face when he said that, because his attitude was so much different from what I was used to hearing from guys. I told Ricky that I was through with asking guys to be my boyfriend. If he wanted to be more than friends, he had to ask.

Ricky said he was from a big family. He had a lot of nephews and nieces. When I asked him about his Dad, Ricky told me his Dad committed suicide when he was a baby. After Ricky had finished telling me that, I told him about Zachariah. We talked for a long time before Ricky had to leave. He pushed me back into my room and gave me a hug. A simple hug without trying to kiss me. That was so perfect. I told him to let me know he made it home safe. I felt so bad for him. While he was visiting me, someone had stolen his bike and he ended up walking part of the way to his home before he called his Mom to pick him up.

I couldn't stop thinking that Ricky was the one I was looking for and how my search was over. Life had worked its magic. To me, Life chose Jeff to convince me to add him on Tagged. Otherwise, I would have never known about the website and never would have met Ricky. Thank you Jeff.

Ricky and I were becoming inseparable in no time at all. He would even go to my therapies with me. It was nice having someone at my side. Ricky had accepted me the way that I was without any trouble. He was willing to help me any way that he could. He didn't mind helping me into the bathroom, putting me into bed, or in my wheelchair. It takes a special person to look past physical disabilities and see the real you. Ricky showed me that it does happen. I couldn't believe that it was happening to me.

On February 7th, 2009, Ricky asked me to be his girlfriend. I was so excited and happy. Everything I wanted was coming true. A man to love me and treat me like a lady, of course I said yes. When I called and told Mom about my news, she told me that it was time for her to meet him. I knew Mom would like Ricky and not judge him.

Ricky and Mom met briefly and they seemed to like one another. Later, Mom and I talked about what she thought of him. Mom said that I was lucky to have met Ricky and she could tell that he was sincere. Even though Mom had hoped that the one I was going to meet would have been a doctor or therapist, Ricky seemed to cherish me and that was the most important thing.

One day Ricky told me that he was going to Wisconsin to pick up a car for someone. While Ricky was on the road, I began working really hard at standing up and pulling up and down my pants. If I could do that, I could go home. I tried and tried, but still had a lot of trouble. I really wanted to reach this goal, so I could live my new life with Ricky. When Ricky arrived back home, the first thing he did was come to see me. He brought with him the most beautiful heart necklace and gave it to me. This was also the first time he said "*I love you*" to me. My heart skipped a beat and I said it back to him. Not because he said it to me first and it was a right thing to say. I said it because I was falling in love with him. After he put the necklace on me, we kissed. I still wear the necklace. I don't take off the necklace unless if I need to for x-rays or surgery.

I was discharged from Mary Free Bed on March second. I didn't meet all the goals the therapist had hoped that I would, but I left the hospital more healthier and stronger than I had been since my first surgery in 2006.

Before I was discharged from the hospital, Ricky was staying with a friend in Grand Rapids. His friend was about to move and Ricky needed to find another place to live. Ricky wasn't working at that time and didn't have money. I told Ricky I would ask Mom if he could stay with us in Lakeview. Mom said he could, but if he turned out to be anything like Blake, he was on his own.

I was so happy to be back home. I had been away for close to six weeks. It seemed like forever. Like I always had done when we pulled into the driveway, I turned my head toward Sebastian's doghouse. There he was, barking a little and waiting for us to get out of the car and let him off his leash. Sebastian was looking old when I saw him. Mom said that he was having a lot of trouble with his hips and he was eating less. She didn't think he would make it through another year. It was sad to think that we might be losing our loving dog.

Couple of weeks after coming home, I felt ready to face my fear of sex. I was so scared, but Ricky was so gentle with me. I couldn't believe how beautiful and wonderful sex could be. Ricky had to help me with everything at Moms. I barely could get around in my wheelchair at Moms. Her house was so small and not set up to accommodate me.

I still needed help with getting in and out of the bathtub because

I couldn't raise my legs high enough to climb in. I also had to have help getting off the toilet because the toilet was so low to the floor. There were a lot of obstacles I had to maneuver wheelchair around also. Ricky and I began talking about finding a place of our own. A place that was specially designed for the disabled.

If I was going to learn to become more independent, I would need to live in a place that is set up for me. Ricky and I looked around Lakeview for an apartment, but no handicapped apartments were available. We then looked around Greenville and found one. The apartment complex was called Maplewood Square Apartments and was located a short distance behind Greenville high school. It would be a perfect place for us to live. I could easily drive my wheelchair to the stores and plus visit the office staff, Gates, and especially O'Brien from time to time.

Ricky and I made an appointment to meet with the landlord. The landlord was very nice and took Ricky and I for a tour of the apartment. It was a one bedroom apartment, but had a lot of room to move around with my wheelchair. The kitchen counters and stove were lowered to where I could easily reach. The only obstacle would be the tub. It was a normal tub, but Ricky could help me in and out of it.

We wanted the apartment, but didn't have the money for the deposit. If we signed a fourteen month lease, our rent would be set at $500.00 a month. Otherwise, the rent would have been a little higher. I called Grandma Sandy and asked her if she could loan Ricky and I the money for the deposit. She said that she could, so Ricky and I took the apartment. Living on my own in an apartment, with the man of my dreams, was truly a dream come true.

Ricky and I were going to be moving in the apartment May 1st, 2009. Money was going to be tight, but I knew we could manage. Mom said that if we needed help, she would do what ever she could. With only my income of $676.00 a month, we would have a total of $176.00 left after paying the rent. That wasn't a lot of money to live on.

Before the big move, I received a letter in the mail from SSI stating that I owed them over $1,200 dollars. They claimed that I was overpaid back in 2007 and it was my responsibility to repay the money back. I just didn't understand why it took two years to inform me. I could have had the matter taken care of. In order to pay back the amount they said I owed, $70.00 was going to be subtracted from my monthly checks until the balance was paid off. I could not believe this. This would mean that for over a year, my income would only be $606.00. Mom said not to worry about it. She would make up the difference each month and she did.

Moving away from Mom was a big step for me, because her and I had been through so much together. I didn't want to leave my sleeping buddy, Sebastian. I was going to miss him so much. He was always there by my side when I needed him the most. Mom said that our journey we were on was completed. We made it through some very challenging times and came out winners. Now, a new chapter in my life was unfolding.

Life had brought to me the love of my life and it was time to begin that life with Ricky. Anyway, Mom and I would talk on the phone everyday and she was only twenty-five minutes away if I ever needed her. I was going to miss seeing Mikey and Katie, along with all the people coming in and out of Mom's house.

For so long, I didn't think I would ever be allowed to live how I wanted to live. I felt like an adult now and not like a child that needed to be told what to do and how to do it. Life was good and I was ready to move forward with Ricky. I just knew everything was going to work out for Ricky and me.

When Ricky said he was from a big family, he wasn't lying. I met some of his family a few weeks before the two of us moved out of Mom's house. Meeting Ricky's family was important to me. Since he was a part of my life now I wanted to know everything about him. Ricky drove me to Plainwell to his Aunt Becky's house. His Mom and Grandma Judy were also there to meet me. Ricky introduced me to everyone and it felt like I had known them for years.

Right off, I called Ricky's Mom, Mom. She didn't mind. So, she was now Momma Rose to me. They were all so nice and asked me questions about why I was in a wheelchair. I answered them all and felt like it didn't matter to any of them that I was handicapped. Each of them saw past my disability, just as Ricky had at Mary Free Bed. I asked Momma Rose if she had any baby pictures of Ricky. That was always the first thing Mom brought out when ever any of us kids brought someone home to meet Mom. Momma Rose said that all of

Ricky's baby pictures were destroyed in a house fire years ago.

I loved meeting his Aunt, Grandma, and Momma Rose. I couldn't wait to meet the rest of his family. I didn't have to wait long because a few days after meeting his Grandma Judy, she passed away. It was a sudden death that caught all of us by surprise. Meeting at a funeral wasn't how I imagined I would be meeting the rest of his family. Yep, Ricky was right. The Robinson family was big and in no time at all, his family became my family as well.

CHAPTER FIFTY-SIX

RIVING HEATHER TO HER CONSULTATION at Mary Free Bed, stirred up a lot of memories. It seemed like forever since I had stepped foot into the hospital. While Heather and I waited to see Dr. Kuldanek, I began telling Heather several stories about her stay in rehab when she was little. Once incident in particular still remained vivid in my mind, as if it happened just yesterday. I love telling this story because it just brings to the surface of how accepting of others, children can be.

Just a few days before Heather's discharge from rehab back in 1992, I was invited to attend Heather's therapies. When it came time to take Heather down to the physical therapy room, I began wheeling her to the elevator. As Heather and I approached the elevator, I noticed two nurses pushing a hospital bed into the elevator. Laying on the bed was a woman whom had been severely burned in a house fire.

One of the nurse's noticed Heather and I approaching and signaled for us to enter. She said there was plenty of room for Heather and I if we wanted to join them. Personally, I felt a little awkward being near the burned victim and wasn't certain if Heather would become frightened by the sight of the patient. Plus, you know how children can be. I thought for sure Heather would suddenly blurt out something inappropriate about the woman's appearance, because the woman laying on the bed, barely looked human. Her face was badly scarred and she only had a few patches of hair left on her head.

Not wanting to appear ungrateful of the nurse's gesture, Heather and I entered the elevator. When the elevator door closed, Heather looked up at the woman and out of the blue, reached upward and placed her hand on the woman's hand. The woman slowly turned her head and looked down at Heather. The two of them made eye contact before the woman smiled and whispered "Hi." Heather automatically presented the woman with one of her magical smiles in return. The two of them remained focused on one another and held hands until the elevator reached the floor we all had to get off on.

The encounter between Heather and the woman was so incredibly moving. Heather's total acceptance of others, without discrimination, was definitely a reminder of how I too had the capability of showing more empathy toward others. Somewhere, along the way while growing up into adulthood, I had seemed to have misplaced that virtue. I guess once I had reached the age where I surrounded myself with the notion of how my own welfare needed to be addressed first and foremost, empathy toward others lessened. Perhaps, Heather's purpose in life included assisting those around her, in becoming more aware of their own perspective they each had formed, toward the indifference among people.

Retelling my favorite memories to Heather while waiting was suddenly interrupted, the moment Heather's name was called out. Hearing Heather's name being called out sounded like music to my ears. I had been anticipating this visit for a very long time. How does that saying go? "Don't put all of your eggs in one basket?" Well, I had and could only hope my certainty, regrading Dr. Kuldanek's ability to help Heather was not about to be shattered.

Heather and I were led to the examination room, where her vitals height and weight were recorded. Later, Dr. Kuldanek would tell us that with Heather's height being only 58.5 inches and her weight totaling eighty-nine pounds, Heather was well below the fifth percentile for her age. Heather was indeed tiny for her age and her weight was what worried me the most. She hadn't regained any of the weight she had lost after her first surgery. Losing fifteen pounds may not seem like much, but on Heather, the lost of that amount of weight made her look so fragile and sickly.

While examining Heather, Dr. Kuldanek, and the team of therapists noted mild spasticity and weakened muscle tone affecting Heather's upper body. Severe spasticity and scissoring were noted in her bilateral hip abductors (muscles of the inner thigh). Spasticity was also seen in Heather's hip flexors and extensors. The team also commented on the among of spasticity with Heather's hamstrings and how this made it difficult for Heather to fully extend her legs outward. Before this journey with Heather began, I never took into consideration just how many muscles and tendons are involved with our daily movement. What a magnificent creation our bodies really are.

When asked to sit upright on the edge of the mat table in the examination room, Heather demonstrated good sitting balance. She also was able to complete sit to stand with little assistance. Heather managed to maintain standing for a few seconds before needing to sit again. With assistance, Heather was able to move from sitting to side lying.

Based on the opinion of Dr. Kuldanek, along with the team of therapists, Heather was believed to have had a good chance of becoming more independent with transfers and self care skills. Each felt that her potential would increase if her spasticity and pain were better controlled.

At last! I was in the company of others who supported my belief all along. Rid Heather of her pain first, then focus on rehab. It was a great feeling to know that a different approach in helping Heather was about to take place. That is until Dr. Kuldanek mentioned something about using Baclofen as a means to reduce Heather's spasticity.

I immediately broke in and voiced my concerns I had with placing Heather back on the very drug she had recently overdosed on. Dr. Kuldanek then stated that she was aware of the overdose and wasn't considering oral Baclofen. Heather and I were given a pamphlet detailing the method, in which Dr. Kuldanek was seriously considering, as a way to administer Baclofen into Heather's system without the need to be taken orally.

The device, which required a surgical implant, would disperse doses of Baclofen right into the spinal fluid, thus eliminating the need for oral consumption. Oh my God, this is exactly what Heather needed. Think of it. Heather's spasticity would be better controlled without Heather feeling drugged up. No more feeling overly tired and no queasiness. Heather's appetite would not be affected nor would the Baclofen affect her emotional well being. I knew all along and repeatedly told others that Heather's lack of progress was not due to lack of trying on Heather's part, it stemmed from the side effects Heather experienced from the drugs that were prescribed to her. Perhaps, those whom shared this view would change once they see what a difference it did make, with Heather being off of oral medication.

Everything about the pump sounded encouraging. However, since Heather's spine had been fused at the time of her first surgery, Dr. Kuldanek feared that Heather's spine would not be accessible for a Baclofen test procedure, nor for the catheter which needed to be positioned into the spine. The Baclofen test procedure would determine if Heather could tolerate the higher dosage of Baclofen needed to reduce her spasticity. If a site was located and if Heather tolerated the Baclofen successfully, Dr. Kuldanek would then proceed to contact the surgeon. So, a lot depended on whether or not a site could be found. I personally believed that Heather's overall recovery rested on getting the pump implanted.

Before leaving the examination room, Heather said that if she were to be admitted into rehab, she wanted to be sure that the therapists knew what they were doing. She actually came right out and asked. I was taken back by her directness. Everyone in that room was. I know I wouldn't have had the courage to ask such a daring question.

Heather really had shown how she wasn't going to just go along with whatever was suggested anymore. She was now taking control of her own care. Her question wasn't meant to discredit those in the room, the question simply revealed the amount of mistrust Heather had formed toward doctors and therapists. Those in the room knew Heather wasn't being disrespectful, for they understood how Heather could have developed that kind of mistrust.

A date was scheduled for Heather's spinal x-ray before Heather and I left the hospital. Heather and I returned back to Mary Free Bed a few days after Thanksgiving for the x-ray. It wasn't until after the New Year when we finally heard back from Dr. Kuldanek, with the news that there were several sites accessible along Heather's spine. We could now proceed with the Baclofen test. If all went well, Heather would then be referred to the surgeon.

All did go well and within a week, Heather and I met with the surgeon. He was very confident Heather would benefit from the Baclofen pump and was eager to move ahead with surgery. January 23, 2009, Heather was admitted into Spectrum hospital in Grand Rapids, for the implant of the pump. The following day, she was transported by ambulance, to Mary Free Bed Rehabilitation Hospital, where she was about to undergo some serious rehab.

CHAPTER FIFTY-SEVEN

*P*RIOR TO HEATHER'S ADMITTANCE INTO Mary Free Bed, her functional independence was evaluated by the team of therapists. This gave each therapist an idea of Heather's overall strengths and weakness which helped determine what approach to therapy might be the most beneficial to Heather. Few of the activities, Heather was evaluated and rated on were performed during the evaluation. The rest were rated by how Heather and had described her ability to perform the activity at home. The scores ranged from zero to seven. Zero being no activity and seven bring independent.

Eating: was rated a 7. Preparing her meals was a zero. Heather didn't prepare her meals while living with me. The counter tops, stove, and microwave were all too high for her to work with.

Toileting/Hygiene: 1 (Total, assist)

Transfer bed to chair: 2 (Maximal assist)

Transfer chair to toilet: 2 (Maximal assist)

Locomotion walk/wheelchair: 5 (Supervised) Heather was able to propel her wheelchair independently a few feet around the house. She was also capable of taking 1-3 steps with the use of her walker.

Dressing upper body: 3 (moderate assist)

Grooming: 4 (minimal assist) If all of Heather's personal items were set out for her, such as; makeup, comb and hair pins, tooth brush and toothpaste, and so on, she was able to complete her grooming independently.

Dressing lower body: 1 (Total assist)

Bed mobility: 2 (Maximal assist) Heather could not get in and out of bed on her own. With her pain in her lower back and hips, the twisting it took to go from sitting to side laying caused her to much pain. She was able to roll over in bed during the night, by holding onto and pulling herself over, using the clothes line rope we had strung along the sides of the bed.

Bathing: 1 (Total assist) Heather could not step in and out of the tub. She was able to wash her hair, face and upper front body while sitting on the shower chair. Bending over to wash her lower body was impossible. Not only because of balance issues, but also the bending would trigger pain and spasms in her lower back and hips.

Taking into account of Heather's limited mobility and functional scores, the estimated length of stay in rehab was set at three to four weeks. The following were Heather's rehab goals set by her therapists.

1) Maximal independence with self care and mobility.

2) Independence with bed mobility and to move from lying down to sitting position.

3) Transfer to chair with minimal assist or less.

4) Minimal assist or less for bathroom transfers.

Begin walking longer distances with walker.

1) Minimal assist with upper body dressing.

2) Minimal assist with upper body bathing.

3) Moderate assist with lower body bathing.

4) Moderate assist with lower body dressing.

5) Minimal assist or less for toilet transfers.

6) Moderate assist for toilet hygiene.

Again, Heather was faced with the challenges of relearning how to master basic daily activities. This would mark the third time in which she has had to either relearn how to or learn a different approach to everyday activities. The first experience being during her infant to toddler stage. The second time Heather had to learn the basics of self care and even eating, was in rehab right after her illness back in 1992, at the age of two and a half years old. Now at the age of nineteen. Heather had the task of discovering what was the best way to complete an activities accordingly to her limitations she had at the present time. So in a way, Heather was starting from scratch.

Heather's therapy began rather simple. Lots of stretching and some sitting. It wasn't until the pain in her abdominal lessened did she begin a more intense program. One week after the pump implant, Heather's pain in her lower back and hips had gone completely away. One week. I'll write that again. One week. After over three years of constant pain, enduring spasms in her back, hips and legs, it only took one week for the pump to perform its magic. This was mind boggling to me.

Not only had her pain disappeared, but her range of motion in her lower extremities increased as well. It was noted that Heather was able to weight bare on her legs without cringing in pain. She was able to maintain her legs in extended positions, where as before, she tended to draw her legs upward while laying down. There was also improvements in Heather's hip and knee extension. Only mild improvements were noted in hamstring extensibility at both knees.

I knew from here on out, Heather would gradually grow stronger. There was little holding her back. Heather may not reach all the goals set for her while in rehab, but I knew in time she would get there. Her muscle tone had become weak from her inactivity during the past three years. Strengthening her muscle tone was the key to Heather's independence.

When I visited with Heather during her second week in rehab, I noticed her color had come back. She no longer looked sickly and pale. The dark circles under her eyes were fading away and there seemed to be a new radiance beaming throughout her. Her eyes were sparkling and she had the most energy I had seen in her since before her first surgery. Being off of oral pain medication made a world of difference.

Heather was said to be very positive and cooperative throughout her stay in rehab. A complete turn around from her demeanor at the other hospital. Says a lot about the differences between the two hospitals and the way each approaches their patients. Not once did Heather call home and ask me to rescue her while she was in rehab at Mary Free Bed. As I had claimed throughout this entire journey, Heather's determination to become independent was within her all along. It just took a long three years to find the help that allowed Heather to regain that independence.

As amazing as the pump appeared to be, there were possible side effects related to the pump. One may experience dizziness, drowsiness, headaches and nausea, along with weakness. These symptoms were usually reduced or eliminated by adjusting the dosage. Constipation is a common side effect of Baclofen. Rather the drug is orally ingested or dispensed by the pump. Heather has had dealt with constipation ever since her illness back in 1991, so this was nothing new to her.

The more harmful side effects are likely to occur if the Baclofen in the pump is not filled on time or stops working properly. Convulsions/seizures are known to occur, but it is not that common among users. The majority of side effects are experienced during the process of discovering the correct dosage that works best for the patient. To date, Heather has not experienced any significant side effects.

During the course of Heather's stay, she made some remarkable gains in therapy. Heather was in time, able to pull up her pants over her hips with the aid of a reacher grabber, as Heather calls it. Heather managed to walk eighty feet with sitting down once after forty feet. She now was able to complete sit to stand with the aid of her walker using one hand. Able to stand upright with the aid of her walker for seven minutes. Forty five seconds while supporting herself with her walker using one hand. The greatest accomplishment Heather achieved was finally being able to wipe herself . When Heather told me she could now wipe her own butt, we both rejoiced.

Heather may have not met all the goals that were set for her, but she reached her own set of goals she had set for herself . That is all that mattered to Heather, coming out of rehab with the skills to build upon in order to live on her own. It wasn't Heather's goal to master walking anymore.

The two of us had discussed the importance of her walking on many occasions. As much as I would have liked to have seen Heather independent of her wheelchair, I knew for this to happen, more surgeries would most likely be required. Having Heather healthy, happy, and alive was more important than walking. I'm not sure why others found it difficult to accept Heather's stance on walking. There always seemed to be higher expectations placed on Heather, than what Heather could reach or wanted to reach.

When Heather informed me that she had met someone, I was overjoyed for her. That is, until she mentioned that she had met him over the internet. Ricky, *the stray*, as I referred to him, was not exactly the type of man whom I had in mind for Heather. I was hoping more along the lines, Heather would become involved with a therapist or perhaps a doctor. A mother can wish, right? The reason for referring to Ricky as a stray, was because he had no home. Before her discharge, Heather would ask if Ricky could come live with us. That's my Heather, asking to bring home someone she barely met who needed a place to stay.

The day Heather first introduced me to Ricky, I was quite disappointed. He failed to meet my expectations of a compatible suitor for Heather. Like many others whom would later meet him, I automatically judged him merely by the social standards we, as people, seem to use when determining one's worth. Such as, level of education, family background, type of job one held (in Ricky's case, no job,) where one lives, and the list goes on.

Then, when Ricky moved in with us, I began to observe the two of them together, without any preconceived notion of how Ricky should be. I discovered by doing so, Ricky and Heather fit perfectly. Ricky was a bit odd, Heather has always been odd, but together they completed one another. What can be more perfect than that? The amount of care and love Ricky offered Heather while living with me had won me over. I had no reservations about him thereafter.

Whenever anyone, whether it was a family member or friend, made a comment regarding Ricky's lack of job, I would quickly jump in and defend him. How was it that others could not see that Ricky did in fact have a job? He was taking the greatest care of Heather. That in itself should have been greatly appreciated by everyone. I know it was by me. Probably, because I knew firsthand the amount of work it took to take care of Heather. Perhaps, if others had noticed the gift Ricky brought into Heather's life as I had, then their approval of Ricky would not have had to be based on whether or not he had a job.

Heather wanting to move out and begin her life with Ricky was not surprising. My role in Heather's life naturally shifted from being center stage to just being a loving Mom. The journey we were on had come full circle and our dependency on one another was no longer needed to the full extent that it had been.

Like all parents, I didn't want to see my child have to struggle financially. She had been through enough hardships already in life. Moving into an apartment and making ends meet with only Heather's income would definitely be a challenge but manageable. That is why I became so outraged when Heather received the letter, informing her that she had to pay back over $1200.00 to SSI.

The amount of money Heather received while living with me had been based accordingly to the household income. My income had not changed during the period Heather supposedly had been over paid. Therefore, whomever granted the allowance made the error and in my opinion, should have been held accountable, not Heather. Furthermore, I strongly believed that all of Heather's needs, throughout her entire life span, should have been provided for by the institution which mandated or recommended childhood vaccinations. That would be the United States government. Unfortunately, that is nothing more than a pipe dream.

The sad truth is, the government has pretty much left those, whom have been injured by a vaccine, in a position to fend for themselves. Very few victims are awarded any type of compensation through the federal government program created as a no fault alternative to suits filed against drug manufacturers and health care providers. However, under the National Childhood Vaccine Injury Act, citizens were given the right to file suits against pharmaceutical companies for *partial* liability, for not making the vaccines more safe, when federal compensation was denied. This right to do so, was wrongfully taken away just recently.

February, 2011, the supreme court shielded drug manufacturers of *ALL* liability. No drug manufacturer can not be held accountable by a jury of peers, in the court of law. With this new ruling and little chance of receiving federal compensation, how does the government expect individuals, such as Heather, to live within their means? What ever happened to *"We the People, for the People"* being the foundation of our government? Why not just rewrite the phrase, starting with *,"We the Government, for the Government..."* because it seems that today's government has failed its citizens in many ways.

The only financial help Heather qualified for was SSI. With SSI, she was placed in the Medicaid program and was automatically eligible to receive food stamps. There are some states which has a state funded program that pays out extra money for living expenses, on top of the SSI benefits. Michigan is one of those states that offers this type of program. Every 3 months, Heather would receive an additional $42.00.

With having to pay over $1200.00 back to SSI, Heather and Ricky's struggle to survive financially would only heighten. I couldn't allow this to happen. Until the amount was paid in full, I made up the difference in Heather's monthly income. There were others who had stepped in and offered help to Heather and Ricky, by way of bringing food to them or what ever else the two of them needed.

I didn't experience no wheres near the separation anxiety I thought I would, when Heather moved out and into her own apartment. I think Sebastian experienced the majority of it. The two of them, Heather and Sebastian, were best of pals. He was always by her side except for the day Heather fell and he ran upstairs. The house seemed quite empty without Heather's presence, along with her wheelchairs and walker taking up space.

It took a few weeks to actually accept that Heather had moved out. Those were the weeks where I had the greatest difficulty with finding what to do with all the free time I now had. I honestly didn't know what to do with myself or where to start. Interesting, how my own sense of self became lost during Heather's ordeal and how bewildered I felt afterward.

There was one bright side to my new way of life, I now was able to fully enjoy smoking a cigarette without interruption. I know this may seem trivial, but to those who smoke, I know each will catch my meaning. I kid you not, no matter what the time, where I was in the house, or in the garage for that matter, as soon as I lit up a cigarette, Heather would suddenly be in some type of need requiring my help.

It was also during those first weeks, when I really noticed how I had aged. I looked old and for the first time since our journey began, I really became aware of how I overlooked my own well being while caring for Heather. With all the chaos we had dealt with, I had little energy left to even care about my appearance or health. Both were pushed on the back burner, so to speak. I had heard it from others, time and time again, "You need to make time for yourself." I wasn't comfortable doing so. I didn't feel right doing something leisurely while Heather was suffering.

In time, I adjusted to my new life and moved forward as expected. It now became possible to spend some much needed quality time with Katie. I had missed out on a great deal of Katie's discoveries, not to mention her soccer games, while she was growing into a teenager.

The saddest realization for me was, how no longer were Mikey, Heather, Katie and I inseparable as we had been for so many years. Each of us were moving in our own direction in life. The cycle of parenting was coming to a closure for me and all I could do was watched the transformation take place.

It gives me the greatest satisfaction to witness how compassionate and positive each of my children have grown to be. It's like I always told Heather,*"We did it. We made it."* My kids and I endured many years that were filled with adversity. In that adversity, we managed to retain a close knit bond. As a parent, this bond signifies a job well done by me. That is all I really aimed for as a parent. Raising children who carried with them little or no regrets regarding their childhood.

CHAPTER FIFTY-EIGHT

HEATHER'S WORDS

THE DAY RICKY AND I were going to move into our own apartment finally arrived. I had been waiting for this day a very long time. Freedom was mine. I wanted freedom so badly and I was pushing and pushing to get it. When it seemed like I would never be on my own, I became so angry. Up until now, it just wasn't meant to be.

I asked Dad if he could help Ricky and I move my power wheelchair over to the apartment. With Dad's trailer, my wheelchair could easily be loaded and unloaded. The apartment Ricky and I were moving into wasn't furnished. Ricky and I had no furniture of our own. Dad and Momma Denise offered to give us their old couch and Lazy Boy chair. They also gave us some pictures to hang on the wall. Grandma Sandy brought over a full size bed, along with a table and chairs. Ricky found an old TV that someone had put out by the curb for free. He brought that to the apartment. The TV worked fine, but the volume was really low on it. Ricky already had an old computer and Mom gave us her old computer desk.

We didn't have to buy any household things. Mom helped buy pots, pans, and bake ware. I already had bought plastic cups, plates and bowls. I didn't want any glassware because I knew I would end up dropping or breaking them. I also had silverware and towels. I bought all those things back when Blake and I were talking about getting our own apartment.

I am so thankful that I was going to my life with Ricky instead. At least I knew that I would be taken good care of by Ricky and wouldn't have to worry about living on the street. I don't mean to sound harsh, but I really think that is where I would have ended up if I went out to California with Blake.

After everyone had left our apartment on moving day and as Ricky was busy unpacking, I wheeled my chair over to the sliding glass door in our living room. I sat there in front of it looking out and thinking how excited I was to be on my own and having a boyfriend who loved me the way I was. Someone who would always take care of me.

Ricky and I were so perfect for one another. The two of us were comfortable letting each other to do what ever we wanted. If Ricky wanted to pick up and go see his family he would. If I wanted to go spend the weekend with Mom I would. It was the greatest feeling to know that Ricky wasn't a controlling person, who told me what I could and could not do.

Soon after the move, I learned how to get in and out of bed on my own. I didn't have a bed rail to hold onto to support me for transfers, so I had to come up with a different way of getting in and out of bed. I discovered by placing my manual wheelchair next to the bed, I could use it for transferring. Plus, I was able to hold onto it while rolling over on my side. My walker wouldn't work for transfers or support, because it tipped too easily.

I would park my power wheelchair next to the bed, slightly behind my manual wheelchair. I then would grab the handles of my manual chair and stand. I stood on the foot rest of my power wheelchair, because I was then high enough to just twist and sit on the edge of the bed. If I stood on the floor, I wasn't tall enough to just sit down. The mattress was too high. Once I was seated on the edge of the bed, I would use my left hand to hold up my left leg, then simply fall backwards. I then would roll onto my side and push my body upward to my pillow. It turned out to be a lot of work just to lay down.

It was much easier getting out of bed. I simply swung my legs over the side of the bed, grabbed the handles of my manual chair and pulled myself upright. I would stand on the floor and lift one foot on the foot rest of my power wheelchair then sit. Then I would grab my right leg and lift it the foot rest. I would side back and be on my way. On the nights when I was too weak from being tired, Ricky would help me into bed.

I was able to get into the shower on my own, but Ricky needed to help me get out. I could easily slip and fall on the wet flooring in our bathroom. I used a shower chair in the shower, so Ricky would balance my upper body with one arm as he swung my legs over the side of the tub with his other. He would hold my walker in place as I grabbed onto it and used it to stand.

I washed the dishes while standing on my foot rest of my power wheelchair as well. This made me a little taller and easier to reach the faucet. I did a lot of the cooking and laundry. There was a laundry room right next to our apartment. I was so grateful for that, because it would have been a hassle having to go to a laundromat in town. I was gradually becoming more independent, but I had to learn how to do everything while in a wheelchair. Not as easy as one might think.

Financially, starting off was very hard. Mom would take me shopping once a month for toiletries. Such as; shampoo, pads, toothpaste, along with buying us some food. I was so grateful she did that for us. Before Ricky and I applied for Food Assistance, we went around to different churches and received free food. Aunt Shirley and Uncle Kurt would put aside a couple of trash bags of returnable cans each month for us to cash in. Grandma Sandy would always bring a goodie box for Ricky and I, every time she came to visit us. I asked Dad only a couple of times if he could bring us over something that we needed. I stopped asking when he began reminding me of how he couldn't always be buying us things, followed by asking, *"Has Ricky found a job yet?"*

I would always get so pissed when a family member asked me that question. Didn't they see, mainly Dad, that Ricky did have a job? Taking care of me and seeing to it that I was safe, happy and healthy. I guess they thought Ricky should be bringing in some money. To me, Dad and the others were more concerned about money than my well being. Not me, I had a roof over my head, a man who loved me, and I was happy. Also, there was food in the house. I didn't go without. Mom has always said, "Life will always provide you with what you need. It's those things that you want that you may not get."

Couple of months after moving, Ricky and I learned that Ricky could receive money from the State for taking care of me. The sound of that was great. The extra money would certainly help out. I contacted the Michigan Department of Human Services. After all my information was taken over the phone, a date was set up for an in home visit. The lady who came to our apartment was very nice. Together, we went over a check list of tasks helped me with. The tasks Ricky helped me with included, dressing, bathing, shopping and more. With all that he was doing, he became qualified to receive money. There, Ricky now had a paying job. Everyone who had criticized Ricky for not working should now be happy.

Ricky's first check was over $500.00. Then the amount was set at $480.83 every month. It was enough to carry us through with a little extra to go out and make memories. Ricky and I were told by the lady who visited us, that if Ricky and I were to get married, he would no longer receive any money. I didn't understand why it made a difference. Ricky still would be helping me in the same matter. To me, I believed it was wrong to stop receiving the money because of being married. Unfortunately, the state of Michigan sees it differently.

Living in town was so perfect, especially during the summer. If Ricky and I had extra money, I would drive my power chair to my favorite store, Dollar General, and buy what ever we needed. Soon, I became well known by the employees. Sometimes I would just go over to the store and say "Hi." I also made trips to the high school, in order to hang out with O'Brien, Gates, and the office staff. I'm so glad I was able to do so, because it was the last year Gates would be there. He was going to retired after the school year ended. Summer time was when Ricky and I would go on walks around town. Ricky had a friend who lived nearby us, so we made several trips over to Perky's house and visited with him and his family.

My life with Ricky was better than I could have ever dreamed of. We never argued. With all the time we spent together in such a tiny apartment, you would think we would. Ricky would keep himself busy by playing video games on the computer and also on our Wii. I began writing short stories to occupy my time. I thought if I were to write a book, it would be so cool to have the book placed next to one that Nicholas Sparks had written, on a shelf in Wal-Mart or a book store. Nicholas Sparks is my all time favorite author.

Yes, life was great and it was going to get even better. During a visit with Dr. Ausiello, I asked if I could stop taking Prozac. I no longer felt depressed and thought it was a waste to keep taking a drug I didn't feel I needed. Dr. Ausiello agreed along with me.

I was placed on an anti-depressant during my first rehab stay at Advanced Care Hospital. Every reason for taking Prozac no longer applied to me. All that was behind me now and had changed when I had the pump implant. The pain I had lived with along with losing my independence, had a huge effect on my way of thinking. Becoming so discouraged and giving up was so over whelming. No matter how hard I had tried to fight against the depression I couldn't. The depression completely consumed me.

Have you ever sought help for a certain condition, only to find a solution years later? Well, this happened to me. I developed toenail fungus when I was younger and no matter what was tried, the fungus would not go away. My toenails became so brittle and deformed because of it. Mom had asked several times while I was at Advanced Care Hospital, to have a specialist look at my toenails or at least have them trimmed. No specialist was contacted and no trimming was done. Instead, I was given a strong drug used to get rid of the fungus. At $75.00 a tablet, you would think it worked.

Later when I went for a check-up at Dr. Ausiello's office and told him what drug I was taking, he told me to stop. The drug was known to cause liver damage. Dr. Ausiello suggested soaking my feet in bleach mixed with water. My feet and toes became so raw and sore by doing that, so I quit. I also tried using some type of cream, but that only caused my skin to start peeling away from my toes. Toenail fungus was something I was going to live with for the rest of my life I didn't care about that, I just wanted to find someone who could trim my nails without causing them to start bleeding or causing me so much pain.

Dr. Ausiello told me to make an appointment at Greenville Family Foot care. He said that the doctor there would trim my nails the right way. My toes had become so sore from the mis-shaped toenails from years of being improperly cared for. The doctor I went to see, ended up numbing my big toes before he could even begin to trim the nail. That was how tender my toes had become.

He ended up using a small hand held sander to trim my nails. I continue to see him once a month and I no longer have the discomfort of mis-shaped toenails. When I was given a business card at the end of my first visit, I started laughing. On the card, I noticed that he had an office right in Lakeview at that time. Since then, he has closed his office in Lakeview. I could have been going there all along when I was living with Mom. We never knew who to go to for help. I guess, we expected the doctors, we had asked for help, to know and tell us where to go. This would only happen to me.

I am a person who likes to help out others. well, Life was about to teach me that helping others may not always turn out good. No Matter what, I would never choose to take back my offer to help out my friend, Jacob. I met Jacob while I was still going to school. He was a year behind me. Jacob was somewhat of an outsider, but always friendly to me. I guess because we both were a little different.

I had seen him in town shortly after Ricky and I had moved. The two of us began catching up on each others life. He said that he needed to find a place to live, while he looked for work. *"Heather to the rescue,"* as Mom would say. I went home and asked Ricky if Jacob could stay with us until he found another place to live. Ricky said yes and before long, Jacob moved in. It was great at first. Kinda crowded, since our apartment was only one bedroom. Jacob slept on the couch and didn't have a lot of belongings. He helped out with the housework for a while, until he lost interest in it. Then he began inviting his girlfriend over to stay, without asking Ricky or I if we minded. I know right then this wasn't going to work.

I felt as though he was taking his stay for granted and wasn't even worried about finding another place to live. I finally told him that he had to leave. He wasn't angry at me or anything, but we did lose touch with one another after he moved out. I think of him often and hope that he is well and happy.

I guess we had to make the same mistake again before Ricky and I realized that we needed to put ourselves first. This time, a family member needed help. Ricky's younger brother didn't have a place to stay and was sleeping in his truck. We offered him our couch and told him he could stay until he found a job and saved up for his own place. He assured Ricky and I that he was getting food assistance and would help out with food. We found out quickly that he was lying.

Again, Ricky and I felt that we were being taken for granted and eventually we asked that family member to leave. I then realized that Life was showing Ricky and I how we needed to focus on our own life and take care of one another. It was time to stop putting others first. At first, I felt selfish for thinking this way, but I was tired of Ricky and I being used.

As much as possible, I continued to work on my short story. One day while on Facebook, I began chatting with my Spanish teacher I had in high school. Mrs. Paulsen, asked me what I was up to. I told her that I was writing a short story. Upon hearing this, she began telling me about a local author who might be willing to help me with my writing. She told me his name was Richard Ashland.

Richard already had one book published and was working on a sequel. He also worked for Encompass Magazine, as Director of Marketing and Staff Writer. Mrs. Paulsen said that she would mention me to Richard. I gave her my e-mail address to pass on to him, in case he wanted to contact me. Maybe, just maybe, he would help me with my writing and perhaps, I would get a book published and on a shelf for people to read after all.

I thought it was a nice gesture by Mrs. Paulsen, but I didn't think I would hear from Richard. It sounded like he was a very busy man. Too busy to take time out of his schedule to contact me. He didn't even know me. How wrong I was. In a matter of days after chatting with Mrs. Paulsen, I received an email from him. In his e-mail he asked me what kind of short story I was writing. I told him that the it was somewhat of a love story. He offered to read through what I had written so far and he would pass along any suggestions, if I was willing to send the writing to him. I was surprised that he had offered and told him I would send him my story right away. Shortly after I sent him the story, Richard emailed me back saying that he would like to meet me.

When I first met him, I thought he looked like Elvis Presley and sounded like him also. Richard and I instantly took to one another. It was like we had known each other for years. Right off, he took me under his wing and since then, we have grown very close. He liked the way I wrote and encouraged me to continue with my story. He helped me with my writing and also allowed me to read his work.

After a few visits, he finally asked why I was in a wheelchair. I told him my story, which he thought would make a great book to read. I mentioned to him that Mom had said the same thing, how her and I should write a book about me. She wanted me to write how I felt about growing up handicapped and what I went through after my first spinal surgery. Mom would write about what it was like going through my illness when I was little and also what she went through after my first surgery in 2006. Richard became excited when I told him this and he wanted to meet with Mom.

Once again, Life had worked its magic. Starting with my chat with Mrs. Paulsen. She in turn, brought Richard into my life to inspire Mom and I to write my story. Not only that, but he said he would help us with getting the book published and with setting up book signings. Without meeting Richard, I'm not sure if Mom and I would have ever follow through writing with writing our book.

Mom and I started writing our book in January, 2010. Mom said that I should fill out a request to get a copy of all my medical files and x-rays, since there was a lot of things we had forgotten. After all these years, Mom still had all my files dating back to 1991, when I first became sick after the shot. Mom said she didn't know why she held onto those files, but I guess it was for this book. When I received the call telling me that my files were ready for pickup, I called Mom because she was the one who would be driving.

Mom thought the entire family should go to together, to mark the end of the journey we all were a part of. Mom also said that she was going to see if Holly could make time to see us while we were at the hospital. This would give us the opportunity to say our final farewell and to thank her. Mom was able to talk with Holly and said that Holly was anxious to see how well I was doing. Then as a way to celebrate our journey's end, Mom thought we should go to Olive Garden and feast.

With Katie going along, I knew our trip was going to be interesting. Katie is known for her unique personality. You never know what she might do or say in any given moment. Mom, Mikey and Katie came to the apartment to pick me up the morning we went to Ann Arbor. After giving Ricky a kiss, we were on our way. I couldn't believe that this was going to be my last trip to the hospital, along with seeing Holly. What a journey I had. So happy that I was now free of pain and depression.

As usual, Mom stopped at Burger King in Ionia to get breakfast, then we were off to the city. Three hours later, we pulled into the parking lot in front of the building where my medical files were. The first stop we made was at the hospital, because Mom and I thought that was where my medical files were. They wasn't. We had to drive to another building, a short distance from the hospital.

The parking lot we drove into was almost empty, so Mom parked in a handicap space. Mom never got around to getting a handicap sticker for her car. She always parked like a mile away from any store we went into. Well, maybe not a mile, but usually far away from other cars.

Mom said since her and I were just going to be in the building only for a second, parking in the handicap space would be okay. While Mom and I went into the building, Mikey and Katie remained in the car. As they were waiting, Katie came up with this brilliant idea. Mom had one of those Yankee Candle air fresheners hanging down from her rear view mirror. Katie took it down and drew the symbol of the wheelchair, you usually see on a handicap tag. Then she hung the air freshener back up.

When Mom and I walked back to the car, we noticed Katie pointing at the air freshener. We didn't know what she wanted us to see, but once we got into the car, Mom and I broke out in laughter when we saw Katie's art work. Only Katie would think to do something like that. The symbol was so small, people would never have had seen it. I wondered what Katie would do next while we were waiting at the hospital to see Holly. I knew one thing, our wait was not going to be boring.

Once we all were in the hospital, the first place we headed for was the gift shop. Any time we went to that hospital, we rarely left for home without walking through the gift shop. Sometimes, Mom would buy a stuffed animal (or two) and other times Mikey and I would drag her out before she had a chance to buy anything. Today, we were at the gift shop to buy! Mom had been saving her money for this trip and she planned to make a lasting memory for us all. Mom told us to pick out what we wanted and not to worry about the price.

I saw what I wanted right off. There was a big white tiger in the window staring at me. Wanting me to take it home. Mom bought herself a stuffed bear, Katie ended up picking out a strange looking beaver, along with a pelican. Mikey chose to get a clown fish puppet. After paying for our animals, we headed off to the Orthopedic waiting area. Remember when I wrote how I was wondering what Katie would do next?

Well, the area we chose to sit in had several plants sitting on the end tables. A few of the plants were pretty big and bushy. Katie gathered up all our animals and placed them around this one tree like plant and also on the branches. She then began taking pictures while talking like she was an animal hunter. Narrating the hunt in a fake Australian accent, trying to sound like the Crocodile Hunter. Mom and I were laughing so hard. Mikey was just sitting in his chair shaking his head. No other people in the waiting area saw any humor in what Katie was doing. In fact, one man sitting near us stood up and moved to the other side of the area. This is what I love most about our family outings. We are always goofing off and having fun. Time just seems to go by so fast when we are together. It was an interesting moment. Only Katie, 4.0 GPA.

When my name was called out, the animals were gathered and we all were led into a room to wait for Holly. When Holly walked in, I gave her a big hug. I thanked her for doing what she could for me and told her how happy I was. I also let her know that I was no longer in any pain, then I showed her where my pump had been implanted. Holly said she had never heard of such a pump like the one I had. I told her if she ever had another patient like me, try using the pump. Holly was happy to see how well I was doing and told me she wanted a signed copy of our book, once I told her how Mom and I were writing one. Before leaving, Holly gave both Mom and I a hug. The visit didn't last very long, because Holly had other patients waiting to see her. I was so glad that Holly took the time to see me. It meant a lot.

As the four of us were walking out of the hospital, I felt a weight being lifted off of me. I think I needed to have this final visit with Holly in order to let her know I wasn't angry at her and to thank her. Maybe, the reason I felt lighter, was because any disappointment I still carried, was being left behind and I no longer needed to carry it with me.

CHAPTER FIFTY-NINE

HEATHER'S WORDS

*I*N EARLY JULY, 2010, MOM called me with the news that Sebastian was having trouble walking. He also was losing control of his bowels and he was eating less. Right away I knew if Sebastian was eating less, something had to be very wrong. Aunt Shirley told Mom that Sebastian would begin to have hip and joint problems as he grew older. This was common for the kind of dog he was; Rottweiler and Lab mix. I knew by the sound of Mom's voice, she was going to put Sebastian, my best friend, down. I didn't want him to leave yet, but at the same time, I knew his time was up on earth.

Mom had already made it clear a long time ago, that she would never allow Sebastian to suffer needlessly just so we could keep him with us. We all agreed with Mom. Sebastian was the greatest and had lived such a full life. I remember how he used to get stuck in the fence when he was just a pup and how he used to run a lap around the house, when ever Mom unleashed him. I'll never forget how he would wait patiently at the kitchen table, for someone to drop a crumb of food on the floor, while we were eating. Sebastian could clear out a room with one of his deadly farts. When I was younger and would stay the weekend with Mom, she would purposely feed Sebastian chicken, knowing how bad he would stink up the bedroom I slept in.

I made plans to go see Sebastian before Mom took him to see Doc. Dr. Lepley had been Sebastian's vet, since he was a puppy. Mom said the Doc would tell her if she was doing what was best for Sebastian, by putting him down. Ricky and I drove to Mom's house a few days before Sebastian went to see Doc.

After eating dinner, I watched Sebastian as he hopped up on the couch cushion and laid down. I noticed how hard it was for him to lift his back legs up. I wheeled myself over to where he was laying and looked into his eyes. I felt like Sebastian could sense that this was going to be the last day seeing each other, until we met again somewhere else.

I leaned forward and held onto his paw. I whispered to him how I loved him and thanked him for keeping an eye on me throughout my recovery and being my sleeping buddy. I also told Sebastian to watch over Mom and have fun where ever his next journey would be taking him. After saying what I needed to say, he gently licked my hand, as if it was his way of saying goodbye to me. I felt a tear rolling down my cheek and wiped it away before leaning in more to give him a kiss on his head. I whispered "I love you" one more time before I wheeled myself away.

I asked Mom if she wanted me to go with her, when she took Sebastian to see Doc. She said that she needed to do this by herself, which I understood. Sebastian was her baby and Mom felt that since she was the first person he saw in our family, she should be the last he would see. Sebastian was such a loving dog. We still talk about him often. Once in a while, I can hear him snoring underneath my bed. His way of letting me know that he is around me and still watching over me.

Ricky and I had been together for over one year before I started talking about starting a family. I really wanted to experience pregnancy. To feel the baby grow inside me and have that sensation women talk about, when the baby begins kicking. Ricky and I both love children and by watching Ricky interact with his nieces and nephews, I knew he would make a wonderful Dad. I asked Dr. Kuldanek if she thought I was able to have children and she didn't see any reason why I couldn't. Dr. Kuldanek said that with my limitations, I most likely would be placed on bed rest later in the pregnancy. I was willing to go through that, if it meant I could have a child.

Boy, I stirred up a lot of controversy when I mention to the family that Ricky and I were trying to start a family. Mom was most concerned with health issues and if I would be able to carry the baby full-term. She then said that if I was willing to risk the health issues, not only regarding me, but also the baby, then I should go for it.

Other members of the family wasn't liking the idea of Ricky and I having a baby at all.

I was asked so many questions like, Who will take care of the baby, Ricky? Whats going to happen if Ricky leaves you? You're not even married, why would you want to start a family before getting married? Once again, I felt like others saw me as being a total cripple, who couldn't do anything, I thought that I should have been given the benefit of doubt, but I wasn't. You know what? I didn't care what the family thought. Ricky and I believed that we would manage just fine. Ricky and I had talked about marriage, but he hadn't proposed to me yet. I told Ricky that if he wanted to marry me, he had to get down on one knee and propose. I still believe the man should be the one to ask. Guess, I am a bit old fashion.

One morning when I got out of bed, Ricky stopped me in our bedroom doorway. He bent down on one knee with a ring in his hands. I was so excited and laughing. He asked me to marry him. I said "yes." Ricky placed the ring on my finger and I wrapped my arms around him. I didn't want to let go.

Before I even began trying to get pregnant, Ricky told me that he might not be able to have kids. In his previous relationships, his other girlfriends didn't get pregnant, but would become pregnant in another relationship. Maybe it wasn't Ricky's time to become a dad back then. Ricky and I tried for months to get me pregnant. I even went to my gynecologist to have tests ran, in order to find if I was fertile or not. I was, so maybe Ricky was right about not being able to have children.

There was one month I skipped my period and we were so excited, until I took a pregnancy test. The test was negative. We didn't stop trying, but finally accepted that if I was going to become pregnant I would. To me, this is the only way to look at life. If something is meant to happen it will, if it doesn't happen, that is the way it is supposed to be. Still, I couldn't help but feel discouraged every month when my period started.

Ricky didn't like seeing me that way. After months of trying, the two of us talked about breaking a rule in the apartment rule book. The rule of "No Pets Allowed." I am not a person who goes behind people's back or breaks rules just to get what I want. I am the worst lair and I feel so bad afterward, that I come out with the truth. The only thing working in Ricky and my favor, was that hardly anyone associated with the building, ever came over to check on the apartment. With that in mind, Ricky and I took a trip to the pet store in town, Anne's Pet Shop.

Ricky wanted a puppy, but a puppy would make a lot of noise and we would definitely be caught. Birds, fish, or any kind of reptile was out of the question. I wanted a kitten and Ricky agreed to it. I wanted a female kitten and Ricky wanted a male kitten. He said that males were more lovable. I didn't know if that is true or not, because I always have been around female cats. Maybe, I take after Mom when it comes to pets. She always had a female cat and usually a male dog.

My heart was set on getting a female kitten. Had to. I already had the name picked out; *"Molly Anne Robinson."* It is so hard to look at the puppies and kittens without wanting to take them all home. It was going to be hard to pick just one kitten. But, when I looked up, there was a little black and white kitten staring down at me. I knew Ricky and I were meant to pick that kitten. The kitten was the only one looking at us, the others were fast asleep in the cage. We asked the worker to check the sex of the kitten, all the while crossing my fingers, hoping the kitten was a girl. The kitten was, so Ricky and I paid for the kitten and took our baby Molly home.

The only thing we heard all the way back to our apartment, was Molly's cute meow. Here I was trying to make her stay in the box, when all she wanted to do was jump out. Ricky and I managed to get inside our apartment without Molly being noticed. What a relief.

With having a small animal running around the apartment, I always had to watch out for her while I was using my wheelchair. Molly soon began to sit on my foot rest and took rides with me. She really liked that. There had been a few times when I accidentally drove over the tip of her tail. But in time, she learned to stay out of the way of my chair, if she wasn't hitching a ride on it.

Like all kittens, Molly was very playful and always making Ricky and I laugh. I couldn't wait until Molly was old enough to be declawed. Man, those claws of hers were sharp. Not only was Molly declawed, we also had her fixed. Nothing sounds worse then a cat in heat. For sure, with all the meowing she would have done, Ricky and I would have had been tossed out.

Molly was supposed to be my cat, but she had taken to Ricky

more. I thought this was funny, because Ricky didn't like cats all that much. He is more of a dog person. It didn't matter, Molly had a way of melting Ricky's heart. The two of them could be found napping together, with Molly snuggled up against Ricky.

Cats can be so finicky. Molly did not like drinking water from a bowl. When ever we put a bowl of water on the floor for her, she would tip it over on purpose. The only liquid Molly would drink out of a bowl was milk. Molly preferred to drink water from a dripping faucet, so Ricky and I kept the faucet on all the time.

Later on, Molly earned the nickname, "Maw Maw." Every time we gave her can cat food, she would maw it down. It was only when she was naughty did I call her "Molly Anne!" Her favorite toys were hair ties. She loved to play with a hair ties when I dropped one on the floor. Soon, I began snapping them in the air for her to jump at and play with. I would pick up the hair ties with my reacher grabber and once again snapped them in the air. I bet we had at least sixty or more hairs ties laying around the apartment. Maw Maw was growing into a very skittish cat. Loud noises would scare her and when company came over, she would run and hide underneath our bed. Not a socializing cat at all.

When the lease on our apartment was almost up, I told Ricky that I didn't want to hide Molly anymore or get caught with having a pet. I've began looking around for another apartment to rent. One that allowed pets. We found the perfect apartment. Not in Greenville, but in Belding. Wood-Haven Apartments allowed small Pets, plus the rent was income based. The apartment complex included forty separate apartments. The building was a single story structure, equipped with handicap door opening. The apartment Ricky and I looked at was bigger than the one we were living in.

The entire apartment was handicap accessible and also had emergency devices installed that when the string was pulled, an alarm would go off and a light above the apartment door would begin flashing. The tub had a section cut out of the side, which would make it so easy to get in and out of the shower.

Ricky and I liked the apartment and said that we wanted it. When I called Mom with the news she was happy for us. Then I told her that the other occupants were all senior citizens. Mom's reaction was quite funny.

"What? You and Ricky are moving into a nursing home?"

"Not a nursing home, Mom," I answered back laughing. "Its a regular apartment building, but with older people living in it."

"A retirement community?" Mom then asked.

"I guess, but the rent is cheaper and best of all, we can have Molly."

"Well, if nothing else," Mom said. "You will probably be spoiled by those living there, because you know they will soon be treating you like a grandchild.'"

I love my mom's sense of humor. Ricky and I moved into our new apartment October 27, 2010, on Ricky's birthday. It didn't bother Ricky nor I being the only young couple in the building. I was glad that I was living with older people. I have a harder time with getting along with people my age because they seem to be more judgmental. Plus, I'm limited to what I can do. I just can't pick up and go do things without having help.

I soon became addicted to putting together puzzles. Mom found this to be funny, since I never liked to do jigsaw puzzles before. Not enough patience, I guess. There is always a puzzle in the process of being put together, on a table in the main lobby. Anyone could stop and work at finishing it. There were also tables in the community kitchen, where puzzles were being done. Every Tuesday and Thursday, Bingo was played. Anyone in the building could come and play. I had played a few times, until I put everything on hold in order to finish this book.

Out of everyone I had met in the apartment complex, Daisy and Ethel, had become my closest friends. Not everyone living in Wood-Haven is sociable. Some like to gossip and criticize the other occupants. I prefer not to associate with them. Most of the time I keep to myself. I go out to the main lobby long enough to collect our mail. I hang out with Daisy and Ethel if they are out there, but not for very long.

Once Ricky and I were all settled in, we were ready to set our wedding date. Mom came up with the perfect idea. Since I told her how I would love to get married in Uncle Jon's backyard, she suggested getting married during weekend we were having our family reunion. By having the ceremony at that time, most of the out-of-state relation would already be in Michigan. So, the date of our wedding was set for June 25, 2011. This gave Ricky and I well over six months to prepare. Ricky and I both wanted an informal wedding. Having a fancy wedding wasn't me. I always thought a fancy wedding was more for show than anything else.

I asked Uncle Jon and Aunt Cindi if Ricky and I could hold our wedding in their backyard. Both of them felt honored and offered to help out with anything that Ricky and I may need. My plan was to not ask anyone for help. I didn't want to hear how much it cost them by helping me. Mom said that if anyone offered, then allow them to help. It would mean a lot to them if they were a part of making your dream come true.

So, we had a place to hold our wedding. Now, Ricky and I needed to find somewhere to have the reception. Uncle Jon and Aunt Cindi made arrangements to rent out the Lakeview VFW Hall. As a wedding gift to Ricky and I, they paid for it as well.

I asked Katie to be my maid of honor. I asked her because she had gone through a lot with me and I wanted her to know how much I loved her for that. Ricky asked his friend, Matt, to be his best man. Matt and Ricky had been friends for a long time and Matt was the one Ricky was living with when I was at Mary Free Bed. Next, we needed to find a pastor who would marry us.

One day while visiting Richard Ashland, and his wife, Mary, the subject of our wedding came up. I mentioned how we needed to find a pastor. Rick said that the pastor of the church he attends, might be able to. Ricky and I contacted Pastor Wayne and set up a day to meet. Right off, I told Pastor Wayne that neither Ricky nor I attend church and how I didn't believe in traditional religion. I asked him if that was going to be a problem. Pastor Wayne said it wasn't a problem and from the way Rick talked about me, it would be an honor to be the pastor who married you and Ricky.

Ricky and I had to attend several classes with Pastor Wayne, before he could marry us. I was so grateful that Pastor Wayne never tried to push religion onto Ricky nor I. He is such an unique Pastor and the passion for his work shines brightly through his eyes. He has a way of touching people in the most heartfelt manner.

While surfing the web and looking at different styles of dresses, I found the perfect dress for me. A simple summer dress. The dress was white with large flowers that were outlined in brown, with patches of turquoise and olive colors splattered inside the flowers. The dress was trimmed in turquoise and brown. Ricky decided to wear a pair of jean shorts and a white polo. Matt, intended to wear Khaki shorts and a turquoise polo. Katie chose to wear a simple white spring dress. Our date was set, the location for the wedding and reception was taken care of, we found a pastor and bought our clothing. Now, I needed a wedding cake and to pick out invitations.

As a wedding gift to Ricky and I, Grandma Ski and Mom offered to pay for our cake. Grandma Ski took Mom and I over to meet her friend and neighbor, Dottie Wood who makes cakes for all different occasions. I took along my wedding dress so Dottie could see the exact colors I wanted on my cake. It was hard to choose just one cake from all the pictures Dottie was showing me. I finally chose a cake that Dottie never had made, but wanted to try making. It was a three layered cake with a staircase attached to two smaller cakes. Dottie also planned on placing a fountain on the cake table, with flowing turquoise colored water.

The wedding and reception invites were just simple invitations. I divided the invitations into two groups. Family and close friends were sent an invitation to the wedding and reception. All the rest of my friends were sent an invitation to just the reception. I wanted everyone one to be at my wedding, but I didn't want to overwhelm Uncle Jon and Aunt Cindi. They already had the majority of relatives, up for the family reunion camping out in their back yard.

As a surprise, Mom asked Uncle Jon if he would drive Ricky and I to the reception in his Model A, that he had recently restored. Uncle Jon said if the weather was nice, he would be honored to. This was perfect. The Model A used to be Grandpa Ski's and I remember him giving all of us grand kids rides in it. A lot of memories are connected to that car.

Mom and I went flower shopping in Grand Rapids. I wanted to use silk flowers to decorate the gazebo Ricky and I were getting married on. Richard and Mary, brought over a beautiful bridal bouquet for me so I didn't have to worry about buying one.

Everything was in order. Mom and her boyfriend, Jeff, built a ramp leading up to the floor of the gazebo. The two of them also decorated the gazebo the morning of our wedding and set up the sixty lawn chairs, Grandma Johnson supplied us with. Richard Ashland, along with Ricky's Aunt Ruthy, who was an notorious picture taker of the family, were going to be our photographers. My cousin Kelly, the one who visited me in rehab, was going to do my hair. Ricky and I picked the song, *"This I Swear."* sung by Nick Lachey, as our wedding song. The song would be playing as Mikey was pushing me to the gazebo. Yes, Mikey.

I asked Dad to give me away. Most fathers would say yes and be excited to give their daughter away. But, mine; a whole different story. Dad told me that he wasn't going to give me away to Ricky. I knew Dad never approved of Ricky, but that shouldn't have had stopped him from giving me away. Dad wasn't going to live with Ricky, I was. But, Dad was still having a fit about the two of us getting married. I would wait another week and ask him again.

Mikey had said all along, that he should be the one who gave me away. I know that he has always watched over me and has helped take care of me. He was more of a father figure than brother at times. But, I still wanted my Dad to give me away.

When I called Dad back after waiting a week, he still refused to push me to the gazebo and give me away. So, I asked Mikey to. I then asked Dad if he would at least give me a kiss after Mikey gave me away. At first, Dad wasn't willing to do that, but changed his mind. I was so happy that he did. Dad's side of the family offered to decorate the hall and furnish the food and drinks, since Mom helped out with the wedding. I felt honored that they wanted to do this for me.

I was so excited the morning of my wedding day. The weather was going to be perfect; sunny and warm. The wedding was scheduled to start at eleven O'clock. Mom's house was so busy with people coming and going. When I was finished with dressing and my hair done up, I headed out the door to go to Uncle Jon's house.

The first thing that happened when I was wheel out the door, I rolled right over a huge pile of dog crap. There was dog crap all over my wheelchair wheel. Mom just busted out laughing and said, "There is always something that has to happen unexpectedly. Now, with that out of the way, the wedding will go smoothly."

When I finally made it to Uncle Jon's, I remained hidden in his pole building until our wedding song began to play. As Mikey began pushing me around the corner of their pool and toward the gazebo, I was surprised to see all the people who came to share this day with Ricky and I. All sixty chairs were filled, plus there were others standing.

It is my nature to laugh when I get excited or nervous. I wasn't nervous, I was just so excited. Halfway to the gazebo, I noticed Ricky brushing a tear away. My husband to be, couldn't have had shown the amount of his love for me,in any better way. When Mikey and I reached the ramp we stopped. Pastor Wayne said a short prayer and asked the question, which Mikey proudly answered; *"I do."* Then Dad walked up to me and gave me a kiss, before Ricky took over and finished pushing me up the ramp.

Ricky positioned my wheelchair in the center of the gazebo, then sat down on a chair to face me. By this time, tears began streaming down my checks. I was so happy. There are no words to describe how happy I was. I loved Ricky so much and so grateful that Life had brought us together. When it came time to exchange vows, I couldn't talk. I just broke down crying. The pastor, Ricky and everyone waited patiently for me to regain my composure. It was beautiful. The ceremony was absolutely beautiful. Life was beautiful.

The reception went well. A lot of people came and went. Sitting alone in the midst of others, was O'Brien. It meant the world to me to see him there. After being at the reception for an hour or so, I was beginning to get tired. Definitely tired of smiling for all the pictures that Aunt Ruthy was taking. As a special tribute to Ricky and I, Richard Ashland took us to the back of the hall, where there was a microphone set up and sang , "I can't Help Falling in love with You" by Elvis Presley. Rick's voice sounded just like Elvis.

Rick and Mary had already reserved a really nice hotel room in Cadillac, as a wedding gift, for Ricky and I to spend our wedding night in. So, after the reception, Ricky and I headed up to the hotel. Once we were checked in and after calling mom, I went and took a shower then passed out. The following afternoon, Ricky and I attended his brother, Tommy's Graduation Open House. Then we drove back to our apartment, where our Maw Maw was waiting for us. Shortly after our wedding, Daisy and Ethel threw Ricky and I a party for all of the occupants who wanted to attend our wedding, but couldn't. Another journey was beginning for me. I would begin this journey as "Mrs. Heather Robinson."

Epilogue

PART ONE

HEATHER'S WORDS

*M*OM SUGGESTED WRITING AN EPILOGUE, including thoughts and feelings that I might like to share with our readers. Kinda like a summary of what I discovered about myself, others and about life. So, I guess this will be my final chapter of our book. Mom and I worked together writing our book for the past two years. I didn't think we were ever going to reach the end, but here we are.

Throughout the book, Mom has helped me to find my words whenever I got stuck. I am not saying that my chapters are not mine, but there were times when I couldn't put into words what I wanted to say. Plus, I have always had a lot of problems with my writing skills. Mom said that it's because I went to Greenville schools and not Lakeview. She is always making that remark, but it's all in fun.

When I was younger, being handicapped was no big deal to me. In fact, if Mom didn't take videos of me being able to walk, run and play like a normal child, I would have never known I was any different from the way I am. I don't have any memories of being normal. I knew that I was different from Mikey when I was young because Mikey could do more things than me. But, that was okay. What I couldn't do Mikey did for me. Like getting my toys around for me, pushing me around the house in my stroller, or carrying me up and down the stairs. Mikey played with me like any brother would a sister, including making me cry from picking on me. Mom said that I always got my revenge in some way or another.

Also, when I was young, I remember my family and relatives

were always giving me encouragement. No matter how small my achievements were, I was praised. It was okay to work at my own pace at anything. There wasn't any pressured placed on me by anyone to meet certain goals. I think the family was so grateful that I survived my reaction from the vaccine, that no one was concerned. over what I could or could not do. Being alive and still with the family was more important.

I was lucky to have had many teachers, friends and family who helped me develop a healthy self esteem. Mom asked me where I got my courage to stand up for the special education students at school, whenever I saw the students being bullied or made fun of. I told her my courage came from her and all the others who had given me the feeling that I was no different from anyone else.

I felt liked I needed to stand up for the students who couldn't or wouldn't stand up for themselves. I didn't care what others called me, because by that time, I knew my body didn't make me who I was; my heart did. I guess some of the kids making fun of the students, as well as me, didn't believe that we had similar likes and dislikes like them. All they saw and mocked us about was our disabilities. Didn't they realize that those students, nor I, asked to be handicapped or slow learners?

I accept that there will always be those who look down upon others who are different. To me, everyone should be accepted for the way they are. Thankfully, there are others who can look pass the disabilities and indifference of others. Those people are the ones who make all the difference in life.

Like so many other kids in school, I thought I needed to wear brand name clothes in order to fit in. I always had brand name clothes while living with Dad. When ever I would go shopping with Mom, she would always roll her eyes and shake her head, anytime I asked her to take me into Old Navy, American Eagle, Aeropostale and other stores like those. Mom was always saying, "It's just cloth. Why do you need to buy the expensive clothing?"

It wasn't until I moved in with Mom, when I realized that brand name clothing didn't make me who I was, my personality did. Seeing Mom wear what ever she wanted and not caring what others thought, I wanted to be that way also. So, I did. Shopping at Goodwill and Walmart is where I now buy my clothes. Sweatpants and Tees has become my favorite clothes to wear. To me, if my body is covered, it's good enough.

The hardest time I went through when I was younger, was going back and forth to Mom's house and Dads. I think it's hard for all kids whose parents are divorced or separated. It wasn't until I was much older did I realize how hard it must have been for Mom, to let me go and live with Dad. I never even given it a thought how Mom would feel when I asked to live with Dad. All I remember is how excited I was when she said I could. Mom had said that I was always so attached to Dad, starting at a very young age.

Dad and Mom had completely different ways of parenting. Mom was always laid back and open minded. Whereas, Dad was more judgmental and strict. I felt as though Dad and Momma Denise were rich and Mom was poor, but in a way, Mom seemed more happy.

The one thing I remember about visiting Mom, was how she never said anything bad about Dad in front of me. It was only when I began asking questions about her and Dad, did she describe her feelings toward him. Dad was more open with his feelings toward Mom. It wasn't hard to see that there was a lot of anger Dad felt against Mom. It made me angry every time Dad said bad things about her, because I loved Mom. I wished he would have kept his feelings to himself or waited until I asked questions, like I did Mom.

When I moved in with Dad, I was told that the only reason I was living with him was because Mom didn't want me. I didn't tell Mom this until I was older. When I did tell her, she just looked at me with her eyebrows raised and asked me, "what do you think?" At first, I did believe what I was told. Any young kid would do the same, but I never let on how I felt to Mom because I was always excited to see her.

By the time I was in fourth or fifth grade, I knew it wasn't true. I knew Mom loved me and would do anything for me. Later on, I would either ignore whatever was said against Mom or talk to her about it. Mom never really became defensive. She would always come back with, "what do you think?" I know now that Mom was letting me discover for myself, what was true about her and what wasn't.

The older I became, the more critical Dad seemed to act toward me. I didn't understand why Dad couldn't just love me for the way I was and not worry about my limitations. I don't think Dad could accept that I was always doing my best. To me, parents should love their children unconditionally. I always felt that Mom had, but I didn't understand why it was so hard for Dad to. I ended up giving him the nickname "*Krusty Krab*", because of his crabbiness.

As long as I can remember, Dad has always been the kind of person who speaks before thinking whether or not, his words will hurt. You know, in spite of Dad's ways, I loved him more than he could ever imagine. It was so important for me to be close to him. I thought of myself as being "*daddy's little girl.*" I always tried my best to please Dad as well, because I wanted him to be proud of me. Things changed between Dad and I when Kaleb and Nibbles were born. I now had to share him. That is why I cherished our Cribbage games we played together. I didn't have to share him with anyone. It was our special time together.

I loved going to Mom's house. No matter what we did, we were always laughing and having fun. Even though Mom was poor, she made sure all of us did something together as a family. To Mom, making memories with us kids was more important than anything else to her. I know there was a lot of times where Mom made sacrifices in order for us to do things as a family.

I'm glad we did things together, because it made our family close. At Mom's house, we would sit around the kitchen table and just talk. Mom called it *table talk*. Not only did we laugh and joke around, but we talked about everything and anything us kids wanted to. Even Mom talked openly to us kids about her mistakes, hopes and childhood. I don't think there is anything us kids don't know about Mom.

Early in life, I felt a strong sense of being a very independent child. Maybe all children feel this. There was a streak of stubbornness that seemed to be my driving force to become independent. If I was told I couldn't do something I wanted to do, I worked hard at achieving what it was I wanted, just to prove others wrong. I guess that could be called a strong will, but I think it was just Great Grandma White's stubbornness I inherited, that give me my strength to push myself . I never thought that stubbornness inside of me would not ever be strong enough to keep me from giving up on anything.

After my first surgery in 2006, what I needed more than anything was encouragement. Especially, when I was depressed. I did receive a lot of encouragement from others, but not from the one person whom I needed it the most from; Dad. He criticized me more than offering his love and support. This hurt me more than the physical pain I was in.

I couldn't understand why Dad couldn't just be loving toward me. I didn't need to hear how I should have been up and walking or how I wasn't working harder in rehab, along with how I wasn't going to graduate. Dad even went as far as saying that I really didn't need the surgery and it was all of Moms doing.

Dad never saw the x-rays of my spine before I had the surgery. If he had, I don't think he would have been so hard on me. To me, Dad acted like he wanted nothing to do with anything I was going through. I felt abandoned by him and over time, I just felt like giving up; which I did. I'm not saying that my giving up and overdosing is all Dad's fault, because it wasn't. What I am trying to say is that I think I would have been stronger and fought harder if he had shown more concern.

Dad would tell me to toughen up and stop taking the easy way out, by not working harder at recovering. With the amount of pain I was in, it was impossible to work hard at anything that involved movement. More than anything, I wished that it was possible to touch someone, back when I was in all that pain and depression and have them feel all the pain and depression I was having, just by my touch. Then I wonder if they (all those who felt I wasn't working hard enough) including Dad, would have considered just how their words and actions would affect me. Mom kept telling me that the pain was temporary. Once we found someone to take the pain away, I would then begin to make progress. She said that it is always easy for others to tell someone what he or she should be doing, when they are not the person hurting.

I am so grateful to have a mom who is the way she is. Her encouragement, along with her weird sense of humor and her way of accepting things the way that they are, helped me through a lot of dark days. The endless talks the two of us would have, helped me see life and others in a totally different way. Mom is my best friend and knows me more than anyone else.

Right after my surgery, Mom picked up on my disappointment with Dad and together we talked out all my frustrations. Not once, but over and over until I reached the point of finally understanding, that I wasn't going to receive the love and support from Dad, in the way I thought he should be giving it to me. Mom kept telling me that Dad loved me in his own way. It was always in his power to either stop his criticism and offer his love and support, or remain detached like I felt that he was.

Mom said that it wasn't my place to expect Dad to become someone he didn't see himself as being. He was comfortable being the way he has always been. Then Mom said something that made me feel really good about myself. She told me that because of me and my situation, I was offering Dad a gift. The gift I was offering Dad, was a chance to become a more loving father.

Mom said that what I was going through had to be Life's way of helping others to see how important love and compassion is. I'm not sure if what Mom said is true and the reason why I had to go through the hell I went through, but it does make some sense to me.

Over time, I began accepting that Dad wasn't going to change. I began to feel better and could feel the love he did show me, without needing more. I still hurt at times, from not being as close to Dad like I would like to be, but I don't allow this to determine my worth, like I did in the past. My attachment to Dad has been broken. I wonder if other girls go through this. For me, I always wanted to remain *daddy's little girl*, but I guess I couldn't be once I grew up.

Dad and I are beginning to establish a much closer relationship now. All because I did accept him for the way he is and stopped wanting him to be the way I wished he was. It's a great feeling. The two of us talk on the phone every Sunday, which I enjoy very much. He still is crabby, but I have learned to laugh at him and not take him seriously. I know he loves me and that is really what is important. I realize now that he has always loved me and had show me that love, the best way he knew how. While I was growing up and up until now.

As for Mom and I, we remain being best friends. We talk everyday. Sometimes, we talk for a few minutes, then there are days where we talk for an hour before we even realize it. Mom still takes me shopping and I will spend the weekend with her, Katie, and Mom's boyfriend Jeff. I think Mom has finally found the perfect man to share her life with.

I have accepted that I am not going to have a baby, but if Ricky and I were meant to have a baby, I would make sure that I was just as open as Mom was with Mikey, Katie and I. It took me a while to let go of that dream of experiencing pregnancy, but I have. Right now, I am very content with my life with Ricky and our beautiful cat; Maw Maw. If we ever get a home of our own, Ricky and I plan to add another member to our family; a puppy. Maw Maw is definitely going to have a fit over that.

Before Ricky and I moved to Belding, I noticed that I was leaning to the side while sitting. Mom noticed it too. She told me to call Dr. Kuldanek and request a spinal x-ray. One year had passed since my last x-ray. I wouldn't have believed that my spine would return back to the way it was before my surgery at Advanced Care, but it had. The curvature in my spine was at sixty-five degrees. The same as it was when I had my first surgery. None of us could believe this.

Dr. Kuldanek set up an appointment for me to be examined by a spine specialist in Grand Rapids. Mom and I went to see the specialist and was not impressed at all with him. His attitude toward us was rude and disrespectful. So, I chose not to see him again. As luck would have it, Mom nor I could find another specialist in Grand Rapids that would see me. Either they didn't accept my insurance or they didn't specialize in scoliosis. So, I called the first specialist I went to see and asked to be seen by him again. Life had other plans for me, because when I called and talked to the receptionist, she told me that the specialist probably would not see me again since I had said that I didn't like him.

Mom told me not to worry. Life will guide us to the perfect doctor who will help me. All we needed to do was search the web. The specialist will stand out among others and grab our attention. We'll know when we see him. Sure enough, Mom sent me the web site of a well known spine specialist; Dr. Herkowitz. Mom said this was our surgeon, but she wasn't sure if he accepted my insurance. Mom told me to check out the web site, read the reviews, and look at Dr. Herkowitz's eyes. Mom and I both believe the eyes tell how kind and compassionate people are. The eyes are the windows to our soul. That is what Mom says and I believe her.

I checked out the site and like Mom, knew right off that Dr. Herkowitz was the specialist I needed to see. I called his office and was so surprised when the receptionist said that I could be examined by him. They accepted the type of insurance I had as well. Plus, I didn't need a referral to see him.

Mom, Mikey, Ricky and I all went to Royal Oak, Michigan, to meet Dr. Herkowitz. Royal Oak is near Detroit and the hospital the surgeon works at is William Beaumont Hospital. On our way to see Dr. Herkowitz, I just felt that this was where I should be going. It's hard to explain how I knew that he was the surgeon for me, but I could feel it.

The four of us met Dr. Herkowitz's assistant first. Nema, was very nice and funny. He was just as down to earth as us, which made me feel at home. I brought with me all my medical files from Advanced Care Hospital and the x-rays taken of my spine, before my first surgery and after the rods were removed. The thickness of the medical files were about the size of an encyclopedia.

Nema skimmed through the files and began asking questions about my current condition. For the first time I felt like I was in charge of my own care. Nema didn't look to Mom to answer the questions, he was asking me. I felt like I existed as a person and was capable of knowing what was going on. I didn't get this type of acknowledgment very often. I think when people see me, they automatically think I am mentally slow.

Before Dr. Herkowitz come into the room we were in, I asked Nema if Dr. Herkowitz chose not to be my surgeon, if he would help find us a surgeon who would. I told him that we didn't know where to go for help. Nema looked surprised by the question. I told him right out that I didn't want to go through *HELL* again. I needed a surgeon who was going to take care of me, because I didn't want to go through what I did at that other hospital. Nema said not to worry. He would personally help us find a good surgeon if Dr. Herkowitz decided not to treat me. I had to give Nema a hug for that. He didn't seem offended by me asking that and to me, it said a lot about his concern for others.

When Dr. Herkowitz first entered the room, I think he was surprised to find the amount of people waiting with me. He introduced himself to all of us and shook all our hands. The first thing I did when he approached me was look deep into his eyes. His eyes revealed to me that he was a kind and caring man. I instantly felt safe in his presence. We briefly went over my medical files, before he asked the reason for seeing him. Was I there to get a second opinion, or was I seeking treatment? I told him that I was seeking treatment.

But, I had to ask him one question before continuing on. "Will you take good care of me, if I need surgery?" I think the question took him by surprise. His reply was, "I take good care of all my patients." I believed him.

After reviewing the newest x-rays of my spine, surgery was decided on. I was to undergo spinal surgery February 21st, 2012. Unfortunately, there were a few tests I wasn't able to get done before the day of my surgery. Because of this, I had to rescheduled my surgery for April 19th, 2012. Believe it or not, my surgery had to be rescheduled again. This time, the date was set for August 7, 2012.

Well, here I go again. Another journey is about to begin for me. Wish me luck. I have this feeling that I am in good hands with Dr. Herkowitz as my surgeon. I believe, Life is going to see to it that I will not go through what I had before. I can't imagine that there is something more that I need to learn in life, which involves more hardships. Mom said that she didn't think there was. She told me that I have been through enough and believes that Life, is now in the process of healing me physically. Life healed me emotionally, by bringing Ricky into my life. Ricky is everything to me and brings me the greatest joy I have ever felt.

Before writing this epilogue, I told Mom that I wanted to tell the readers to never give up when you're feeling down or defeated. Because, in the end, things will get better. From my own personal experience, I know that it's hard to even hold onto such a thought like, *"never give up."* That is why it is so important for others to step in and fight along beside you. It is their love and support that becomes your strength. I know. At times, Mom's strength did become my strength. Mom never gave up fighting, even when I chose to. She somehow understood that I wasn't strong enough to keep fighting and did what she could to carry me through, until I grew stronger. Her love and the love and compassion from others saved me.

I guess the biggest discovery I made about myself, others and life, is that it is so important to feel loved by others. I think that is what our lesson is in life. Not so much getting the love you want, but offering your love and compassion to those in need. The amount of love and compassion shown to others makes a difference. The lack of love and compassion shown to others also makes a difference. Like Mom has asked us kids many times, *"What kind of person do you choose to be?"*

PART TWO

Helen Keller is quoted as saying,"The struggle of life is one of our greatest blessings. Our character cannot be developed in ease and quiet."

This is the message Heather and I have tried to convey throughout *Strength of Character*. With every life experience, an opportunity is offered for the growth of one's character. However, whether or not one benefits from the experience, is solely up to the individual and the perspective he/she chooses to attach to that experience.

For some, personal growth may not be an area of interest in which he/she chooses to pursue. Whether it is an area of interest or not, at some point in time, should we not ask ourselves what is the basis of being human? As Pericles had beautifully stated,"What you leave behind is not what is engraved in stone monuments, but what is woven into the lives of others."

I intentionally decided upon *Strength of Character,* as being the absolute perfect title for our book. I believe, strength of character is what carries each one of us through the many obstacles in life. Whether it be the strength to physically endure, or mentally withstand the challenges we're faced with from time to time.

Not only does this refer to the individual confronting the challenge, but also includes the strength of character of all those personally connected to that individual, along with those in a position to help the individual whom is in need. The character of those individuals, is often revealed by the amount of compassion and involvement, each person is willing to invest in helping the one suffering overcome his/her predicament. I chose to use the word *predicament,* because it implies a complicated situation where it is hard to free *oneself* from, which perfectly describes Heather's predicament following her first surgery in 2006.

By closely watching the way each medical professional approached Heather's care at Advanced Care Hospital, I noticed how each repeatedly applied a similar tactic every time he/she dealt with Heather. Even when it became obvious that their methods wasn't making a difference. It just seemed to me, all those whom were involved with Heather's treatment and care following her surgery, had grown very comfortable in approaching their patient's care and treatment a certain way. Kinda like a *one size fits all* mindset. Perhaps, having had successfully treated and healed many patients similar to Heather, each had taken it for granted that Heather was going to be another text book success story.

What if Life had other plans for the team who worked with Heather? What if, it was a part of Heather's destiny to challenge the medical staff? A challenge that required all those involved in Heather's care to step away from their comfort zone and question their methods of treatment in a totally new way?

Heather remained in the care of the medical team, long enough for them to recognize that their methods of treatment wasn't producing any positive results. Rather than approaching Heather's condition in a new direction, each continued with the method of treatment which had worked best, for their patients in the past.

It seemed to Heather and I, that it was much easier to somehow pin the lack of progress on Heather personally, rather than seeking other treatment options. The answer to the puzzling question, "What can be done to help Heather?" was always available. All that was needed, was a willingness to become more personally involved and seek out that answer.

As Heather and I see it, no one chose to do so. By not choosing to do so, Heather and I experienced the consequences of their actions. I'm not saying, the fault lies totally on the medical staff involved with Heather. I too, played a role in our experience. I had put all my trust into the medical staff, believing they would pull through for Heather. Because of this, I did not take charge of our situation early on.

Am I suggesting Heather's destiny in life was to become a martyr? Perhaps, in a way I am. Are there not those among us, whom seem to have been *chosen* to undertake the role of martyrdom for the benefit of others? These are the individuals whom are capable of shaking our life up just enough, to bring about personal change and awareness in ourselves.

The two of us recognize that every individual involved with Heather, following her surgery, had done what they *believed* to be in Heather's best interest at that time. Perhaps, because of Heather bringing to Holly's attention, the availability of a Baclofen pump, it may in turn benefit other patients. The pump may replace the need for some patients to undergo numerous Botox injections, as Heather had during her care. Not only are those procedures expensive, but relief the injections offer is limited. In any case, there is now another treatment option at that hospital, available to those patients similar to Heather, because of Heather.

The day Heather became, Mrs. Heather Robinson, was truly magical. Her wedding didn't center on lavish decorations or designers gowns. In fact, the simplicity of her wedding was what made the day magical. Vows exchanged with the most heartfelt emotion, made all those present teary eyed. Once again, I had witnessed another monumental moment in Heather's life; my heart took a picture.

Heather is an amazing young woman who has gone through a lot of difficult times, but still manages to smile. That in itself is a strength of character, which is inspiring to others, as well as myself. She absolutely loves life and is very content in being who she is. How many people can honestly say that?

In August of 2012, Heather underwent another spinal surgery. Prior to her surgery, Heather and I met the surgeon, whom we discovered was recognized throughout the country as being the best. Apparently, the vertebrates in Heather's upper spine did not fuse together like we had hoped. Therefore, Dr. Herkowitz recommended the surgery, in which he would fuse her upper back, along with rod placement,extending just below her shoulder blades. The shorter rods would allow Heather more flexibility with bending and twisting.

Surgery went well and when Heather was medically stable, she was transported from William Beaumount Hospital in Royal Oak, Michigan, to Mary Free Bed for rehab. She spent a total of three weeks in rehab, before she was ready to return home. Unfortunately, to date, Heather is again experiencing some breathing difficulties and stomach issues. Right off, we all suspected the cause for her discomfort had to be associated with her spine. Heather arranged to see Dr. Herkowitz for an examination and to get his opinion.

After reviewing Heather's latest x-rays of her spine, Dr. Herkowitz assured us that Heather's spine was not the underlying cause. Heather's spine had not regressed in any way. Dr Herkowitz recommended that Heather be seen by a Gastroenterologist, for her stomach issues and a Pulmonologist, for her breathing difficulties. Heather is now in the process of doing just that. Before leaving our visit with Dr.Herkowitz, Heather gave him a *high five*, while telling him; "Finally, a surgeon, who got my back surgery right." Dr. Herkowitz, as promised, has taken good care of Heather.

In late March of 2011, I walked away from my home in Lakeview. Without sufficient income, I was not able to keep my house. Before locking the door behind me as I left, I gave thanks to the home that kept us warm, safe and dry. I had recently driven by the house and was delighted to see that the house is now owned by another, whom is in the process of remodeling it. I always had known, the house had potential.

As for Mikey, he had met someone shortly before Heather went into rehab at Mary Free Bed in 2009. Like Heather, he had met his soul mate; Danielle. It was looking like nothing but good was happening to our family unit. There was a feeling in the air, that 2009-2010 was going to be a year of endings and new beginnings. Some would cause sadness, while others created a boundless sense of joy.

Truth be known, it took some convincing from Heather, Katie and I, to get Mikey to go out with Danielle in the beginning. Although he hasn't yet thanked us yet for doing so, he is now the happiest that I have seen him. The two of them have started a life together and along with that, I have now become a Grandmother of three beautiful children; Fayth, Raven"pumpkin", and Adam Micheal. Mikey is great at being a dad. Should be, since he acted as a father figure with Heather and Katie, while the two of them were growing up.

Katie is now seventeen and soon will be graduating from high school. She managed to rise above all the adversity she endured while growing up. Katie has grown into a very confident young woman, with the ability to achieve anything she sets her mind to. Here I thought, it would be a miracle, if she lived past the age of six. What a handful she was. Her temperament when she was younger, earned her the nickname *Katie Ka-Boom*. Anyone familiar with the show, *Animaniacs*, will know the meaning behind the nickname.

In closing, I would like to ask every reader to take a moment and say a little pray for all the children, past and present, who has experienced a reaction to a childhood vaccine. These children are the victims of a society, who believes that the benefits of immunizations out weighs the potential risks of adverse reactions, along the hardships families will endure following a reaction.

Adverse reactions to immunizations are not going to go away. If anything, the amount of reactions may surely rise. Thirty years ago, government officials were recommending and ordering doctors to give twenty-three doses of seven vaccines to children. Today, children are being given 63-70 doses of sixteen vaccines. Thankfully, Michigan is one of only seventeen states that continues to support the right of parents and individuals, to make their own decisions regarding vaccines. The remaining states do not allow this freedom. In fact, police powers and punishment can be used to *FORCE* citizens to get vaccinated, if the state chooses to do so, or if the government orders it. Imagine that.

About the Authors

Photo courtesy of Katie Johnson

Heather Robinson, lives in Ionia, MI, with her husband, Ricky, along with Sady and Molly.

Barb Johnson, lives in Lakeview, MI. She is the mother of three children.

Made in the USA
Monee, IL
11 March 2020